D0148814

Gandhi
The South African Experience

Gandhi

The South African Experience

Maureen Swan

Ravan Press   Johannesburg

Published by Ravan Press (Pty) Ltd
P O Box 31134, Braamfontein,
Johannesburg, 2017
South Africa

© Maureen Swan 1985

All rights reserved. No part of this publication may be reproduced, stored in a retrieval system, or transmitted in any form or by any means, electronic, mechanical, photocopying, recording, or other wise, without the prior permission of the Copyright owner.

First published 1985

ISBN 0 86975 232 4

Cover design: The Graphic Equalizer
Cover photograph: Courtesy of the Johannesburg Public Library
Typeset by: Opus 61

Printed by Galvin and Sales (Pty) Ltd., Cape Town

For William Swan

Contents

List of Illustrations

Photographs

Author's Note: For the photographs reproduced in this book I am grateful to two sources: the Johannesburg Public Library (JPL) and the History Workshop Photographic Collection of Early Working Class Life on the Rand (HWPC), compiled by Peter Kallaway and Patrick Pearson. I am particularly grateful to Patrick Pearson for the assistance which he gave in locating the photographs and providing prints.

Tables

Acknowledgements

This book is based on a DPhil thesis for Oxford University. I would
like to thank Adrian Graves, Gyan Panday and Christopher Saunders
who read and commented on parts of the original manuscript, and
Ashok Tayal who spent a great deal of time computerizing data from
ships' logs in Durban. I benefited in particular from the insights of
Tapan Raychaudhuri (who supervised) and Shula Marks and Stanley
Trapido (who examined) my thesis. Peter Delius, a constant source of
encouragement since the final stages of the thesis, has eliminated many
of my more immoderate turns of phrase. I, of course, am responsible
for the weaknesses which remain.

A variety of scholarships and grants helped fund the research for my
thesis. Thanks are due to the Bartle Frere, Beit, McKenzie King and
Rhodes Trusts. The book assumed its present form in the course of a
post-Doctoral Fellowship at the University of the Witwatersrand
during which Charles van Onselen was unfailingly helpful.

Abbreviations

BIA	British Indian Association
DIS	Durban Indian Association
HYMA	Hindu Young Men's Association
INC	Indian National Congress
NA	Natal Archives
NIC	Natal Indian Congress
NIPU	Natal Indian Patriotic Union
PRO	Public Records Office, London
SABIC	South African Indian Committee
SABA	Union Archives, Pretoria
SADF	South African Defence Force Archives, Pretoria
TABA	Transvaal Archives, Pretoria

Orthography

In general, I have used contemporary orthography, except where changes have taken place in well known names such as Loanda (Luanda). Where variants of names occur, I have used the one most frequently noted in the primary sources.

Preface

In 1893 Mohandas Gandhi was hired by a Durban-based Indian merchant company to assist in the preparation of a lawsuit against an Indian merchant in the Transvaal. He spent most of the next twenty-one years in South Africa. During that period he developed the moral doctrine and the political technique and skills which became the basis of his idiosyncratic style as one of India's foremost nationalist politicians. Indeed, the international reputation which he had acquired in South Africa by 1914 provided the entrée into Indian nationalist circles which had been denied him on his first attempt to penetrate the upper levels of nationalist politics a dozen years earlier.

As one of the twentieth century's most charismatic figures, Gandhi has been the subject of a vast literature. Naturally, the majority of these studies concentrate on his years as a nationalist politician in India. However, many of them include an introductory section on the crucial, formative South African decades. Some recent works concentrate on that period. The sheer volume of this literature suggests that no aspect of Gandhi's life or career could possibly require further exploration. That was my own first reaction when the topic for the study which produced this book was first suggested to me. It was only then that I began systematically reading the Gandhian literature. I very quickly learned that the existing work on Gandhi in South Africa not only obscures an understanding of this key period in his life, but ignores or distorts what was also the crucial, formative period in the history of the South African Indians. This preface is a brief attempt to explain how and why this has happened.

The general consensus of the existing literature[1] is that the history of the South African Indians was made by Gandhi between 1894 and 1914. He is supposed to have been confronted on his arrival in South Africa with demoralized, apolitical Indian communities, divided on the basis of religion, and suffering the first onslaughts of discriminatory legislation in Natal and the Transvaal. In the words of one of Gandhi's earliest and more celebrated biographers, 'the Indians in Africa were not equipped to struggle. They had no power, no will, no faith. They were demoralized and without organization. They needed a leader.'[2]

Some variation of this arresting verbal portrait provides the familiar backdrop for a history which sees Gandhi as the unique figure who chose to resist this oppression, and to rally his countrymen behind him. The contrast between Gandhi and the rest of the Indians, 'dispirited and sunk in apathy, accepting their depression without protest',[3] is so stark that a later and equally celebrated biographer asks rhetorically, 'Why, of all the people, did it occur to Gandhi to resist the evil?'[4] Another writer's answer, which captures the flavour of the literature as a whole, is that 'he was deeply introspective — a moralist and idealogue who all his life wrestled with conscience and the spirit, Truth and Right.'[5]

There is no real place in this discourse for anyone but Gandhi. The assertion that 'organized Indian political expression in South Africa owes its origins to M K Gandhi'[6] acquires a seemingly irrefutable logic within this framework. Thus one readily accepts the dominant theme of the literature which portrays Gandhi as the man who organized, united and led the Natal and Transvaal Indians in a movement of protest against discriminatory legislation — the man who 'remained twenty years fighting the battle for Indian rights [and] won.'[7] One can find no quarrel — within this problematic — with a description of Gandhi which sees him as 'the champion of indentured labourers',[8] and the author of a 'startling new philosophy of revolution'.[9]

The flaw in all of this is that analyses which concentrate on Gandhi to the exclusion, or virtual exclusion, of his constituents, inevitably offer a superficial, and thus often distorted, picture of the social and political reality in which the doctrine and techniques of *satyagraha* (passive resistance) were worked out. The reasons for this Gandhi-centric superficiality are less suprising than they might seem at first glance. In some instances it derives from the hagiographic nature of the studies in question — a burden which has been imposed on many colonial nationalists beside Gandhi. But Gandhi was unusual even for a colonial nationalist, and the well-known asceticism of his lifestyle in later years provided a further impetus to hagiography. By virtue of hindsight, many of his biographers have projected the

'Mahatma-ness', the 'saintliness', of the 1930s and 1940s backwards into his early life.

But superficiality has also, in many instances, derived from a too heavy reliance on Gandhi's historically inaccurate autobiographical writings, *Satyagraha in South Africa* and *The Story of My Experiments with Truth*. Surely no other politician's memoirs have been — or should be — accepted as uncritically as these? They were written years after the events which they describe. It scarcely needs be said that Gandhi, like all of us, interpreted, and thus rewrote, his past in the light of subsequent experiences. But more than this, the 'soldier of Truth' was also a teacher, and these works were meant to be, as Eric Eriksen suggests, pedagogic: they were meant to convey certain moral lessons to their readers.[10] As such, they are of use more as reflections of what Gandhi was thinking in the 1920s than as the historical documents they are so often taken to be. Remarkably, however, an awareness of this did not prevent Louis Fischer from basing the South African chapters of his biography almost exclusively on these sources.[11] Indeed, they are the standard source for the years 1894 – 1914.

More recent studies of this period, notably Huttenback's *Gandhi in South Africa* and Pillay's *British Indians in the Transvaal* (which deals with some of Gandhi's most important constituents and includes a chapter specifically on Gandhi), move beyond his memoirs into some of the documentary sources. However, despite the promise of their prefaces, neither Huttenback nor Pillay systematically explores the political and social reality of the turn-of-the-century South African Indians. By concentrating on official documents, both studies confine themselves mainly to a discussion of the relations between the imperial government, the South African governments and Gandhi. The social and ideological bases of Indian politics are scarcely examined: the 'Indians' appear as a virtually undifferentiated mass. Thus stratification within the Indian communities, and the relationships of the different strata to each other, and to Gandhi, are lost.

This book has taken as its starting point Gandhi's constituents rather than Gandhi. I have tried to explore and to understand divisions within the Indian communities, and the way in which, and the extent to which, these were reflected in organized politics. Although concentrating on those strata which were represented by the political parties, I have also attempted to identify and investigate the others which remained outside of or inadequately represented by Indian politics, the reasons for this inadequacy, and the consequences of lack of representation for those outside the political community. But, in particular, I have tried to assess Gandhi's role in South African Indian politics between 1894 and 1914 — to explore his contribution to these politics and their contribution to the development of his unique political style. Much of Gandhi's mature moral and political philosophy was already apparent by the early years of this century. I have therefore tried to root the development of that philosophy in the social and political context in which it was worked out. I have tried also to understand the nature of Gandhian passive resistance in South Africa, the extent to which and the reasons why it was 'successful', and the limitations of that success. This has seemed to me important not only because the South African experience informed Gandhi's approach to Indian nationalism, but also because his political technique and, indeed, elements of his philosophy have provided an enduring legacy for the continuing struggle against racial and class oppression in South Africa.

A very different picture of Gandhi emerges when he is viewed thus — within the context of the Natal and Transvaal Indian communities, rather than above or beyond them as he has been in the past. I find contribution to South African Indian politics has been greatly overstated. The role of 'leader' which is generally attributed to him is entirely inappropriate before 1906, and must be carefully qualified for the period after 1906. The constituency which Gandhi represented throughout most of the period under review was very select, and consisted of the highest strata in the Indian communities. The underclasses, especially the indentured labourers with whom he has so consistently and so wrongly been identified, formed part of his constituency only for a very brief period, and for a very special reason. It is also particularly noteworthy that as a politician Gandhi was never more than a reformist in terms of goals and ideology, even when the passive resistance movement was transformed into a truly mass movement. Gandhi was a social 'rebel' to the extent that he had made the commitment to moral autonomy, and sought to convert others to moral individuation. But he was a revolutionary only to the extent that the technique of mass passive resistance implies elements of a revolutionary style.

Notes

1 Frene Ginwala's unpublished D.Phil thesis — 'Class, Consciousness and Control: Indian South Africans 1860-1946' (Oxford, 1975) — is an exception. Her works suffers, however, from lack of access to the key South African sources, and although her mainly materialist analysis is sensitive to the need to move beyond the leadership level, she lacks the evidence to do so successfully.

2 R Rolland, *Mahatma Gandhi* (Zurich, 1925) p.13. This, and the quotes which follow, have been chosen for the way in which they capture the essence of the literature as a whole.

3 R F Hoernlé, 'A South African Tribute', S Radhakrishnan (ed.), *Mahatma Gandhi: Essays and Reflections on His Life and Work* (London, 1939) p.116.

4 L Fischer, *The Life of Mahatma Gandhi* (London, 1951) p.56.

5 R Huttenback, *Gandhi in South Africa* (Cornell University Press, 1971) p.47.

6 B Pillay, *British Indians in the Transvaal* (London, 1976) p.112.

7 Fischer, op cit., p.60.

8 Ibid., p.63

9 Huttenback, op cit., p.vii.

10 E Eriksen, *Gandhi's Truth* (London, 1970). See, for example, pp.57-61.

11 Fischer, op cit., p.546.

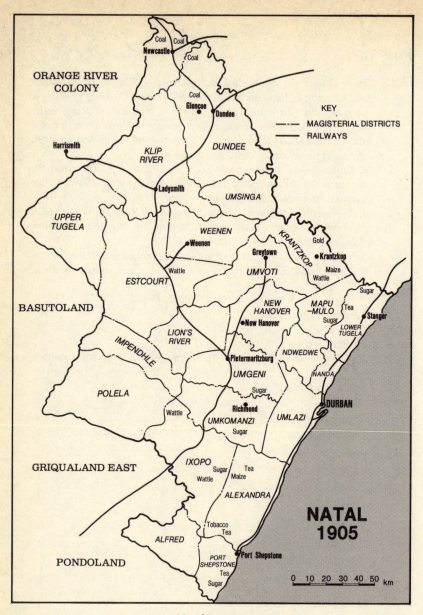

Natal in 1905

CHAPTER ONE

Merchants and Migrants: Social Stratification and Politics

The Indian community in Natal has its origins in an indentured workforce which was imported between 1860 and 1911.[1] Natal offered its Indian workers a five-year term of indenture which began on the day of arrival in the colony. A free return passage was available after five years indentured plus five years free labour. Until 1890, an ex-indentured worker had the choice of exchanging his return passage for a plot of land.[2] The unfavourable conditions in India which were in large part responsible for pushing workers into colonial recruiting nets will be discussed later. For the present it is enough to note that lack of opportunity at home, combined with an endemic shortage of cheap labour in Natal,[3] resulted in some 52 per cent of migrants staying on in the colony after their contracts had expired.[4] Thus the indentured workforce gave rise to a permanent group of ex-indentured labourers and their descendants (the 'colonial-born', or 'colonials', as they came to be known) some thousands of whom drifted north to the Transvaal Republic in search of higher wages before the Anglo-Boer war.[5] Only fifteen years after the first indentured worker had appeared in Natal, the colony's growing Indian population began to attract Indian merchant immigrants: 'passengers', or those who had paid their own passage, as distinct from the great majority who migrated under contract. Again, significant numbers of these eventually made their way to the Transvaal.

Contrary to the impression created by the existing literature on Gandhi in South Africa, the Indian political community in Natal and the Transvaal during most of the period under review was very small.[6] An essentially male community, their numbers fluctuated, as will become clear in subsequent chapters. It is worth noting at the outset, however, that even during the latter part of the period under review — leaving aside the peaks of the passive resistance campaign in 1908 and 1913 — their numbers never exceeded some 2 000 men in Natal, and around 1 000 in the Transvaal. In Natal this represented 3,5 percent of the non-dependent male adult Indian population during the census year 1911. In the Transvaal, with a much smaller Indian population, it represented 15 per cent of the non-dependent male adult Indians.

These few thousand men comprised the most privileged strata of the Natal and Transvaal Indian populations: merchants, petty traders, professionals, white-collar workers and prosperous farmers. Their political associations were created in response to perceived threats to their relatively privileged positions, and attempted to maintain if not improve those positions. The following outline of Indian social stratification in Natal and the Transvaal is thus meant to demonstrate, firstly, the needs and aspirations of the Indian elites, which were expressed in formal, modern political associations. But it is also meant to demonstrate the needs and aspirations of the underclasses. Contrary to the rhetoric of elite politics and, indeed, the existing literature, the grievances of Indian urban and rural wage labourers, and petty cultivators and hawkers, were largely ignored by the elites during most of the period under review, unless representing them could be seen to serve elite interests in some way. Nor was cohesive formal political protest generated by the underclasses themselves. It is thus necessary to understand the generally unrecorded grievances of Indian workers and cultivators in order to appreciate, (a) the limitations of Indian politics in Natal and the Transvaal, (b) the pressure exerted on the oldest political organizations after 1908 when new organizations began to emerge in Natal which claimed the mass of the people as their constituents, (c) the massive response when the social base of elite politics in Natal was finally widened in 1913.

The Commercial Elite

The original political community in Natal and the Transvaal was a commercial elite. Some of them invested in property and finance; but most of their capital went into trade, and they were generally loosely referred to as merchants or traders regardless of the size of their enterprise. The three major political associations which they created, the pre-Gandhian Indian Committee, the Natal Indian Congress, and the Transvaal British Indian Association, were almost exclusively merchant in membership, created to protect merchant interests, and in the main used to further these interests.

There is very little quantitative evidence directly concerned with the social origins of the merchants. But a variety of evidence, including qualitative assessments made during the period under review, suggests that the majority were Gujerati Muslims who had emigrated to South Africa at their own expense. The heterodox Gujerati trading communities — Bohras, Khojas and particularly Memons — appear to have been well represented.

The best source of evidence in support of these contentions is the South African press which contains a wealth of biographical information on the merchants, some of which will be introduced later. In addition there is the fact that characteristically Muslim names predominate in their political and social institutions. Again, this will become apparent later. More general evidence for the composition of the group derives from the labels which were applied to them, or which they used themselves. In the early days in both Natal and the Transvaal the commercial elite were known as 'Arabs'[7] — an inaccuracy which is probably attributable to their mode of dress as well as their religious affiliation. Later, they were referred to as 'Bombay merchants', or 'Bombay traders', labels which they sometimes used themselves.[8]

One of the most striking aspects of the commercial elite is the fact that the few most financially powerful and politically active members had significant economic interests in both Natal and the Transvaal. Thus it is possible to make sense of their politics only within the framework of a 'Natal-based' and a 'Transvaal-based' elite rather than from the perspective of two separate elites. The links between the Indian merchants in the Transvaal and Natal, as well as the commanding economic position of the few individuals who dominated their politics, are demonstrated in the following discussion of the shared economic interests which fuelled those politics.

Abubakr Amod, the first passenger merchant, arrived in Natal in June 1875.[9] Like some of the other Gujerati passengers he came via Mauritius where he retained trading contacts. Amod was closely followed to Natal by Abdullah Haji Adam,[10] who was to become a founder member of both the Indian Committee and the Natal Indian Congress. When they arrived in the colony the total Indian population numbered almost 10 000. The importation of indentured workers which had ceased in 1866 had just been resumed and some 6 000 workers were imported between 26 June 1874 and 1 May 1875. The Indian population expanded rapidly after this. By 1880 it had topped

20 000 and by 1885 it was over 30 000. Although the majority of these were under indenture with little money to spare for trade goods, the ex-indentured population which numbered only about 4 000 in 1874 increased steadily after 1879 as successive groups of labourers worked out their five-year contracts.[11]

This growing ex-indentured community was served by ten Indian stores when the passenger merchants began to arrive. The storekeepers included two Naidoos, a Panday, a Naik and three Singhs,[12] all of whom were ex-indentured and all of whom belonged to higher castes than was usual for a migrant labourer. For a time the ex-indentured storekeepers held their own against their new competitors. By 1880 at the peak of their commercial success they held 30 of the 37 retail shop licences which had been issued to Indians in Durban, the colony's main urban centre. The decline from this peak was rapid. By 1885 there were around 66 Indian stores in Durban, 60 of which belonged to passengers. The remaining six ex-indentured storekeepers had difficulty keeping their businesses afloat.[13]

There is insufficient evidence to determine conclusively how and why the passengers came to dominate Indian commerce in Natal and, later, the Transvaal. But such evidence as there is suggests that the mechanisms were not particularly complex. The passengers, especially those who came earliest, appear to have arrived in Natal with relatively large sums of capital against which ex-indentured labourers found it increasingly difficult to compete. Property ownership in Durban illustrates this well. In 1877 passenger holdings comprised two properties owned by one man for a total value of £270; 17 properties were owned by 12 ex-indentured labourers for a total value of £3 685. By 1884, four passengers owned 40 properties valued at £16 000, and 78 ex-indentured labourers owned 96 valued at £17 605. In less than a decade the average property investment of ex-indentured workers had declined from £300 to £225, and the average passenger investment had risen from £135 to £4000. The remaining passenger merchants, of whom there were about 40 in Durban at the time, rented stores at 'very expensive rates'.[14]

The nature of passenger businesses also worked to their advantage. They were generally of the family type where proprietors, managers and assistants are related. In the absence of relatives, fellow Gujerati passengers were employed: the commercial elite associated with the ex-indentured community only 'so far as trade and labour compel[led] them'.[15] Thus, as the old stores were bought out by newcomers,[16] ex-indentured labourers were gradually excluded from prominent positions in Indian commerce. A quarter of a century passed before that situation was challenged. By then, the entrenched privilege of the passengers had received legal sanction.[17]

Once they had established themselves at the coast the passenger merchants fanned out across Natal and into the neighbouring Boer republics. In 1885, a decade after the arrival of the first passenger, they owned 60 stores in Durban and 20 branches throughout Natal, the Transvaal and the Orange Free State.[18] By 1904, when new applications for trade licences were systematically rejected in Natal and the Transvaal (and Indians had been prohibited from trading in the Orange Free State)[19] 1225 Indians were licensed in Natal, and 581 in the Transvaal.[20] Table 1 shows the distribution of Indian trading licences in Natal between 1895 and 1908. Although the records are incomplete, it is clear that commerce was concentrated in the major areas of Indian population — Durban, Pietermaritzburg and the coastal sugar-growing districts of Umlazi, Inanda and Lower Tugela. The smaller pockets of commercial activity in the north (Ladysmith, Newcastle, Dundee and Estcourt) reflect the sizeable Indian labour forces in the coal mines and on the Natal Government Railway. No comparable statistics exist for the Transvaal. But Table 2 is of use in demonstrating the overwhelming concentration of Indian commerce in Johannesburg and Pretoria.

The spatial distribution of these businesses reflects the nature of their trade. In Natal the Indians dealt to a large extent in commodities most suitable to a low income Indian clientele. These included rice, *ghee*, condiments, inexpensive jewellery and cloth. In the Transvaal, a low income clientele, though less specifically Indian, was attracted by inexpensive household goods and garden produce, which were also important staples of the Natal merchants.[21] In both areas, numbers of rural merchants, and a few in the urban centres, specialized in the 'kaffir truck trade' — the sale of cheap cloth, trinkets and tobacco to the Africans.[22] Some of the bigger merchants imported directly from India and elsewhere, and some even exported abroad. But most merchants in both Natal and the Transvaal bought their imported stock from white wholesalers in Durban.[23]

Beside helping to identify the nature of Indian commerce, and the range of clients on which it depended, the distribution of Indian trading activity provides important information for assessing the extent to which the interests of the commercial elite were interlinked.

Numerous examples indicate the fact that many of the Indian businesses had one or more branches. Indeed, numbers of the stores in northern Natal and the Transvaal were branches of the earliest enterprises in coastal Natal. It is worth identifying some of the key figures who were involved in trading on this scale because these were the men who constituted the most powerful stratum of the commercial elite, and who dominated Indian politics throughout much of the period under review.

Abdullah Haji Adam was one of the earliest passengers to arrive in Natal. He and two others were managing partners in the firm of Dada Abdullah and Company. Based in Durban, the company was one of the largest Indian businesses in South Africa in the 1890s, with fifteen branches scattered throughout the interior. Their interests included two steamers which regularly sailed between Bombay and Durban. Commercial transactions were carried out with firms in England, Germany and India.[24] Like some of the other large companies, Dada Abdullah's served as a point of entry for new passengers. N A Cama, for instance, a Gujerati Parsi who arrived in Natal in 1895, spent several months with them and then moved on to the Transvaal. He became a substantial interest holder in the firm of Cama and Company, as well as trading in his own right. An anomaly in the law of the republic which classified Parsis separately from other Asians enabled him to become, in addition, a landed proprietor in the Transvaal.[25]

Abubakr Amod, the first passenger merchant to arrive in Natal, owned a business house in Calcutta, an agency in Bombay, a company in Durban, and branches in the Transvaal. After Amod's death in 1888 the Pretoria branch of the company was renamed Tayob Haji Khan Abdullah and Company. Tayob Haji Khan Mohamed, the former managing partner in Pretoria, who was also a Gujerati, retained his interests in the original firm and expanded into several other businesses under his own name.[26] Amod's younger brother, Omar Johari, who came to Natal in 1883, worked with Dada Abdullah and Company for two years after he had completed his secondary education in 1890. He returned to India in 1892 and again in 1907 for higher education, but retained his links with the Natal elite as well as the property and commercial interests which he had inherited from his brother. The property investments included a partnership in the 'kaffir market' in Queen Street, Durban, which was sub-let to whites who managed the market.[27]

Mohamed Cassim Camroodeen, Abdul Kadir and Abdul Gani were partners in the Durban-based firm of M C Camroodeen and Company. Kadir managed their holdings in Durban, and Gani managed the Transvaal end of the business. Camroodeen and Company was described as the principal Indian firm in South Africa in the late 1890s.[28] Unlike other leading firms which branched out extensively, Camroodeen seems to have invested much of its surplus in property. The firm had substantial property investments in Durban.[29]

The Coovadia brothers, Moosa, Ebrahim and Amod, emigrated from Gujerat in 1889. They first established themselves in northern Natal, with businesses in Ladysmith, Newcastle, and Charlestown. In 1892 they moved to the Transvaal where they also acquired substantial commercial interests.[30] On a much smaller scale, M A Goga and his brother-in-law E L Amla each managed branches of Goga's firm in Ladysmith.[31] Dada Osman arrived in Natal in the early 1880s. He spent several years with Dada Abdullah and Company and then moved north to establish his own business. By 1898 he had two branches in Umsinga and another in Vryheid.[32] Adamji Miankhan, a member of a prominent Gujerati merchant family, also arrived in the early 1880s. He established the Durban-based firm of G H Miankhan and Company in conjunction with his father and brother.[33]

Among the other newcomers in the early '80s was Rustomji, a Gujerati Parsi who quickly established 'important business interests all over South Africa'. His holdings included commercial and property investments in Durban. His investments in the Transvaal, which comprised joint or exclusive interests in three Johannesburg businesses, had grown out of a partnership in Abubakr Amod's Johannesburg branch.[34] Dawad Mohamed who arrived around the same time reversed the usual order of procedure by starting off in the Transvaal. He became a partner in Ismail Mamoojee and Company in Pretoria, and then a partner of Abubakr Amod's branch in Potchefstroom. In 1884 he moved to Natal, established his own company, and invested in land and property in Durban.[35] Amod Jeeva, from a base in Durban, had expanded north into Estcourt, Dundee and Newcastle by 1898,[36] and Suleiman Essop Vavda owned three businesses in Newcastle by the 1890s.[37]

Ahmed Cachalia presents an unusual case for a Gujerati passenger. He arrived in the Transvaal in 1890 as a hawker. By 1893 he had opened his own business in Johannesburg and a branch in Pretoria.

Later he expanded into Nylstroom.[38] Mohamed Anglia was also
unusual. A fluent linguist in English, French, Dutch and several Indian
languages, he had been a municipal councillor in India. In 1897 he
emigrated to the Transvaal as the managing partner of big Mauritian
sugar merchants. Later, he moved to Natal and opened businesses in his
own name.[39] Haji Mahomed Haji Dada is also particularly noteworthy.
He was senior partner in another of the South African Indians' largest
firms. Dada and Company had holdings in Natal, the Transvaal,
Mozambique and, before 1890, the Orange Free State.[40] It seems likely
that one of Dada's managers or partners was his brother Haji Habib[41]
who arrived in South Africa in 1880, and who was later described by
Gandhi as having quickly established connections with 'important
businesses' in both Natal and the Transvaal.[42] Habib spent most of his
time in the Transvaal where he and Abdul Gani dominated Indian
politics until approximately 1909.[43]

Several interesting points are raised by the biographical information
sketched above. Firstly it is clear that through the wealthiest
merchants elite interests were firmly linked from the coast of Natal to
the interior of the colony and into the Transvaal. Some statistics from
the census year 1904, midway through the period under review, give
an approximate idea of the size of these interests. Z Konczacki has
estimated that profits and other incomes derived from Natal Indian
trade in the year 1903-1904 totalled £502 000.[44] Total Indian
property holdings in the colony were valued at £602 960 for 662
properties in April 1904.[45] No comparable figures are available for the
Transvaal, but it is possible to strike a rough comparison. The total
turnover of Transvaal Indian trading business for the year ending 31
December 1904 was £1 040 542.[46] In June 1904 a Transvaal government commission calculated the average rate of profit on 106 Asian
(Indian and Chinese) businesses at 6,71 per cent per month.[47] If this
rate is applied to the turnover listed above, total profits derived from
Transvaal Indian trade in 1904 stand at approximately £69 713. The
vast discrepancy between the figures for Natal and the Transvaal is
due in part to the fact that there were 1 225 traders in Natal (Table 1)
and only 581 in the Transvaal (Table 2). It is also due to the fact that
the Transvaal economy had been shattered during the war, whereas
Natal, though hovering on the brink of a depression, was still enjoying
the tail-end of a wartime boom. Clearly, though, the discrepancy also
reflects a much smaller Indian commercial investment in the Transvaal
than in Natal.

The gap in property investments is even wider. Legal limitations virtually prohibited Indian property ownership in the Transvaal.[48] Indians could, and did, 'own' property provided that it was registered under the name of a white, but there is nothing to suggest that this practice was widespread. The main point to be noted here, however, is that in a period when the average annual income for the majority of the free Indian population was approximately £12-18, the average for some 1 800 merchants is in excess of £300. And hidden within that average is the fact that a powerful minority, some of whom have just been described, commanded a disproportionate share of total Indian trade profits.

A second interesting point to emerge from the biographical information is the fact that Indian commercial expansion took place through a steady trickle of new merchants and new capital, and that much of the expansion took the form of partnerships between fellow Gujerati passengers, some of whom were newcomers buying into old, established firms. This suggests that as the colonial economy in Natal grew, and Indian trade along with it, the success of new commercial ventures demanded increasing amounts of initial capital investment. That, in turn, suggests that the network of Gujerati partnerships was an additional mechanism in excluding the ex-indentured from the front ranks of Indian commerce, and in consolidating the passenger monopoly.

The elite's common economic interests were not limited to the interdependency of wealthier merchants with multiple branches. Hundreds of the smaller traders in Natal were linked to the biggest firms through property rentals and credit. In 1898, for instance, M C Camroodeen and Company had outstanding debts of over £25 000 among nearly 400 Natal storekeepers and hawkers.[49] This example confirms a confidential government memorandum of August 1898 which claimed that up-country traders in Natal 'were and are "supported" by larger Indian houses which were established in Durban'.[50] In addition, Camroodeen's owned between £18 000 and £20 000 worth of property in Durban. They rented that property to smaller traders.[51] Amod Jeewa did the same with his holdings in Estcourt, Dundee, Newcastle and Durban.[52] Moosa Haji Adam, another 'extensive landed proprietor', was the landlord of probably several dozens of smaller traders from at least the mid-1890s onwards.[53] In the Transvaal, by contrast, where few Indians owned immovable property or land, it is clear that the relationship between big and small traders must have differed. But there is sufficient information to suggest that linkages occurred through the extension of credit by big merchants to petty traders.[54]

Thus the primary relationship which defined the commercial elite in Natal and the Transvaal, both objectively and subjectively,was common — indeed, shared — economic interests. Other levels of consciousness are also clearly definable, but their significance is less easy to assess. The elite created and nurtured many social and religious organizations which celebrated narrow cultural distinctions. In Natal these included the Brahman Mandal, the Anjuman Islam, the Mastic Society, the Hindu Sabha, the Zoroastrian Anjuman, the Memon Committee and the Kathiawar Arya Mandal.[55] In the Transvaal, identifiable sub-groupings, though some were perhaps less formally constituted, included the Gujerati Kunbis, the Konkanis, the Hindu Society, the Gujerat Hindu Society, the Sanatan Veda Dharma Sabha, the Hamidia Islamic Society and the Hamdarde Islamic Society.[56] Muslims in both areas supported the international Red Crescent Society[57] and, for a time between 1905 and 1908, committees which were established in Durban and Johannesburg to collect funds for a 'Holy Railway' from Damascus to Medina.[58]

There is insufficient information available to determine how much of a counter-pull these narrow loyalties might have exerted against the economic imperative which defined the group. It seems likely that they were balanced out by a consciousness — however ill-defined — of themselves as an *Indian* elite. There is an abundance of information to demonstrate that their most extravagant secular social activities were attended by *all* of the group; and though they may occasionally have included guests of other races, these were 'Indian' celebrations.[59] But this is not to suggest that national consciousness generated the politics of the commercial elite. In the discussions of merchant ideology and political activity in subsequent chapters, it will become clear that their politics were based, essentially, on the economic relationship which defined the elite, and that this was both a strength and a weakness of these politics.

The New Elite

A new elite began to emerge as an objectively definable group in Natal between 1905 and 1906. By early 1910, its perimeters were clearly distinguishable, though the group itself still showed signs of groping towards a self-conscious sense of identity. For the most part they were 'colonials', the young Natal-born offspring of indentured or ex-indentured labourers.

The major distinguishing feature between the new elite and the underclasses from whom they had risen was their superior position in the occupational structure. The most successful among them were a few highly trained professionals: lawyers, civil servants, accountants and a lone newspaper publisher. Lower down the occupational ladder were teachers, bookkeepers, clerks, interpreters, petty entrepreneurs and small farmers.

On the rare occasions when individuals within these categories emerge in official records, or the Indian press, little detail is given about their backgrounds. Indeed, some their specific occupations are rarely mentioned. The merchants, by contrast, are well-documented, mainly because so many of them were the subject of petitions to the colonial or imperial government at one time or another. However, it is possible to illustrate the occupational breakdown of the new elite with some concrete examples.

The handful of professionals included men such as James Godfrey, a London-trained barrister,[60] the youngest son of an Indian mission schoolmaster who had come to South Africa from Mauritius. The family's lifestyle was described by contemporaries as European, they spoke English from infancy.[61] Joseph Royeppen was also a London-trained barrister.[62] Royeppen played an active role in the politics of the new Natal elite as well as the passive resistance campaign in the Transvaal.[63] P Subramania Aiyar, a Tamil *brahmin*, was deeply involved in the politics of the new elite for several years, although not, apparently, colonial-born like the others. The Anglo-Tamil weekly *African Chronicle* which Aiyar published and edited was an important means of communication for the group.[64] S R Pather was active until he left to study law in London in 1907.[65] Other active participants slightly lower down the occupational ladder included T M Naicker, the Tamil headmaster of Umbogintwini Indian School;[66] B L E Sigamoney, headmaster of Estcourt Indian High School;[67] Lutchman Panday, a north Indian Brahmin who was an attorney's clerk;[68] and L M Naidoo,[69] S P Pillay[70] (both Tamils) and Suchitt Maharaj,[71] each of whom was a government interpreter. Indian Christians can rarely be identified in terms of ethnic background, but V Lawrence, an attorney's clerk and Tamil language teacher, was clearly a Tamil.[72] The ease with which other Christians integrated with an essentially Tamil group suggests that they were also Tamil. They are exemplified by men like Brian Gabriel, a photographer,[73], and Lazarus Gabriel who was a photographer and Indian eating-house keeper.[74] The most successful farmers included men like Charlie Nulliah Naidoo, a Tamil whose level of prosperity allowed family celebrations lavish enough to excite the admiration of young white neighbours in turn-of-the-century Pietermaritzburg.[75]

Most of the new elite, though, were white collar workers, dependent for a livelihood on the needs of the colonial administration: they numbered a little over 300 in 1904.[76] Their salaries obviously varied but it seems accurate to suggest that until around 1905-1906 most were economically comfortable if not wealthy. Konczacki estimates their average annual income for 1904 at over £65[77] — nearly five times that of the average worker, and about one-fifth that of the average merchant.

For many of the new elite, occupational achievements rested on a western education. Most of them had obtained as good an education as Natal had to offer Indians, and the mere fact of their having obtained any at all was another significant distinguishing feature between them and the mass of the people. By the census year 1904, out of a total population of 100 918,[78] only 5 211 (5 per cent) of the Natal Indians were literate in English.[79] This low rate is attributable to several factors. Firstly it reflects the fact that those who came to the colony as adults were rarely able to acquire a working knowledge of English. But still, the rate is far lower than it would have been if all school-aged children had received an education: in 1904, for instance, there were 16 311 Indians in Natal between the ages of 6 and 14.[80] Part of the cause of the low literacy rate must therefore be attributed to inadequate educational facilities. In 1904 there were 40 Indian schools in Natal.[81] Ten of these were privately run 'Muslim' schools, one a private 'Tamil' school. The other 29, all English medium schools, were predominantly missionary establishments, some of them government-aided, most of them not. They were poorly distributed leaving some areas with no educational facility at all.[82] And finally, the parents of many school-aged children could not afford to let them attend school. They were required to contribute to the family income either by wage work or by taking care of the household and releasing their mothers for work.[83]

The fact that the new elite had acquired a western education, despite the obvious difficulties they faced, suggests some important deductions about their backgrounds. It suggests that they came from families who had grasped the significance of education in the process of vertical mobility in South Africa, and who were so committed to raising themselves above the general level of the mass of the people that they were willing to undergo whatever hardships were necessary in order to equip their children properly. Indeed, a 1914 Union Government Economic Commission reported that those who had succeeded in obtaining an education 'in many cases owed this to the self-sacrifice of [their] lowly indentured parents.'[84] The next question to be approached — the cultural diversity of the new elite — which is raised primarily as a means of demonstrating some of the difficulties which they had in generating a sense of group identity, is thus also of interest as a commentary on those who were willing to make self-sacrifices. It reveals the fact that Indian upward mobility, far from being a random process, conformed to very specific patterns.

Only the leadership level of the new elite can be analysed with any degree of accuracy. What little detailed information exists for individuals is confined almost exclusively to those who were the driving force behind the group's four major proto-political or political organizations, the Hindu Young Men's Association (HYMA), the Durban Indian Society (DIS), the Natal Indian Patriotic Union (NIPU), and the Colonial Born Indian Association (CBIA). The two dozen men who by overlapping memberships filled some 45 leadership positions in these organizations[85] were by no means representative of the migrant labouring population from which they had risen. There was an imbalance between the two major ethnic groups which comprised the underclasses. South Indians and their descendants who were an estimated minimum 57 per cent of the labouring population during the census year 1911[86] (the only year for which such data are available) filled 86 per cent of the new elite's leadership positions. Their names suggest that most of these were Tamils, but characteristically Telegu names are also apparent. North Indians and their descendants, an estimated 22 per cent of the labouring population,[87] made up the remaining 14 per cent.

In terms of religious composition the imbalances in the group are even more striking. Christians, who were a small minority of the labouring population (8 per cent)[88], made up 28 per cent of the total leadership level despite the fact that none of them was a member of HYMA. Muslims, an equally small minority of the population,[89] were not represented at all. South Indian Hindus were proportionately represented (58 per cent) and North Indian Hindus were underrepresented (14 per cent). In addition, Hindu members of the new elite were invariably drawn from higher castes than the majority of the migrant labourers. As the names of those who have been mentioned indicate, they included *brahmins*, and members of communities which in their home districts in India claimed *kshatriya*[90] or *vaisya* status in the late nineteenth century, though they were not accorded this status by census officials.[91] No member of the new elite's leadership was a *panchama*. The only confirmed *sudras* were Modaleys, a title used by the Vellala whose occupations in Madras ranged from peasant proprietor to clerk, merchant or shopkeeper, and some of whom petitioned to be recorded as *vaisyas* in the 1871 Madras census and who were described in the 1901 census as being 'by general consent', the highest of the Tamil *sudra* castes.[92]

Since the majority of Indian schools in Natal were mission schools, the disproportionate number of Christians among the western educated is not surprising. Education was represented as a desirable end in itself for Christians. Their prominence in the new elite goes far towards explaining the over-representation of South Indians vis à vis North Indians. In a random sample of over 1 500 male immigrants from Madras, Christians emerge as the fourth largest 'caste' grouping.[93] There are none at all in a similar sample of over 900 male immigrants from Calcutta.[94] The fact that the 'higher' castes among the ex-indentured and colonial-born Hindus predominated is particularly interesting. This suggests that despite the extent to which caste was of necessity broken down under the conditions of indentured labour, the 'higher' castes made a concerted effort to adapt to new circumstances in such a way as to regain the relatively privileged position in the socio-economic hierarchy which they had held in India. For them, western education can thus be viewed as a means of social and economic upgrading. It is worth re-emphasizing that the difficulties entailed in achieving a western education indicate that the commitment to upward mobility was strong.

It is not surprising, then, to find that the new elite began to emerge as a separate group during the post-war depression in Natal when it became increasingly difficult for western educated white collar workers to maintain existing standards, far less realistically aspire to anything higher. Hitherto, in the classic pattern of an upwardly mobile group, their ambitions had been expressed in an alliance with those above them in the Indian social and economic hierarchy, the merchants. They had followed the leadership of the commercial elite and supported their politics from the moment the Natal Indian Congress was founded.[95]

They had shared the merchants' secular social functions and sought their patronage for social activities of their own which the merchants did not care to join.[96] During the Anglo-Boer War they had served as unpaid leaders of the Indian Stretcher Corps whose war effort became an integral part of the merchants' attempts to validate their claim to the rights and privileges of citizenship.[97]

The fact that the Congress did little or nothing on behalf of the western educated did not weaken their allegiance between 1894 and 1905. Their numbers were so small and the Indian community so polarized in terms of social, economic and even legal status, that the mere fact of their acceptance by the merchants had its uses. It served to reinforce their distance from the underclasses and helped them escape the stigma of the crude legal definition which classified Indians as 'passengers' or (indentured) 'immigrants', and which was popularized as 'Arabs' or 'coolies', regardless of the personal achievements of non-passengers. Thus, involvement with the Congress offered the western educated social esteem and valuable support against the omnipresent threat of petty harassment by whites, whether public or officials. At this level, then, their alliance with the merchants can be viewed as another investment in social upgrading like the western education which made the alliance possible in the first place.

The other part of the explanation for the continued alliance lies in the paradoxical fact that until 1905 or so the economic position of the western educated was far less vulnerable than that of the merchants themselves. Indian interpreters, policemen, court clerks, magistrates' assistants, hospital compounders and the like, were essential to the smooth running of the administration in a colony whose population included over 100 000 Indians. Magistrates' replies to an official circular issued in 1901 show that interpreters performed valuable clerical functions, often handling much of the Indian business which passed through the magistrate's office. In fact all of these minor functionaries appear to have been highly valued by their white superiors. Examination of a number of cases of bribery or extortion brought against Indians in such positions between 1897 and 1909 reveals a series of dismissed cases, acquittals or, at worst, transfer to another post despite the fact that charges were often accompanied by an impressive weight of evidence against the accused.[98]

During the post-war depression, however, the upward mobility of the western educated received its first serious check, and even existing standards were eroded by widespread salary cuts and the introduction of a new form of taxation.[99] With their economic interests threatened for the first time since 1894, the compensations derived from involvement with the Congress were outweighed by disadvantages. It became clear that the party did not adequately represent the interests of the western educated and was even opposed to them in some instances.[100] It was during this period that the process of differentiation which gave birth to the new elite first became apparent.

Late in 1905, young, western educated Tamil colonials in Durban and Pietermaritzburg established twin branches of an organization called the Hindu Young Men's Association.[101] Apart from sports' clubs, which dated as far back as the 1890s,[102] HYMA was the earliest effective non-passenger organization in Natal. Its establishment turned out to be the first in a series of steps which culminated in March 1911 in the formation of the Colonial Born Indian Association. The CBIA, which looked to the mass of the people for its constituency, reflected the first clear expression of both the new elite's perceived interests, and the ideology which served to define them as a group. Thus within a brief time period after the birth of HYMA, the young colonials redefined their relationship with the merchants, forging, in the process, a common identity for themselves, and re-interpreting their relationship with the underclasses from whom they had risen. The realignment of relationships, and the two political associations which expressed this (the Natal Indian Patriotic Union and the CBIA) will be the subject of chapter 5. For the purpose of the present chapter it is necessary only to discuss the two proto-political associations, HYMA and DIS (the Durban Indian Society), and the role which they played in helping to define the sense of community which prepared the young colonials for separate politics.

The two branches of HYMA were established in October 1905 under the guidance of Professor Parmanand, a visiting Arya Samajist missionary from the Anglo-Vedic College in Lahore.[103] It is impossible to assess how much impact, if any, Arya Samajist doctrines had on the Natal Hindus at this time. In any event the real significance of Parmanand's visit was that it produced the chain reaction from which the new elite's first political associations emerged. The enthusiastic response to the establishment of a non-passenger organization, and the fairly rapid development of events within the next few years, make it clear that the emerging elite would have begun to realign their loyalties sooner or later anyway. As it happened, though, the catalytic agent which started the sequence of events was a Hindu missionary, and there seems little doubt that whatever advantages were derived from HYMA it was disadvantageous in two respects. Its religious nature excluded prominent members of the emerging elite (Christians) while the decision to use Tamil as the Association's official language discouraged still others (non-Tamils).

The speeches at the first Annual General Meeting of the Durban branch on 20 April 1907 offer a good indication of HYMA's orientation. The joint secretaries, T M Naicker and K R Naidoo, urged members to encourage the study of Tamil which, they said, had been neglected in the colony, and to 'work strenuously for the noble cause of their religion'.[104] In Pietermaritzburg a Tamil school had already been opened by HYMA in 1905;[105] and in 1909 when Hindu religious festivals first began to be celebrated publicly on a large scale, the school was reported to have drawn attention to Divali by organizing an exhibition for the festival in Durban.[106]

However, HYMA served other needs than the purely religious or cultural. The wide-ranging programmes of the weekly meetings included mock trials, and discussions on *swadeshi*, 'truth', the need for industrial training facilities for Indians and the benefits of education for women.[107] Thus despite its origins and despite the fact that it probably helped delay the establishment of the emerging elite's first non-sectarian organization, HYMA certainly did not obstruct its creation. The Pietermaritzburg branch of NIPU was founded at a meeting which took place in the HYMA hall in August 1908,[108] and six of the fourteen officials who have been identified for the Durban and Pietermaritzburg branches of NIPU were HYMA officials. Of the rest, five were Christians.[109]

NIPU reflects a significant step in the creation of a unifying ideology and the realignment of loyalties for the emerging elite. With the establishment of the party they had passed beyond traditional bases of differentiation and although in 1908 they had yet to define consciously a basis for social regrouping they seemed to be moving towards identifying themselves as 'colonials': South Africans who happened to be of Indian descent. One of NIPU's earliest public statements stressed the fact that the party's members were loyal British subjects and that 'their home was this colony'.[110] In this respect they echoed the persistent merchant claim to the right to be treated as 'responsible citizens', adding the weight of the claim derived from their local origin. Unlike the Congress, however, the early membership of NIPU included some workers, although they were few in number. In any event the party clearly sought to identify itself with the underclasses from whom its leaders had risen.

The purpose of NIPU was stated to be 'to ameliorate the present distressed condition of their fellow men and also to assist them in every possible way to a better condition of life'[111]: the party's earliest activities demonstrate that this was more than mere political rhetoric. Enthusiasm ran high at the beginning of this first attempt at independent politics. By January 1909, NIPU had branches in Durban, Pietermaritzburg, Sea Cow Lake, Springfield, Isipingo, Tongaat and Newcastle.[112]

Shortly after NIPU was established, however, the advances which it represented received a damaging set-back. While the party was still in its infancy Professor Parmanand's successor, Swami Shankeranand, arrived in Natal for a prolonged visit. Within months of Shankeranand's arrival, religious divisions had reappeared in the slowly coalescing but still fragile elite in a new, intense form. The Pietermaritzburg branch of the party split off from the main Durban branch and the membership of both began to drop. NIPU continued to exist for some time but the enthusiasm which had characterized its origins was lost and its early promise remained unfulfilled.[113]

The Durban Indian Society was established during the winter of 1909,[114] while Shankeranand's disruptive influence was at its height. Eight of DIS's thirteen most active members were NIPU officials,[115] and membership appears to have been completely open. The old, close links between the emerging elite in Durban and Pietermaritzburg were reaffirmed when officials of DIS opened a branch in Pietermaritzburg in April 1910.[116] But despite the continuity of the leadership level from HYMA, through NIPU and DIS, the Society offered a means of retrieving lost ground rather than an advance from NIPU's position. Although speakers at the weekly meetings included the secretary of the local branch of the Social Democratic Federation and the acting secretary of the Cape Town based African Political Organization,[117] DIS was not primarily a political association. Its own political activity was confined to occasional resolutions about Indian grievances, and muted rumbles of discontent about the unrepresentative nature of the Congress.[118] DIS's value lay in the fact that it kept open the lines of communication between members of the emerging elite. It provided the organizational framework for regular meetings after NIPU had ceased to be effective. When the Colonial Born Indian Association (CBIA) was established in March 1911, most of its leadership level was drawn from DIS. The CBIA marked the emergence of the new elite as a self-conscious social unit, their perceived unity defined in terms of their relatively privileged position in the occupational structure, as well as their common South

African origins. The CBIA also confirmed — though with some ambivalence — the chosen role of the colonial-born as the spokesmen for the Natal Indian underclasses.

The Underclasses

The base of the Natal Indian population was built on the flow of indentured labour which began in 1860. Between 1860 and 1911, when the importation of Indian workers ceased at the request of the Union Government, 152 184 were shipped to Natal out of Calcutta or Madras.[119]

Tables 4 and 5 show the caste breakdown of a random sample of 929 male and 455 females shipped out of Calcutta between 1860 and 1906, and of 1 572 males and 751 females shipped out of Madras. Table 4 is of interest in demonstrating that some 50 per cent of the migrants from Madras were drawn from castes above, or at the top of the *sudra* level. Indeed, many of the *sudras* listed here claimed *vaisya* or *kshatriya* status in their home districts in India, though they were not accorded this status by census officials.[120] Tables 6 and 7 show the districts of origin of the random samples. Table 6 is of particular interest in demonstrating the heavy flow of labourers from three districts in Madras: North and South Arcot, and Chingleput. These three Tamil-language districts produced nearly 60 per cent of the South Indian migrants to Natal, which may offer part of the explanation for the vitality of the ex-indentured Tamil community in Natal. Tables 8 and 9 show the age distribution of the sample population. Predictably, the highest numbers of migrants were in the most productive age groups, 20 to 24 and 25 to 29. The relatively high proportion of 'dependent' minors — approximately 22 per cent of the migrants from Madras and 17 per cent from Calcutta — illustrates the lengths to which recruiters were prepared to go in order to recruit able-bodied adults.

By reducing the migrants to statistical expressions, however, the tables fail to illustrate the human sorrows which are all too evident in the meticulous details of the ships' logs: the vulnerability of a single woman with children in an impoverished society; the many young migrant families with infants-in-arms whose recent child evidently proved one dependent too many; the young men who had prematurely become heads of joint families, and who thus supported not only wives and children, but also sisters and elderly mothers; the sudden crises in fragile village economies, which cleared thirty or forty people out of a single village in one shipment. An understanding of the process of recruitment for indenture illuminates the harsh reality of nineteenth-century India which these details reflect. This process has been described by Hugh Tinker in *A New System of Slavery* which discusses the export of Indian labour between 1830 and 1920. Recruitment for Natal fits the general pattern which emerged from Tinker's research: the single most important factor which shaped the process was unwillingness to emigrate. Recruiting statistics and official correspondence leave no doubt that few Indians would voluntarily exchange even a subsistence level existence for emigration. But the increasing pressure on land as the nineteenth century advanced produced a situation of growing rural indebtedness and swelled the ranks of landless labourers. With subsistence margins reduced to a bare minimum, rural wage labourers and peasants were increasingly unable to support the burden of a hostile ecology and the demands of landlord and tax-collector, particularly in seasons when natural disaster struck and whole crops were lost to drought or flood. Officials were frank in their recognition that it was the 'floating population who live from hand to mouth' upon whom the recruiters depended. And even they were loath to emigrate except in 'times of scarcity' when the 'starving inhabitants' would 'troop to the depots'.[121] In addition, fraud and kidnapping were often resorted to, especially in years when there were good rains and a healthy crop.[122] Thus the bulk of Natal's indentured labourers came to be made up of the distressed, the despairing, the diseased, and even the disabled; products of a socio-economic system which offered at best subsistence, but too often only starvation.

The sugar industry in Natal was founded on this cheap labour. Indian contract workers were also the mainstay of up-country farms and wattle plantations. Increasingly after the 1890s they were used in industry as well, mainly on the Natal Government Railway and the northern coalfields. They were also valued as domestic servants in private residences, hotels, boarding schools and hospitals. However, indentured Indians in Natal were primarily agricultural labourers. Agriculture rarely absorbed less than 75 per cent of the total indentured workforce.[123]

Some 52 per cent of these migrants stayed on in Natal after their terms of indenture had expired. From there, several thousands drifted north to the Transvaal before the Anglo-Boer war; but most of them remained in Natal.[124] Initially many of them, and their descendants, enjoyed modest material success. Natal was a young and growing colony. The severe depression of the late 1860s which had put a temporary stop to labour importation gave way to a period of increasing white settlement and economic growth. Free Indian labour was in constant demand by whites in the coastal areas. And, by the early 1890s, the railway extensions in up-country Natal and the Rand gold mines, with wages far in excess of those offered by white planters and farmers, were drawing ex-indentured workers away from agriculture.[125]

More importantly, there were numerous opportunities for involvement in petty enterprises which required little or no capital investment. Fishing, market gardening, and fruit and vegetable hawking were monopolized by ex-indentured Indians in the late 1870s.[126] The fishermen formed a small community on Salisbury Island in Durban Bay, where their catch was salted and dried. There was a steady market for their produce among Indians on the mainland.[127] Market gardeners rented holdings of 5 to 15 acres around Durban at rents between 15 and 25 shillings a year which they generally managed to pay in advance. An occasional particularly successful migrant was able to buy a few acres for as much as £20 an acre. Total Indian smallholdings were estimated at over 3 000 acres in 1877.[128]

By 1897, Indians cultivated 25 340,25 acres. The total market value of their crops during that year was £111 890. Livestock was valued at £17 875.[129] In 1899, the Protector of Indian Immigrants claimed that many ex-indentured labourers had recently bought land around Durban, paying as much as £25-£60 an acre.[130] By 1904, smallholders' profits were estimated at £355 300.[131] The 1904 census lists thousands of head of Indian-owned livestock and poultry.[132] The total acreage cultivated by Indians had risen to about 41 000 by 1907.[133]

In general, Indian cultivators sought the economic security of crop production: vegetables, sugar and, in particular, maize. Tobacco was also an Indian staple from the earliest days. By 1906 Indians were producing annually nearly three million pounds of tobacco for sale, rough dried, to the Natal Africans. In addition the 1891 census shows an Indian involvement in coffee production. But this is absent from later records.[134]

The Protector of Immigrants' files reveal numerous examples of the striking failures and successes of this period. A statement of the assets of some two dozen deceased ex-indentured labourers in 1890 averages out at a few pence over a pound. They had been in the colony, on average, eight years.[135] There are periodic lists of destitute ex-indentured Indians being shipped back to India free of charge. Almost invariably they were suffering from some form of disease.[136] Less numerous are the striking successes. Jowahir, who died on 1 November 1900, left behind £88.1s.8d. plus a one-third share of a 93-acre property which he had owned jointly with his two elder brothers. The surviving partners valued Jowahir's share of the property at £124. Chunga Reddy, who died in February 1896, had owned a wood and iron house and a horse and cart. He had 24 acres under cultivation. A list of accounts for his estate between March and May 1897 shows that African workers — as many as sixteen at a time — were hired on a daily basis at a shilling a day. Akloo, who died some seven years after the end of his term of indenture, had managed to accumulate £200 and a house on leasehold land. Mootoosamy died in August 1890 leaving an iron house and 21 acres of freehold property. £15 was still owing on the purchase price of the property.[137] Until around 1905 these examples of relative affluence and destitution seem to have been the extremes between which fell the majority of ex-indentured labourers in Natal. Konczacki notes that generally low Indian incomes are reflected in data on house rentals which show that in the early years of the century the majority of Indians occupied the most inferior types of dwellings.[138]

Links between the ex-indentured community and the commercial elite were limited and well defined. An important point of contact was merchant marketing of Indian produce. Between the early 1890s and 1910 most Indian market gardeners and petty farmers sold their produce in the Durban 'Mosque Market'. The only reference to the origins of the market states that some time in late 1892 or early 1893 Durban's leading Indian merchants were approached by a deputation of producers who complained about the lack of marketing facilities. Some land owned by the Porbunder Madressa was then set aside by its trustees as a market ground. The fee for the use of this ground was an optional donation to the school.[139] At some point after this a mandatory fee was established, and by 1909 the Madressa's annual income from the market was estimated at £1 400 or £1 500.[140] It is ironic that Durban's main Muslim school should have been so handsomely supported by Indian cultivators, few of whom were Muslim, and whose children were sadly lacking in educational facilities. The question of feeding market returns back into the community became the major issue which Swami Shankeranand used to mobilize popular support during his brief involvement in Indian politics between 1909 and 1910.[141]

A more onerous and increasingly more important link between the commercial elite and the ex-indentured Indian community in both

Natal and the Transvaal was usury. It is impossible to quantify the extent of the merchant credit network, but all available evidence suggests that it was widespread and that the interest rate for people who had no security was 'very high'.[142] One source suggests that the rate was as high as two shillings and sixpence in the pound per month.[143] Thus the ex-indentured population had easy access to credit, which may have appeared to offer them a competitive edge over their struggling African fellow-cultivators in Natal, as one recent work suggests.[144] However, it is clear that the vicious circle of usury once entered into must have have been very difficult to escape. Indeed, it is known that in at least some instances merchants established what seems to have been a bondage relationship with newly freed Indian labourers, setting them up on smallholdings under conditions which one observer found as stringent as the indenture which they had just completed.[145] In addition, a 1911 Magistrate's report noted that some tenancy agreements included the condition that the cultivator's produce must be sold to the landlord at an essentially unfavourable rate.[146]

The real pressure on the ex-indentured community came during the post-war depression in Natal. Again, the paucity of statistical data makes it difficult to assess exactly how widespread and how severe were the hardships experienced by the underclasses during the period from around 1905 to 1913. But there is more than enough information to suggest that thousands of ex-indentured Indians in Natal were profoundly affected by the double burden of the depressed economy and the annual £3 tax to which those who had entered indenture after 1895 were subjected.[147] Heavy indebtedness, and widespread unemployment and destitution are recorded in a variety of sources.[148] Indeed, one source reported some 28 000 'destitute coolies' in 1907.[149] The NGR and the plantations lowered their wage levels for free Indian labour so that even those who were employed experienced unusual pressure.[150] In addition, the Rand gold mines which had attracted Indian wage labourers before the war were virtually closed to Natal Indians after the Transvaal administration started clamping down on Indian immigration in 1903 and 1904:[151] the 1911 census shows only 3 121 male and 1 055 female Indian wage workers in the Transvaal.[152] The pre-war opportunities which had existed for Indian hawkers in the Transvaal were, of course, similarly restricted: only 2 966 'Asiatics' were licensed to hawk in the Transvaal in 1905.[153] However, the most illuminating examples of the hardships suffered during these years are found in the records of Indian labour on the Benguela railway, and in statistics for re-indenture.

In April 1907, some 2 000 Indian men, women and children sailed from Durban for Lobito Bay in Angola. 'Almost all' of them owed the Natal government between £1 and £14 in tax arrears. They 'were for the most part out of work and clamouring to be allowed to engage themselves on the Benguela Railway at the liberal wages offered'.[154] Within months the Natal Protector received letters from workers alleging brutal conditions and a high mortality rate. The British consul at Luanda was instructed to visit and inspect the railway construction camp. Consul Mackie found the conditions favourable.[155] Griffiths and Company, who had contracted the workers, denied the allegations of ill-treatment and claimed that a high desertion rate resulted from attempts to avoid payments on the £3 tax arrears, which were deducted from their wages.[156] Since deserters tried to make their way back to Natal,[157] where there were no jobs, and where the tax was owing, this seems highly unlikely. Some figures provided by the Natal government suggest a disastrous experience:[158]

	Men	Women	Children	Total
Left Natal April 1907	1 212	423	639	2 274
Disembarked before sailing	39	–	–	39
Total who left	1 173	423	639	2 235
Reported dead or missing, Lobito Bay	386	91	150	627

Increasingly, then, ex-indentured workers were driven back into the privations of contract work, where payment of the tax was suspended for the duration of the contract. Table 10 shows the steady rise in the percentage of men and women under second or subsequent terms of indenture between 1901 and 1913. The figures are calculated as a proportion of the workers who ended a term of indenture, or became 'free', in each year. Second or subsequent indentures were usually for two-year periods. It is not possible to know how many re-indentured labourers had been free for some time between terms. Table 11 suggests that at least 1 000 men and women went directly from one contract to the next. The key evidence, however, is provided by the 1913 Protector's Report which shows that 65,25 per cent of the entire indentured workforce was under second or subsequent indenture during the year ending December 1913, some four years after the end of the depression.[159] Most of these were on the sugar plantations.

In theory every aspect of the indentured workers' material existence was dictated by the terms of their contracts which conformed to Government of India regulations. These stipulated that the working week should consist of six nine-hour days. The basic wage for men over seventeen was ten shillings a month during the first year of indenture, with annual increments of one shilling a month in each subsequent year. Women and minors were paid half these amounts. Food rations were also covered by the contract. Migrants over the age of twelve were entitled to two pounds of *dhal*, one pound of salt, two pounds of salt fish and one pound of *ghee* or oil monthly; and daily either one and a half pounds of rice, or two pounds of maize meal on three days of the week and rice for the remainder. Migrants under twelve were entitled to three-quarters of an adult ration. Employers were also expected to provide free medical attention in case of sickness, and accommodation in good repair. In addition, Natal employers issued a set of clothing to each migrant at the point of embarkation.[160]

On paper the terms of indenture appear adequate. Indeed, at first glance the migrants seem to have been considerably better off than their free counterparts in rural England.[161] Like any other system, though, this one was open to abuse and it is necessary to examine the extent to which it was abused in order to arrive at a clear picture of the conditions of existence of Indian indentured labourers in Natal.

A close reading of the Protector of Immigrants' files suggests that in agriculture — and particularly on the labour-intensive sugar plantations where some 60-70 per cent of indentured Indians worked — employers sought to keep costs low by denying workers their contract rights and by a concomitant reliance on labour-coercive techniques.[162] Plantation labourers were overworked (as much as a seventeen or eighteen hour day during the overlapping crushing and planting seasons),[163] malnourished and poorly housed.[164] These aspects of their existence gave rise to abnormally high disease and death rates which, an official medical service notwithstanding, remained fairly constant throughout the period under review.[165] In addition, the Natal indentured labour system offered little room for even such basic human comforts as family life. Women, and particularly family women, were so reluctant to emigrate that Natal, like other recruiting colonies, had difficulty in even fulfilling the terms of Government of India legislation which demanded that four women be exported for every ten men. There was thus a serious imbalance in the male:female ratio, and the possibility of establishing or maintaining a family unit was made even more remote by the prevalent employer practice of refusing to ration or to pay any non-working Indian.[166] In short, there is a solid weight of evidence in the Protector's files to suggest that overwork, malnourishment, and squalid living conditions formed the pattern of daily life for most agricultural workers.

For a variety of reasons which I have discussed more fully elsewhere,[167] the conditions of other indentured Indians were somewhat less oppressive. Briefly, the infant coal-mining industry, still characterized by heavy capital expenditure, and suffering the same dificulties competing in the world market as the sugar industry, was equally concerned with cost-cutting. However, widespread reluctance on the part of Indians to sign up for mine work forced the coal industry to offer slightly better terms than the plantations.[168] In addition, extra productivity was encouraged on some mines by a cash and ration bonus system which could earn workers a consistent 15 to 20 per cent increment over contract terms. The even more favourable conditions enjoyed by the Natal Government Railway workers[169] seem to have derived from the fact that the railway could maintain a satisfactory rate of profit without resorting to a comparable degree of exploitation. Finally, the much sought after experienced domestics were indentured as 'Special Servants' under contracts which offered salaries from £1 to £5 a month: two to ten times that of an agricultural worker.

It is clear, however, that the vast majority of Indian indentured workers suffered extreme privation. Elaborate layers of formal and informal controls were used to keep them on the job under these conditions. The extent and nature of control[170] varied with the harshness of conditions, ranging from employer/official encouragement or sanctioning of palliatives (drug and alcohol abuse, gambling and money-lending, for instance), to sjambok-wielding gang bosses, and a legal system that was heavily stacked in favour of employers. 'Leaving the estate in a body' was illegal and punishable by fines or jail sentences, even if the workers had left to complain about a breach of the contract, and even if that complaint were upheld by the Magistrate or Protector. Indeed, no indentured Indian could move more than two miles beyond his place of work without a written ticket of leave. If, despite all this, a worker did show signs of political awareness, such as trying to organize others in his compound, or even his work-gang, he was immediately transferred elsewhere — the final divisive mechanism.

Given these constraints on worker action it is not easy to assess the nature of the indentured workers' ideology. Throughout the whole period under review they attempted to protest their conditions. But these protests were usually individualistic and mainly of a type which required little or no prior organization — malingering, absenteeism, petty larceny, destruction of employers' property, and desertion, for instance. Before 1909-1910 the incidence of collective action was extremely low. There were no more than a handful of 'strikes', and these were short-lived, rarely transcended the accommodation units or work-gangs into which plantation, mine and railway workforces were further sub-divided, and were generally concerned with specific gross abuses of the contract. The elaborate network of controls erected by employers and the state was in itself almost enough to have ensured this. But, equally importantly, it must not be forgotten that the workers — even the re-indentured — were at most only a few years removed from the pre-industrial Indian countryside. Both the nature of their protest (spontaneous and without organization), and the fact that the contract had evidently replaced the workers' notion of customary justice (and flagrant breaches therefore represented intolerable injustice) are consistent with George Rudé's characterization of 'pre-industrial' protest informed by a 'traditional' or 'inherent' ideology.[171] Indeed, the detailed discussion of the massive 1913 strike in Chapter 6 shows that when, for a unique combination of reasons, a prolonged, widespread work stoppage did become possible, many workers drew on popular forms of Indian culture to explain their actions. As noted, however, there is more than enough evidence to indicate that though they may have lacked an appropriate ideological framework within which to organize and structure protest more suited to industrial employment, indentured workers certainly felt a profound sense of grievance about their living and working conditions. And, as the percentage of reindentured workers rose sharply after 1906, bringing into the contract workforce the new set of grievances that stemmed from their inability to remain free, the rate of protest began to increase.[172] These acts of resistance were still, however, mainly individualistic and incapable of producing any significant change in their conditions.

What is particularly important for present purposes is simply to underscore the more pressing grievances of both indentured and ex-indentured workers by the first decade of the century, and their inability to effectively represent, far less redress, them. Nor, contrary to the rhetoric of the merchant-dominated Natal Indian Congress, were their grievances represented by the Indian elite, unless this could be seen to serve their interests in some way. Indeed, the only real linkages between the elite and the underclasses were the essentially exploitative patron-client relationships formed by money lenders, shopkeepers, and the owner-operators of the Durban produce market. Thus, as the new white-collar Indian elite began to emerge, to develop a unifying ideology, and to create a separate political identity, the field was clear for them to claim this vast potential worker constituency.

Notes

1   A total number of 152 184 labourers, shipped out of Calcutta and Madras, entered Natal during the years of importation, 1860-1866 and 1874-1911. C.O. 551/27/19319, Annual Report of Protector of Indian Immigrants, 1911, part v, encl. in Gov. to Sec. St., 5 June 1912.

2   *Report on Emigration from the Port of Calcutta to British and Foreign Territories for the Year 1894* (Calcutta, 1895) p.4.

3   See, for example, NA, C.S.2857, Mines Commission, Evidence and Papers, 1909. Particularly evidence of W T Heslop, a spokesman for the Natal Mine Managers' Association, pp.263-4. See also, *Supplement to Natal Government Gazette*, 31 March 1908, 'Report of Customs Union Tariff Commission', particularly evidence on Indian role in the soap and match-making industries, pp.37, 50. See also *Indian Opinion*, 29 July 1911, citing evidence of J Kirkman, a spokesman for the Natal sugar industry given before the 1911 Union Government Commerce and Industry Commission; and ibid., evidence of W R Hindson, T G Colenbrander and J Reynolds-Tait on behalf of the Natal Tea Planters Association.

4   C.O. 551/27/19319, Gov. to Sec. St., 5 June 1912, encl. Report of Protector of Indian Imms., 1911, part v. Of the 152 184 Indians shipped to Natal under indenture, 49 853 had returned to India or otherwise left the province by 1911. There is no way of knowing how many of the 22 547 who died during that period had, or would have, chosen to stay on.

5   See, for example, NA, I.I.1/77/66/95, District Supt., N.G.R. Newcastle, to Prot. Imms., 11 Jan 1895; ibid., 209/95, District Supt., N.G.R. Newcastle, to Prot. Imms., 11 Feb. 1895; ibid., 380/95, District Supt., N.G.R., Newcastle, to Prot. Imms., 12 Mar. 1895; ibid., 1/79/1147/95, District Supt., N.G.R., Newcastle to Prot. Imms., 12 Aug., 1895; ibid., 1/80/1799/95, District Supt., N.G.R.,

Newcastle, to Prot. Imms., 17 Dec. 1895.

6   'Political community' is used here to describe those who were involved, to however limited an extent, in formal institutional politics.

7   See, for example, NA, G.H. 1589/(unnumbered document), Report by Durban Supt. of Police, 21 Feb. 1885; or Transvaal Law 3 of 1885 which applied to 'Coolies, Arabs and Mohamedan Subjects of the Turkish Empire'.

8   See, for example, C.O. 179/183/16781, Dept. Gov. to Sec. St. 25 July, 1892.

9   NA, G.H. 1589/(unnumbered document), Report by Durban Supt. of Police. 21 Feb. 1885, p.1.

10   *Indian Opinion*, 3 Feb. 1912.

11   L M Thompson, 'Indian Immigration into Natal (1860-1872)', *Archives Year Book for South African History*, ii (1952), pp.65,69.

12   NA, G.H.1589/(unnumbered document), Report of Protector of Indian Imms., 1877.

13   Ibid., (unnumbered document), Report by Durban Supt. of Police, 21 Feb. 1885, pp.1-2.

14   Ibid., pp.4-5.

15   Ibid.,pp.2-3.

16   Ibid., p.2. Some 24 'old' Indian firms had been bought out by 'passengers' by 1885.

17   See below.

18   NA, G.H.1589/(unnumbered document), Report by Durban Supt. of Police, 21 Feb. 1885, pp.1,4.

19   Ordinance 1 of 1885 and Ordinance 23 of 1890.

20   See Tables 1 and 2.

21   The best sources of information on Indian trade goods are the merchants' advertisements in *Indian Opinion* and *African Chronicle*.

22   See, for example, NA, C.S. 2594/49/1904, Town Clerk Greytown to Princ. Under Sec., 12 April 1904; ibid., G.H. 1589/(unnumbered document), Report by Durban Supt. of Police, 21 Feb. 1885, p.4.; *C.W.*, ix, 168, 'Interview to *Rand Daily Mail*', 25 Jan. 1909.

23   *C.W.*, vii, 160-61, Acting Chair. BIA to *Rand Daily Mail*, 12 August 1907, and advertisements in *Indian Opinion*, 31 Dec. 1903. See also references under fn.32 below.

24   *Indian Opinion*, 3 Feb. 1912. For partners (Abdullah Karim Haji Adam, Joosab Abdul Carim) see advertisements in *Indian Opinion*, 1903, passim, and *C.W.*, ii, p.299, 'The Position of Indians in Natal'.

25   *Indian Opinion*, 18 Jan. 1908; 3 July, 1909.

26   *Report of the Indian Immigrants Commission, 1885-1887* (Pietermaritzburg, 1887) pp.196,197; *C.W.*, iii, p.11, 'Notes on the Test Case'.

27   *Indian Opinion*, 4 May 1907, 11 May 1907; 31 Dec. 1903; *C.W.*, v, pp.395-6, Gandhi to Haji Ismail Haji Aboobaker Johari, 14 Aug. 1906; ibid., iv, p.314, 'The Kaffir Market in Queen Street', 17 Dec. 1904.

28   *C.W.*, iii, p.18, 'Dada Osman's Case' (the firm is described as 'Mohamed Cassim and Company' in this document); ibid., p.179, 'Telegram Regarding Permits'; ibid., p.284, 'Indian Position in New Colonies'.

29   CO 179/205/3039, Gov. to Sec. St., 14 Jan. 1899, encl. Petition to Sec. St. by M C Camroodeen, Dada Abdullah, and others, 31 Dec. 1898.

30   *Indian Opinion*, 3 July 1909.

31   Ibid.

32   *C W*, iii, p.18, 'Dada Osman's Case' and Petition to Sec. St., cited in fn.29 above.

33   *Indian Opinion*, 9 Feb. 1906.

34   Ibid., 22 Aug. 1908.

35   Ibid.

36   Petition to Sec. St., cited in fn.29 above.

37   Ibid.

38   *Indian Opinion*, 26 June 1909. It is highly unlikely that Cachalia was able to open a new branch in the Transvaal in 1907 as is asserted here. The date for the Nylstroom branch should probably read 1897.

39   *Indian Opinion*, 22 Aug. 1908; CO 281/141/10735 Pres. Brit. Indian League Cape Colony to Sec. St., 9 Mar. 1909, and encl. extract from *Cape Times*, 9 Mar. 1909.

40   *C.W.*, i, p.207, 'Petition to Lord Ripon, May 1895', Appendix G; ibid., ii, p.5, 'The Grievances of the British Indians in South Africa'; CO 179/184/22145, encl. Dada to Sec. St. 10 Oct. 1892.

41   Their relationship is mentioned in *C.W.*, ix, p.369, Gandhi to H S L Polak, 26 Aug. 1909.

42   TABA, G.G. 716/15/669, Statement of Transvaal British Indian Case, July 1909.

43   See below, Chapters 3 and 4, passim.

44   Z Konczacki, *Public Finance and Economic Development of Natal 1893-1910.* (Duke U.P., 1967), Table 6A, p.198.

45   TABA, Lt.G.95/97/2, Schedule Re Indian Population, Values, and Licenses, 1870-1903, issued by Town Clerk's Office, Durban, 13 April 1904.

46   See Table 2.

47   TABA, Lt.G.96/97/2/2, Table D.

48   See below, Chapter 3, p.80.

49   Petition to Sec. St., cited in fn.29 above.

50   NA., G.H. 1592/363/A/98, 'Disabilities of British Indians in Natal', Conf. Memo for the High Commissioner, 22 Aug. 1898.

51   *C.W.*, iii, p.18, 'Dada Osman's Case'; ibid., p.40; Petition to Sec. St., cited in fn.29 above.

52   Petition to Sec. St., cited in fn.29 above.

53   CO 179/250/28435, SABIC to Sec. St., 4 Aug. 1908. encl. Moosa Haji Adam to Durban Town Council, March 1908, in which it is noted that ten to twelve of M H Adam's stores had usually stood empty since the passage of the Dealers' Licences Act (1895).

54   See below, Chapter 4.

55   Occasional mentions of all these societies are scattered throughout the Natal Indian press. See, in particular, *Indian Opinion*, 16 Nov. 1912; *African Chronicle*, 24 July 1909; *C.W.*, vi, p.465, 'Farewell to Omar Haji Amod Zaveri'.

56   See below, chapter 4. See also, *Indian Opinion*, 'Souvenir of the Hon. Gopal Krishna Gokhale's Tour in South Africa, October 22-November 18, 1912'.

57   See, for example, *Indian Opinion*, 18 Jan. 1913. See also *Rand Daily Mail*, 17 Feb. 1914.

58   *Indian Opinion*, 16 Dec. 1905; *C.W.* ix, p.8, 'Johannesburg Letter', 31 Aug. 1908.

59   See, for example, *Indian Opinion*, 4 May 1907; ibid., 5 Oct. 1907; *C.W.* iii, pp.101,106,109, 'The Second Report of the Natal Indian Congress'; *African Chronicle*, 25 Mar. 1911.

60   *C.W.*, v, p.306, 'Johannesburg Letter', 5 May 1906.

61   Ibid., iii, p.84, 'The Indian Question in South Africa', 12 July 1899.

62   *Indian Opinion*, 18 May 1907.

63   Royeppen joined the passive resistance movement soon after his return from London. *African Chronicle*, 25 Dec. 1909.

64   See below, Chapter 5, passim.

65   *Indian Opinion*, 4 May 1907.

66   *African Chronicle*, 25 Dec. 1909. Naicker was active in HYMA and DIS: ibid., 13 Nov. 1909, 4 Sept. 1909.

67   Ibid., 26 Mar. 1910. Sigamoney was active in the Higher Grade Indian School Old Boys' Association and DIS; ibid., 5 Mar. 1910.

68   CO 179/192/2281, Gov. to Sec. St., 30 Nov. 1895, sub-encl., *List of Members of the Natal Indian Congress*. Panday was active in NIPU and the CBIA. *African Chronicle*, 1 Aug. 1908, 25 Mar. 1911.

69   NA, C.S. 2593/277/1901. Conf. circular re. Indian interpreters attached to Magistrates' Courts, 29 Nov. 1901. Naidoo sat on a committee which established a private Higher Grade Indian School in Pietermaritzburg. *Indian Opinion*, 31 July 1909.

70   NA, C.S. 2593/277/1901. Conf. circular re. Indian interpreters

attached to Magistrates' Courts, 29 Nov. 1901. Pillay was active in HYMA, *Indian Opinion*, 4 May 1907.

71   *Natal Govt. Gazette*, 12 May 1908, p.361. Maharaj was active in NIPU and DIS. *Indian Opinion*, 25 Dec. 1909; *African Chronicle*, 2 July 1910.

72   C. W., ii, p.348, Gandhi to Town Clerk, Durban, 3 Sept. 1897. Lawrence was active in NIPU and DIS. *African Chronicle*, 1 Aug. 1908, 2 Aug. 1909.

73   CO, 179/192/22881, Gov. To Sec. St., 30 Nov. 1895, sub-encl., *List of Members of the Natal Indian Congress*. Gabriel was involved in the first of the colonial-born Indians' attempts to widen NIC's social base. See below, Chapter 5.

74   CO, 179/192/22881, Gov. to Sec. St., 30 Nov. 1895, sub-encl., *List of Members of the Natal Indian Congress*. Lazarus Gabriel was involved in NIPU, DIS and the CBIA. *African Chronicle*, 1 Aug. 1908, 2 Oct. 1909, 25 Mar. 1911.

75   Interview, Miss S Aydie, Pietermaritzburg, Sept. 1976. Nulliah was active in NIPU. *African Chronicle*, 29 Aug. 1908.

76   Konczacki, op. cit., p.196.

77   Ibid.

78   Colony of Natal, *Census 1904*, Table 293.

79   Ibid., Part V, Table II.

80   Ibid., Part I, Table IV.

81   Ibid., Part V, Table IV.

82   Ibid., Part V, Table IV. Newcastle and Dundee, for instance, had only private Muslim schools.

83   See, for example, *African Chronicle*, 1 Jan. 1910, reporting observations of Rev. J Thomas, headmaster of Wesleyan Indian Methodist School. See also, *Natal Mercury*, 3 Feb. 1914, evid. of Rev. A A Bailie, Supt. of Indian Schools, given before the Indian Enquiry Commission.

84   U.G. 12, 1914. *Report of the Economic Commission*, Jan. 1914, p.39.

85   See Table 3.

86   U.G. *Census, 1911*, Table clxxxviii, Schedule E.

87   Ibid.

88   Ibid.

89   Ibid.

90   Historically, Hindu society has been structured by an elaborate, hereditary, hierarchical division of labour. The major divisions, or *varnas* (usually translated as 'castes') are, in order of precedence: *brahmins* (priests, teachers), *kshatriyas* (warriors, aristocrats), *vaisyas* (merchants), *sudras* (workers). Beneath these, and consigned to the most menial occupations, are the so-called 'untouchables', or

panchamas.

91   This is true, for instance, of the 'Nayakers' (Naickers) and 'Pillays' titles used by the Palli who, in 1871, petitioned the Government of Madras to be returned as *kshatriyas* in the census. In 1900, Pallis in the Godaveri district again claimed *kshatriya* status. The titles 'Nayaker' and 'Pillay' denote 'authority, bravery and superiority'. E Thurston, *Castes and Tribes of Southern India* (New Delhi, 1975) vi, pp.1,9,14.

92   Ibid., vii, pp.361, 366, 373-4.

93   Table 4.

94   Table 5.

95   See below, Chapter 2, pp.52-53.

96   In particular, sports. See, for example. *Natal Mercury*, 5 Mar., 1 April 1902.

97   See below, Chapter 3, pp.89-90.

98   See, for example, NA, C.S. 2576/5/1898; ibid., 2593/54/1902; ibid., 2593/88/1902; ibid., 2594/15/1903; ibid., 2594/78/1903; ibid., 2594/19/1904; ibid., 2597/74/1906; ibid., 2599/40/1907; ibid., 2600/4/1908; ibid., 2600/46/1908; ibid., 2602/78/1909; ibid., 2602/91/1909.

99   On reduction of civil service salaries, for instance, see the mass of documentation in NA, C.S. 2596. The £1 Poll Tax on all adult males who were not under indenture, and who were not subject to the Hut Tax, was meant specifically to 'get at the native and the coolie'. Quoted by S Marks, *Reluctant Rebellion* (Oxford, 1970) p.141.

100   See, below, Chapter 5, passim.

101   *African Chronicle*, 17 Oct. 1908, 28 Nov. 1909.

102   The Pietermaritzburg District Indian Football Association celebrated its seventeenth anniversary in 1909. *African Chronicle*, 15 May 1909.

103   *African Chronicle*, 17 Oct. 1908, 28 Nov. 1909.

104   *Indian Opinion*, 4 May 1907.

105   Ibid., 29 May 1909.

106   *African Chronicle*, 13 Nov. 1909.

107   See, for example, *Indian Opinion*, 4 May 1907, *African Chronicle*, 13 Nov. 1909, 4 Dec. 1909.

108   *African Chronicle*, 22 Aug. 1908.

109   Table 3.

110   *Indian Opinion*, 12 Sept. 1908.

111   Ibid., 25 April 1908.

112   See below, Chapter 5.

113   Ibid.

114   DIS's activities began to be reported in *African Chronicle* around mid-1909.

115   Table 3.

116   *African Chronicle*, 30 April 1910.

117   Ibid., 25 Sept. 1909, 25 Dec. 1909.

118   Ibid., 2 Oct. 1909.

119   Table 3.

120   See fn.91 above.

121   NA, I.I. 1/102/1621/01, Calcutta, Em. Agent to Protector, 10 Mar. 1902; ibid., 1/80/1371/95, Calcutta, Em. Agent to Protector, 23 Aug, 1895. And see, ibid., 1/100/464/01, Circular, Indian Immigration Trust Board of Natal, 25 March 1901 and ibid., 1/102/1389/01, Madras Em. Agent to Protector, 4 Oct. 1901, about the difficulty of obtaining recruits after a good harvest.

122   *Report of Emigration from the Port of Calcutta to British and Foreign Colonies for the Year 1894* (Govt. of India, 1895) p.10. See also, NA, I.I. 1/104/2063/01, Madras Protector of Emigrants to Natal Em. Agent, 23 May 1901, for similar cases.

123   In 1904, for instance, the mining industry and the NGR, which were agriculture's main competitors for Indian contract labour, employed respectively, 1837 and 997 of a total indentured workforce of 28 428. *Natal Departmental Reports*, 1904, 'Report of the Protector of Imms.', p.12; ibid., 'Report on the Mining Industry of Natal', pp.40-41; ibid., 'Report of the Gen. Manager of Railways', p.27. The figures for the year ending 31 Dec. 1908 were 3 107 (mining), 2 798 (NGR), 33 280 (total). *Natal Departmental Reports*, 1908, 'Report on the Mining Industry of Natal', pp.1-2; 'Report of the Gen. Manager of Railways', p.20; 'Report of the Protector of Indian Imms.', p.7.

124   CO 551/27/19319 Govt. to Sec. St., 5 June 1912, encl. Report of Protector of Indian Imms., 1911, part v; NA I.I. 1/77/66/95; ibid., 380/95; ibid., 1/79/1147/95; ibid., 1/8031/799/95.

125   *Natal Departmental Reports*, 1890, 'Report of the Protector of Indian Imms.', p.A42. See also fn.5 above.

126   NA, G.H., 1589/ (unnumbered document), 'Report of the Protector of Indian Imms.', 1877.

127   *Natal Official Handbook, 1886*, p.90; *Report of the Indian Immigrants Commission, 1885-1887*, (Pietermaritzburg, 1887), pp.75-6.

128   NA, G.H. 1589/ (unnumbered document), 'Protector of Indian Imms. Report', 1877.

129   *Natal Departmental Reports*, 1899-1900, 'Protector of Indian Imms. Report', Annexure S, p.A42.

130   Ibid., p.A16.

131   Konczacki, op. cit., p.198. Table 6.A.

132   Colony of Natal, *Census 1904*, Table 385.

133   E T Mullins (Minister of Agriculture), 'The Economic Side of Agriculture in Natal', *Natal Agricultural Journal and Mining Record*, x, part 7, 1907, p.737.

134   *Natal Department of Agriculture: Agricultural Statistics of Natal, 1905-1906* (Pietermaritzburg, 1907) p.36. See also *Natal Departmental Reports*, 1890-1891, Annual Report of Res. Mag. Lower Tugela Division, p.B37; ibid., 1904, Report of the Sec. to the Min. Agriculture from 1 Jan. 1903 to 30 June 1904, p.12; NA G.H. 1589(unnumbered document), 'Protector of Indian Imms. Report', 1877.

135   NA, I.I. 1/58/1140/90.

136   Ibid., 1/55/545/90; ibid., 1/54/1434/90/; 1/54/248/90; 1/59/289/95.

137   Ibid., 1/100/353/01; ibid., 1/85/463/97; ibid., 1/77/1433/90; ibid., 1/58/1034/90.

138   Konczacki, op. cit., Table 4A, p.113.

139   *African Chronicle*, 19 June 1909.

140   Ibid., 9 July 1910.

141   See below, Chapter 5.

142   *Natal Departmental Reports, 1905*, 'Report of the Protector of Immigrants', p.13.

143   *Report of the Indian Immigrants' Commission, 1885-1887*, op. cit., pp.193,200, evid. of George Mutukistna and Telucksing. See also, NA, I.I. 1/55/540/90, Protector to Res. Mag. Klip River Div., 24 June 1890; ibid., C.S. 2596/112/1905, Dr E Nundy to Col. Sec., 8 Dec. 1905 and Protector to Col. Sec., 12 Dec. 1905.

144   C Bundy, *The Rise and Fall of the South African Peasantry* (London, 1979) p.183.

145   NA, C.S. 2596/112/1905, Dr E Nundy to Col. Sec. 23 Nov. 1905.

146   Report by Alexandra Magistrate reprinted in *African Chronicle*, 4 Nov. 1911.

147   See below, Chapter 2 and Chapter 5, passim.

148   See, for example, *African Chronicle*, 5 Dec. 1908, letter to editor from R N Modaley reporting widespread Indian unemployment; NA C.S. 2596/112/1905, Dr E Nundy to Col. Sec., 8 Dec. 1905 and Protector to Col. Sec., 12 Dec. 1905, reporting heavy indebtedness among free Indian cultivators due to the fall in the price of maize; *Report of the Indian Immigrants' Commission*, 1909 (Pietermaritzburg, 1909) p.7, reporting a 'startling number' of destitute women in the Verulam district.

149   *The Natalian*, 6 Sept. 1907.

150   *Natal Departmental Reports, 1908*, 'Report of the Gen. Manager of Railways', p.20; ibid., 1905, 'Report of the Protector of Indian

Imms.', p.13.

151   See below, Chapter 3.

152   U.G. *Census, 1911*, Table clxxxix, Schedule E.

153   TABA, Lt.G. 96/97/2/3, Trade Licences Issued to Asiatics by Receivers of Revenue and Local Authorities Throughout the Transvaal during April 1905.

154   CO 179/244/10983, Gov. to Sec. St., 4 Mar. 1908.

155   Ibid., 249/5973, F.O. to C.O., 18 Feb. 1908 and encl. Mackie to F.O., 31 Dec. 1907.

156   Ibid., 250/18112, Griffiths and Co. to C.O., 19 May 1908.

157   Ibid., 249/5973, encl. Mackie to F.O., 31 Dec. 1907.

158   Ibid., 245/24214, encl. Return showing numbers of Indians who left for Lobito Bay.

159   CO.551/56/12682, Gov. Gen. to Sec. St. 21 Mar. 1914, encl. Report of Protector of Indian Imms., 1913, Section V. Konczacki defines the period of depression as 1904/1905 to 1909. Op. cit., p.26.

160   *Report on Emigration from the Port of Calcutta to British and Foreign Colonies for the Year 1894*, (Govt. of India, 1895) p.4. See also, NA, I.I. 1/100/713/01, Natal Emigration Agent to Chief Officer, SS Congella, 11 April 1901.

161   Cf. for example, some of the autobiographical sketches in J Burnett (Ed.), *Useful Toil* (London, 1975).

162   This was an attempt to compensate for a 'long term decline in soil productivity and prices'. P Richardson, 'The Natal Sugar Industry, 1849-1905: An Interpretative Essay' (Queen Elizabeth House, Oxford, Unpubld. research paper, 1980) p.27.

163   NA, C.S. 2584. Commission on the Treatment of Indians on Messrs. Reynolds Brothers, Esperanza, Alexander County (hereafter referred to as 'Commission: Esperanza'), evid. of D.O. in charge of Umzinto Police; evid. of labourers Peramal and Mari; evid. of Renaud (mill overseer 1887-1894); evid. of Peddie (former junior overseer); evid. of Mellon (mill overseer 1884-1890, 1896-1897, 1899-1900). And see M J Tayal, 'Indian Indentured Labour in Natal, 1890-1911'. *Indian Ec. and Soc. Hist. Rev.*, XIV, no.4 (1978), pp.519-547 for additional detail on all aspects of the conditions of agricultural indentured labourers.

164   See fn.163 above. See also NA, I.I. 1/141/954/06, Report on the Heavy Mortality in the Year 1906 among Indian Labourers on the Tongaat Sugar Cos. Estates.

165   The average annual death rate between 1890 and 1911 was 16,2 per thousand, M J Tayal, 'Indian Indentured Labour', op. cit., Table 1.

166   See, for example, Commission: Esperanza; NA, I.I. 1/100/720/01,

Protector to Princ. Under-Sec., 1 Feb. 1901.

167 Tayal, M J, 'Gandhi: the South African Experience', D Phil (Oxford, 1980) p.41-55.

168 Mine wages started at 12s per month for surface work, and 15s in the pits.

169 Wages started at up to 20s per month, depending on previous experience.

170 For elaboration, and documentation, of the material summarized on the next two pages, see Tayal, 'Gandhi', op. cit., pp.36-40, 44-50.

171 G Rudé, *Protest and Punishment* (Oxford, 1978) pp.52-54; G Rudé, *Ideology and Popular Protest* (London, 1980) pp.30-33.

172 The number of 'strikes' — shortlived and localized though they may have been — increases after about 1909. See, for example, CO 551/27/19319, Gov. Gen. to Sec. St., 5 June 1912, encl. Report of Protector of Indian Imms., 1911, part XVII, which shows a particularly high incidence of workers convicted for 'leaving the estate in a body' (645 convictions), and 'absence from roll-call and disobedience of orders' (725 convictions). The figures for 1912 and 1913, although less striking, are still higher than in previous years: CO 551/38/11530, Gov. Gen. to Sec. St., 19 March 1913, encl. Report of Protector of Indian Imms., 1912; ibid., 56/12682, Gov. Gen. to Sec. St., 7 April 1914, encl. Report of Protector of Indian Imms., 1913.

1 *New arrivals awaiting health officer*, 1909 (JPL)

2 *Indentured workers cutting cane*, circa 1894 (JPL)

3 *Indentured workers on a tea estate, 1896 (JPL)*

4 *'Special Servants', Royal Hotel, Durban (JPL)*

5 *Itinerant Indian trader, Transvaal* (JPL)

6 *Indian tailor, Johannesburg 1916* (JPL)

7 *Indian market women, Johannesburg, 1890s* (HWPC, Scenes and Life in the Transvaal, *Johannesburg, c.1897*)

8 *Fruit and vegetable hawkers, Johannesburg* (JPL)

CHAPTER TWO

Merchant Politics I: Natal, 1895 — 1906

Gandhi became involved in the politics of the Natal merchants in mid-1894. By that time their political priorities had already been firmly established and a tentative start made on political organization. Gandhi was drawn into merchant politics when there was an urgent need for a full-time organizer, preferably fluent in Gujerati and English and with a legal training. Gandhi was perfectly suited to the merchants' needs from the point of view of linguistic and legal qualifications, and of ideological compatibility. As their hired representative he ensured the continuity of merchant political philosophy and practice between 1891 and 1906.

Pre-Gandhian Indian politics in Natal reached a peak of activity in the early 1890s. As early as 1885 merchants had petitioned the British government about a variety of grievances in regard to both Natal and the Transvaal; but systematic political activity began only in 1891 when they had already been expelled from the Orange Free State, their business interests were under threat in the Transvaal, and they feared that Natal would soon follow in the steps of the two republics. Thus in many ways the years 1890-1892 were critical for the commercial elite. White attitudes towards Indian commercial success first became fully apparent during this period, and the merchants' response to attacks on their economic interests set the pattern for their politics over the next decade and a half.

The roots of the political activity in the early 1890s go back to 1885 when the Free State and the Transvaal had first begun to turn their attention to Indian merchants. Under the terms of Ordinance 1 of 1885, all Indian merchants in the Free State were required to register with the magistrate of the district in which they did business. There were only nine Indian merchants in the Republic. None of them bothered to register, and despite this they were routinely granted annual trading licences for several years.[1] In the Transvaal, the merchants came more directly under attack when Law 3 of 1885 was introduced in response to the whites' appeals to curb 'Asian' — which included Indian — trade competition. Law 3 held that all Asians should be prohibited from acquiring landed property or citizenship rights. It also provided for the government to 'point out to [Asians] their proper streets, wards and locations, where they should reside'.

Since the Transvaal was subject to British suzerainty under the terms of the Pretoria Convention of 1881, Colonial Office permission had been sought before the discriminatory legislation was framed. On the advice of the British High Commissioner to South Africa, the Colonial Office made a class-based distinction which later developed into a firm policy respecting British Indians in South Africa: they agreed that the Transvaal should be free to regulate the conditions of presence of Indians provided that the vested interests of the Indian merchants in the Republic were respected. The wording of Law 3 derived from the fact that the Colonial Office had given permission for legislation in regard to 'coolies' (workers), which the Transvaal State Secretary took to mean all Asians.[2]

The law thus produced a lengthy correspondence between the Colonial Office and the Transvaal State Secretary which culminated in an apparent compromise two years later. Two 1886 amendments to the Law provided that the government could confine Asians to designated locations in the interests of public health, and prohibited Asian ownership of fixed property except in such locations. This left room for negotiations on both sides, and correspondence between the two governments continued. The Colonial Office claimed that the amendments could not be used as an excuse to move established merchants to 'Locations' — the word which came to be used to designate 'non-white' ghettoes. The Transvaal government insisted that all Asians were insanitary, and in the interests of public health all should therefore be confined to Locations for business as well as residential purposes.[3] They were strongly backed by the Volksraad, with resolutions in June and July 1888 which called for the immediate implementation of Law 3 and, indeed, a Bill to prohibit the immigration of Asians.[4] Their interpretation of the Law was further confirmed by a Transvaal High Court judgement of August 1888 which decided against an Indian merchant's application for a licence to trade in the town of Middelburg.[5]

Thus, although the Colonial Office continued its correspondence on Law 3, the situation was increasingly uncertain for Indian merchants.

In September 1890 it worsened abruptly when legislation was introduced in the Orange Free State which prohibited Indians from owning land or carrying on trade in that republic unless they were registered under the terms of Ordinance 1 of 1885. Since none of them had, in fact, registered, the new ordinance provided for the elimination of Indian commerce in the Free State.[6] Three months later, in December 1890, a select committee of the Natal legislature produced a draft constitution for the introduction of responsible government to the colony. The draft did not contain adequate provision for safe-guarding the interests of Indians in Natal,[7] the area of maximum Indian commercial investment and the base from which many holdings in the interior, and even some in Mozambique and India, were operated.

The more powerful among the Natal merchants, and particularly those with holdings in the Transvaal or the Free State, viewed the series of events in Natal and the two republics towards the end of 1890 as part of a larger pattern which would ultimately deprive them of their trading rights and vested interests in all three areas. Thus far, they had met each threatening situation with legal counsel and an occasional petition of protest to a colonial or imperial official. They had made no attempt to form a permanent organization or evolve a coherent strategy to protect their interests. In January 1891 they began a wider and more well organized, if still somewhat unsophisticated, campaign in an attempt not only to salvage what they could from the Free State, but also to prevent a further deterioration of the situation in the Transvaal, and to make it impossible for Natal to move in the same direction as the two republics. This was the genesis of the politics of the Natal Indian merchants and in many ways it set the pattern for their political activity throughout the next fifteen years.

Merchant politics were spearheaded by Haji Mohamed Haji Dada and Dada Abdullah who controlled the biggest Indian commercial interests in Natal which, between them, had multiple branches in Natal, the Transvaal, the Free State, Mozambique and India.[8] Although there is little information on individual merchant holdings it is known that in the Orange Free State, where none of the Indian firms had big investments, Haji Dada was left with approximately £2 000 worth of goods after part of his stock had been sold by public auction following the passage of Ordinance 29 of 1890.[9] In addition, he had approximately £50 000 invested in stock in the Transvaal in 1891.[10] His investments in Natal, where his firm was based, were probably higher. Dada Abdullah's total investments may have been even larger.

His firm was later described by Gandhi as having 'probably owned the largest Indian business throughout South Africa' in the 1890s.[11] Haji Dada and Dada Abdullah headed the Durban Indian Committee[12] which met on an ad hoc basis to discuss 'important . . . political and other subjects'. Haji Dada was voted to the chair at every committee meeting, and one of the partners in Abdullah's firm served as secretary.[13] In January 1891, the Committee began the first South African Indian political campaign. The goal of the campaign was to protect the commercial interests of the Indian merchants in Natal, the Transvaal and the Orange Free State.

The campaign started with a list of grievances which were sent to Fajalbhoi Visram, a fellow merchant in Bombay. On behalf of the Durban Indian Committee, Visram and a group of other merchants prepared a memorial for the Governor of Bombay.[14] Because of the initial decision to enlist the aid of merchants in India, the memorial attracted far more attention than it otherwise would have done. It eventually passed through the Government of Bombay, the India Office, the Colonial Office, the Natal Colonial Secretary's Office, and the office of the Natal Protector of Immigrants.[15]

This was not the first time that the merchants had protested against some aspect of their conditions in South Africa; but it was the first time that the protest served any useful purpose. When the memorial first passed through the hands of the various governments, none of them knew much about the South African Indian merchants. The Colonial Office thought that they 'came in as indentured coolies'.[16] The Natal Colonial Secretary apparently shared this belief: he applied to the Protector for information about them. The Protector, whose duties were confined to dealing with indentured and ex-indentured labourers, knew 'nothing which would permit him to give government reliable information'.[17] Ultimately, the memorial led to an investigation of the conditions of Indians in Natal. Although the investigation did nothing for the merchants, in that their complaints were dismissed as 'without foundation or frivolous', a report on the conditions of Indians was routed back through the same channels as the memorial had taken.[18] Together the two documents served to bring the commercial elite firmly to the attention of appropriate officials in England, Natal and India. The report also served to introduce the various governments to the fact that the merchants considered themselves separate from, and superior to, the mass of the Natal Indian people. The investigation had been delayed for over two months because the Indian Committee considered it an 'indignity' to have been approached by the Protector, who was informed that 'we are not in any way connected with your department, neither do we see what your department has to do with us'.[19] Their demand to deal directly with the government was ultimately respected,[20] reinforcing at the official level the distinction between merchants and workers which the Colonial Office had earlier been advised to make in the Transvaal.

The original memorial and the subsequent investigation were significant for the future of merchant politics in other ways too. This unaccustomed response to complaints served to encourage the use of slightly more sophisticated political techniques. By the end of 1892 the merchants were preparing the first printed pamphlet on Indian grievances in Natal, the Transvaal and the Orange Free State. At the same time they re-appealed to the Colonial Office, addressing themselves specifically to Lord Ripon, the new Secretary of State, on the basis of his known sympathy towards Indians.[21] Shortly afterwards they made their first contact with Dadabhai Naoroji who also knew little about the South African Indians, but who was now drawn into what was to be a very lengthy involvement with them. In October 1891 the merchants petitioned by cable for the first time, further widening the number of persons with whom they were in contact. Telegrams were sent from Durban and Pretoria to the Colonial Office, and from Pretoria to Queen Victoria, Naoroji, and Gladstone, who was Prime Minister at the time.[22] In June 1893, a second pamphlet, which dealt exclusively with the Orange Free State, was sent to the Colonial Office.[23]

The list of complaints which the merchants advanced is also significant as the earliest statement of what was to be the major thrust in their politics. In the cases of the Orange Free State and the Transvaal their appeal was straightforward. In the hope of having the recent discriminatory legislation reversed by Colonial Office pressure, they pointed to the extent of Indian commercial investment in the two republics, claiming the right to protection as British subjects.[24] By contrast the list of Indian grievances in Natal included lengthy references to the oppressed conditions of indentured and ex-indentured labourers. These seem particularly anomalous given the fact that the investigation of their grievances was delayed for over two months because the merchants refused to be identified with the Indian underclasses. Thus the inclusion of workers' grievances can be understood only as part of the merchants' attempts to protect their own interests. Labour conditions were included in a far more general statement of Indian grievances in Natal which contained instances of petty harassment of the elite, and the fact that an attempt to deprive them of the franchise several years earlier had been prevented only by immediate action on the part of the Indian Committee.

The purpose of listing these grievances — workers' as well as merchants' — was to convince the Colonial Office that Natal was unfit for responsible government which, the merchants claimed, 'would do us incalculable harm'.[25] In other words, they feared that constitutional advance in Natal would soon be followed by the same kind of discriminatory legislation as was already threatening their interests in the Transvaal, and which had led to their expulsion from the Orange Free State. The question of the conditions of Natal's '50 000' Indian workers (in fact the number was closer to 35 000), was raised to demonstrate how 'important' it was that the colony remain under direct imperial control.[26] This tactic represented the beginning of another distinct trend in merchant politics: on numerous occasions over the next twenty years workers' grievances were used by the elite in attempts to protect their own interests.

One or two other minor aspects of pre-Gandhian politics are also noteworthy. During the course of the first political campaign the necessity of being able to delegate responsibility became apparent. An important memorial to the Colonial Office was held up for months because Haji Dada was ill and unable to deal with it.[27] Dada Abdullah, engaged in a £40 000 law suit against an Indian merchant in the Transvaal, was also preoccupied with other matters.[28] Yet, given the lack of an organizational structure, there was no-one besides these two capable of carrying on the campaign. Also, since so much of the elite's political activity was based on interpretations of the law, the need for legal counsel was constant.[29] Since few of the merchants spoke English, the advantage of a lawyer who was fluent in both Gujerati and English requires no emphasis. These facts go far towards explaining the way in which Gandhi was particularly suited to elite political needs.

By 1893, then, a number of the trends which were to shape the future of merchant politics had become apparent. The South African governments had demonstrated their intention to express a generalized anti-Indian hostility in discriminatory legislation. It is difficult to analyse the dynamics of this hostility. It is clear, for example, that while Indian commerce threatened some, their generally lower prices benefited others. It is equally clear that the cheap Indian labour which benefited employers threatened white labour in Natal. Even when Indians were not in direct competition for jobs — and they very seldom were — their low wage rates helped depress the colony's wages as a whole.[30] Similarly, the Natal Indian market gardeners whose low-priced produce and door-to-door deliveries were welcomed by white housewives, were resented by white plantation owners to whom they represented the loss of both labourers and cultivable stretches of ground.[31] Wherever Indians threatened the economic interests of some whites, they served those of others. Yet no significant white counterweight to any of the anti-Indian lobbies was organized. It is thus difficult to assess whether economic, political, social or completely irrational factors, or, indeed, some permutation or combination of these factors, mobilized the hostility of any given group.

The important point for Indian merchant politics is that whatever the root cause of the anti-Indian hostility in Natal, the form in which it was manifested was racial discrimination. It was this in particular that the commercial elite fought. In order to protect their extensive economic interests they sought to distinguish themselves from the Indian underclasses, and to claim exemption from anti-Indian hostility on the basis of this distinction. Their politics, far from unifying the Indian community as has been asserted in the past, were directed specifically towards attaining white recognition of the fundamental differences between the two major social groups in the community: merchants and workers. As already indicated, the inclusion of workers' grievances in the merchants' political platform can therefore be understood only in terms of attempts to safeguard their own interests. In the following chapters it will become apparent that the elite did not, ever, seriously challenge the ideology of the dominant white minority which rationalized the low wages and oppressive conditions of Indian labourers — indentured and free — in terms of their assumed inferiority.

Elite political techniques, though still somewhat unsophisticated in 1893, nevertheless represented an improvement over the past. The merchants had learned to diversify the contacts on whom they depended for assistance, and to appeal to private persons as well as government officals. They recognized the additional impact to be derived from preparing lengthy printed statements of grievances, and the sense of urgency conveyed by the use of telegrams. It had become apparent that the preservation of their commercial interests in South Africa would demand increasing political activity on their part and that the loosely structured Indian Committee was unequal to such a task. It had also become apparent that political activity, even of the sort they had attempted in the past, was a time-consuming business difficult to combine with managing large-scale commercial enterprises. In 1894, shortly after Natal had been granted responsible government, when the elite's political prognosis about the colony proved correct, the need for more efficient political organization and for someone to undertake the task of organizing on a full-time basis suddenly became critical.

On 25 April 1894 a Bill to Amend the Franchise was announced during the opening speech of the second session of Natal's first parliament under responsible government.[32] The terms of the Bill were threatening to the merchants. Except for those who already held the parliamentary franchise, 'no persons belonging to Asiatic races not accustomed to the exercise of franchise rights under parliamentary institutions' could in future qualify to vote. Less than 300 Indians exercised their franchise rights in 1894. Thus there was little chance, nor on the part of the merchants any great expectation, that they would be able to outweigh Natal's 10 000 white voters at the polls in the forseeable future.[33] They recognized the indirect importance of the franchise though, and had unsuccessfully fought off an earlier attack on what they called their 'only right' in the colony.[34] The real significance of the franchise question lay in the fact that it reflected the hostility of the ruling white minority towards Indians. In 1892, during their first political campaign, the merchants had informed the Colonial Office that they were enjoying what they felt would be the last period of calm before the storm which would break with responsible government.[35] During the first parliamentary sessions under the new constitution there was more than enough antagonism manifested in the Legislative Assembly debates to make it clear that the Franchise Amendment Bill was indeed the beginning of a major assault on Indian commercial interests.

Among the issues raised in the Assembly was the question of imposing an annual residential tax on ex-indentured labourers. The tax was linked to the introduction of a Bill to remove an annual £10 000 grant which was paid out of the general revenue towards the cost of importing Indian labour.[36] Although on the face of it these questions seem only to relate to Indian workers, it was clear from the Assembly debates that they also implied a serious threat for Indian merchants. Both questions reflected the vigorous opposition to the Indian presence in the colony. Although in 1894 indentured labour was vital to Natal agriculture, and the legislature was dominated by representatives of planting and farming interests,[37] white opposition to Indians remained strong. The question of continuing labour importation had been an important issue in the recent elections.[38] The agricultural lobby was powerful enough to prevent the stoppage of importation, but the Bill to remove the annual subsidy demonstrated the strength of the opposition. As one of the members put it, he objected to the colony 'becoming a dumping ground for the scum of India'.[39] The proposed residential tax was thus a compromise measure seen as a means of driving workers out of the colony, or back into indenture, on the expiry of their contracts. The fact that a number of the agricultural representatives themselves favoured the tax indicates that they supported the general hostility towards Indians who were not of direct or immediate use to them.[40] The implied threat which this widespread hostility towards non-indentured Indians held for the merchants was made explicit by the Attorney General during a debate on the subsidy for labour importation when he added the presence of the merchants to the other disadvantages of indentured labour which had already been raised. He pointed out that Indian merchants 'invariably did follow in the spoor of the Coolie, with the intention of extending their trade among that class of people and but for the introduction of these Indians . . . [merchants] would not, at any rate, have arrived in such large numbers as they had.'[41]

The debates on the Franchise Amendment Bill also made it clear that some of the support for the Bill reflected a specific hostility towards Indian merchants. Henry Bale, who later became Premier of Natal, suggested more than once that those Indians already on the voters' roll should be struck off.[42] In addition, the Governor of Natal, explaining the reason for the Bill to the Colonial Office, included the fact that Indian merchants — those who would have been most likely to qualify for the franchise in the future — were not even welcome in the colony.[43] Inevitably the question of the Indians' continuing right to exercise the municipal franchise was also raised by a number of the members of the legislature. Ultimately this question was dropped for fear of prejudicing the chance of having the Franchise Amendment Bill accepted by the Colonial Office; but not before the Attorney General had given the House his assurance that the government would 'take care' of the municipal question.[44]

Two other related issues which were raised during the same parliamentary session left little doubt that Natal would follow in the footsteps of the Boer republics' attack on Indian commercial interests if given the opportunity. A Bill was introduced to augment the powers of the municipal corporations which were said to require increased authority to regulate sanitary conditions. The Premier's contention that this was necessary not only in Durban 'but in other parts of the colony populated by Asiatics'[45], could not have failed to remind anyone reading the reports of the debates in the local press that the Transvaal government was currently using an alleged danger to public hygiene in its attempts to remove Indian merchants to designated locations. As it turned out, the Premier had, indeed, given an advance warning of Natal's intention to use the increased municipal powers as a means of refusing trade licences to Indian merchants on alleged sanitary grounds: this practice became increasingly frequent as the 1890s wore on.[46]

The fact that the Legislative Assembly's generalized hostility towards Indians included specific antagonism towards Indian commercial interests was nowhere more evident than in the proposal for the government to introduce a Bill 'providing that no person of Asiatic race, birth or descent, should be allowed to take out a licence for the purpose of trading as a storekeeper, and for the better regulation of those who had become licence holders'.[47] Like some of the other issues raised between May and July 1894, this one was also dropped — probably, again, for fear of jeopardizing Colonial Office acceptance of the Franchise Amendment Bill. It was resurrected in 1897, and although much more subtle in form, when used in conjunction with the amended Municipal Corporations Bill, it achieved the same damaging results as had been envisaged in the original proposal.[48]

By 1894, then, the merchants' political prognosis of two years earlier was already proving correct. Natal's first Legislative Assembly under responsible government had demonstrated an implacable hostility towards non-indentured Indians, with unmistakable indications that commercial interests would be a future target of attack, as they had already been in the Transvaal and the Free State. There can be no doubt that the merchants would have followed the reports of the Assembly debates in the press. Their interests in Natal were too great, and their awareness of what responsible government could do to them too keen, for them to have done otherwise. In previous years they had kept a close watch on discussions in the Natal legislature and, indeed, in the Transvaal Volksraad. There is no reason to suppose that they were any less knowledgeable about what was taking place in Natal in mid-1894. Nor could they have been unaware of the scale of political activity which would be required to defend their interests. They had gained sufficient experience in the earlier campaign to know what the demands of a new and more important one would be. These were the circumstances under which Gandhi was inducted into the politics of the commercial elite.

The background to Gandhi's arrival in South Africa is too well known to require extensive repetition here. Early in 1893, he had been hired by the Porbunder branch of Dada Abdullah's firm to assist in the £40 000 law suit against a Transvaal merchant which was occupying so much of Abdullah's time. According to Gandhi's autobiography the offer of a first-class return fare to South Africa and a fee of £105 for a job that would take no more than a year to complete came as a welcome relief to him. He had been called to the London bar almost a year earlier and since then had tried unsuccessfully to establish a legal practice; first in Bombay, then in Rajkot, his family home. The autobiographical account of his early days in Natal and the Transvaal, working for Dada Abdullah, is also well-known: timid, inexperienced, and painfully shy of public speaking, he was so deeply shocked by the indignities which the Indian elite routinely suffered at the hands of the whites that he overcame all these handicaps in order to voice his objection to gratuitous insults.[49]

The events surrounding Gandhi's actual entry into politics are unclear. What is clear is that the autobiography offers a highly romanticized — though generally accepted — version of these events. As Gandhi recalled it years later, he was responsible for bringing the Franchise Amendment Bill to the attention of the Natal merchants. Their initial reaction is remembered to have been: 'What can we understand in these matters? We only understand things that affect our trade . . . what can we know of legislation?' Gandhi then explained to them that if the Bill were passed it would be 'the first nail into our coffin. It strikes at the roots of our self-respect'. The merchants therefore persuaded him to stay on, plying him with legal retainers, so that they could fight under his direction. He immediately began to organize a petition to oppose the Bill, and his involvement with Natal Indian politics had begun. 'Thus God', as he put it, 'sowed the seed of the fight for national self respect'.[50]

By contrast, there is sufficient evidence, as noted earlier, to suggest that the merchants were well aware of the significance of the Bill as the probable prelude to an attack on their commercial interests and that Gandhi, particularly suited to their needs with his legal training and fluency in Gujerati and English, was therefore hired to handle the time-consuming administrative and legal work of a second campaign. In any event the important point to clarify is that whether it was Gandhi, or the merchants, who first became aware of the implications of the Franchise Bill, the campaign against it was conducted on the basis of its potential significance for Indian commercial interests. One of the early letters to Naoroji which Gandhi drafted on the question pointed out that 'Natal is not a bad place for the Indians. Good many traders can earn a living here. The Bill, if it becomes law, would be a very great blow to further Indian enterprise'.[51] Thus whether Gandhi became involved in politics in order to lead the merchants, as he recalled, or to be their representative, as seems much more likely, the essential continuity with pre-Gandhian politics was preserved. The major thrust in the elite's political activity remained an attempt to protect their commercial interests, and it was to remain so throughout the period under review.

The innovations in elite politics after Gandhi had become involved in May 1894 were for the most part tactical only. Three major strategic decisions were made however: to establish the Natal Indian Congress, to start the newspaper *Indian Opinion* and to found a communal settlement at Phoenix, near Durban. The Congress, *Indian Opinion*, and Phoenix in its capacity as the location of the press which produced the paper, became the main political institutions of the commercial elite in Natal.

The Natal Indian Congress

The Natal Indian Congress was founded on 22 August 1894. The origins of the Congress are, like Gandhi's entry into politics, unclear. It is generally assumed that the initiative for a permanent political organization came from Gandhi, and although even his autobiography does not make this claim, it is certainly implicit in the passage which discusses the founding of the party.[52] On the other hand, the first annual report of the Congress attributes its origins to the fact that 'all the Indians recognized the absolute necessity of establishing a permanent institution that would cope with the legislative activity, of a retrograde character, of the first Responsible Government of the Colony with regard to the Indians, and protect Indian interests'.[53] More specifically, a letter which Gandhi wrote to the *Natal Mercury* in September 1895 pointed out that the 'Congress was formed chiefly by the efforts of Mr Abdullah Haji Adam'.[54] Abdullah Haji Adam was, in fact, the party's first president. He was a partner in Dada Abdullah's firm and had been one of the key members of the Indian Committee. It is therefore quite likely that the initiative to form a standing political organization did come from him. As noted earlier, the experience of the first campaign, and the awareness of the increased political activity which responsible government would demand, was more than enough to have demonstrated the need for a permanent organization. However, as with Gandhi's entry into politics, the point which requires clarification is that, whether the initiative to establish the Congress came from Gandhi, or from the merchants, the new political organization was, in terms of ideology and leadership, a direct descendant of the Indian Committee.

Insofar as the merchants had an articulate secular ideology, it was fairly typical of any merchant class, and certainly typical of the Gujerati trading communities from which they had migrated. Maximum emphasis was placed on protecting their privileged economic position. Socially and politically they were conservative: they worked within the framework of the existing social and political order and when they protested manifestations of the whites' discrimination against themselves, they protested as a class rather than a race. At the same time, they shared all of the whites' prejudices about the Natal Africans. Less usual was the emphasis which the merchants placed on the distance between themselves and the Indian underclasses. This was a requirement of a colonial situation in which legal distinctions were increasingly being made on a racial basis, and in which the major threat to the merchants' economic interests thus happened to be posed in terms of their being identified as part of a certain group which was placed low in the racial hierarchy, and for whose majority restrictive legislation already existed.[56] Protection of their interests therefore required frequent reference to their claim to be separate from, and superior to, the rest of the group. This was important in several ways. It precluded the merchants from developing a nationalist ideology such as was increasingly being subscribed to by their counterparts in India at the turn of the century; an otherwise not improbable theoretical basis for their own political activity. Despite the reality of the relationship between elite and masses in India, there was no barrier to the political elite at least claiming common cause with the mass of the people. In Natal, however, there could be no attempt to construct a sense of Indian community so long as the distinction between the merchants and the underclasses was a logical requirement of the merchants' ideology. At the same time, the irrational conviction that Africans or 'coloureds' were, *ipso facto*, inferior to themselves, helped prevent any attempt at alliance with the articulate, politicized elements in the African or coloured communities.[57] The politics of the Natal Indian Congress, like the politics of the Indian Committee, reflected an essentially exclusive and self-serving ideology.

Throughout the entire period from 1894 to 1906 and, indeed, until 1914, the leadership of the Congress was drawn from the former Indian Committee. Of the fifteen so-called 'prominent members' of the Committee, ten were among the original vice-presidents of the Congress. The names of some of them disappear from the records after the mid-1890s, but others stayed on. Each of the Congress presidents who served between 1894 and the split in the party in October 1913 had been a so-called 'prominent member' of the Indian Committee: Abdullah Haji Adam, 1894-1896 (temporarily returned to India); Abdullah Karim Haji Adam, 1896-1898 (resigned); Cassim Jeewa, 1898-1899 (returned to India, accidentally drowned October 1899); Abdul Kadir, 1899-1906 (temporarily returned to India); Dawd Mahomed, 1906-1912 (left on a pilgrimage to Mecca); Abdullah Karim Haji Adam, 1912-1913 (split with the party).[58] Abdullah Haji Adam and Abdullah Karim Haji Adam were brothers and partners in Dada Abdullah and Company, a powerful Natal-based firm with extensive investments in the Transvaal. Abdul Kadir was a managing partner of the equally powerful M C Camroodeen and Company which also had significant investments in the Transvaal.[59] Dawd Mohamed, a land and property owner in Natal — and, indeed, an employer of indentured Indian labour — owned 'large business interests' in the Transvaal before the war, if not also after it.[60] Leaving aside the brief presidency of Cassim Jeewa, then, the Congress was run during the entire period under review by the owners of three single companies whose economic interests in not only Natal, but also the Transvaal, were extensive. These men, and the other powerful Durban-based merchants whose biographies appear in Chapter 1, made up the firm but flexible core of the Congress which ensured continuity despite the frequent absences of various merchants.

The Congress secretaries formed another level of continuity. Gandhi was honorary secretary between August 1894 and October 1901 when he returned to India. During his temporary absence between 1896 and 1897 his place was filled by Adamji Miankhan, one of the original vice-presidents. In 1902, Gandhi was succeeded by M H Nazar and R K Khan who were joint secretaries until their resignation some time before May 1905.[61] Nazar, who first arrived in Natal in 1896, had been involved with the Congress ever since.[62] There is little information available on Khan except that he was an advocate whom Gandhi brought back with him when he returned to South Africa in 1897.[63] Both he and Nazar, like Miankhan, were fluent in English. They were succeeded by Omar Johari and, again, Adamji Miankhan, acting as joint secretaries.[64] Johari, as noted in Chapter 1, had temporarily returned to India in the early 1890s, but became involved in the party on his return. Adamji Miankhan resigned in March 1906, Johari in April 1907.[65] They were replaced by M C Anglia and Dada Osman who informally assumed the leadership in 1913 when the party was breaking up over the question of extending the passive resistance movement to Natal.[66] Anglia, who had been in the Transvaal before the war, was a relative newcomer to the Congress when he became secretary. Dada Osman was one of the original up-country members of the party.[67] Like the other secretaries, Dada Osman, Johari and Anglia were also fluent in English.

Although in theory membership in the Congress was open to 'any person approving of [its] work', in practice the annual dues of £3 placed clear limitations on the socio-economic strata from which the party could draw.[68] Inevitably, the membership was dominated by merchants. Although the records of the Congress cannot be traced, there exists a full list of the early members which appears to date from December 1894. The list shows a total membership of 222. Of the 166 whose occupations were also listed, 85 per cent were merchants. Twelve per cent were from the white-collar occupations (overwhelmingly clerical). The remainder comprised a fisherman, a barman, a waiter and a hawker. At least in the early days the party had a disproportionately large standing committee. In 1894 it numbered 70, three quarters of whom were merchants, one quarter clerks. The 27 vice-presidents were all merchants. The Congress claimed 11 branches in 1894, but its membership was concentrated in Durban, the main Indian commercial centre (62 per cent). The only other sizeable branches were in Pietermaritzburg, the administrative centre of the colony (18 per cent), and Verulam, a small town 19 miles north of Durban in the heart of the sugar-growing district (16 per cent),[69] both of which were also Indian commercial centres, though much smaller than Durban in this respect. The fact that 62 per cent of the total membership and 85 per cent of the committee were from Durban reflected its importance as the headquarters for Indian commercial acitivity in Natal. Indeed, during the years that followed, all significant decisions were made in Durban, and the small branches do not appear to have been effective at all. The name of only one original up-country member (Dada Osman, Umsinga branch) appears in the later Congress activities, and by that time he had moved to Durban.

It is particularly interesting that western educated white collar workers, who had not been in any way involved in merchant politics before 1894, were members of the Congress from very early days. According to Gandhi's autobiography they had been shunned by the merchants in the past in the belief that since many of them were Christian they must be 'under the thumbs of the white clergymen, who in their turn were subject to the government.'[70] It seems reasonable to accept, as Gandhi implies, that the decision to incorporate them resulted from his pointing out the value of their fluency in English. Certainly, this seems to have been put to good use by the party. At least in the early days the western educated members, despite their small numbers, made up 25 per cent of the standing committee.[71]

Notwithstanding the Congress's heavy annual dues, this alliance was even more important for the western educated themselves. In 1894 it looked as if they too were about to be adversely affected by forth-coming legislation.[72] Their interests had been singled out for both generalized and specific attacks in the Legislative Assembly like those of the merchants and the ex-indentured workers. An amendment of the Education Law, introduced in April 1894, disqualified those who were not white from attending government secondary schools. One of its supporters in the Assembly expressed the widespread hostility towards what he called 'coolies' by pointing out the 'danger of educating the black races in our midst to a point which rendered them eligible for ousting sons of white colonists from official and other positions'.[73] Two months later when the House was in Committee on a Civil Services Bill, a proposal to debar Indians from the Civil Service — one of the major career outlets for the western educated — was defeated only by the chairman's casting vote. Again, the debates left no room for doubt that the proposal was laid aside only for fear of prejudicing acceptance of the Franchise Amendment Bill. And, again, it was made clear that the question could be solved even without legislation. The Premier pointed out that since the task of selecting candidates would fall to the proposed Civil Service Board, 'that of itself would be a check against the appointment of improper persons'.[74] Thus the western educated were drawn into elite politics at a time when their specific interests appeared to be under immediate threat. In fact the threat did not materialize for over a decade, but the other benefits which they derived from an alliance with the merchants, which have already been described, made it worth their while to remain in the Congress.

There is little hard information available on the organizational structure or decision-making processes of the party. The rules which were drawn up when the Congress was established have survived along with the first two annual reports.[75] But none of these is particularly helpful. The rules proved impracticable after attendance at Congress meetings had dwindled drastically within a year or so of its creation; and the reports provide no real indication of the roles played by various officials, or their relationship with the rest of the members. However, from a close reading of *Indian Opinion* and the *Collected Works*, it is possible to put together what is probably a reasonably accurate picture of the workings of the party. The picture which emerges suggests that whatever the Congress may have been in theory, in practice it operated like a very small private club.

Firstly, as noted, despite nominal branches throughout the colony, the Congress existed primarily in, and for, Durban. The president and vice-presidents were elected, presumably by the entire active membership since there is nothing to indicate otherwise. Secretaries were appointed by the working committee.[76] Once an official had been elected he retained his post until he chose to resign.[77] It does not appear that the vice-presidents played a significant role; in fact it is doubtful that the office existed in any meaningful way after the first year or so. Secretaries were clearly chosen for their ability to command the English language, and presidents on the basis of their financial standing in the community. When the party was founded it was intended that the working committee would constitute the decision-making mechanism through regular meetings. Business for discussion in the committee could only be accepted if it had been proposed and seconded by committee members. After business had been discussed, proposals were to be framed and voted on by the committee whose chairman had the casting vote. No business could be transacted unless there were ten committee members present.[78] Apart from the fact that a disproportionate number of the original committee were western educated, and that it included the vice-presidents, president and secretary of the party,[79] there is nothing to indicate the basis on which members were selected.

But in any event, this system was short-lived. In the early days members were so eager to participate that the notion of separate committee meetings was dropped.[80] Within a year, however, attendance at party meetings had become 'very poor' and by 1899 there were only 37 paid-up members, and it was 'difficult to form even a quorum' at meetings within an hour and a half after they had started, as regulations decreed.[81] By 1902 the party's activity was described as having 'become slack', and by March 1906 no funds had been collected 'for a long time'.[82] Under the circumstances it is clear that whatever mechanisms may have existed for decision-making at the theoretical level — in 1906, for example, there was still a 'committee' — in practice decisions were generally the work of the handful of members who participated on a regular basis.

There were occasional exceptions to the general rule of decison-making, however. In June 1903, for instance, the Congress succeeded in mobilizing 'members' throughout the colony when the Mayor of Durban proposed to his Council that the government should be petitioned to pass legislation confining Indian merchants to designated locations. The party held a meeting in Durban where the Mayor's proposal was discussed, and resolutions condemning it were framed and voted on by representatives from various parts of the colony. The resolutions were then forwarded to the Natal government.[83]

Clearly on occasions such as this a democratic decision was valued for the extra weight which it would carry with the government. Reports of the meeting in *Indian Opinion* stressed the fact that 17 delegates had come from Ladysmith alone.[84] This example highlights the fact that the key to mobilizing the merchants was to challenge a direct threat to their economic interests. This point will be raised again later and dealt with more fully in the following chapter. The example also serves to illustrate the fact that almost a decade after its inception Congress machinery, although badly rusted, did exist in some form or another throughout the colony. But all available evidence suggests that after the first year or so the Congress's decision-makers (which is to say the party's regular supporters) generally comprised mainly, and perhaps even solely, the wealthiest merchants — those with multiple branches and extensive property holdings who would face tremendous financial loss if the Natal government followed in the footsteps of the Transvaal and the Free State.

Much of the surviving information on the workings of the Congress deals with fund-raising. The problems experienced in collecting membership subscriptions, let alone any additional funds, corroborate the contention that few besides the wealthiest merchants maintained an ongoing interest in the party's activity. The annual membership dues were £3, but in the early days all of the wealthiest merchants and, indeed, a number of others, pledged upwards of £6. Abdullah Haji Adam and Abdul Kadir subscribed as much as £24 each, and Dawd Mahomed £15. But by the end of the Congress's first year, the only group of subscribers which was fully paid-up was that whose members had undertaken to pay £24 and £15. The total deficits in the projected receipts for the other groups were increasingly larger as the annual subscriptions were lower: annual subscription £12, total projected receipts from the group £120, deficit in the projected receipts 22 per cent; subscription £6, projected receipts £132, deficit 32 per cent; subscription £3.1.0, projected receipts £6.2.0, deficit 10 per cent; subscription £3, projected receipts £559.10.0, deficit 51 per cent.[85]

Between 1894 and 1895, and again in 1896, fund-raising drives were conducted to try to bring in overdue subscriptions and attract new subscribers. The most active participants on both occasions were men like Dawd Mohamed, Moosa Haji Adam, Mohamed Cassim Jeewa, Abdul Kadir, Abdul Karim Haji Adam and Rustomji. Sometime around May 1896 the Congress became a landlord in an attempt to come to grips with its financial problems. A building in Durban was bought for £1080. The rentals paid by the Tamil labourers who tenanted it came to approximately £10 per month. By September, though, the Congress's liabilities stood at around £300-£400.[86] Several years later, at the beginning of 1907, the party was functioning on a bank overdraft guaranteed by Dawd Mahomed and Omar Johari.[87] After the first few years Congress activity was thus financed more or less out of the pockets of the wealthiest merchants.

Thus, although in theory the Congress was an open organization, in practice the annual dues of £3 made it almost as exclusive a body as its ideological predecessor, the Indian Committee. At times the party successfully mobilized most of the merchant and the western educated white collar workers whose interests it had been created to protect. But, in general, throughout the period 1894-1906, the elite were politically apathetic. The extent to which this apathy might have resulted from the party's inability to protect their interests will be discussed shortly. For the moment it is enough to note that during its first decade the Congress was for the most part financed, organized, led and indeed, actively supported, only by the comparatively small number of merchants who made up the highest strata of the Natal Indian elite.

Indian Opinion

Indian Opinion began publication in June 1903. The decision to start an Indian newspaper had been made as early as 1896 during the first flush of enthusiasm for organized politics. But the idea was abandoned at the time because Gandhi, according to his autobiography, did not have time to run a newspaper and he could find no-one else to do it. In 1898, at Gandhi's suggestion, Mandanjit Vijavaharik, an active member of the Congress, opened the International Printing Press in Durban. In 1903, advised and encouraged by Gandhi, Mandanjit began printing and publishing *Indian Opinion*. His editor was M H Nazar, the Congress joint secretary.[88]

The time lapse between the opening of Madanjit's press and the establishment of *Indian Opinion* was certainly not due to lack of expertise, which had made the idea of a paper impracticable in 1896. Between 1901 and 1903 a small Pietermaritzburg weekly, *Colonial Indian News*, had been published and edited by P S Aiyar. Although Aiyar was a member of the Congress his paper was aimed prematurely at what later became the new elite, as its name suggests. The *News* started off in both English and Tamil, but was reduced to Tamil only in April 1902. The English edition of the paper contained 'Notes and News' from India which included reports of nationalist activities; extensive coverage of Natal Indian sporting events; a weekly 'Market Report' which listed produce prices in the Pietermaritzburg market, and reports of the ill-treatment of indentured labourers. Nearly all the advertising space in the *News* was bought by Tamil petty traders. The paper folded in 1903, probably for lack of funds. Unlike its successor, *African Chronicle*, which will be discussed in Chapter 5, there is nothing in the contents of the *News* to suggest that it could have had a wide enough circulation to pay its way.

Rather than lack of expertise, then, the long-delayed establishment of *Indian Opinion* reflects the general apathy surrounding merchant politics during this period. The Congress itself was labouring under a shortage of both funds and members, and the Anglo-Boer war disrupted both white and Indian political activity. Late in 1901, after seven years of political failure, Gandhi returned to India in the belief that the Congress cause was lost in Natal.[89] By January 1903, however, he was back in South Africa — at the invitation of the Congress — poised for action in the Transvaal on the assumption that under British rule, 'our position in the Transvaal is and ought to be infinitely stronger than elsewhere'.[90] However, within weeks of his return it seemed apparent that the Milner regime intended to enforce Transvaal Law 3 of 1885 which called for the removal of Indians to designated locations. By May he had committed himself to working in the Transvaal for an indefinite length of time.[91] These were the circumstances under which the decision was taken to launch *Indian Opinion.*

Indian Opinion served primarily as a spokesman for the Indian merchants in Natal and the Transvaal. In this respect it took the place of the countless letters 'to the editor' which Gandhi had composed for South African and Indian newspapers over the previous decade: at least during the paper's first two years, over 500 complimentary copies of each edition were sent out to prominent persons in South Africa, Britain and India.[92] The paper's other important function was to keep the elite informed of Indian political activity in Natal and the Transvaal. Although it was edited first by Nazar, briefly by H Kitchin after Nazar's death, and then by H S L Polak,[93] the editorial policy was set by Gandhi throughout the remainder of his stay in South Africa. Indeed, most of the editorials written between 1903 and 1914 have been credited to Gandhi.[94]

The paper started with weekly editions in English, Gujerati, Tamil and Hindi. In February 1906 Gandhi decided to drop the Tamil and Hindi sections. His contention that 'we do not give the right stuff. We are not in a position to do so',[95] underlines the reality of the gap which existed between the elite and the Tamil and Hindi-speaking underclasses despite Congress and *Indian Opinion* claims to represent the community as a whole. P S Aiyar who had run an Anglo-Tamil weekly between 1901 and 1903 and who started another in 1908 was not, apparently, invited to edit the Tamil columns of *Indian Opinion.* This has the appearance of an attempt by Gandhi to isolate a potential political rival.[96] Although a member of Congress, Aiyar was something of a maverick who eventually became a harsh critic of it as well as a spokesman and sometime leader of the new elite.

From the day of its first issue *Indian Opinion* suffered the same financial problems as the Congress, despite the fact that most of the workers on the paper were unpaid volunteers and that it was run on a non-profit basis. Advertising space was bought by merchants who were also expected to subscribe to the paper as well as try to sell new subscriptions.[97] As with Congress, whatever general enthusiasm existed for *Indian Opinion* in its infancy soon dissipated. During the paper's first eighteen months, Gandhi, the Congress and its Transvaal equivalent, the British Indian Association, were all required to contribute to running costs.[98] By the end of 1904 when advertising sales had slipped badly and there were only 887 paying subscribers, the paper's finances were in a chaotic state.[99] When Gandhi came down from the Transvaal in October 1904 to review the situation, the trip resulted in the establishment of his first communal settlement.

Phoenix

Much has been written about the creation of the settlement at Phoenix. In his autobiography Gandhi recalls that as he was about to leave for Durban, H S L Polak, a sub-editor on the *Transvaal Critic*, who was beginning to take an interest in South African Indian politics, loaned him a copy of Ruskin's *Unto This Last*. Gandhi read the book on the train journey south and, determining 'to change his life in accordance with [its] principles', arrived in Durban with a solution for *Indian Opinion*'s financial problems.[100] He had decided to move the paper to a farm where the workers could support themselves on two acre plots of land and draw only a nominal salary for their work. When the move was reported in an *Indian Opinion* editorial in December 1904, Gandhi described one of its benefits as the fact that 'the workers could live a more simple and natural life, and the ideas of Ruskin and Tolstoy be combined with strict business principles.'[101] Thus the original inspiration for the first of Gandhi's communal settlements is always attributed to his readings of Tolstoy and Ruskin. What has been overlooked in the past, however, is the fact that a far more immediate influence on Gandhi may well have been the example of the successful rural commune which predated his own settlement at Phoenix. John L Dube, an American-educated Zulu, editor of the weekly *Ilanga Lase Natal*, was already directing a communal settlement at Phoenix when Gandhi decided to buy land in the same area. Dube's settlement included a school and training facililties for various trades,[102] all of which Gandhi's own commune was eventually to offer. If Gandhi had no prior knowledge of Dube's work, then the establishment of his commune, in the same area, is a most striking coincidence.

Phoenix became significant to Gandhi, personally, both as the model for a second settlement in the Transvaal, and as a staging point for the final phase of his passive resistance campaign in 1913. During the period up to 1906 and, indeed, until the 1913 Congress split when many of the merchants dissociated themselves both from Gandhi and *Indian Opinion*, Phoenix served the elite in its capacity as the headquarters of the paper. Whatever the original source of inspiration for the settlement, as an element in elite strategy Phoenix represented a distinct departure from the political norm. There can be no doubt that Gandhi was the sole author of this innovation.

Strategy and Tactics

The elite's strategy and tactics were strictly constitutional in nature. The merchants claimed exemption from disabilities on the grounds that they were British subjects and, moreover, desirable citizens. On every possible occasion the colonial and imperial governments were reminded that the elite considered themselves distinct from and superior to the Indian underclasses and the Natal Africans. However, all legislation which discriminated against Indians *eo nomine*, or which was framed in such a way as to permit discrimination against Indians, was opposed on the grounds that it was part of the Natal government's broader strategy for eliminating Indian trade competition. The intensity of the opposition varied notably. The imposition of a new legal disability on indentured workers merited a brief and mildy-worded reproach to the Natal government; discrimination against ex-indentured workers was more firmly contested on the basis of its being one aspect of the general attack on free Indians which was intended to drive the merchants out of Natal; and, finally, direct or indirect attacks on the merchants themselves were the object of sustained campaigns employing the full range of tactics.

The tactics which the Congress used were those of polite constitutional protest: petitions and delegations to government officials, letters to the press and to prominent public figures, editorials in *Indian Opinion*, court cases and official notification to the government of resolutions passed at party meetings. Strenuous attempts were made to bring pressure to bear on Natal through the governments of India and Great Britain. The most effective point to which the party could legitimately apply pressure was the question of Natal's continuing use of indentured labour. The significance of the labour question was discovered soon after the Congress was established and from then onwards the party routinely used demands for the stoppage of labour as a lever for trying to extract concessions for the free Indian community from the Natal government.

Thus both strategy and tactics changed subtly after 1894: the use of a full-time organizer was apparent in the merchants' politics. New institutions were created, and if not always widely supported they at least provided a framework within which responsibility could be delegated so that the load was evenly distributed to ensure that political activity could be sustained over a long period. Strategic and tactical innovations were made and though they did not — with the exception of Phoenix — by any means represent a radical departure from pre-Gandhian politics, they bore the imprint of more careful planning and of continuity of institutions and personnel. Gandhi left Natal in 1901, but he remained in close touch with the Natal merchants. He was their chief strategist and tactician throughout the period 1894 to 1906.

Political Campaigns

Elite political activities between 1894 and 1906 fall into two distinct phases. The first, between 1894 and 1897, was an attempt to forestall the passage of damaging discriminatory legislation. The second, between 1897 and 1906, reflected the failure of phase one and was characterized by an attempt to mitigate the effects of a series of potentially discriminatory laws passed in 1897.

Political activity between 1894 and 1897 revolved around the campaign against the Franchise Amendment Bill which began with Gandhi's induction into Natal Indian politics. The first major step against the Bill was a petition signed by some 9 000 people which was submitted to the Colonial Secretary in July 1894.[103] The level of organization and activity reflected by the petition far exceeded in scale anything which had taken place before Gandhi's arrival or, indeed, anything which took place in Natal during the next two decades.

A number of factors mitigated against the use of widespread signature campaigns after 1894. Firstly, the ideological limitations of the merchants precluded them from even raising most of the issues around which a mass response could have been built. Secondly, the effectiveness of the merchants' organizational machinery was severely curtailed after the early enthusiasm for the Congress had dissipated. Finally, the 1894 petition was counter-productive. The Natal government used it to support their contention that unless Indians were disenfranchised they would soon become serious rivals for political power in the colony. The number of signatures on the petition was particularly convenient in this respect since it almost exactly equalled the number of white voters in Natal.[104]

After the July 1894 petition the campaign continued steadily while the Franchise Amendment Bill was under consideration by the Colonial Office, but no further attempt was made to give the appearance of mass support. During the next two years Gandhi drafted repeated petitions, memorials and letters to the Natal Assembly and Council, the Secretary of State for the Colonies, the Viceroy of India, Dababhai Naoroji and the British Committee of the Indian National Congress.[105] In addition numerous letters were sent to the Natal *Mercury, Advertiser,* and *Witness*.[106] An open letter and a questionnaire on attitudes towards Indians were sent to prominent whites in Natal.[107] In all, Gandhi averaged about one item a month. Petitions were submitted in the name of the president of the Congress and a handful of others. Letters to the press were signed by Gandhi alone; thus he was soon identified by the Natal whites as the chief Indian 'agitator'.[108]

In June 1896, Gandhi returned to India to fetch his wife and family. During the five months which he spent there, he made a concerted effort to mobilize support among the Indian elite. Gandhi carried with him a document authorizing him to 'represent the grievances the Indians are labouring under in South Africa before the authorities and public men and public bodies in India'.[109] Although it was less than two years since the Congress had been established, support had dwindled to the extent that there were just over forty signatures on the document. Only about a dozen of them are familiar as staunch supporters of the party and as Natal's most powerful merchants. Nevertheless the document served Gandhi well. In Bombay he met major nationalist leaders such as Pherozeshah Mehta, Gopal Krishna Gokhale and Lokamanya Tilak who organized large meetings which he addressed under the auspices of the Bombay Presidency Association and the Poona Sarvajanik Sabha. In Madras he spoke at a meeting organized by the Mahajan Sabha.[110] He also wrote letters or gave interviews to a number of newspapers including the *Statesman*, the *Englishman*, the *Times of India* and the Madras *Hindu*.[111] Wherever Gandhi went, reference was made to his first substantial publication on the South African question, *The Grievances of the British Indians in South Africa: An Appeal to the Indian Public*. The Green Pamphlet, as it was known for short, dealt mainly with Natal. The Transvaal and the Free State were also well covered and there were brief sections on the Cape and Zululand.[112] The demand for the original edition of the pamphlet was so great that a second edition of 4 000 copies was ordered in Madras midway through Gandhi's tour. By the time he returned to South Africa in December 1896, the ground had been laid for pressure to be applied to the government of India through the nationalist movement.

There was a contradiction in the logic of the campaign against the Franchise Bill. A new tactic introduced by Gandhi sought to give a firm constitutional basis to the Congress's demands by claiming equal rights for Indians and whites in Natal on the basis of the royal proclamation which followed the assumption of crown rule in India in 1858.[114] However, since the Natal government was clearly not prepared to accept all Indians as fellow subjects on principle, and nor, indeed, did the Congress's ideology lend itself to the notion of equality for all Indians, the campaign also aimed to gain acceptance specifically for the merchants in terms of their being 'desirable citizens'. Thus discrimination against Indians qua Indians was opposed. Over and over again objections were raised to the disabilities — formal and informal — of the elite on the grounds that they were what Gandhi called 'respectable' Indians, those suffering 'the non-recognition of the just place of the better class'.[115] He made it clear, though, that the merchants had no ambitions to share political power with the whites, far less pave the way for 'coolies' (Indian workers) to vote.[116] Direct links were made between the Franchise Bill and the continuing security of Indian commercial interests. 'There would have been no franchise agitation', Gandhi claimed, 'had not an attempt been made to tread upon their commercial pursuits'.[117] For this reason also, opposition to the 1895 Immigration Amendment Law Bill under whose terms freed labourers were to pay an annual £3 tax, and which was seen as a first step towards ridding the colony of non-indentured Indians, was a minor but important feature of the campaign. Its role was perhaps best expressed in a lengthy petition to the Colonial Office which began with the contention that the 'ultimate extinction of the Indian as a free man is the goal of the Colonist, and that every disability placed on the Indian becomes the forerunner of many more, and that his position is to be so reduced that he cannot exist in the Colony except as (to quote the Attorney General of Natal), "a hewer of wood and a drawer of water" '.[118]

The question of labour importation was crucial to the campaign and it was used consistently after it was first raised in August 1895. This was a particularly sensitive issue which could easily have backfired if mishandled. Gandhi and the Congress wanted continuing importation to be made dependent on better treatment for the free Indian community.[119] But it would have been disastrous if the government of India had, in fact, stopped the labour flow. This would almost certainly have invited swift and merciless retaliation from the planter and farmer interests that were dominant in the Natal Assembly. Thus Gandhi took care to emphasize that the calls for an end to labour importation did not imply that workers' conditions in Natal were worse than elsewhere, or that this question was 'part of the general grievances of the Indians in the Colony'.[120] When the Green Pamphlet came under harsh attack in Natal he even went so far as to inform the *Times of India* that 'the lot of the indentured Indian cannot be very unhappy; and Natal is a very good place for such Indians to earn their livelihood.'[121]

The reaction of the Natal government, press and white public became increasingly hostile as time passed and the Colonial Office refused to give a decision on the Franchise Bill. Early in January 1895 the Prime Minister of Natal suggested to the governments of the Cape, the Transvaal and the Orange Free State that a conference should be convened to 'establish common principles of policy and action in dealing with the future position and relations of the Asiatic races that are so rapidly acquiring a footing in South Africa.'[122] The press frequently stated that when the time came for a federation of the South African territories Natal would be an outcast if she had been forced to make concessions on the Indian question. By September 1895, the imperial government was being accused of 'culpable negligence' and 'contemptible weakness'. The mutinous air of the colony was expressed in the *Times of Natal* declaration that the 'white man should never consent to meet the black man at the ballot box; if the electoral franchise should be extended to the black man — native or imported — then will it be the signal for the whites to leave the country'.[123]

Inevitably the Congress and Gandhi also became objects of attack as the Indian campaign continued. The Congress's power was exaggerated out of all proportion and used, like the 1894 signature campaign, as further justification for disenfranchising Indians. F S Tatham, a member of the Legislative Assembly, claimed, typically, in a press interview that the 'Arabs wish[ed] to climb to power' and that disallowance of the Franchise Bill would mean 'government by the coolie in Natal'.[124] A Farmers' Association meeting, called to discuss the Indian question, made similar remarks. Information from Indian witnesses, whose sworn depositions alleged that the Congress used intimidation and boycotting in an attempt to swell their membership and collect funds, was used by the Prime Minister to show the Colonial Office 'that the gravity and urgent importance of this [franchise] question cannot be exaggerated'.[125] In the Assembly he referred to the party as a 'very powerful body in its way, a very united body, though practically a secret body'.[126]

The biggest demonstration of anti-Indian hostility in Natal came from the white working class, however. The origins of working class hostility had nothing to do with the elite's political activity. But their profound sense of grievance about what they saw as unfair competition from Indian workers was fanned by the increasingly anti-Indian tone of the press and the Assembly, and fed on rumours until it focused on the elite in general and Gandhi in particular.

In August 1896 while Gandhi was in India, the president of the Tongaat Sugar Company was granted permission by the Indian Immigration Trust Board to bring in some dozen skilled workmen under indenture at wages far below the market rate.[127] Rowdy mass meetings of white workers were held in Durban to demand cancellation of the agreement and the introduction of legislation to ban the importation of skilled workers under contract. The Trust Board was harshly criticized, and so were the government and the white capitalist class. But the worst criticism was directed at fellow victims of the system rather than the system itself. Indian workers were condemned for their ability to exist on sub-minimal wages 'huddled in mud huts or in cabins of packing cases . . . living like beasts.' 'They breed like rabbits', one demonstrator said, 'the worst of it is that we can't shoot them down'.[128] Tongaat quickly withdrew its application for skilled workmen and the hostility temporarily subsided.[129] It resurfaced in mid-December when Gandhi returned to Natal on board Dada Abdullah's ship the *Courland*, which arrived on the same day as another Indian-owned ship, the *Naderi*. Both were filled with passengers from Bombay — about 800 in all. It was widely rumoured in Durban that they were skilled workmen being brought in by Gandhi and the Natal Indian merchants to work at sub-market rates. The ships were kept at anchor in Durban Bay for nearly a month on slender evidence that they might have been in contact with plague. During that time increasingly threatening white working class demonstrations were organized in Durban. Members of the government publicly indicated their sympathy for the demonstrators. On 11 January 1897 when the Indian passengers were finally cleared to land, thousands of demonstrators massed at Durban Point to prevent their coming ashore. They dispersed only after the Attorney General had given his assurance that the whole Indian question would be dealt with in an early session of parliament.[130] Gandhi, who went ashore late in the evening, was set on by a small crowd and physically assaulted. The Durban Police Superintendent's wife cleared away the crowd and took him to her home. Later that night the police escorted him out of the back entrance disguised in police uniform while the crowd milled about in front singing 'We'll hang old Gandhi from the sour apple tree'.[131]

These events dominated Natal press headlines and correspondence between the governor and the Colonial Office for over a month.[132] By April 1897 the Natal Assembly had used them to do exactly what the Congress had been formed to prevent them from doing: they drew up bills to restrict Indian commercial activity and the immigration of free Indians.[133]

Colonial Office policy during these formative years, although marked by the difference between Ripon's and Chamberlain's priorities, gradually assumed the direction which it was to take over the next decade and a half. Ripon, who was Colonial Secretary from 1892 to 1895, was unusually sympathetic to the Natal Indians, as the Indian Committee had estimated he would be. But there is nothing to indicate that the Congress activities had anything to do with Ripon's attitude. He saw the Franchise Bill as an affront to Indians which would almost certainly cause dangerous repercussions in India if it were passed. The India Office was behind him in condemnation of the Bill,[134] but no clear-cut decision had been given on it by the time a new ministry assumed office in June 1895. By contrast, within three months of Chamberlain's appointment as Colonial Secretary the guidelines of future policy towards Natal had been laid down. The Indian question was viewed in terms of the belief that federation probably lay in the future for the South African territories and that such a federation should not be hostile to Britain. The Colonial Office interpretation of Natal and Transvaal press reports, Natal Assembly debates, and official correspondence on the franchise question, led to the conclusion that disallowance of the Bill would achieve the 'almost impossible . . . the union against us of the whole of South Africa over a political question. All the other colonies and states would join and we should eventually give way after an infinity of harm is done'.[135] Thus Chamberlain consented to legislation which served to discriminate against Indians provided only that they were not named in the legislation, and that existing rights were preserved.[136] This compromise, the essence of British policy towards the Natal Indians over the next fifteen years, placated the India Office and, more importantly, served broader South African policy considerations as well.

By May 1896 a new and more subtly worded franchise bill, designed to do the same job as the old one, was passing through the Natal Assembly. By August the Colonial Office had assented to the Bill.[137] The following year the Natal government, using as justification the intense, popular anti-Indian demonstrations of December 1896 — January 1897, drew up an Immigration Restriction Bill and a Dealers' Licences Bill. Both were carefully worded, both provided the springboard for an attack on Indian economic interests. The Immigration Restriction Bill required that intending immigrants possess £25 and written knowledge of a European language.[138] For the past twenty years the expansion of Indian commerce had depended on a steady, if small, influx of new passengers. Further free Indian immigration was virtually stopped by the new bill. The Bill to Amend the Law Relating to Licences for Wholesale and Retail Dealers stipulated that applications for trading licences, or renewal of existing licences, were to be submitted to municipal licensing officers appointed by the corporations.[139] This bill, in conjunction with the amended Municipal Corporations Act of 1894, provided the Natal administration with the means to deny licences to Indians on the grounds of insanitation. Both bills met Colonial Office requirements: they were necessary in order to ensure the maintenance of amicable relations between Natal and the imperial government; they did not discriminate against Indians *eo nomine*, nor — at least in theory — did they interfere with existing rights. Thus despite a lengthy correspondence between the India Office and the Colonial Office on the question of whether or not adequate provision had been made for safeguarding existing rights,[140] both bills eventually received royal assent in the form in which they had been drawn up.

Colonial Office acceptance of the Franchise Amendment Bill, the Immigration Restriction Bill and the Dealers' Licences Bill, established the framework within which the Congress worked for the next decade. Having failed to prevent the introduction of new legal disabilities which served to erode the position of the elite, the party had no alternative but to fall back on attempts to mitigate the effects of the implementation of the legislation.

The Congress's tactics remained much the same as they had been since its inception. Gandhi drafted petitions to the governments of Natal, India and Britain, and wrote letters to the press, to Naoroji and Gokhale.[141] But the output of letters and petitions of protest was much smaller than it had been during the campaign against the franchise bill, and when Gandhi returned to India in 1901, convinced that the Congress's cause in Natal was lost, official protests which focused on the legislation of 1896 - 1898 had already ceased. The active number of Congress supporters had, not surprisingly, dropped sharply, and funds were low. Some critics even viewed the Congress's work as counter-productive. They saw the damaging legislation of 1897 as white retaliation against Indian political organization.[142]

Increasingly, as the Dealers' Licences Act was enforced, the Congress's activity came to revolve around court cases which challenged refusals to renew old licences, or unsuccessful attempts to transfer a licensed business to new premises.[143] The big merchants who remained the only committed supporters of the party were affected by the Act both directly and indirectly. They were unable to expand by opening a new branch, to break a partnership into its component elements, or to pass on a business to an heir. They were not generally affected by the most usual reasons for the refusal to renew an existing licence — inability to keep books in English, or allegations of maintaining insanitary premises.[144] But those with pro-perty holdings were indirectly affected by the Act if persons leasing business premises from them were refused renewal of licence, and those with debtors among the petty traders stood to lose if their debtors were forced to shut up shop.[145]

When *Indian Opinion* was established the workings of the Dealers' Licences Act were the subject of many reports and editorials in the paper as, indeed, was any other attempt, or rumoured attempt, at further discriminatory legislation. Even after he had left Natal Gandhi continued to advise the Congress on how best to protect themselves from the Act, and he remained involved in the legal cases which arose from its working. But even the legal cases were unsuccessful for the most part, grounded as they were in the party's failure to prevent the discriminatory legislation of 1897. As Gandhi had observed in 1901, the Congress's cause in Natal was lost.

Notes

1   CO 417/109/13485, *Claims of British Indian Merchants against the Government of the O F S for Expulsion* (15 June 1893), Shepstone, Wylie and Binns to Haji Mohamed Haji Dada, Dec. 1892.

2   CO 417/4/2900, High Commissioner to Sec. St. 28 Jan. 1885; C.7911, no.1, Sec. St. to High Commissioner 19 Mar. 1885; ibid., Transvaal State Sec. to High Commissioner, 23 Dec. 1885.

3   This correspondence is printed in C.7911. See also TABA Lt.G. 95/97/2, Sec. St. to Gov., 20 July 1904, which contains an excellent summary of these events.

4   C.5588, no.2, Brit. Ag. Pretoria to High Commissioner, 8 Aug. 1888.

5   C.7911, no.2, High Commissioner to Sec. St., 8 Jan. 1895, encl. 'Explanation of the so-called Coolie Question now pending between Her Majesty's Government and the Government of the South African Republic'.

6   The three remaining Indian merchants in the O F S (Haji Mohamed Haji Dada and Company, Moosa Hajee Cassim and Esop Hoosen and Company) were ordered to cease trading and sell up their stock. CO 417/109/13485, *Claims of British Indian Merchants against the Government of the O F S for Expulsion* (15 June 1893) Shepstone, Wylie and Binns to Haji Mohamed Haji Dada, Dec. 1892.

7   C.6487, no.6, Gov. to Sec. St., 6 Dec. 1890, encl. 'First ad interim Report of the Select Committee appointed on 3 December 1890 to prepare the Draft of a new Constitution for the Colony'.

8   See above, Chapter 1.

9   CO 417/109/13485, *Claims of British Indian Merchants against the Government of the OFS for expulsion* (15 June 1893).

10   CO 179/184/22145, encl. Haji Mohamed Haji Dada to Sec. St., 19

Oct. 1892.

11   *Indian Opinion*, 3 Feb. 1912.

12   The other members of the Indian Committee included Abdullah Haji Adam (Dada Abdullah and Co.), Moosa Haji Cassim, Hoosen Jeeva, Amod Danje, Esop Hoosen, Mohamed Cassim Camroodeen, Amod Mohamed, Mohamed Moosajee, Peeran Mohamed, Mohamed Cassim Jeewa, Ismail Mamoojee and Co. (sic), A Mohamed Tilly, Ismail Suliman, Amod Jeewa. CO 179/183/16781, Dep. Gov. to Col. Sec., 25 July 1892, encl. Haji Mohamed Haji Dada and others to Sec. St., n.d.

13   CO 179/184/22145, encl. Haji Mohamed Haji Dada to Sec. St., 19 Oct. 1892. For other 'Leading Members of the Indian Committee' (Moosa Hajee Cassim, Osman Khan, Ramant Khan, Hoosen Meerun) see CO 417/109/7669, *Record of Correspondence, Memorial to England etc. Concerning Grievances of British Indians, Merchants and Others, in the Colony of Natal, SAR and OFS* (n.d.) p.11, 'To Hon. Fajalbhoi Visram from the Indian Committee', Durban, 1 June 1891.

14   Ibid., 109/7669, *Record of Correspondence*.... pp.2-13, 'Petition by Merchants and inhabitants of Bombay, trading with Mauritius, Natal, Zanzibar, Mozambique, Delagoa Bay, Quillimane, Inhambane and other places in Africa, 9 July 1891; To Hon. Fajalbhoi Visram from the Indian Committee', Durban, 1 June 1891.

15   Ibid., and CO 179/182/6088, Gov. to Sec. St., 1 Mar 1892, encl. Natal Minute No.112; Sec St. to India Office, 6 Apr. 1892.

16   CO 179/183/16781, Minutes on Dep. Gov. to Sec. St., 25 July 1892, by Graham, 1 Sept. 1892, and Lord Ripon, 4 Sept. 1892.

17   CO 179/182/6088, Gov. to Sec. St., 1 Mar. 1892, encl. Natal Minute No.112.

18   CO 179/183/16781, Dep. Gov. to Sec. St., 25 July 1892 and encl. 2, Natal no.119, 25 July 1892, Schedule: 1. Extracts from lists of grievances with Reports by Attorney General and Mr Justice Wragg. 2. Report by Protector of Immigrants. 3. Report by Health Officer, Durban. See also ibid., draft CO to Under-Sec. St. India, 10 Sept. 1892.

19   CO 179/182/6088, Gov. to Sec. St., 1 Mar. 1892, encl. Natal Minute no.112, Haji Mohamed Haji Dada to Protector, 18 Jan. 1892.

20   Ibid., Natal Minute no.112, Assist. Col. Sec. to Haji Mohamed Haji Dada, 22 Jan. 1892.

21   CO 179/184/22145, encl. Haji Mohamed Dada, 29 Oct. 1892. For pamphlet in its final form see CO 417/109/7669, *Record of Correspondence, Memorial to England etc. Concerning Grievances*

of British Indians, Merchants and others in the Colony of Natal, SAR and OFS (n.d. — apparently early 1892).

22   CO 417/88/20107, Telegrams: British Indian merchants in the Transvaal to Sec. St. 13 Oct. 1892; to Queen Victoria 13 Oct. 1892; to Gladstone 13 Oct. 1892, and Naoroji to Ripon, 13 Oct. 1892.

23   CO 417/109/13485, *Claims of British Indian Merchants against the Government of the OFS for expulsion* (15 June 1893).

24   CO 179/183/16781, Dep. Gov. to Sec. St., 25 July 1892, encl. Haji Mohamed Haji Dada, Abdullah Haji Adam and 13 others to Sec. St. (n.d.); ibid., 184/22145, encl. Haji Mohamed Haji Dada to Sec. St., 19 Oct. 1892.

25   CO 179/183/16781, Dep. Gov. to Sec. St. 25 Jul. 1892, encl. Haji Mohamed Haji Dada, Abdullah Haji Adam and 13 others to Sec. St. (n.d.)

26   Ibid.

27   CO 179/182/6088, Gov. to Col. Sec., 1 Mar. 1892, encl. Natal Minute no.112, Haji Mohamed Haji Dada to Col. Sec., 17 Feb. 1892.

28   M K Gandhi, *An Autobiography* (London, 1949), pp.85,109-10.

29   Shepstone, Wylie and Binns, for instance, represented them in their claim against the OFS. CO 417/109/13485, *Claim of British Indian Merchants against the Government of the OFS for expulsion* (15 June 1893) p.5. See also, B Pillay, *British Indians in the Transvaal* (London, 1976) p.27 for lawyers representing Indian merchants on the Transvaal question.

30   TABA, Smuts Collection: Public Papers (b), no.10, Transvaal, Report of the Customs and Industries Commission, 1907, p.6. And see below for reaction of white workers to low Indian wage rates.

31   See below, p.46.

32   CO 179/188/8751 Gov. to Sec. St., 27 Apr. 1894.

33   The number of Indians on the parliamentary voters' roll for the year ending August 1895 was 266 out of a total registered electorate of 10 279. CO 179/189/14248, Minute by Fiddes, 17 Nov. 1894, and Peace to Fairfield, 4 Dec. 1894.

34   See above, p.43.

35   CO 179/183/16781, Dep. Gov. to Sec. St. 25 Jul. 1892, encl. Haji Mohamed Haji Dada, Abdullah Haji Adam and others to Sec. St. (n.d.).

36   *Natal Witness*, 27 Apr. 1894, 1 May 1894, 2 May 1894.

37   Even in 1898 the Gov. claimed that 'under the present system of distribution of seats in Natal . . . [the Assembly] must always contain a majority of representatives of the farming and agricultural interests'. CO 179/204/29101, Gov. to Sec. St., 28 Nov. 1898.

38   *Natal Witness*, 2 May 1894 (Gerland). Also *Natal Times*, 20 Jun. 1894 (O'Meara).

39   *Natal Witness*, 2 May 1894 (Smythe). See also ibid., 1 May 1894 (Hulett) and *Natal Times*, 20 Jun. 1894 (Tatham) and ibid. (Bale).

40   By the early 1890s, it had become clear that ex-indentured labourers, instead of providing an auxiliary plantation labour force, sought alternative means of subsistence whenever possible. (See above, Chapter 1). For the planters and farmers the tax held the potential of building at least part of a labour force from re-indentured Indians, thus eliminating the costs involved in bringing in new workers.

41   *Natal Witness*, 11 May 1894.

42   Ibid., 21 Jun. 1894; *Natal Times*, 27 Jun. 1894.

43   CO 179/189/14248, Gov. to Sec. St. 16 Jul. 1894.

44   *Natal Mercury*, 26 June 1894. See also ibid. (Tatham, Bale and Leuchars) and ibid., 21 June 1895 (Bale, Rethman, Ryley, Baynes, Tatham).

45   *Natal Witness*, 3 May 1894.

46   See below, p.68.

47   *Natal Witness*, 8 May 1894 (Yonge).

48   See below, p.68.

49   Gandhi, *Autobiography*, op. cit., pp.89-91, 105-109.

50   Ibid., p.117.

51   *C W*, i, p.130, Gandhi to Naoroji, 27 Jul. 1894.

52   Gandhi, *Autobiography*, op. cit., pp.123-4.

53   *C W*, i, p.231.

54   Ibid., p.247.

55   The following discussion of the merchants' ideology is based on the clearly definable ideological assumptions which are implicit as well as explicit in their politics.

56   Much of the public debate on the franchise question made it clear that even those whites who sympathized with the merchants were reluctant to concede them any rights which might later be claimed by ex-indentured labourers. See, for example, *Natal Witness* 7 Oct. 1895, *Natal Times*, 8 Oct. 1895, *Natal Advertiser*, 8 Oct. 1895, *Natal Mercury*, 7 Sept. 1895.

57   On merchants' attitudes towards Africans see, for example, *C W*, ii, p.74, 'Address in Bombay', 26 Sept. 1896; ibid., pp.100, 105, 'Address in Madras', 26 Oct. 1896. See also Chapter 3, passim.

58   *C W*, iii, p.109, 'The Second Report of the Natal Indian Congress', after 11 Oct. 1899; ibid., v, p.227, 'The Natal Indian Congress', 10 Mar. 1906; ibid., xi, p.274, 'Speech at Durban Farewell to Pilgrims', 13 Jul. 1912; ibid., p.394, 'Diary 1912', 30 Jun. 1912. The entry notes only that Abdool Karim Sheth was 'elected' at a Congress

meeting. Since this happened less than two weeks before Dawd Mohamed's departure, it is reasonable to assume that he was elected president. The connecting link between Dawd Mohamed and the Indian Committee was his partnership in Ismail Mamoojee and Company. On which, see fn.12 above, and Chapter 1.

59   See above, Chapter 1.

60   *Indian Opinion*, 22 Aug. 1908; NA, I.I. 1/103/1835/1901; Protector to Sec. Indian Imm. Trust Board. And see above, Chapter 1.

61   CO 179/192/22881, Gov. to Sec. St., 30 Nov. 1895, encl. *List of Members of the Natal Indian Congress, Durban*; *C W*, iii, p.102, 'The Second Report of the Natal Indian Congress', after 11 Oct. 1899; ibid., p.236, Gandhi to Khan and Nazar, 31 Mar. 1902 (first indication of Khan and Nazar acting as joint secretaries) and see also ibid., v, p.227, 'The Natal Indian Congress', 10 Mar. 1906.

62   *C W*, v. pp.179-81, 'Mansukhlal Hiralal Nazar', 27 Jan. 1906.

63   Gandhi, *Autobiography*, op. cit., p.169.

64   *C W*, v, p.227, 'The Natal Indian Congress', 10 Mar. 1906.

65   Ibid., p.315, 'Adamji Miankhan', 9 Feb. 1907; ibid., vi, p.410, 'Meeting of Natal Indian Congress', 8 Apr. 1907.

66   Ibid., and see below, Chapter 6, pp.250-251.

67   CO 179/192/22881, Gov. to Sec. St. 30 Nov. 1895, encl. *List of Members of the Natal Indian Congress, Durban*.

68   *C W*, i, p.131, 'The Natal Indian Congress', Aug. 1894.

69   CO 179//192/22881, Gov. to Sec. St. 30 Nov. 1895, encl. *List of Members of the Natal Indian Congress, Durban*.

70   Gandhi, *Autobiography*, op. cit., p.116.

71   CO 179/192/22881, Gov. to Sec. St., 30 Nov. 1895, *List of Members of the Natal Indian Congress, Durban*; *C W*, i, p.131, 'The Natal Indian Congress', Aug. 1894.

72   *C W*, i, p.131, 'The Natal Indian Congress', Aug. 1894.

73   *Natal Witness*, 8 May 1894 (Bainbridge).

74   *Natal Times*, 27 Jun. 1894.

75   *C W*, i, pp.132-5, 'The Natal Indian Congress', Aug. 1894; ibid., pp.231-41, 'The First Report of the Natal Indian Congress', Aug. 1895; ibid., iii, pp.96-110, 'The Second Report of the Natal Indian Congress', after 11 Oct. 1899.

76   See, for example, ibid., pp.96-110, 'The Second Report of the Natal Indian Congress', after 11 Oct. 1899; and ibid., i, p.132, 'The Natal Indian Congress', Aug. 1894.

77   See above, p.51.

78   *C W*, i, pp.129-135, 'The Natal Indian Congress', Aug. 1894.

79   Ibid.

80   Ibid., p.231, 'The First Report of the Natal Indian Congress', Aug. 1895.

81   *C W*, iii, pp.98,109, 'The Second Report of the Natal Indian Congress', after 11 Oct. 1899.

82   Ibid., p.227, Gandhi to Rustomji, 1 Mar. 1902; ibid., v, p.228, 'The Natal Indian Congress', 10 Mar. 1906.

83   NA, G.H. 1595/515/1903, Chairman NIC to Gov., 26 Jun. 1903. The mayor's proposal came within weeks of the Transvaal administration's announcement that Asian 'bazaars' should be set aside in the Transvaal and new licences issued only for trading within bazaars. Ibid., 1594/296/1903, Milner to Col. Sec. 17 Apr. 1903. The Congress's protest was effective. The mayor's proposal was dropped for fear of prejudicing the Natal government's attempt to renegotiate the conditions of labour importation with the government of India. Ibid., 1595/515/1903, P.M. to Gov. 14 Dec. 1903. See also, *Natal Mercury*, 25 Jun. 1903.

84   NA, G H 1595/515/1903, Chairman NIC to Gov. 26 Jun. 1903.

85   CO 179/192/22881, Gov. to Sec. St., 30 Nov. 1895, *List of Members of the Natal Indian Congress, Durban; C W.*, i, p.232, 'The First Report of the Natal Indian Congress', Aug. 1895.

86   *C W*, i, p.235, 'The First Report of the Natal Indian Congress', Aug. 1895; ibid., pp.97-8,100, 'The Second Report of the Natal Indian Congress', after 11 Oct. 1899.

87   Ibid., vi, p.373, 'Natal Indian Congress', 23 Mar. 1907.

88   Ibid., iii, p.256, fn.1, and Gandhi, *Autobiography*, op. cit., p.238.

89   *C W*, iii, p.214, 'Speech at Calcutta Congress', 27 Dec. 1901.

90   Gandhi had written this in a letter to W S Caine, dated 26 Mar. 1902, ibid., p.231.

91   See below, Chapter 3, p.103.

92   *C W*, iv, p.319, 'Ourselves'.

93   Ibid., p.326, fn.3,4.

94   Many of these, including translations from the Gujerati, are printed in the *Collected Works*.

95   *C W*, v, p.174, Gandhi to M H Nazar, 5 Jan. 1906. See also ibid., p.183, 'Our Tamil and Hindi Columns', 3 Feb. 1906.

96   This observation is purely speculative. But see CO 291/113/43192, statement by Gandhi, Oct. 1906, and ibid., 104/41487, minute by Just, 19 Nov. 1906, for Gandhi's remarks about Dr William Godfrey who had organized a petition disputing Gandhi's claim to represent the Transvaal Indians.

97   See, for example, *C W*, iv, pp.409,432-3, Gandhi to Chhaganlal Gandhi, 17 Apr. 1905, 13 May 1905.

98   Ibid., pp.319-21, 'Ourselves', 24 Dec, 1904; ibid., v, pp.289-90,

Indian Opinion, 23 Apr. 1906.

99   **Ibid.**, v, p.289, *Indian Opinion*, 23 Apr. 1906.

100   Gandhi, *Autobiography*, op. cit., p.249.

101   *C W*, iv, p.320, 'Ourselves', 24 Dec. 1904.

102   S Marks, 'The Ambiguities of Dependence: John L Dube of Natal', *Journal of Southern African Studies*, 1, 2, Apr. 1975, pp.162-80.

103   Co 179/189/15016, encl. in Gov. to Sec. St., 31 July 1894. Given the low level of politicization of the vast majority of the Natal Indians during this period, and the remoteness of the franchise question for most of them, it is reasonable to assume that most of the signatories did not know what they were signing. Certainly, the petition did not reflect grassroots political mobilization.

104   Ibid., encl. Minute, P M's Office, Natal, 27 Jul. 1894. Since all signatories of the petition asserted their fitness to vote, it was claimed that the petition showed 'conclusive evidence of the danger that menaces the electorate should Asiatics continue to be admitted to the franchise'.

105   See, for example, *C W*, i, pp.92-6, 'Petition to Natal Assembly', 28 Jun. 1894; ibid., pp.97-9, 'Deputation to Natal Premier, 29 Jun. 1894'; ibid., pp.102-3, 'Deputation to Natal Governor', 3 Jul. 1894, ibid., pp.104-5, 'Petition to Natal Council', 4 Jul. 1894, ibid., pp.105-6, Gandhi to Naoroji, 5 Jul. 1894, etc.

106   These are also printed in the *Collected Works*. See, for example, *C W*, i, pp.112-13, Gandhi to Editor, *Natal Mercury*, 7 Jul. 1894, ibid., pp.244-5, Gandhi to Editor, *Natal Advertiser*, 23 Sept. 1894.

107   *C W*, i, pp.142-63, 'Open Letter', Dec. 1894; ibid., pp.100-1, 'Questions for Legislators', 1 Jul. 1894.

108   See, for example, F S Tatham, M L A, describing Gandhi in a press interview as a 'gentleman who, while nominally a solicitor, appears to devote his time more to raising discontent among the Indians than to his profession', *Times of Natal*, 8 Oct. 1895.

109   *C W*, ii, p.52, 'The Grievances of the British Indians', 26 May 1896.

110   Ibid., pp.70-84, 'Address in Bombay', 26 Sept. 1896; ibid., p.136, 'Address in Poona', 16 Nov. 1896; ibid., pp.94-121, 'Address in Madras', 26 Dec. 1896.

111   Ibid., pp.124-7, 'Interview to the *Statesman*', 10 Nov. 1896; ibid., pp.131-5, 'Interview to the *Englishman*', 13 Nov. 1896; ibid., pp.85-9, 'Indians in Natal', 17 Oct. 1896; ibid., pp.122-3, 'A Message of Thanks', 27 Oct. 1896.

112   The *Green Pamphlet* is reprinted in *C W*, ii. pp.1-52.

113   Ibid., pp.122-3, 'Message of Thanks', 27 Oct. 1896.

114   See, for example, *C W*, i, p.80, 'The Indian Vote', 29 Sept. 1893; ibid., p.311, 'The Indian Franchise', 4 April 1896; ibid., p.336,

'Memorial to Mr Chamberlain', 22 May 1896. The proclamation declared inter alia, that British subjects should be eligible for crown service regardless of race or creed.

115   See, for example, *C W*, i, p.160, 'Open Letter', Dec. 1894; ibid., p.296, 'Indians and Passes', 2 Mar. 1896; ibid., ii, pp.7, 12-14, 30, 'The Grievances of the British Indians in S.A.'; ibid., pp.56,60, 'Notes on the Grievances of British Indians', 22 Sept. 1896; ibid., pp.74, 75, 'Address in Bombay', 26 Sept. 1896; ibid., pp.86, 88, 'Indians in Natal', 17 Oct. 1896; ibid., pp.96,97,100,104, 'Address in Madras', 26 Oct. 1896; ibid., p.127, 'Interview to the *Statesman*', 10 Nov. 1896. See, in particular, ibid., p.133, 'Interview to the *Englishman*', 13 Nov. 1896.

116   Ibid., p.250, 'The Indian Question', 9 Oct. 1895; See also, ibid., pp.265,271, 'The Indian Franchise', 16 Dec. 1895; ibid., ii, p.126, 'Interview to the *Statesman*', 10 Nov. 1896.

117   Ibid., p.271, 'The Indian Franchise', 16 Dec. 1895. See also, ibid., p.130, Gandhi to Naoroji, 27 Jul. 1894; ibid., ii, p.135, 'Interview to the *Englishman*', 14 Nov. 1896.

118   Ibid., ii, p.185, 'Memorial to Mr Chamberlain', 15 Mar. 1897. See also ibid., i, p.127, 'Petition to Lord Ripon', 17 Jul. 1894; ibid., ii, 'Memorial to Mr Chamberlain', 15 Mar. 1897; ibid., i, p.178, 'Petition to Natal Assembly', 5 May 1895. And during the second part of the campaign, see also, ibid., iii, p.240, 'Indians in South Africa', 22 Apr. 1902.

119   Ibid., i, p.230, 'Memorial to Lord Elgin', 11 Aug. 1895. See also, ibid., ii, p.89, 'Indians in Natal', 17 Oct. 1896; ibid., p.156, 'Interview on board the *Courland*', 13 Jan. 1897. On the use of this tactic during the second stage of the campaign, see also, ibid., pp.347-8, 'To Public Men in India and England', 10 Jul. 1897; ibid., iii, p.40 'Petition to Chamberlain', 31 Dec. 1897; ibid., p.51, 'To Press and Public Men in India', 21 Jan. 1899; ibid., p.249, Gandhi to Bhownaggree, 18 May 1902; ibid., pp.250-51, 'Indians in Natal', 20 May 1902; ibid., p.277, 'Petition to Lord Curzon', Jan. 1903.

120   Ibid., ii, p.24, 'The Grievances of the British Indians in S.A.', (1896).

121   Ibid., p.87, 'Indians in Natal', 17 Oct. 1896, and see also, ibid., p.104, 'Address in Madras', 26 Oct. 1896; ibid., p.160, 'Interview on Board the *Courland*', 13 Jan. 1897.

122   CO 179/190/2259, Gov. to C O, 12 Jan. 1895, encl. P M Natal to P M Cape and State Sec. SAR and Govt. Sec. OFS, 11 Jan. 1895.

123   *Times of Natal*, 4 Sept. 1895; *Natal Witness*, 5 Sept. 1895. And see also, *Times of Natal*, 8 Oct. 1895 and *Natal Mercury*, 18 Feb. 1897.

124   *Times of Natal*, 8 Oct. 1895.

125   CO 179/192/19929, Gov. to Sec. St., 19 Oct. 1895, encl. Minute

no. 15/1895 P M's Office, 18 Oct. 1895.

126 *Natal Witness*, 7 May 1896.

127 CO 179/195/18749, Gov. to Sec. St., Separate, Confidential, 13 Aug. 1896.

128 Ibid., and *Natal Mercury*, 12 Aug. 1896. See also, *Natal Mercury*, 10, 13, 15 Aug. 1896; *Natal Witness*, 15 Aug. 1896.

129 *Natal Mercury*, 13 Aug. 1896.

130 This entire incident is well reported in the Natal press. See, for example, *Natal Mercury*, 1, 5, 7, 8, 9, 13, 14, 15 Jan. 1897; *Natal Advertiser*, 6, 7, 12, 13, 14, 15 Jan. 1897; *Natal Witness*, 1, 6, 7, 8, 9, 12, 14 Jan. 1897; *Natal Times*, 6, 8 Jan. 1897. And see also CO 179/197/1/742, Gov. to Sec. St., (free copy of cypher tele.), 8 Jan. 1897; ibid., 2211, Gov. to Sec. St., 9 Jan. 1897, and encls.

131 Killie Campbell Library, Durban, Dawes Collection, m.s. DAW, 2.042, Reminiscences of Ex.-Det. Inspect. J A Stubbs, 1898.

132 See fn.130 above and CO 179/197/1/1104, Gov. to Sec. St. tele. 15 Jan. 1897, and C O minuting; ibid., 1110 Gov. to Sec. St. tele., conf. 15 Jan. 1897, and C O minuting; ibid., 2958, Gov. to Sec. St., 15 Jan. 1897, and C O minuting and encls.; ibid., 3041, Gov. to Sec. St. secret, 15 Jan. 1897, and C O minuting and encls.; ibid., 3919, Gov. to Sec. St., 28 Jan. 1897.

133 CO 179/197/1/5975, encl. Immigration Restriction Bill; ibid., 5976, encl. Bill to Amend Quarantine Laws; ibid., 5978, encl. Bill, Licences to Wholesale and Retail Dealers.

134 See, in particular, CO 179/197/1/14248, minute by Ripon, 17 Oct. 1894, on Gov. to Sec. St., 16 Jul. 1984.

135 CO 179/169/14248, Gov. to Sec. St. 16 Jul. 1894, Minute by Meade, 10 Oct. 1894. See also ibid., Sir R Herbert to Meade, 17 Sept. 1894; ibid., 191/11/17045, Gov. to Sec. St. 6 Sept. 1895, encl. extract from the *Johannesburg Star*, and C O notation.

136 CO 179/192/19528, Gov. to Sec. St. 9 Oct. 1895 (commenting on Sec. St. to Gov. 12 Sept. 1895).

137 CO 179/195/18749, Sec. St. to Gov. 25 Aug. 1896. The Bill disqualified persons who did not enjoy the parliamentary franchise in their homeland. During the third reading of the bill, an M L A noted that 'the word "Indian" is not in the Bill, but the first clause refers to Indians entirely'. *Natal Witness*, 22 May 1896.

138 See fn.133.

139 Ibid.

140 See, for example, Co 179/202/4900, I O to C O, 2 Mar. 1897; ibid., 16007, I O to C O, 21 Jul. 1897; ibid., 23735, I O to C O, 2 Nov. 1897 and Minute by H.W. Just; ibid., 24288, IO to CO., 10 Nov. 1897; ibid., 202/2050, CO to IO 15 Feb. 1898. And see,

in particular, ibid., 197/1/5985, minute by Chamberlain, 5 Apr. 1897, and ibid., 202/12465, minute by Chamberlain on Naoroji to Sec. St., 9 Jun. 1897.

141   These are printed in the *Collected Works*. On Immigration Restriction Act see, for example, *C W*, ii, pp.289-90, 'Petition to Natal Assembly', 26 Mar. 1897; ibid., p.356, Gandhi to Naoroji, 18 Sept. 1897; ibid., iii, p.59, 'The Plague Panic in South Africa', 20 Mar. 1899; ibid., p.266, 'Petition to Chamberlain', 27 Dec. 1902; ibid., v, 'Immigration Act of Natal', 2 Dec. 1905; ibid., pp.220-21, NIC to Col. Sec., 10 Mar. 1906; ibid., p.356, 'Indian Position in Natal', 13 Jun. 1906. The letters and petitions of protest against the workings of the Dealers' Licences Act are more numerous. See, in particular, *C W*, iii, p.26-49, 'Petition to Chamberlain', and appendices, 31 Dec. 1898, ibid., iv, pp.367-8, 'Indian Licences: Need for Vigilance — II', 4 Mar. 1905; ibid., v, 'The Hoondemal Case Again', 23 Sept. 1905; ibid., pp.112-13, 'Dealers' Licences Act', 28 Oct. 1905; ibid., p.283, 'The Ladysmith Licensing Board', 21 Apr. 1906.

142   The criticism was suffcently widespread or forcefully put that Gandhi found it necessary to offer a rebuttal in the second annual report of NIC. *C W*, iii, p.104.

143   See fn. 141 above.

144   NA., G H 1598, passim. (copies of hearings of unsuccessful appeals against the negative decisions of local licensing boards).

145   In 1908, for instance, Moosa Haji Adam complained to the Durban T C that ten or twelve of his stores had usually been unoccupied since the passage of the Act. CO 179/250/28435, SABIC to Sec. St., 4 Aug. 1908, encl. Moosa Haji Adam to Durban T C, Mar. 1908. See also *C W*, iii, 'Petition to Chamberlain', 31 Dec. 1898, and Chapter 1 for other property owners who rented to petty traders.

CHAPTER THREE

Merchant Politics II:
The Transvaal, 1895 — 1906

During the years before the Anglo-Boer war (October 1899 — May 1902), Transvaal merchant politics were in the main a subsidiary branch of Natal politics in terms of both decision-making and levels of activity. Most of the Transvaal merchants moved to Natal during the war, and Indian politics were temporarily suspended. In June 1900 the former republic was annexed by the British crown, and Indian refugees began to trickle back into the Transvaal late in 1902. Beginning in 1903, the changed circumstances created by the new administration dictated a refocusing of the elite's political energy away from Natal and towards the Transvaal. But, for a variety of reasons, the years 1903 to 1906 were the low water mark of their political activity. Then, beginning with the first declaration of passive resistance late in 1906, the social base of elite politics in the Transvaal was gradually widened to include the Tamil petty traders and hawkers whose presence on the fringes of the Indian political community had been noticeable since at least the early 1890s. In what ultimately came close to a complete reversal of roles, the near moribund Natal Congress was soon being eclipsed by the Transvaal British Indian Association: first, in terms of levels of activity and degree of active participation in politics, then in terms of decision-making. The beginnings of this process, which reflected Gandhi's gradual shift from the role of hired representative to that of leader, were already apparent by 1906.

Pre-war Politics

Gandhi's involvement in the Transvaal merchants' politics began in April 1895, almost exactly a year after his entry into Natal politics.[1] Prior to his arrival disabilities in the Transvaal had been handled in the same way as those in Natal, and by the same people. First, white legal counsel had been hired to represent the merchants to the government, the same lawyer sometimes handling problems in both Natal and the Transvaal.[2] Later, the Natal Indian Committee had included the grievances of the Transvaal and, indeed, Free State merchants in their petitions and pamphlets.[3]

When Gandhi became involved the same pattern was continued for a number of years: Indian politics in the Transvaal remained by and large a subsidiary branch of the Natal-based merchants' politics. The reason for their dominance was the simple fact that a handful of them owned most of the Indian capital invested in the Transvaal. This is particularly true of the early 1890s when Dada Abdullah and Company alone held some 50 per cent of the Indian investments in the republic.[4] The Natal Congress, as discussed earlier, was founded 'chiefly by the efforts' of Abdullah Haji Adam, one of the partners in Dada Abdullah's. The Congress presidency was held by either him or by his brother and partner Abdullah Karim Haji Adam, between 1894 and 1898. In 1899, the presidency passed to Abdul Kadir who held it until 1906. Kadir was managing partner of the Natal holdings of the powerful Natal-based firm M C Camroodeen and Company. The firm, like Dada Abdullah's, had significant investments in the Transvaal. What is particularly important is that, even in the absence of hard figures concerning relative weight of investments, qualitative assessments leave no doubt that the Transvaal interests of both Dada Abdullah and Company and M C Camroodeen and Company were a small part of their total South African investments. After 1892 when Natal became self-governing, elite political energy was thus poured into stemming the tide of discriminatory legislation in the colony, despite the fact that merchant interests in the Transvaal had been under heavy attack since 1885.

The Transvaal question was never entirely neglected by the merchants, however. Transvaal legislation, particularly Law 3 of 1885 which prohibited Indians from owning fixed property or residing anywhere but in designated locations, threatened them both directly and indirectly. Through it, those with branches in the Transvaal stood to lose the greater part of their investments in the republic; and, more importantly, as early as 1891 they had recognized that the Natal government might use the example of the Transvaal to validate its own discriminatory legislation.[5] Even at the height of the first full scale Indian political campaign in Natal between 1894 and

1897, a watching brief was therefore kept over the republic. Gandhi's entry into Transvaal politics in 1895 reflected a distinct deterioration in the situation.

In March 1895, in an attempt to end the ten year old dispute over the rights of British Indians in the republic, the diverse views of the British and Transvaal governments were submitted to arbitration. The basic question under consideration was whether or not Transvaal Law 3 of 1885, as amended in 1886 and approved by Britain, permitted the republican government to confine Indian merchants to designated locations for the purpose of trade as well as residence. The arbitrator, Mellius de Villiers, Chief Justice of the Orange Free State, dismissed most of the arguments advanced by each side. Nevertheless, his conclusions, handed down on 2 April 1895, confirmed the right of the republic to interpret the law as it saw fit. De Villiers found that:

> The South African Republic is bound and entitled in its treatment of Indian or other Asiatic traders, being British subjects, to give full force and effect to Law No. 3 of 1885, enacted, and in the year 1886 amended, by the Volksraad of the South African Republic subject (in case of objections being raised by or on behalf of any such persons to any such treatment as not being in accordance with the provision of the said law as amended) to the sole and exclusive interpretation in the ordinary course by the tribunals of the country.[6]

The Indian merchants' immediate response to the 'Bloemfontein Award', as it was called, was a series of petitions. They clearly bore the Congress hallmark and the party claimed credit for them in its 1895 annual report.[7] The first petition was submitted on behalf of the British Indian merchants in the republic.[8] Those which came after claimed to represent all Transvaal Indians in the same way that the Congress claimed to be the spokesman for the Natal Indians.[9] In fact, though, it is likely that the social base of elite politics was even narrower in the Transvaal than in Natal before 1906. Separate petitions were submitted to the government, and even to the Indian National Congress, by ex-indentured Tamil petty traders at regular intervals throughout the 1890s and the first years of this century.

Centred in Johannesburg, the petty traders described themselves variously as 'Indian Merchants of Johannesburg', the 'Indian Committee', the 'British Indian Association', the 'Indian Political Association' and the 'Tamil Benefit Society'.[10] There is very little information available for this level of political activity. But several deductions are possible. Firstly, the petty traders' basic interests were the same as those of the commercial elite: their livelihood derived from commercial investments, however small. Their petitions protested the Transvaal government's attempt to confine Indians to locations. Secondly, the petitions indicate that as early as 1891 formal political organization in the Transvaal had ceased to be confined to the elite: signatories are identified as 'committee member', 'vice president', and so on. It is not possible, however, to assess how effective this organization was. It is possible only to note a certain overlap of officials between 1891 and 1912, and between organizations having different names.[11] This suggests, if nothing else, some continuity in the politics of the Johannesburg petty traders which goes far towards explaining the apparent ease with which Gandhi drew them into elite politics after 1906. Finally, it is worth noting that this level of political activity was dominated by the higher castes of the ex-indentured population, as in Natal. Those who were most successful in the Transvaal were, almost exclusively, Pillays, Padiachays, Naidoos, Naickers and Modaleys.[12]

Thus despite claims to the contrary, at the time of the Bloemfontein Award and for years afterwards, elite politics in the Transvaal appear to have represented only the major commercial interests. The chief signatories of the Transvaal merchants' petitions were Abdul Gani (managing partner of M C Camroodeen and Company's Transvaal holdings); Haji Habib (the evidence points to his being managing partner in his brother Haji Mohamed Haji Dada's vast Durban-based firm); and Tayob Haji Khan Mohamed who had started business in the Transvaal managing a branch of Abubakr Amod's large Durban-based firm.[13] At least two, and possibly all, of these three thus had close economic links with the Natal-based merchants. Each was prominent in Transvaal politics for at least a decade. Tayob Haji Khan dropped out for no apparent reason in 1903, but Gani and Haji Habib remained active until the commercial elite began to withdraw their support from Gandhi in 1909. With all the evidence pointing to the Congress as the decision-making body for Transvaal politics, the continuity in their chief representatives or associates in the Transvaal helps explain the smoothness with which elite politics in the two areas meshed together.

The ideology which informed Transvaal elite politics naturally differed little from the Natal merchants' ideology. However, the exigencies of the Transvaal situation called for a subtle but potentially important realignment of the merchants' priorities. In Natal, the major threat to the elite's economic security was posed in terms of their being equated with the Indian workers for whom special restrictive legislation existed. Thus in order to protect their interests the Natal elite adopted as a central principle their distinctness from and superiority to the Indian underclasses. By contrast, in the Transvaal no legal distinction existed between different classes of Indians. But successive constitutions had denied any equality as between whites and others. Consequently, the major threat to the merchants derived from their being identified with Africans, who represented a precedent for restrictive legislation being applied to 'non-whites'. The Transvaal merchants therefore placed maximum emphasis on their assumed superiority over Africans. They had nothing to gain by stressing the differences between themselves and the Indian underclasses. Thus Transvaal legislation had the effect of tailoring their ideology in such a way that mass-based politics were not logically precluded as in Natal.

There is scarcely any information available on the organizational structure of Transvaal merchant politics before 1903. Although the signatories of petitions occasionally described themselves as a Committee,[14] even this hint of formal organization is usually lacking. This is consistent with the Congress's role as the decision-making body for the Transvaal. Since all that was really needed in the republic was information gathering, the need for an elaborate organizational structure did not exist. In the absence of any evidence to the contrary it therefore appears that the major task of Gani, Haji Habib and Tayob Haji Khan Mohamed was simply to keep the Congress informed of events in the Transvaal. Before the war, travel between the coast and the interior was not rare for Indians, and communication, even on a personal basis, could not have been very difficult. Information received from the Transvaal 'committee' must also have been supplemented by the white lawyers hired to represent the Transvaal merchants to the government.

There is no evidence to indicate that funds were raised in the Transvaal for political activity. Indeed, the fact that Transvaal grievances were generally included in Congress petitions or pamphlets which focused on Natal suggests that costs were borne by the Congress — if only by those members who had commercial interests in the Transvaal — and that some attempt was made to minimize costs. The fact that the Transvaal elite and the Tamil petty traders continued to duplicate each others' efforts despite a shortage of funds thus offers additional evidence that the elite had not appealed (or, at least, not appealed successfully) to a wider group than their own during this period.

The extent to which the Transvaal merchants as a whole participated in politics before 1903 is unclear. Obviously, however, in the absence of an organizational structure, and with decision-making taking place at the coast, room for active participation was strictly limited. It seems highly likely that it was only the few who signed petitions who actually participated in the political process. Thus before 1903, the Transvaal-based merchants lacked even the degree of political experience which had been acquired by their counterparts in Natal.

Strategy and Tactics

The strategy and tactics which had been worked out for Natal were also applied to the Transvaal before 1903. In both areas, the Congress served as the major political institution. In the Transvaal, as in Natal, the merchants fought against legal disabilities at two levels. Firstly, they claimed the ordinary rights of British subjects. In the Transvaal this was a two-step process. Indian equality with other British subjects was claimed in terms of Queen Victoria's 1858 Proclamation, as in Natal. Then, in recognition of their status as aliens in foreign territory, the merchants claimed the rights guaranteed to British subjects under the terms of the 1884 London Convention.[15] At the second level of opposition, because the Transvaal government refused to concede any equality of rights between whites and blacks, relief from legal disabilities was also claimed on the basis of the assumed superiority of Indians over other blacks.[16] In petitions and speeches discriminatory legislation was denounced as serving to 'degrade' Indians to the level of Africans.[17] In this connection, efforts were made to prevent the republican government's use of the terms 'coolie' or Asian 'aboriginal' on the grounds that such terminology when applied to the Transvaal Indians was both insulting and inaccurate.[18] By contrast, however, the elite often used the pejorative term 'kaffirs' to denote Africans, possibly as further proof of Indian superiority.

As in Natal, although the major thrust of merchant politics was aimed at protecting Indian commercial interests, other apparently unrelated instances of discrimination against Indians were also opposed on the grounds that they were part of a broad strategy to eliminate Indian trade competition.[20] And, again, the connection was made between official policy in the various South African territories, and the potential effect on the merchants as a whole. As Gandhi phrased it in 1895, the question did not really concern the street in which a Transvaal Indian should be allowed to live, but rather 'what status he is to occupy throughout South Africa . . . since there seems to be a general consensus of opinion that the question will have to be settled on a common basis modified by local conditions'.[21]

There was little difference between tactics in Natal and the Transvaal. Petitions, pamphlets, letters to the press, delegations to government officials and court cases were all used. The major difference between the two areas was that they were used less on behalf of the Transvaal: the Congress's resources and energy were concentrated on the campaigns in Natal. Attempts were made to interest the government of India in the Transvaal question.[22] But, here too, the attempts were less concerted than for Natal. The merchants lacked a point to which the government of India might be requested to apply pressure on the Transvaal. Indian labour was not essential to the republican economy as it was to Natal's.

During the period up to 1903, then, the Transvaal-based elite lacked a separate political institution. Nevertheless, subtle changes were apparent in the strategy and tactics of elite politics in the Transvaal, as well as in Natal, after Gandhi's arrival. Although no radical departures were made in this period, more careful planning and institutional continuity, as well as continuity of personnel, were apparent in the campaign against the Bloemfontein Award.

The Campaign against the Bloemfontein Award

This campaign falls into two phases. During the first, from April to September 1895, attempts were made to prevent the British government from accepting the Award. The second, from September 1895 until the outbreak of the Anglo-Boer war, was moulded by the failure of the first: in accordance with the terms of the Award, the Transvaal government's interpretation of Law 3 was tested in a court of law.

Phase one of the campaign began with Gandhi's entry into Transvaal politics. His first major step was a lengthy petition to the

Colonial Secretary, Ripon, in mid-May 1895, channelled through the British agent in Pretoria.[23] In an attempt to give the appearance of popular support, over 1 000 signatures were appended to the petition. Gandhi's mass signature campaigns represented short-lived tactical innovations in both the Transvaal and Natal. They were not repeated for well over a decade. In Natal, the 1894 signature campaign had proved counter-productive after the government used it against the elite. In both areas, and particularly the Transvaal, lack of an effective organizational structure militated against the use of such tactics.

A copy of the petition to Ripon was sent to Elgin, the Secretary of State for India, at the same time as the original was despatched.[24] The major thrust of the petitions was a well-planned attack on the validity of the Bloemfontein Award. The nature of the attack reflected the legal expertise which made Gandhi's contribution to the politics of the elite so valuable. The choice of Arbitrator was criticized on the grounds that his known bias against Indians should have disqualified him. The Award itself was declared invalid since it departed from the Arbitrator's terms of reference by delegating responsibility for the interpretation of Law 3 to the Transvaal courts.

These points were followed up by the familiar bi-level strategy which Gandhi had already developed for use in Natal. Equal Indian rights for other British subjects were claimed in terms of Queen Victoria's Proclamation of 1858. In addition, strenuous efforts were made to prove that Indians were desirable citizens, regardless of their legal rights. Since the 1886 amendment of Law 3 held that Indians were to be confined to locations for sanitary reasons, documentation was provided in which numbers of white merchants and medical practitioners attested that the homes and businesses of Indian merchants were clean and hygienic.[25] The Indians were then compared to the Africans who were subjected to discriminatory legislation and with whom the Transvaal government equated them. By implication, Indian superiority was asserted in the contention that, given continuing oppression, Indians 'cannot but degenerate, so much so, that from their civilized habits, a generation hence, between the progeny of the Indians thus in course of degeneration, and the Natives, there will be very little difference in habits, and customs, and thought'.[26] The theme of Indian superiority also emerged when Gandhi, using another element of the strategy developed for Natal, broadened the immediate issue to include numbers of other, apparently unrelated, Indian grievances. These were used primarily in support of his contention that the real reason for the attempt to confine Indians to locations was a desire to restrict Indian commercial competition, but they also doubled as a further implication of Indian superiority. The mandatory registration fee for Indian traders, and the restrictions on property-owning, freedom of movement, and the use of first or second class railway carriages, were all described as 'insults and indignities' which, it was noted, classified Indians with Africans.[27]

Gandhi's petition was received by the Colonial Office on 24 June 1895, two days after Ripon had telgraphed British acceptance of the Bloemfontein Award.[28] It therefore fell to Joseph Chamberlain, who became Colonial Secretary in July, to deal with the Indian protests. During Chamberlain's term of office, before the outbreak of war, Indian rights in the Transvaal were more aggressively protected than ever before, or after, as he and Alfred Milner, the High Commissioner for South Africa,[29] sought increasingly to assert British authority over the Transvaal by intervening vigorously in opposing infringements of the rights of British subjects.[30] In September 1895, however, Chamberlain had little choice but to confirm the decision of his predecessors, pointing out that he had had nothing to do with them, and that since arbitration was entered into without formal terms of reference having been submitted by either side, the Award could not be considered invalid. The petitioners were to be informed only that Chamberlain intended to make 'friendly representations' to the republican government on behalf of the Indian merchants.[31]

The elite's response to British acceptance of the Award was slow to come. The delay appears to have been dictated in part by the fact that the Transvaal government seemed in no hurry to implement the Award, and in part by the fact that events in Natal captured the attention of the elite. During September and October 1895, Gandhi was preoccupied with defending the Congress against its white detractors in Natal. General awareness of the existence of the party emerged from a court case in which an Indian witness in an assault trial testified that members of the Congress had attempted to suppress his evidence through intimidation.[32] They were soon being described by the Natal press as a gang of conspirators who extorted money from Indians for the purpose of fighting the government.[33] Gandhi wrote a number of letters to the press denying these allegations and presenting a more balanced view of the party's objectives and activities.[34] From then, until June 1896 when Gandhi left for India to collect his wife and family, the Congress's energies were concentrated almost exclusively on the Natal franchise question.

During the five months which he spent in India, Gandhi made a concerted effort to mobilize the Indian political elite on behalf of the South African Indians. He met Nationalist leaders such as Tilak and Gokhale, addressed public meetings in Bombay, Poona and Madras, and distributed copies of his first substantial publication on the South African question, *The Grievances of the British Indians in South Africa: An Appeal to the Indian Public.* The focal point of Gandhi's campaign was the Natal Indian question.[35] But some discussion of conditions in the Transvaal was invariably included. This generally consisted of a reiteration of the points raised in the May 1895 petition to Ripon and Elgin.[36] These were presented, again, within the framework of white resentment of Indian commercial competition.

During his tour of India Gandhi also continued to maintain that Law 3 could be used to confine Indians to locations only for residential and not for business purposes,[37] thus making it clear that the merchants intended to challenge the law in the Transvaal courts in keeping with the Bloemfontein Award's recommendations. The challenge was delayed even after Gandhi's return and, when finally raised, it was pursued in an almost desultory manner. Again, this reflected both the Transvaal government's slowness to implement Law 3 as well as the Congress's preoccupation with events in Natal. The initial stages of planning for a test case did not take place until May 1897,[38] two years after the Bloemfontein Award had been handed down. The Transvaal State Attorney's office was slow to make its side of the preliminary arrangements for the case and the question dragged on into 1898. The Congress does not appear to have pressed the State Attorney to hurry: Indian merchants continued to trade at will in the republic and the arrest of 42 merchants for 'illegally trading'[39] without licences was successfully disputed by the British Agent in January 1898,[40] as part of the broader policy of keeping a close watch on violations of the rights of British subjects.[41] The test case, on behalf of Tayob Haji Khan Mohamed, was finally heard in August 1898. The judgement went against the Indians on the basis of a similar case which had been tried in 1888. Despite what semed to be a final and binding interpretation of Law 3, Chamberlain acquiesced in Milner's continued attempts to secure preferential treatment for Indian merchants, thus fulfilling the promise of his response in September 1895 to Gandhi's petition. Milner's negotiations with the Transvaal government were ultimately unsuccessful but they served to delay the order for the removal of Indians to locations still further. The date for their removal was finally set for July 1899.[42]

Some fourteen years had passed since the passage of Law 3 during which time growing numbers of Indian merchants had continued to trade freely in the republic, increasing total Indian commercial investments there by nearly 400 per cent. The delays in implementing Law 3 were due, not to the political activity of the Indian elite, but rather to the intervention of the British Agent, the High Commissioner for South Africa and the Colonial Secretary. This was particularly so after 1895, when infringements of the rights of both white and Indian British subjects were challenged with increasing forcefulness until this challenge was ultimately used as a *casus belli* in 1899. The swiftly deteriorating relations with Britain preoccupied the Transvaal government from mid-1899 onwards. The question of the removal of Indians to locations was thus ignored once again. Locations had been set aside on the outskirts of Johannesburg and Pretoria by the time the war started. But, although numbers of Indian workers and hawkers had chosen to move there, Indian merchants were still trading on their old sites when the war began.[44]

Elite Politics during the Boer War

At the outbreak of the war Indian refugees began to stream into Natal from the Transvaal.[45] The Congress's appeals to the government were instrumental in helping them to bypass the Colony's virtual ban on Indian immigration.[46] The party also organized substantial refugee relief for Indians, at least during the early stages of the war.[47] In addition, less than a week after the war started, Gandhi, under the auspices of the Congress, had begun to organize an Indian ambulance corps for use at the front. He mobilized support on the grounds that participation in the war effort would add substance to the merchants' claim to be desirable citizens. The call for participation thus fitted well with one of the major elements in the elite's strategy which the Congress had pursued since its inception, and the merchants gave generously of their money, if not their services. The Corps was equipped, and provided with small luxuries for distribution to the wounded, by donations from merchants. It was made up, however, of indentured workers, supervised by young, western educated members of the party.[48] During the same period a hospital started by the voluntary efforts of two white doctors, and intended to provide free treatment for Natal's impoverished ex-indentured workers, folded due to lack of funds, despite Gandhi's attempts to secure financial support from the Congress.[49] These two examples of reaction to crisis serve to illustrate again the essence of elite politics. Towards the end of the first decade of organized political activity elite politics continued to be self-serving, and the gap between the merchants and the Indian underclasses in Natal remained as wide as it had always been.

The Anglo-Boer War served to produce a turning point in both Gandhi's political career and his private life. In October 1901, after active Congress participation in the war effort had ceased, he returned to India with the intention of settling there permanently. Little information exists on the reason for this decision, but what there is points consistently towards the conclusion that he returned to India in search of a new political arena which would offer him the opportunities that were lacking in South Africa. The Natal Congress's political activity, which had already declined markedly before the war, was more or less suspended for the duration in the interests of maintaining a working relationship with the whites.[50] Gandhi could see nothing in the party's future except monitoring the administration of the discriminatory laws which had been passed in the 1890s and appealing to the imperial government in the event of new threats.[51] In the Transvaal the situation was less clear-cut in late 1901. The republic was annexed by the British crown in September 1900. At first, not unnaturally, Gandhi 'confidently expected' that the new administration would dismantle the network of discriminatory legislation which had been erected by the Boers.[52] By the time he left South Africa a year later there was considerable doubt as to whether the new regime would be any less hostile to Indians than the old.[53] Indeed, what little political work Gandhi did between September 1900 and September 1901 consisted mainly of alerting the Congress's supporters in England and India to the threatening situation in the Transvaal.[54] However, the political challenge which the Transvaal was beginning to represent was insufficient to prevent Gandhi from making the move that he had been thinking over for at least eighteen months.[55] In October 1901 he sailed for India, and within days of his arrival he had attempted to launch himself at the highest level of Indian nationalist politics.

Gandhi had only one possible political platform on which to stand in India: the South African Indian question. During the year which he spent there he first tried, unsuccessfully, to persuade the Indian National Congress (INC) leaders to make a major issue of South Africa. When that failed he tried, again unsuccessfully, to become involved in work for Gokhale, the only major political figure with whom he was able to make close contact and who represented a means of entering the upper levels of nationalist politics, if at a slightly less exalted level than Gandhi had first striven for.

Gandhi began his attempt to build the South African question into a major issue shortly after he arrived. On 19 December 1901 he addressed a letter to the *Times of India*, pointing out that 'something more' was required on behalf of the South African Indians than the INC's annual critical resolutions. He suggested a top level deputation to the Viceroy backed by a series of public meetings[56] — a tactic which he had already recommended shortly before leaving Natal.[57] Soon after his letter to the *Times*, he left Bombay for the 1901 INC session in Calcutta. He took the same train as Pherozeshah Mehta to try to secure his support for a South African campaign. Mehta destroyed his political platform, and with it his only real chance to gain an immediate entrée into nationalist politics, by pointing out that the INC could do nothing for South Africa as long as Indians had so few rights at home.[58]

Gandhi's resentment of his powerlessness in nationalist political circles during this period showed through years later in his autobiography when he commented that 'I tried to plead with Sir Pherozeshah, but it was out of the question for *one like me* to prevail upon the uncrowned King of Bombay'.[59] His resentment also showed in 1901. He was allotted five minutes of Congress time to speak in support of a resolution condemning the South African situation. While calling again for deputations to the Viceroy and meetings of protest, he publicly disagreed with Mehta's views on the South African question and implied that the INC was responsible for the oppressed condition of the Transvaal Indians and that he, Gandhi, was responsible for saving Natal from a similar oppression:

> Now with due deference to the uncrowned King of Bombay Presidency, I believe that our position is so very bad in the Transvaal and the Orange River Colony, because proper steps were not taken to withstand an attack on our rights as British subjects, and had no steps been taken in Natal, the position would be infinitely worse there today than it is.[60]

Despite his performance at the INC, or perhaps because of it, Gandhi shortly afterwards accepted the impossibility of engineering a campaign with the help of the party. He gave two further speeches at public meetings in Calcutta in the next few weeks. Both of them were concerned with South Africa, but in neither of them did he call for demonstrations in India.[61]

After a brief visit to Rangoon, Gandhi returned to his home town of Rajkot in the Kathiawar peninsula in February 1902.[62] Mehta's rejection appears to have weighed heavily on him. In the first instance of what Erik Erikson notes as a recurring feature in Gandhi's life,[63] a crisis in his political career was attended by illness. His doctor advised him to take 'complete rest' for several months.[64] Nevertheless, between March and August he continually pressed Gokhale about a suggestion — whether his or Gokhale's is not made clear in his letters — that he should become involved in a national fund-raising campaign which Gokhale was to organize for a memorial for Ranade. Although Gokhale occasionally replied to these letters the question of Gandhi's involvement in a national-level project went unanswered.[65]

As 1902 progressed Gandhi's position became increasingly precarious. He had failed to become involved in nationalist activities on his own terms, or any others. In Rajkot he found obvious difficulties in working on South African issues.[66] He was low on funds and believed that he could not even support himself as a lawyer there. He wanted to move to Bombay, but could not afford to.[67] The Natal Congress bailed him out with Rs.3 000 and he arrived in Bombay in August 1902 with the intention of resuming his political work as well as his legal career.[68] Again he went to Mehta for his 'blessing', and again he was rejected. Mehta advised him that he 'would be foolishly wasting away in Bombay [his] small savings from Natal'.[69] By November, although he professed no anxiety about the future, he had still not 'begun to feel [his] way about' Bombay, when he received a telegram from the Natal Congress asking him to make an official visit to London and then return to South Africa.[70]

NIC's request was an important potential turning point for Gandhi. During his year in India he had failed to establish himself either politically or professionally. South Africa offered professional success, but it had appeared to be a political dead end when Gandhi made his decision to leave. This is important because it is abundantly clear, even from the slender amount of personal data which survive, that Gandhi sought to become a career politician. He wired NIC for further information, but wrote to a friend that he doubted if he could stand the 'mental strain' of complying with their request.[71] It was only when he learned that he was wanted in connection with Chamberlain's proposed visit to South Africa that he decided to return.[72] Chamberlain was expected to make a decision on the extent to which republican legislation concerning Asians should be maintained in the Transvaal and the Orange River Colony. Gandhi viewed this decision as crucial for the South African Indians. He believed — and this was the panoramic vision that he had asked the INC to share with him — that if Chamberlain fulfilled the promise of his pre-war policy and called for the removal of discriminatory legislation in the two new colonies, then Natal would have to follow suit.[73] Chamberlain's tour therefore appeared to hold the possibility of reversing the Natal Congress's failures of the 1890s in both the Transvaal and Natal. These were the circumstances under which Gandhi returned to South Africa.

Post-war 'Asian' Policy in the Transvaal

By the time of Chamberlain's tour, and Gandhi's return to South Africa, it was over two years since Britain had annexed the Transvaal and more than six months since the Treaty of Vereeniging which formally ended the war. No clear-cut policy statement had been made on the future of the Indians during this period. In fact, little consideration had been given to the matter. Although Colonial Office minutes referred to the Indian question as a 'difficult' one in mid-1901, it was considered less pressing than the 'native' question.[74] Milner, the High Commissioner for South Africa, was asked to take the matter under consideration at that time only after the flow of letters to the Colonial Office which had been the result of Gandhi's last round of work for NIC before he left for India.[75] Some nine months passed before the Colonial Secretary pressed Milner for his report. This time, the Indian question was due to be raised in Parliament.[76]

Milner was Governor of the Transvaal and the Orange River Colony until March 1905. As Shula Marks and Stanley Trapido have shown in a recent article, Milner's major policy consideration in the Transvaal — and in this he enjoyed the support of both the imperial government and his own administrators — was to service the needs of the mining industry. This policy dictated, first of all, the erection of a modern bureaucracy. It also dictated the co-option of the generally anti-capitalist white working class and rural notables. Equally importantly it demanded, ultimately, the creation of a system of 'reserves' for 'non-whites' in order to reproduce and regiment the vast cheap labour force required by the mines.[77] Although the Transvaal Indians were rarely more than a minor consideration in the massive task of transforming the Transvaal into a modern state, Milner's policy towards them was perfectly consistent with his broader strategy for reconstruction.

Indians were the subject of lively and often virulent debate in the Transvaal, as they had been before the war.[78] Indeed, the burgeoning poor white post-war population added an extra dimension to the debate: 'White Leagues' were formed throughout the colony, and 'Vigilants' Associations' — the names speak for themselves. The amicable relations between the Transvaal whites and the colonial administration, which were an indispensable element in Milner's reconstruction programme, therefore depended in part on a satisfactory solution of the 'Asian' question.[79] When he did turn his attention to the Transvaal Indians, Milner was in complete agreement with his officials who favoured implementing as much of the former republic's legislation as the Colonial Office would permit.

Early in 1901 on the advice of F N Gillam, the Supervisor of Indian Immigrants, the military Governor of Pretoria had ordered that Indians should be restricted to the Pretoria location for both residential and trading purposes in keeping with Law 3 of 1885. (Gillam also noted, for future attention, his belief that steps should be taken to lower the wages of Indian workers in Pretoria 'who show great independence'). By June 1901 all but two of the 29 Pretoria merchants who had stayed on during the war had moved their shops into the location.[80] The Johannesburg Indians were saved from a similar upheaval only because the Town Council claimed to find the site of the pre-war location so insanitary that they recommended that the entire area be cleared and a new site chosen.[81]

In October 1901 the administration was already trying to come to grips with the shortage of cheap labour which hindered reconstruction of the mining industry. Both the Commissioner for Mines (W Wybergh), and Gillam's superior, the Commissioner for Native Affairs (G Lagden), deprecated the importation of Indian labour as a possible solution.[82] Lagden and Wybergh enlarged on their views of the Asian question in the following months as Milner tried to put together a report for the Colonial Office. Lagden, on the basis of information received from Gillam, advised against any modification of Law 3. He justified his advice on the grounds that 'the attitude of British colonies in other parts of the world illustrates the necessity of guarding against the misguided efforts of those who advocate that British Indians be allowed to insinuate themselves wholesale into the domestic life of a society which is alien'.[83] In order to avoid 'the foundations of further embitterment between races having a substratum of mutual antipathy towards each other', Lagden recommended that all but certain high-class Indians should be confined to locations for residential as well as trading purposes. He was aware of Indian views on the question and suggested that locations should be renamed 'townships' or 'bazaars', since location was 'supposed to be an offensive term'. And, finally, he laid down proposals for an immigration restriction act designed to prohibit the entry of virtually all Indians unless they came under a work contract.[84]

Wybergh agreed with most of what Lagden had to say.[85] Like other officials of the time he too rationalized his solution to the Asian question in terms of protecting alien cultures from each other.[86] 'I am strongly in favour', he reported, 'of adopting segregation as a fundamental principle in our dealings with all Asians in South Africa both in their own interests and in those of the European population'. In addition, Wybergh went beyond the generally accepted idea of segregation in the urban areas, suggesting that Asians should be allocated the warm northern and eastern districts of the lowveld, and that the cool districts in the highveld be reserved for whites.[87]

Other members of the Executive Council who reported to Milner early in 1902 were in substantial agreement with Lagden and Wybergh,[88] and maximum consideration was undoubtedly given to their reports. With reconstruction of the mining industry one of Milner's top priorities, Wybergh's views must have weighed heavily. Lagden, responsible for the administration of both Native and Asian affairs,[89] was even more influential: it was his report which formed the basis of the Milner administration's first attempt to delineate Asian policy.[90] Milner disagreed with Lagden only on the question of immigration restriction. He agreed that Lagden's proposal to prohibit the entry of all but contract labourers 'might be desirable to take up, if we could stick to it'. He did not think that Lagden's position could be maintained, however, and his own alternative went into the Executive Council Resolution which grew out of the reports submitted early in 1902.[91]

Executive Council Resolution 97 of 1902 is worth quoting in full since most of it was eventually translated into legislation:

Resolved to submit the following scheme, as a basis for Asiatic legislation, for the approval of the Secretary of State:

1   All Asiatics, whether now resident in the Transvaal or hereafter entering it, unless specifically exempted, to take out certificates of registration to be annually renewed at a charge of £3.

2   Registered Asiatics, unless living on the premises of a European employer, to reside and carry on their business in special quarters of town set apart for the purpose, and under regulations framed for their benefit: the site of these Asiatic townships to be determined by Government: their control for sanitary purposes to be exercised by the local authorities in accordance with Municipal regulations approved by the Governor.

3   Certificates of registration may be refused on the ground that the persons applying for them are,
      a. suffering from a loathsome or infectious disease,
      b. of bad character,
      c. without employment or visible means of subsistence.

4   Exemption from registration to be granted to Asiatics possessing a certain degree of education and civilized habits of life: such exemption to relieve from the operation of all laws relating exclusively to Asiatics.

In addition to the above, a majority of the Council also approved the following:

5   The laws prohibiting Asiatics from owning real property to be repealed but the rights of Asiatics to acquire such property to be restricted to town areas for a period of five years.[92]

The Transvaal Executive Council's first policy statement on Asians thus reaffirmed Law 3 of 1885, with exceptions to be made only in special cases. Points 1 and 2 of the Resolution outlined a mechanism to facilitate the implementation of the Law. Point 3 outlined a means for restricting Indian immigration which had been absent from the statute books of the South African Republic.

The Colonial Office attitude towards the Transvaal Indian question began to emerge more clearly in response to Resolution 97. Colonial Office minuting reveals sympathy for Milner's position; but there was reluctance, as long as Crown rule existed, to sanction any measure which contradicted pre-war policy and which the Colonial Office would thus be unable to defend in parliament or before the Government of India.[93] H W Just, one of the principal clerks in the Colonial Office, summed up what seems to have been the general feeling when he wrote, 'for the present it would be impossible, I think, to come down at one leap to the position which is advocated by Milner'.[94] The official reply to Resolution 97 reflected Colonial Office ambivalence on the Indian question. Milner was informed that in keeping with pre-war policy there could be no discriminatory legislation unless it were defensible on sanitary grounds, but the proposals in Resolution 97 were not dismissed entirely. Chamberlain simply observed that 'I doubt whether we could prohibit business outside the locations'.[95]

A few months later during Chamberlain's tour of South Africa, Milner was informed that the Colonial Office would sanction the implementation of Law 3 only if the Transvaal Indians agreed to it,[96] as Milner had earlier claimed they would.[97] Since Chamberlain already knew that the Indians were opposed to Law 3, this condition was apparently intended to prevent the Transvaal administration from producing another set of unacceptable proposals, thus placing the burden of dealing with hostile white opinion on the administration rather than the Colonial Office. Chamberlain may also have intended to convey to Milner that the Colonial Office would agree only to legislation affecting Indians which would not prove controversial. Either Chamberlain failed to impress on Milner a firm policy guideline,[98] or else Milner tried to beat him at his own game. On 8 April 1903, Transvaal Government Notice No. 356 was issued. The 'bazaar notice', as it is usually known, reasserted that the majority of Indians must be confined to 'bazaars' (Lagden's new name for locations) for both residence and trading.[99] This was an improvement over Resolution 97 only in that additional exemptions were offered for those who had held pre-war licences to trade outside locations. Thus the burden of choosing between white hostility or Indian hostility was shifted from the Transvaal to the Colonial Office.

The Colonial Office was saved the necessity of dealing with the bazaar notice. In May 1903 in an attempt to speed up reconstruction of their railway system the Transvaal administration proposed the importation of 10 000 indentured Indian labourers, provided that they could be repatriated on completion of their terms of indenture.[100] Milner was informed that the Government of India would not agree to the Transvaal's proposals unless all Indians who had traded before the war — whether with or without licences — were now given licences to trade in their pre-war sites.[101]

The Government of India's proposals brought Milner the closest that he came to a significant departure from republican anti-Asian legislation. In December 1903 the Transvaal Colonial Secretary proposed an amendment to the bazaar notice which would have validated the trading rights of all those who claimed to have traded before the war, whether they were licensed by the republic or not. A great deal of hostility was manifested by unofficial members of the legislative council during the debate on the amendment, and a compromise solution was found in a resolution to renew only the licences of those traders who could prove before a commission of enquiry that they had actually traded before the war.[102] Despite legislative council hostility Milner was still prepared in January 1904 to try to push through as many as possible of the Government of India's demands.[103] But, by April, the availability of Chinese labour on satisfactory terms, and the continuing hostility of the council and the white public, allowed Milner to 'despair of introducing any measures which would satisfy the Government of India.'[104] Thus, in early April 1904, Milner and Arthur Lawley (the Lieutenant Governor of the Transvaal), reverting to their earlier policy, sent lengthy despatches to the Colonial Office supporting their recommendations for the introduction of legislation to carry out the proposals in the bazaar notice.[105] On 16 June, only days before the next session of the legislature was due to begin, Milner followed this up with a telegram pressing the Colonial Secretary for a pronouncement on the Asian question.[106]

Faced with specific legislative proposals, the Colonial Office responded to the Milner-Lawley despatches with its first official postwar policy statement on the Transvaal Indians. Chamberlain had resigned in December 1903, but the considerations which moulded his successor's statement did not differ from those which had been at the forefront of Colonial Office thinking since the war. Lawley's despatch was described as a 'convincing argument against attempting to maintain the older and more liberal traditions of the Empire'.[107] Arthur Lyttelton, the new Colonial Secretary, found it 'a very able one, and much weight is properly to be attached to it'.[108] But, on the other hand, the events of the past year had placed the Colonial Office in the indefensible position which they had sought to avoid since 1902. A petition from the Transvaal British Indian Association, and a lengthy covering letter from Sir Mancherji Bhownaggree, were considered 'to show clearly the weakness of our position in that we have allowed Crown Colonies to take measures against [British] subjects which are quite contrary to our traditions and go beyond anything done either in the Responsible Government colonies or the late South African

Republic'.[109] On 11 May, a new Supreme Court decision on another test case which had been brought by the British Indian Association held that Law 3 of 1885 could not be used to restrict the trading activities of Asians.[110] This rendered an already weak position untenable. Repeated questions in the House of Commons during May and June while the Colonial Office worked on a reply to the Milner-Lawley despatches served as constant reminders of the price which would have to be paid for continued support of Milner's position.

The Colonial Office policy statement on the Transvaal Indians was embodied in a despatch sent to Milner on 20 July 1904.[111] In the face of hostility from the whites, and from the Indians and their allies abroad, the Colonial Office fell back on the same solution which it had found for Natal a decade earlier: an immigration restriction act which would virtually put a stop to further Indian immigration; and, in return for this, protection of Indian vested commercial interests.

In officially proposing to modify Law 3 of 1885 for the first time since the war, the Colonial Secretary pointed out that Indian commercial interests comprised only a small percentage of total commercial activity in the Transvaal, and that these interests would become proportionately smaller as immigration dried up. A similar prospect had been sufficient to satisfy the Natal government at a time when legislation curtailing the rights of passenger Indians was a new phenomenon. In the Transvaal, with its history of restrictive legislation and of successes in the face of Colonial Office opposition, there was much less willingness to settle for the Natal solution — even on the part of Milner who, as recently as January 1904, had noted that 'we have been fairly successful hitherto in getting the C O to come along with us [on the Asian question] and it is most important that we keep up the touch'.[112] The official members of Milner's government therefore supported the Transvaal legislative council's response to the Colonial Office policy statement. A resolution introduced by one of the nominated members and passed on 16 August 1904 called for a ban on granting trading licences to Asians pending a commission to investigate the extent of Asian commercial activity in the colony.[113]

Although Milner was not made aware of it, the Colonial Office was prepared to violate the newly enunciated Lyttelton policy if the legislative council resolution of 16 August proved to be the start of concerted opposition in the colony.[114] They were committed to nothing except an Indian policy which could be justified to critics in the House of Commons and the Government of India. Strong pressure from the Transvaal — the prospect of 'Briton, Boer and Foreigner' united against the government[115] — would have rendered defensible the otherwise indefensible 'final betrayal of the British Indians'.[116] This was particularly so because the Lyttelton policy statement had been followed immediately by an announcement in the House of Commons that representative institutions would soon be reintroduced into the Transvaal. Erosion of the Lyttelton policy could more easily be justified under pressure from an elective assembly.[117]

Paradoxically, the announcement of forthcoming constitutional reform delayed a determined challenge to the policy. After an initial outburst of protest in the Transvaal, attention was turned to the constitution. The Asian question was relegated to the background in the months leading up to the introduction of representative government. The Colonial Office thus escaped the pressure which would have revealed their lack of commitment to the Lyttelton policy. Indeed, they were even able to avoid an official response to the legislative council resolution of 16 August. Milner was privately informed that there could be no departure from Lyttelton's policy statement; but he was instructed to let the matter drop if possible.[118] This he was able to do.

Milner left South Africa in April 1905, a few days after the letters patent for the Lyttelton Constitution had been issued. His successor, Lord Selborne, arrived in South Africa with the simple intention of keeping both whites and Indians 'in a reasonable frame of mind'; of holding the Indian question open until responsible government, neither attempting to settle in favour of the Indians, nor permitting new restrictions to be imposed upon them.[119] Selborne's plans, supported by the Colonial Office,[120] and implying a retreat from the Lyttelton policy, offered a means of riding out the remainder of crown rule.[121]

Early in 1906, however, when negotiations were under way to replace the Lyttelton constitution which had proved unworkable, Selborne chose to introduce two draft ordinances concerning Asians. On the surface the drafts appeared innocuous, even favourable to the Indians. They were to submit to registration with a view to determining who had the right to reside in the Transvaal, after which the British administration would permit no further immigration. In exchange for this restriction the drafts proposed that the former republican government's £3 poll tax on Asians be eliminated; Asians be permitted to hold land for religious purposes; the heirs of Abubakr Amod be

permitted to inherit the land purchased by him before the promulga-
tion of Law 3 of 1885, and temporary permits be made available for
Asians to visit the Transvaal.[122] On closer inspection (see below), the
ordinances were, on balance, unfavourable to the Indians. Indeed,
they became the object of Gandhi's first declaration of passive
resistance. The questions to be raised from the point of view of British
policy, however, are why, on the eve of responsible government,
Selborne chose to introduce new legislation at all, and why the
Colonial Office initially assented to his controversial proposals.

The ordinances appear to have stemmed directly from an Indian
deputation to Selborne in November 1905. The deputation criticized
the working of the Peace Preservation Ordinance which was used to
deny entry permits to would-be Indian immigrants. They also
repeated their standing criticisms of Law 3; the general question of
Indian inability to hold land; the specific question of the inability even
to own the land on which mosques had been built; and the republican
poll tax.[123] The deputation was followed up by letters requesting
Selborne to modify the workings of Law 3 and the Peace Preservation
Ordinance.[124]

Selborne's immediate response to the deputation was to transfer the
administration of Asian permits to the Colonial Secretary's Office.
Here the question came under the scrutiny of Lionel Curtis, one of the
stars of Milner's 'kindergarten', the man who had risen from
nominated clerk of the Johannesburg Town Council to Assistant
Colonial Secretary, heading his own branch of the Colonial Secretary's
Office. Early in May, Curtis submitted a lengthy report on the
Transvaal Indians to Selborne.[125] The draft ordinances do not differ in
substance from Curtis's report which, Selborne noted, was 'as usual
admirable'.[126] Curtis's report was based, in turn, on a lengthy
confidential memorandum prepared in mid-April by M Chamney, the
Protector and Registrar of Asiatics.

Chamney's memorandum came soon after three months leave which
he had spent in Britain. Interestingly enough, the thirty-page
document is prefaced by a summary of his discussions with what he
called the Indian 'wire pullers' in Britain. He reported that Sir
Mancherjee Bhownaggree found Gandhi too idealistic and that
although he offered support for the Indians in parliament there would
be no support in Britain for the principle of equality between whites
and the class of Indians who emigrated to the Transvaal. Indians of
this class did not deserve any better treatment abroad than they

received in India, according to Bhownaggree. Dadabhai Naoroji went further: he 'dismissed the subject in a few words. He said the subject was after all a small one and that the real question for Indians was India'.[127] Chamney's memorandum therefore has the appearance of a reappraisal of the Indian question, confident in the knowledge that the Indians had been shorn of their support in Britain.

Colonial Office assent to the Chamney-Curtis-Selborne proposals was an attempt to come to grips with the failure to implement the Lyttelton policy. The policy statement had called for protection of Indian commercial interests in keeping with the Supreme Court decision of May 1904, and an amendment of Law 3 to permit Indians to own the property on which their businesses stood. In exchange for this, an immigration restriction act of the Natal type would be permitted. When Selborne gave notice that his drafts were on the way, it was observed in the Colonial Office, belatedly and with patent insincerity, that an attempt should be made to get Law 3 off the statute book before the Transvaal received responsible government.[128] When the drafts arrived it was noted with far greater interest that Selborne's covering despatch could be used to justify the fact that though his ordinances represented a retreat from the Lyttelton policy, they did imply some measure of relief, and were the best that could be done on the eve of responsible government without inviting retribution from a responsible ministry.[129] Thus the Selborne proposals appeared to offer the Colonial Office the final defensible position in which to sit out crown rule.

The Indian reaction to the ordinances was hostile. The first passive resistance pledge was taken at a mass meeting in Johannesburg, and Indian criticisms were delivered in person to the Colonial Secretary by a deputation headed by Gandhi. His most potent criticism was the refusal to accept Selborne's contention that the proposed legislation was in the interests of the Indians. He pointed out that virtually every Indian in the Transvaal had already paid the republican poll tax which it was now proposed to abolish; that releasing Abubakr Amod's land to his heirs and permitting Indian ownership of mosque grounds did not constitute the relief from property restrictions that Indians were seeking; and, finally, the proposed registration scheme — particularly the suggestion that ten fingerprints would be required from every registrant — was an oppressive piece of legislation which duplicated Milner's registration of the Transvaal Indians in 1904, with the added indignity of a full set of fingerprints.

Faced again with a position which could not be justified, at a time when responsible government was imminent, the Colonial Office withheld assent to the ordinances. As Winston Churchill, the Under Secretary of State for the Colonies, put it, 'We are in a wholly indefensible position . . . the new parliament may shoulder the burden. Why should we?'[130] The logical conclusion to this line of thought appeared in another C O minute: the matter should 'be fought out under Responsible Government. If it is necessary to adopt a policy of expediency, we can at least say that we have a clear and un-questionable expression of the wishes of the Transvaal community'.[131]

Post-war Politics

Chamberlain's tour of South Africa, as indicated earlier, was seen as critical by Gandhi. He believed it might result in the repeal of discriminatory legislation in the Transvaal and thus, ultimately, all of the South African colonies. But Chamberlain did not annul the legisla-tion, or even promise the Transvaal Indians continued imperial government assistance to oppose it. Indeed, he advised the deputation — led by Gandhi — which waited on him in Pretoria on 7 January 1903 that they must negotiate the conditions of their existence with the colonial government rather than appeal to Britain for help.[132] The new Transvaal administration had already demonstrated that if left to its own devices crown rule would be even more hostile to merchant interests than republican rule had been. The government had given notice that trading licences were to be issued only to those traders — a minority — who had actually been licensed to trade by the republic.[133] In addition, a special Asiatic department had been set up to administer Indian affairs,[134] institutionalizing the republican practice of treating Indians separately from other British subjects. Shortly after his return to South Africa, then, Gandhi found himself with both the political and professional opportunities which he could not find in India, or even in Natal. It was not long before he committed himself to staying indefinitely in the Transvaal.

One of Gandhi's first moves in the Transvaal was the creation of a political party formed around the commercial elite. The British Indian Association, established early in 1903,[135] paralleled the Natal Congress in many respects. The names of members in the records indicate that, like the Congress, BIA was dominated by Gujerati passengers, merchants of some substance. Gandhi described the membership as 'most of them traders of long experience'.[136] The president of the new party was Abdul Gani; the Pretoria Committee — Pretoria was the largest centre of Indian commerce in the colony — was presided over by Haji Habib.[137] Gani's role as president ensured the continuation of close links with the Natal-based merchants. Gani was, as mentioned earlier, managing partner of the Transvaal interests of the powerful Natal-based firm M C Camroodeen and Company. Abdul Kadir, his managing partner in Natal, was president of the Natal Congress between 1899 and 1906. Gandhi was secretary and chief strategist and tactician of BIA — as he was, still, of the Congress.[138] The ideology of the new party did not differ from elite ideology as it has already been analysed.

The British Indian Association differed fundamentally from the Congress, however, in terms of structure. It lacked the written constitution,[139] the formal membership roll, and thus the well-defined leadership level and fund-raising devices with which the Congress had been endowed. Business was carried on by way of a general meeting at which, in theory, delegates from every Indian community in the Transvaal were present. It was the task of the general meeting to elect a central committee. When matters of importance to the merchants arose, the central committee called a mass meeting by way of advertisement. Much later, BIA was described as having been founded 'not on western lines but on lines well recognized in India'.[140] Gandhi's gradual shift away from conventional western political techniques will be discussed shortly. For the moment it is worth noting that whatever else the loose structuring of BIA reflected, it was certainly appropriate to Gandhi's perception of the political reality with which he had to deal. Seven years experience in Natal had convinced him that formal regulations, a membership roll, dues and the like, would be ignored by the elite.[141]

Although there is occasional mention of the BIA committees in Johannesburg and Pretoria, it is unlikely that these had any more meaning than the Congress committee had come to assume after its first few years of existence — 'committee' seems to have been the word used to designate whoever were the active participants in these two centres at any given time. There is no mention of elections to the central or any other committee in *Indian Opinion*, the usual repository of information on merchant politics. It should be noted also that though so-called committee members changed, the most dedicated were Gani (Johannesburg) and Habib (Pretoria), who had alread been at the forefront of Transvaal political activity — such as it was — for some eight years.

Apart from the two major commercial centres, the only other centre which generated any significant political participation was Potchefstroom. This reflected the high degree of politicization of Abdul Rahman, secretary of the 'Potchefstroom Indian Association' which worked in concord with the British Indian Association to the extent that it may well be described as another branch.[142] Rahman had emerged in elite politics shortly before the war when he accompanied Gandhi, Haji Habib and H O Ally on a deputation to the British agent in Pretoria.[143] There is little information available on Rahman except that he was one of the first four merchants for whom Gandhi tried to negotiate permits to re-enter the Transvaal after it had been annexed by Britain during the war.[144] Each of the others whose names were put forward at the same time — Gani, Habib, and M S Coovadia — had substantial investments in the colony, and it seems fair to assume that so did Rahman.

Until the first declaration of passive resistance in September 1906 the British Indian Association failed to gain support and was relatively ineffectual. Though it prevented the implementation of Law 3 insofar as trading in bazaars was concerned, it did not succeed in its aim of having the Law removed from the statute books. The sum total of the party's endeavours between early 1903 and late 1906 comprised three 'mass' meetings, six deputations to goverment officials, and a handful of petitions, addresses and letters of protest.[145]

The low level of elite political activity in both Natal and the Transvaal during this period is best exemplified by an *Indian Opinion* editorial written in December 1903 when Milner's bazaar notice was due to come before the Transvaal legislative council for amendment. The editorial congratulated the Transvaal Indians on their 'most praiseworthy' recent activity. Between Tuesday and Friday of the same week, it was noted, BIA had petitioned the legislative council, addressed a long circular letter to its members, and convened a meeting thought to have been attended by over 500 people: 'a very creditable performance worthy of imitation by us in Natal'.[146]

Two separate issues are thus raised. Firstly, what were the reasons for BIA's failure to gain support between 1903 and 1906; and then — to be discussed later — how and why were 3 000 people suddenly mobilized for passive resistance in September 1906?

Several reasons suggest themselves for BIA's lack of support. As with the Congress there is nothing to indicate that the party attempted to appeal to the Indian underclasses, far less other 'non-whites' (though the size of the mass meeting in December 1903 suggests the beginning of the co-option of the petty traders). The party's base of support was therefore limited to the Indian commercial classes. The central issue addressed by BIA, indeed its *raison d'être*, was Law 3 of 1885, the question of whether or not it would be enforced by the British administration and, if so, who would be exempt from its workings.

The possibility of being forced to live and trade in bazaars and the obvious economic dislocation which this would cause were certainly of vital interest to the merchants. But the question had been at issue for almost 20 years. During this time, despite minimal political activity on their part, Indian merchants had continued to trade successfully in the Transvaal. Political apathy in the Transvaal can thus be seen in part as a reflection of the relative success of doing nothing. Paradoxically, the same apathy which gripped the Natal-based elite during this period reflected the failure of the early Congress campaigns against the imposition of discriminatory legislation in Natal.

At one level imperial and colonial government policies appeared to justify merchant apathy. In official statements these policies were characterized by the tension between the anti-Indian hostility of the Transvaal and the apparent fairness of the Colonial Office. The pro-tracted negotiations which grew out of this stance offered precisely the situation in which Indian commercial interests had flourished and grown before the war.

At another and more fundamental level of political reality, however, the activities of the post-war Transvaal administration offered far less justification for apathy than had their predecessors'. Despite the Colonial Office's rejection of Milner's bazaar notice, the 1904 Supreme Court decision which re-interpreted Law 3 in favour of the Indians, the Lyttelton policy statement, and the Colonial Office refusal to suspend the licensing of Indian traders pending an investiga-tion of the extent of their holdings — despite all this, the British administration surveyed and set aside Indian bazaars throughout the Transvaal between 1903 and 1906.[147]

The republican regime had also attempted to set aside locations, as they were then called, but never as systematically as the British. In addition, the regulations drawn up by the British for the inhabitants of bazaars were harsher than the previous regulations had been. The republic had permitted outright ownership of land in the Johannesburg location, where some 1 600 Indian workers, petty traders and hawkers continued to live after the war. They had also permitted 99-year leases in Johannesburg, and sub-letting to members of other races at least in the Johannesburg and Pretoria locations. Indeed, Gandhi claimed that the high rental income from stands (plots) leased to Indians as well as Africans in both Johannesburg and Pretoria were an important source of revenue for the merchants. The British administration, by contrast, was prepared to allow only short-term (21-year) leases, no sub-letting and no land ownership.[148] And, by 1906, it was trying to reorganize the old Pretoria and Johannesburg locations to exclude Africans.[149]

Probably the most ominous indication of the intentions of the British administration was the siting of the bazaars. These were uniformly condemned by the small active core of BIA who had independent assessments made by white professional men of their suitability for residential as well as trading purposes. The most usual criticism of a proposed site was that it was too far from the centre of the adjacent town to attract the business of anyone but inhabitants of the bazaar itself.[150] Nowhere was this more true than in Johannesburg. The old republican location had been expropriated by the Johannesburg Town Council in September 1903, allegedly because of its insanitary condition and the consequent need to find a new site. The inhabitants of the location continued to live as tenants of the municipality, and no attempt was made to improve conditions.[151] After much debate, a decision was finally reached by the local government in August 1906 to establish the new Johannesburg bazaar at Klipspruit, more than thirteen miles from the centre of the city.[152] As long as Law 3 remained on the statute books this decision held serious consequences for the entire Johannesburg Indian population. In terms of the Law any Indian could be compelled to reside in a location (bazaar) for reasons of public hygiene. The Colonial Office had long held that this applied to hawkers and workers who, despite Gandhi's assertion to the contrary, clearly stood to be severely affected by so great a distance between residence and workplace.[153] It scarcely need be added that a reversal of the 1904 Supreme Court decision under the circumstances would have ruined the Johannesburg merchants. Even as things stood, an upheaval of this nature threatened them indirectly. During the 1904 plague outbreak, 1 600 Indian inhabitants of the

Johannesburg location were removed to Klipspruit temporarily. Gandhi claimed that the merchants suffered heavy losses from this dislocation because many of those who were moved were indebted to merchants and could no longer meet their liabilities.[154]

In the face of this, the question must be raised of the extent to which lack of political awareness might have been responsible for the Indian merchants' continued and unjustifiable indifference to the growing threat in the post-war Transvaal. Gandhi, their strategist and tactician, was certainly aware of the increasingly threatening situation as bazaars were surveyed and laid out. BIA, as noted, documented the unsatisfactory nature of the bazaars and submitted their criticisms to the government. The Lyttelton policy statement, made in the light of the favourable Supreme Court decision, and the single most important official statement during the period under review, was dissected and criticized for its failure to address the question of discrimination against Indians *per se*.[155] By responding to the Milner-Lawley proposals with a simple demand for guaranteed protection of vested commercial interests, rather than calling for the elimination of Law 3, the Lyttelton statement for the first time offered imperial government support — albeit tacit — for the principle of racial discrimination against Indians in the Transvaal. This was the principle which, Gandhi had always thought, if once admitted would open the floodgate of restrictive legislation. These insights were made available to the merchants clearly and in detail through the columns of *Indian Opinion*. In any event, the merchants — or some of them at least — had never been lacking in comparable political insights themselves. And yet, in the post-war Transvaal, they failed to support the organization created to protect their own interests.

Gandhi claimed increasingly in the post-war period that Indians were incapable of organizing, of uniting for a common purpose. These criticisms clearly stemmed from the failure of either BIA or the Congress to generate support during this period. As such, they suggest that the failure of the parties was due to some inadequacy on the part of their constituents rather than inadequacy in the parties themselves. In this, Gandhi's repeated editorials in *Indian Opinion* are very like P.S. Aiyar's in *African Chronicle* some five years later. The major difference is that Aiyar's criticisms tended to be directed at the emerging elite in Natal rather than at the established commercial elite. In both cases, the criticisms were misdirected. The political crisis of the emerging elite will be analyzed more fully in Chapter 5. Gandhi's view of the crisis in the merchants' politics scarcely needs to be discussed. His own experience in Natal and the Transvaal belies his criticisms. The Natal merchants had responded well to formal organization during the first two or three years of the Congress's existence. Indeed, they had been formally organized even before the party was created. Support for organized politics fell away only after NIC's failure to prevent the introduction of damaging legislation. But, even after the war, NIC was still capable of mobilizing the Natal merchants in moments of perceived crisis, as we have seen. In the Transvaal, effective merchant organization helped combat the 1904 outbreak of plague in the Johannesburg location. Gandhi commented favourably on their activity in *Indian Opinion*.[156]

Gandhi's claim that Indians were incapable of forming themselves into a united group for a common purpose was thus not only invalid, but also myopic. The problem, then, comes down to this: the Transvaal-based merchants with few exceptions, had never been actively involved in politics. The British Indian Association offered neither a mechanism for active participation nor, more importantly, a strategy capable of effecting political mobilization, far less generating continued support.

Strategy and Tactics, 1903-1906

Within weeks of his return to South Africa Gandhi made the first of the significant compromises which were to become a major characteristic of his political career. He abandoned his demands for full equality for all British subjects in the Transvaal. These were replaced by the once unacceptable Natal solution to the Indian problem: a virtual ban on Indian immigration in exchange for freedom to trade subject to licensing by the municipalities.[157] He thus conceded half the Transvaal battle before it had even begun, ensuring, as we have seen, that when the Colonial Office was finally forced into making a policy statement it would not exceed these demands. The only real improvements over Natal which Gandhi sought for the Transvaal were *guaranteed* protection for vested interests, and special immigration rights for merchants' employees.[158] The latter request is of special interest as one of several instances which demonstrate that despite his increasingly important role in elite politics, Gandhi was still simply a representative of the merchants. Politically the demand was foolish.

The claim that merchants were unable to fulfil their employee needs from among the resident population, and the implication that established merchants would have an ongoing need for new employees from India, suggested that every merchant was a magnet for new immigrants. This was one of the very things that the Natal solution proposed to end, and Gandhi can certainly not have been unaware of the contradiction in his proposals. Nevertheless, the demand for special immigration rights was forwarded to the government regularly.[159]

The post-war strategy which Gandhi chose to pursue in the Transvaal, then, was one of compromise; his tactics the same uninspired and uninspiring letters, petitions and occasional low-key deputations which had been the essence of his political style since his entry into politics. It may be that Gandhi felt — and perhaps rightly at one level — that he had no other choice than compromise. He had failed to gain support in India for a more panoramic and radical vision: the belief that a high pressure campaign spearheaded by the INC would result in the elimination of discriminatory legislation in the Transvaal whose precedent would have to be followed by the other British colonies in South Africa. The interview with Chamberlain in January 1903 had eliminated any hope of support for this strategy from the imperial government. In any event, shortly after his return to South Africa, Gandhi abandoned his radical vision and fell back on a strategy aimed simply at trying to prevent government policy in the Transvaal from exceeding the unsatisfactory Natal policy. The limited rights which he claimed for his constituents were justified sometimes in terms of pre-war British policy towards Transvaal Indians, but more often in terms of the fact that they were now British subjects in a British colony.

It may be, as indicated, that this compromise appeared to Gandhi to be the most appropriate response to the reality with which he had to deal. But that reality was multi-dimensional and if compromise was appropriate to one dimension, it was inappropriate to others. The timid strategy which grew out of Gandhi's compromise could not produce an issue capable of effecting mobilization in a group of merchants in many of whom political consciousness was poorly developed, and whose own uni-dimensional view of their reality lent itself to political apathy. Equally importantly, this strategy could not be expected to gain the active support of the Natal Congress, the only institution with an organizational infrastructure capable of mobilizing the commercial elite. The strategy offered no hope of improving conditions in Natal; indeed, it held only the possibility of reproducing in the Transvaal the same set of conditions which had marked the failure of the early Congress campaigns and the party's subsequent loss of support.

The political apathy which gripped both Natal and the Transvaal in the first years after the war must thus be seen more as a function of an inadequate strategy and unimaginative tactics, than as a reflection of some intrinsic deficiency of the commercial elite.

Passive Resistance: The First Declaration

Before moving on to an explanation for the massive support given to passive resistance — that most unexpected of all conclusions to nearly four years of ineffective leadership on one hand and political apathy on the other — it is necessary to examine the changes which were taking place in Gandhi's moral and political thought as he slowly developed the philosophy out of which passive resistance grew. These changes are documented in *Indian Opinion*, the journal which at its outset was said to be a medium for informing whites and Indians about each other, but which became increasingly a vehicle for the moral uplift of its Indian readers as Gandhi strove to impart to them the moral framework which he was beginning to articulate for himself.

In the columns of *Indian Opinion* Gandhi tried to come to grips with what he perceived — mistakenly, I have suggested — to be the fundamental problem in the crisis of merchant politics: the elite's inability to unite and organize. Through his examination of this question, he reached the conclusion that the main barriers to unity, and thus effective political action, were self-absorption and self-interest — the failure to share a sense of common duty to the wider community, to put public interest before personal interest. He returned to these shortcomings again and again between 1904 and 1906, offering his readers examples of the benefits to be derived from overcoming them.

The examples which Gandhi used to support his contention that a sense of unity and of shared duty were essential prerequisites of successful political action were numerous. They were drawn mainly from what was happening in the international arena at the time. The

Japanese victory in the 1904 Russo-Japanese war was discussed repeatedly and at considerable length in this context. The successful Chinese boycott of American trade, and the widespread strikes in Russia in 1905 served as further examples. The partition of Bengal and the ensuing *swadeshi* movement naturally excited a great deal of attention.[160]

Nowhere, however, did Gandhi completely address the question of why some people unite for political action in some places and at some times, yet not others. His vision was restricted, looking always to a deficiency in the individual rather than expanding to encompass the institution, the ideology, or the goal which is meant to carry him.

The defects in Gandhi's political insight are of dual significance. On one hand they were, as suggested, an important part of the reason for the failure of merchant politics in Natal and the Transvaal during the immediate post-war years. In this respect it is important to remember that in choosing not to attempt to ally with the articulate politicized elements in either the coloured or African communities,[161] Gandhi facilitated the implementation of the divisive segregationalist policies which helped ease the task of white minority rule in South Africa. Indeed, where the Transvaal whites insisted on separate facilities for themselves, Gandhi demanded further subdivision to separate Indians from other blacks.[162] In fact, in his eagerness to compromise, to conciliate, to ensure the white South Africans their predominant position,[163] he was sometimes even ahead of them in advocating separate facilities for whites and others.[164]

To a large extent, these decisions were based on political expediency,[165] which in itself is an unusual motivation to be attributed to Gandhi. But it goes far beyond this. Gandhi was a racial purist, and proud of it. In September 1903 in response to the White Leagues' fear of the possible consequence of mass Asian immigration into the Transvaal he declared in *Indian Opinion* that 'we believe as much in the purity of race as we think they do, only we believe that they would best serve the interest, which is as dear to us as it is to them, by advocating the purity of all the races and not one alone'.[166] Or, again, in December 1903 in response to similar fears voiced by the all-white Transvaal Chambers of Commerce Conference: 'If there is one thing which the Indian cherishes more than any other, it is the purity of the type'.[167]

Working class Indians evidently did not share Gandhi's distaste for 'commingling'[168] of the races. This was still the period when even in the Transvaal racial segregation had yet to permeate the urban working classes. In Ferreiras, a working class suburb of Johannesburg, the population breakdown in late 1904 was listed as 288 Indians, 58 Syrians, 165 Chinese, 295 Cape Coloureds, 75 blacks and 929 whites.[169] Gandhi could do nothing about a place like Ferreiras, but he claimed the right to a say on the racial composition of the Indian locations. In February 1904 he informed the Johannesburg Medical Officer that 'of course, under my suggestion, the Town Council must withdrew the Kaffirs from the [Johannesburg] Location. About this mixing of the Kaffirs with the Indians, I confess I feel most strongly. I think it is very unfair to the Indian population and it is an undue tax on even the proverbial patience of my countrymen'.[170] The only reason that the removal of Africans from the locations did not become one of the consistent demands of BIA would thus seem to be the fact that many merchants profited from black rental income as noted earlier. Indeed, in March 1906 in a clear contradiction of his own principles Gandhi, on behalf of the party, protested the proposed removal of the blacks from the Pretoria location on the grounds that it was inimical to merchant interests.[171]

While still at the level of political thought it is important to note that despite the universalist ring of his ever increasing editorials on duty to the wider community, the public weal, public service, and so forth, Gandhi was as yet no more a politician of the people than he had ever been. There is nothing to indicate that Gandhi meant anything more by 'wider community' than the merchant class as a whole. This is borne out by some of his other concerns during this period. He strenuously protested against the proposal to import indentured Indians into the Transvaal, particularly if their contracts included a repatriation clause. He referred to the proposed scheme as slave labour.[172] But his major concern was evidently the belief that the Indian 'problem is complicated enough without their presence',[173] and that hostility to Indian traders would be fed by a vast influx of Indian workers.[174] That his concern was for the future of the merchants, and not the 'slave-labourers' *per se*, is obvious in that he offered sincere congratulations on the decision to import Chinese instead of Indian workers.[175] In 1906 he actually recommended to the Colonial Secretary that Natal merchants be allowed to bypass the Immigration Restriction Act and import Indian clerks and domestics on the understanding that they must leave the colony at the end of the service with their masters. This was an attempt to break what was described as the 'monopoly' created by local Indian clerks and domestics,[176] and cannot be described in any other way than an indenture scheme complete with below market wage rates and a repatriation clause. Gandhi continued to claim that the 'general condition of the indentured labourer [in Natal] is satisfactory',[177] and though by late 1905 he had advanced far enough to think that contract labour was used 'regardless of any fellow feeling for the indentured labourer' he was 'not prepared to subscribe to any general charge of ill-treatment'.[178]

What little Gandhi knew about the conditions of indentured workers seems to have been gleaned from the Natal press which regularly reported court cases of gross mistreatment of labourers.[179] Despite the fact that his experimental commune at Phoenix lay in the heart of Natal's sugar country, there is nothing to indicate that Gandhi had ever visited a labour compound, whether on a mine, an up-country farm, or a sugar plantation. He was equally removed from Natal's ex-indentured worker population, slipping back into second or third terms of indenture under the crushing burdens of the annual £3 tax on ex-indentured labourers, low-paying jobs and growing unemployment. As the post-war depression in Natal deepened, a £1 poll tax was imposed on all citizens. In an *Indian Opinion* editorial Gandhi devoted a paragraph to the 'heavy burden' which the tax placed on the ex-indentured. Typically, this was followed by a much lengthier treatment of the 'cruel injustice' of imposing such taxes on passenger Indians who already suffered the burdens of not being considered desirable citizens of the colony.[180]

Gandhi's glib assumption that Indian workers in Natal were not badly off was based on ignorance, but he was in a position to know the condition of workers in the Transvaal. In 1904 he was actively involved in treating plague victims in the Johannesburg location where the majority of working class Indians lived. If the fact that they could not escape indebtedness even when living 45 to a stand[181] made any impact on him, he did not record it. His major concern at this point, as noted earlier, was that their temporary removal from the location made it impossible for Indian merchants to collect debts from them.

Even while Gandhi's politics in both theory and practice continued to be the politics of the elite, racially and socially exclusive and self-serving, he was beginning to formulate the moral doctrine out of which his universalist, humanistic principles grew. As indicated, this formulation was articulated within the framework of his perception of the crisis of merchant politics. It thus appears both as another significant consequence, and as a cause, of his limited political insight.

Gandhi's belief that only defects in the individual prevented the merchants from engaging in effective political action in an increasingly oppressive situation led him to explore the question of moral determinism: to ask himself to what extent the individual is, or should be, guided by his own principles, his own will, and to what extent by those of others. He came to view what seemed to him the passive acceptance of increasing material and, therefore, increasing moral degradation as a reflection of a people who had become incapable of exercising internal moral authority, and one of its most potent manifestations the inability or unwillingness to share a sense of responsibility for their community as a whole. It thus became Gandhi's concern to effect a moral transformation in his constituents, to change them from passive objects of someone else's will to free and independent moral agents, masters of their own destiny. The means which Gandhi chose to effect the transformation to moral individuation in this early period was also an end in itself: the attempt to inculcate a sense of group solidarity, of responsibility to and for the group as a whole.

Gandhi does not seem to have expected the Transvaal Indians to experience en masse the moral transformation which he thought was needed to give them the will to start fighting back against an oppressive situation in which, as he saw it, moral degradation permitted — invited even — further degradation. What he did expect was that sufficient numbers of men would come forward who accepted and firmly believed in the principle of moral autonomy, and that these men would form a kind of moral leadership which would weld together the rest of the group in the first step away from oppression. Again he offered through his writings in *Indian Opinion* numerous examples of how he thought entire communities, and even nations, are the beneficiaries of the strength and courage of exceptional individuals working in society for society. The 'heroes' whom he eulogized were for the most part the larger than life figures of European history — Elizabeth Fry, Lord Nelson, Joan of Arc, Sir Thomas Munro, Mountstuart Elphinstone.[182] He believed that India had failed to produce a sufficient number of such heroic figures in her recent past and that this failure was a good part of the reason why she was subjugated by a foreign power; and, indeed, why she *should* be.[183]

Much of Gandhi's mature philosophy was thus already apparent in the first years of the century: the emphasis on internal regulation; the belief that a truly moral being must engage in positive action rather than thought alone which, as Raghavan Iyar puts it, 'led him to assert that the duty that a man owes to himself is also owed by him to his fellow men',[184] and the concept of the heroic exemplary individual whose strength can become the strength of a whole community. But Gandhi seems not to have recognized in this period the foundation of his own moral stance. He had yet to formulate (or, at least, clearly articulate) what later became his cardinal principle: the notion that the active pursuit of truth, through moral autonomy and manifested in service to the community, suffering if needs be the consequences of one's own convictions, is its own reward. The active pursuit of truth alone offers inner equilibrium, self-respect, self-realization; it is, to use the religious terminology in which Gandhi's philosophy was usually clothed, both the means to salvation and salvation itself.[185] Here, then, is the incentive for the will to say no, and to go on saying no, to degradation present and future. And here also, to move from the ethical plane back to the plane of practical politics, is the means to political mobilization.

This is certainly not the only way to effect either a moral transformation or political mobilization, but it was to become Gandhi's way. In the first years of the century, however, he had not yet thought out, or not yet expounded, the ontology which later was to form the basis of both his moral philosophy and his politics — the belief that every living being has not only the capacity, but the duty, to himself and thus to all mankind, to be the master of his own destiny.[186] The call to action in the years leading to the first declaration of passive resistance was thus based largely on tired old saws such as, God helps those who help themselves, to do one's duty is to please God, a just cause is its own strength.[187] Or, more rarely, when Gandhi grew impatient with the inactivity of his constituents, he fell on them with harsh criticisms, the most biting and telling of which was, perhaps, 'when we are told of our duty, we continue to be indifferent, keep our houses dirty, lie hugging our hoarded wealth. Thus we live a wretched life acquiescing in a long tormented process ending only in death'.[188]

It is impossible to pinpoint exactly when or why Gandhi himself experienced the moment of metaphysical rebellion out of which passive resistance grew. Because the first declaration of passive resistance took place in September 1906, and because Gandhi has laid much stress on his activity as a stretcher bearer in the Zulu rebellion immediately before this,[189] it is generally assumed that the critical turning point occurred during his military service. It should already be clear from what has been written above that most of the major elements of Gandhi's philosophy had already been thought out well before mid-1906. Indeed, Gandhi's first call for passive resistance took place not in September 1906, but in January 1904, a fact which seems to have been consistently overlooked. This call to action was closely followed by a series of articles in *Indian Opinion* on the virtue of self-sacrifice. Some ten months later, in December 1904, Gandhi responded to the paper's financial crisis by moving the press to Phoenix, his first, experimental, communal settlement in whose running he took a deep personal interest.

The first call to passive resistance brings us firmly back to the political reality in which Gandhi's philosophy was worked out. The circumstances of the call were the appointment of the Asiatic Traders' Commission which grew out of the December 1903 legislative council debate on a proposed amendment to Milner's bazaar notice. Despite the adoption of a resolution to convene a commission, the government on its own initiative ordered the Receivers of Revenue to issue licences for the new year only to those Indians who could tender proof that they had traded before the war. In other words, traders who had been issued licences by the British administration in previous years were to submit proof of pre-war trading first to a Receiver of Revenue, and then to the Commission, in order to have these licences renewed for the coming year. The situation was patently absurd — exactly the sort of humiliating last straw that could prove catalytic for someone who had already begun to probe deeply into the nature of his own conscience. Gandhi advised the Transvaal merchants that they should make 'respectful representations to the Government, but they should also firmly decline to give proof to the Receivers of Revenue, offering to do so before the Commission that is to be appointed'. If there were prosecutions for trading without a licence, 'the person prosecuted should rise to the occasion, decline to pay any fines, and go to gaol'.[190]

Two days later on behalf of BIA Gandhi telegraphed Milner to 'humbly request' his intervention 'as [the] traders fear prosecution'.[191] The next two issues of *Indian Opinion* contained Gandhi's articles stressing the need for self-sacrifice, the need for each individual to accept responsibility for the well-being of the group as a whole, and to take action aimed at furthering that well-being. He 'drew the particular attention of our brethren in the Transvaal to [the second article] because the condition there is disorganized and saddening'.[192] It is thus clear that the merchants were unwilling to invite jail sentences. Perhaps a realistic assessment of the situation had convinced them that an urgent appeal to Milner would solve the problem. In the event, they were correct: the government undertook not to prosecute even those who were refused licences for 1904 pending the findings of the Commission.[193] By the time the Commission reported, BIA had won the test case against Law 3 which Gandhi had proposed at the same time as his call for passive resistance. The Commission's findings therefore became irrelevant. What is most important about this for present purposes, however, is that it clearly marked the intensification of Gandhi's exploration — in writing at least — of the question of moral determinism, just as it was the first manifestation of his own act of rebellion.

In order to understand the 1906 declaration of passive resistance and the shape of the campaign which followed, it is crucial to bear in mind, then, that for Gandhi the political context was secondary and in no way extraordinary. Selborne's two ordinances were 'abominable',[194] yes, but then so was most of the Natal and Transvaal legislation dealing with Indians. They confirmed the principle of legislation which discriminated against Indians *eo nomine*; also Indians were 'reduced [by them] to a level lower than the Kaffirs'.[195] In these respects they violated political principles which Gandhi — and even the Indian Committee before him — had for years striven to uphold. As the only significant piece of legislation dealing with Indians under British rule in the Transvaal they offered a far from satisfactory example for the responsible ministry which was soon to come into power. But Gandhi did not particularly stress these aspects of the ordinances. In fact his criticisms tended to be emotional as much as intellectual. He spoke in generalized terms of oppression, complete degradation, humiliation, all of which is beyond question but none of which was new or unusual in legislation affecting the Natal and Transvaal Indians.

However, when examining the first passive resistance declaration within the only context in which it can properly be examined — Gandhi's developing philosophy — it becomes clear that the ordinances were of significance to him primarily as catalysts, with the potential to elicit the moral response which his teachings in *Indian Opinion* had failed to effect. The first *Indian Opinion* editorial to announce the proposed passive resistance (it preceded the mass meeting at which the resistance pledge was taken) confirms this contention. Once again, Gandhi turned to heroic examples of self-sacrifice for the good of the community, and again the examples were drawn from Russia. Although the violence of Russian resistance to oppression was condemned, Indians were described in comparison to Russians as 'children in political matters . . . [who] do not understand the principle that the public good is also one's own good'. The article went on to say that 'the time has now come for us to outgrow this state of mind . . . and the new Transvaal ordinance offers an excellent opportunity'.[196]

Within its proper context, then, but only within that context, Gandhi's reaction to the draft ordinances is simple enough to understand. They offered him the first issue since January 1904 around which a rebellious response might conceivably be built.

The larger question for the moment, given the political apathy of the Transvaal elite, is how and why Gandhi was able to gain their support, even for a pledge, in September 1906. All the evidence indicates that despite Gandhi's hope for his constituents, the 3 000 strong crowd at the mass meeting represented a political rather than a moral response on the part of the Transvaal Indian merchants. Whatever the wellspring of his own desire for rebellion, Gandhi, using a tactic developed more than a decade earlier in Natal, represented the registration ordinance as a first piece of discriminatory legislation from which others would inevitably flow: the first step on the road to segregated Indian bazaars, the beginning of the end of merchant commercial success not only in the Transvaal, but also in Natal where the headquarters of the biggest Indian firms were located.[197] It is possible — although there is no evidence to corroborate this — that the otherwise tenuous link between Selborne's ordinance and removal to bazaars was given point by the Johannesburg municipality's recent decision to establish the new Johannesburg bazaar at Klipspruit, some thirteen and a half miles from the centre of the city.[198]

The success of the mass meeting was also attributable in part to the emotional atmosphere in which it was held. Merchants, petty traders and hawkers closed their businesses, as requested by Gandhi, and crowds began to gather at the appointed place hours before the meeting was due to start. The press reports of the speeches leave no doubt that Haji Habib and H O Ally were the main drawcards. It was they who proposed a jail-going resolution, who made the most fiery speeches, and who received the most enthusiastic response from the crowd. Haji Habib, speaking in Gujerati, and railing *inter alia* against Christian persecution of the Turkish empire, turned the jail-going resolution into a solemn oath before God, and had no difficulty carrying with him the mixed crowd of Hindus, Muslims and Christians, the vast majority of whom could not understand his language. They 'understood' the tenor of his speech, and in that emotion-charged atmosphere this was enough. Buoyed by the euphoria of open opposition for the first time, 3 000 Transvaal Indians rose to their feet to repeat after Haji Habib that they would go to jail rather than submit themselves to registration under the new ordinance.[199]

But none of this would have been possible without a swift and solid organizational effort. Organization was the work mainly of the Hamidia Islamic Society,[200] a Johannesburg Muslim benevolent society, established only three months earlier in July 1906. The first of its kind in the Transvaal, it had no written constitution, formal membership roll or regulations governing conditions of membership. It was founded by Haji Ojer Ally who became its first president.[201] A list of officials published in *Indian Opinion* in August 1907 shows Imam Abdul Kadir Bawazeer as chairman; M P Fancy, secretary; E S Coovadia, treasurer; E S Mian and Abdul Gani, patrons.[202] (Ally had already left the Transvaal rather than redeem his passive resistance pledge). The society was thus another merchant organization. All of the officials above, including the Imam, had significant holdings in the Transvaal. In October 1906 the society was described as being in a flourishing condition with several hundred members.[203] This must have included a sizeable majority, and certainly the wealthiest, the most powerful, of the Transvaal merchants.

H O Ally's role in mobilizing support for the mass meeting seems to have been the most critical. One of the few Transvaal merchants with actual experience in participatory politics, Ally, married to a Cape Malay, had been involved in Coloured politics in the Cape in the early 1890s. In 1892 he was elected chairman of the Coloured People's Organization which subsequently sent to London a petition with 22 000 signatures protesting an attempt to deprive the Coloureds of their franchise rights.[204] He moved to the Transvaal some time after 1892 and became involved in the low level politics of the Indian elite.

Ally's powerful role in the early stages of the passive resistance campaign must be deduced from the few direct references in *Indian Opinion*. Gandhi himself described Ally as the prime mover in organizing the mass meeting. Shortly after the declaration of resistance, when Gandhi and Ally were preparing to leave for London to present the Indian ultimatum to the Colonial Secretary, their plans were abandoned under the mistaken belief that the ordinances had received royal assent. It was to Ally that the politically active turned for 'consent' to revive the deputation when it was learned that the ordinances were still under consideration.[205] In London, with Ally ill and barely able to take his place as a member of the deputation, Gandhi did much of the groundwork himself; but it was Ally's approval which he anxiously sought for the idea that a permanent London committee to support the South African Indians should be established and funded.[206]

The other main speakers at the mass meeting provide further indication of the intermediaries who were used to mobilize support: Abdul Rahman, the active secretary of the Potchefstroom Indian Association; Essop Mian and E S Coovadia, both of Johannesburg and both officials of the Hamidia Islamic Society (Coovadia was also an official of the British Indian Association); Haji Habib, the popular chairman of the BIA Pretoria committee; H O Ally; and Gandhi himself. The meeting was opened by Abdul Gani, president of BIA and a patron of the Hamidia Society.[207] Gandhi thus had behind him the officials of the Transvaal's two elite organizations — the colony's most powerful merchants. The way was prepared for a mass meeting with articles in *Indian Opinion*, and a speech given by Gandhi to the Hamidia Society two days before the meeting where the intention to pass a jail-going resolution was announced, and the audience was informed that all would be expected to close their shops and attend.[208]

Once these officials had committed themselves to action it is not difficult to understand how attendance at the meeting was swelled to 3 000, taking in at least the Johannesburg hawkers, and probably numbers of the Johannesburg workers and petty traders. Both hawkers and workers, as indicated earlier, were linked to the merchants by a credit network which is known to have extended at least throughout the Johannesburg location where the majority of them lived. It is reasonable to assume that a merchant could command the presence of his employees and debtors at the meeting.

Similar sets of linkages probably existed between the more powerful merchants and the petty traders. The documentary evidence is fragmentary for the Transvaal, but such linkages are — as noted earlier — well documented for the Indian commercial classes in Natal.

In any event, the petty traders had as much of a direct interest in resistance as the merchants. They stood to lose equally with them if Indians were confined to bazaars for business as well as residential purposes. They too had been organized politically since at least the 1890s. The petitions and letters of protest generated by their organizations shared the same concern as the merchants': protection of vested commercial interests. This, and the presence of the petty traders Peter Moonlight Modliar and Thambi Naidoo as minor platform speakers at the mass meeting, suggests that the petty traders were recruited for resistance — at least initially — by representation of their own leaders at the leadership level of the fledgling movement.[209] Their inclusion in the movement was doubly important. Most of them were Tamils and Hindus. Thus they provided an additional set of links between the merchants, who were mainly Gujerati Muslims, and the hawkers and workers who were mainly Tamil Hindus.

During the crucial years when Gandhi was working out the philosophy which later was to inform his politics, he believed that the political apathy of the elite in the Transvaal and Natal reflected a moral crisis. Evidence suggests that the crisis was political, as much as moral; that the loosely structured British Indian Association, the strategy of compromise, and the ritual of polite constitutional protest were insufficient to mobilize the elite so long as their commercial interests were not directly or immediately threatened.

How then is one to explain the support given by the elite to the notion of passive resistance which represented for Gandhi, its author, the solution to a political problem interpreted as a moral problem? Is one to believe that the desired moral transformation had taken place, and that the new enthusiasm for politics expressed simultaneously an assertion of the individual will as well as the realization that 'the public good is also one's own good'?[210]

Again, evidence suggests that the key support for passive resistance which was given by the most powerful merchants represented a political and not a moral response. The solid organizational basis of the mass meeting, which is reflected in the careful choice of speakers, and which was in large part due to the work of the newly formed Hamidia Islamic Society, is evidence of this response. If a mass meeting on this scale was previously unknown in the Transvaal, so too was an organizational effort of this magnitude.

There is one final question left. How was Gandhi able to channel

the organizational capacity of the Hamidia Islamic Society into tackling
what was for him essentially a moral problem; and how, indeed, to
recapture the enthusiasm of the Natal Congress which had run on a
deficit for years, but which now came forward to contribute heavily to
the expenses of the deputation to London? One returns to the question
of strategy and tactics. The registration ordinance was presented to the
merchants as the beginning of the end of commercial success in both the
Transvaal and Natal. Passive resistance, in theory at least, was
therefore eminently suited to elite ideology. The commercial elite had
actively participated in politics only once before. At that time, the
introduction of discriminatory legislation in Natal had been viewed as
the beginning of an attack on merchant interests which would spread
throughout South Africa. The politics of polite constitutional protest
had been tried and found wanting in Natal. The politics of confrontation can thus be seen as an attractive alternative, in the face of precisely
the kind of threat which had mobilized the elite in the early 1890s. It
was only when the passive resistance pledge was put to the test in 1907
and 1908 that its flaws as an elite political strategy and its weakness as a
vehicle of mass mobilization became apparent. These renewed political
crises led to further refinements of Gandhi's moral doctrine.

Notes

1   Although Gandhi's first existing communication on the Transvaal
     question dates from 1895, one of the leading Transvaal-based
     merchants later claimed that he began advising them in 1894. *C W*,
     iii, p.269, Tayob Haji Khan Mahomed to Col. Sec., 2 Jan. 1903.

2   See, for example, C.7911, sub-encl. in no.5, append. B, I O to C O
     27 Mar. 1889 (H Escombe, M L A Natal, forwarding complaints of
     Transvaal merchants to the Col. Office).

3   See above, Chapter 2, pp.40-42.

4   *C W*, i, p.187, 'Petition to Lord Ripon', May 1895, and see above,
     Chapter 2, p.40. The total Indian merchant investment in the
     Transvaal was estimated at £100 000 in May 1895: Dada
     Abdullah's investment in stock was estimated at £50 000 in 1891.

5   See above, Chapter 2.

6   C.7911, no.5, Lt Gen. Goodenough to Sec. St., 9 Apr. 1895, encl.
     Award of the Arbitrator.

7   *C W*, i, p.236.

8   CO 417/148/8665, High Comm. to Sec. St., 29 Apr. 1895, encl.
     petition to British Agent, 16 Apr. 1895.

9   C.7911, no.10, De Wet to High Comm., 30 May 1895, encl.

petition to Sec. St. for Colonies, May 1895, petition to Sec. St. for India, May 1895.

10   CO 417/148/10832, I O to C O, 27 May 1891, encl. petition signed by A Appasamy, Indian Chief Committee Member, and some 70 Johannesburg Tamils, addressed to Govt. Madras before 3 Apr. 1895; ibid., 8108, High Comm. to Sec. St., 20 Apr. 1895, encl. petition signed by four Tamils for the British Indian Community, Johannesburg and suburbs, 10 Apr. 1895; *C W*, iii, pp.22-3, 'Petition to I N C', 28 Nov. 1898, signed by five Johannesburg Tamils, (it is odd that this petition is attributed to Gandhi); TABA, P S 261/G.579, petition of the British Indian Association, Johannesburg, signed by 25 Tamils, addressed to the Gov. of the Transvaal, Dec. 1902; CO 291/61/14411, I O to C O, 20 Apr. 1903, copy of the Dec. 1902 petition, addressed to the Viceroy of India; TABA, Lt Gen. 95/97/1/I, petition by Indian merchants of Johannesburg, signed by two Tamils, addressed to Lt Gov., Transvaal, 28 Mar. 1903; ibid., 97/97/112, petition of Indian Political Assoc., Johannesburg, signed by 13 Tamils, addressed to Lt Gov., Transvaal, 15 Dec. 1904. Although the Tamil Benefit Society became the backbone of the passive resistance movement and some of its officers became officers of BIA, it remained a separate organization. See below, Chapter 4, passim.

11   P Catha Padayachee signed the 1891, 1895 and 1902 petitions; A Pillay in 1898 and 1902; C Poonoosamy in 1902 and 1903; T D Iyar in 1902 and 1904; A Kistnasamy Naidoo in 1895, 1898, 1902; V S Pillay in 1891 and 1902; V Chetty in 1898 and 1902; Athmoola Padiachey in 1903 and 1904; A Appasamy in 1891 and 1898. This allows for occasional anomalies in transliteration of names, as in Kristneisamy, A Kestnasamy, A Kistnasamy Naidoo, P Catha (Leathe, Catha), Padayachee, or V Chetty (Chettiar) who also later became Chairman of the Tamil Benefit Society (*Indian Opinion*, 10 Aug. 1912). Peter Moonlight Moonoosamy (Modelliar) who was Chairman of the executive committee of the British Indian Association in Nov. 1902, also became an officer of the Tamil Benefit Society (*African Chronicle*, 6 Jul. 1912).

12   See fns. 10 and 11.

13   See above, Chapter 1.

14   See, for example, petition to British Agent, 16 Apr. 1895, fn. 8 above.

15   Ibid., and petitions to Sec. St. for Colonies and Sec. St. for India; also fn. 9 above.

16   And see also the *Johannesburg Star* which wished the South African states and colonies to 'give Mr Chamberlain to understand, in the

plainest and shortest terms, that the colonists of South Africa do not, and will not, accept or carry into practice the absurd theory of the "British Subject" '. Quoted in *Natal Witness*, 5 Sept. 1893.

17   See fns. 8 and 9 above, and *C W*, ii, p.74, 'Address in Bombay', 26 Sept. 1896.

18   Gandhi apparently shared the Transvaal government's view of Asian aboriginals. During a speech in Bombay in Sept. 1896, he pointed out that 'the Santhals of Assam will be as useless in South Africa as the natives of that country'. *C W*, ii, p.72, 'Address in Bombay', 26 Sept. 1896.

19   See, for example, petition to Sec. St. for Colonies, fn. 9 above.

20   Ibid.

21   Ibid., and cf. strategy of the Indian Committee and the Congress, Chapter 2.

22   See fn. 9 above.

23   Ibid.

24   Ibid.

25   This documentation was also used to challenge the legality of Law 3 on the grounds that its departure from the terms of the London Convention was based on the invalid assumption that Indians were insanitary. Petition to Sec. St. for Colonies, fn. 9 above.

26   Ibid.

27   Ibid.

28   C.7911, no.9, Sec. St. to High Comm. 22 Jun. 1895.

29   Milner became High Commissioner in March 1897.

30   In March 1899, Chamberlain went so far as to enquire rhetorically whether the British public would support a war in South Africa on the question of the Transvaal's oppression of Indians. Minute by Chamberlain, 15 Mar. 1899, quoted by B Pillay, *British Indians in the Transvaal* (London, 1976), p.71.

31   C.7911, no.14, Chamberlain to High Comm., 4 Sept. 1895.

32   CO 179/192/19929, Gov. to Sec. St., 19 Oct. 1895, encl. depositions before the R M, Durban, 28 Sept., 1 Oct., 4 Oct., 16 Oct., 1895; ibid., 21561, Gov. to Sec. St., 9 Nov. 1895, depositions before the R M, Durban, 24 Oct., 30 Oct., 31 Oct. 1895; ibid., 22878, Gov. to C O, 28 Nov. 1895, depositions before the R M, Durban, 13 Nov., 15 Nov. 1895; ibid., 193/2599, Gov. to Sec. St., 8 Jan. 1896, depositions before the R M, Durban, 27 Nov., 13 Dec. 1895.

33   See, for example, *Natal Advertiser*, 26 Sept., 8 Oct. 1895.

34   See, for example, *Natal Advertiser*, 25 Sept., 10 Oct. 1895, and CO 179/192/22881, Gov. to Sec. St., 30 Nov. 1895, encl. Gandhi to Col. Sec., n.d.

35   See above, Chapter 2.

36   *C W*, ii, pp.27-31, 'The Grievances of the British Indians in South
      Africa', 1896; ibid., pp.63-8, 'Notes on the Grievances . . . .', 22
      Sept. 1896; ibid., p.80, 'Address in Bombay', 26 Sept. 1896; ibid.,
      pp.97,112-3, 'Address in Madras', 26 Oct. 1896; ibid., p.134, 'Inter-
      view to the *Englishman*', 13 Nov. 1896.

37   *C W*, ii, p.29, 'The Grievances of the British Indians in South Africa',
      1896.

38   Ibid., p.314, Gandhi to British Agent, 18 May 1897.

39   Traders often tendered licence money to officials who refused to issue
      licences although accepting money. Cd.2239, no.1, encl. Bhownag-
      gree to Sec. St., 21 Dec. 1903, and CO 417/109/4726, Naoroji to Sec.
      St., 20 Mar. 1893, encl. Haji Abdullah Haji Dada, 16 Feb. 1893.

40   In this instance, the Agent's case was helped by the fact that some of
      the arrested traders actually had valid licences. Pillay, op. cit., p.65.

41   See also, for example, C.8423, no.117, High Comm. to Sec. St.,
      2 Mar. 1897; TABA, Smuts Collection: Public Papers (b), XCVI,
      no.20, Br. Agent to Smuts, 23 May 1899.

42   These events are summarised in TABA, Lt.Gov., 95/97/2, Lt.Gov.
      to Gov., 20 Jul. 1904.

43   The liquidated assets of the Transvaal merchants were estimated at
      'nearly £100 000' in 1895 (Petition to Sec. St., fn. 9 above). By 1899
      this figure had risen to 'about £375 000', *C W*, iii, p.87, Gandhi to
      Br. Agent, 21 Jul. 1899.

44   TABA, Lt.G. 95/97/2, Lt.Gov. to Gov., 20 Jul. 1904.

45   Some 1 400 appear to have remained in the Transvaal during the
      war. TABA, SNA, 10/1255/02, Supervisor Indian Imms. to SNA,
      13 Jun. 1901; ibid., 614/01, Supervisor Indian Imms. to S N A,
      2 Nov. 1901 and encl. Superintendent Indian Imms. to Supervisor
      Indian Imms., 26 Aug. 1901.

46   *C W*, iii, pp.111-12, 'Relief to Indian Refugees', 14 Oct. 1899; ibid.,
      p.113, 'Congress Resolution on Refugees', 16 Oct. 1899.

47   Ibid., pp.120-21, 'Gandhi to W Palmer', 13 Nov. 1899.

48   Ibid., pp.113-14, 'The Indian Offer', 19 Oct. 1899; ibid., p.129,
      'Indian Ambulance Corps', 13 Dec. 1899; ibid., pp.146-7, 'Indian
      Ambulance Corps', 18 Apr. 1900.

49   Ibid., p.110, 'The Second Report of the Natal Indian Congress', after
      11 Oct. 1899; pp.144-5, 'The Indian Hospital', 11 Apr. 1900.

50   Ibid., p.160, 'Notes', after 3 Sept. 1900.

51   Ibid., p.231, Gandhi to W S Caine, 26 Mar. 1902.

52   Ibid., p.162, 'Notes', after 3 Sept. 1900.

53   Early in 1901, Chamberlain announced that the new administration
      would adopt Boer legislation 'so far as possible' ibid., p.183, 'A

Circular Letter', 20 Apr. 1901. By that time it was apparent that the new regime was reluctant to permit the return of Indian refugees, and the anti-Asian laws of the former Republic were being enforced. Ibid., p.179, Gandhi to High Comm. tele., 25 Mar. 1901.

54   Ibid., pp.183-5, 'A Circular Letter', 20 Apr. 1901; ibid., p.189, 4 May 1901; ibid., p.191, 'Letter to East India Association', 18 May 1901.

55   Ibid., p.148, 'Letter to Leaders of Ambulance Corps', 20 Apr. 1900.

56   Ibid., pp.211-12, 'Appeal for Deputation to Viceroy', 19 Dec. 1901.

57   See fn. 54 above.

58   Gandhi, *Autobiography*, op. cit., p.167.

59   Ibid., (emphasis added).

60   C W, iii, p.214, 'Speech at Calcutta Congress', 27 Dec. 1901.

61   Ibid., pp.216-7, 'Speech at Calcutta Meeting', 19 Jan. 1902; ibid., pp.219-24, 'Speech at Calcutta Meeting', 27 Jan. 1902.

62   Ibid., pp.224-5, Gandhi to Gokhale, 30 Jan., 2 Feb. 1902; Gandhi to P B Desai, 26 Feb. 1902.

63   E Erikson, *Gandhi's Truth* (London, 1970), p.371.

64   C W, iii, p.227, Gandhi to Rustomji, 1 Mar. 1902.

65   Ibid., pp.229, 234, 238, 242, 260, Gandhi to Gokhale, 4 Mar., 27 Mar., 8 Apr., 1 May, 1 Aug. 1902.

66   Ibid., p.227, Gandhi to Rustomji, 1 Mar. 1902.

67   Ibid., p.225, Gandhi to P B Desai, 26 Feb, 1902; ibid., pp.255-6, Gandhi to Nazar and Khan, 3 Jun. 1902.

68   Ibid., p.260, Gandhi to Gokhale, 1 Aug. 1902.

69   Ibid., p.261, Gandhi to Devchand Parekh, 6 Aug. 1902.

70   Ibid., p.262, Gandhi to D B Shukla, 3 Nov. 1902.

71   Ibid., and p.263, Gandhi to D B Shukla, 8 Nov. 1902.

72   Ibid., p.264, Gandhi to Gokhale, 14 Nov. 1902.

73   'All the available energy must, for the present, be devoted to the question in [the Transvaal and Orange River Colony], and, if full justice is done there, Natal would soon have to fall in with them'. C W, iii, p.234, 'Notes on the Indian Position', 27 Mar. 1902. These Notes 'were prepared at the instance of the Congress', ibid., p.236, Gandhi to Khan and Nazar, 31 Mar. 1902. And see also, ibid., pp.245-6, 'Notes on the Indian Question', 6 May 1902.

74   CO 291/35/23977, Minute by Lambert, 13 Jul. 1901, on Bhownagree to Sec. St. 24 May 1901.

75   C W, iii, pp.183-6, 'A Circular Letter', 20 Apr. 1901 (sent to Sec. St. for Colonies, Gov. of Bombay and 'friends' in England); CO 291/35/23977, Bhownaggree to Sec. St., 24 May 1901, and minuting; ibid., 33/26758, Chair. Council of the East India Assoc.

to Sec. St., 29 Jul. 1901; ibid., 32/29575, IO to CO, 22 Aug. 1901.

76   TABA, Gov. 579/P.S. 261, Sec. St. to Gov., tele. no.1, 20 Mar. 1901.

77   S Marks and S Trapido, 'Lord Milner and the South African State', *History Workshop*, 8(1979), pp.50-73.

78   See, for example, TABA, Gov. 579/P.S., Klerksdorp Ch. of Commerce to Gov., 24 Oct. 1902; ibid., SNA, 10/1255/02, Memo for Col. Sec. by Assist. Col. Sec. and see also *Johannesburg Star* (weekly ed.) Oct. and Nov. 1902, and numerous letters of protest about Asians from vigilante associations, public meetings and chambers of commerce throughout the Transvaal, in TABA Lt.G., 96/97/2/2.

79   In Aug. 1904, commenting on a spate of petitions and public meetings protesting against the unrestricted issue of trading licences to Asians, Milner remarked that most of the white traders in the Transvaal were British and that 'it is a serious matter to alienate our only friends in the country districts besides running counter to the British sentiment in the whole Transvaal', TABA, CS, 1084/066/1904, Gov. to Sec St., tele.conf., 4 Aug. 1904.

80   TABA, SNA, 10/1255/02, Super. Ind. Imms. to SNA, 13 Jun. 1901; ibid., 2/46/01, Super. Ind. Imms. to Priv. Sec. to Legal Adviser to Transvaal Admin. 3 Jun. 1901.

81   CO 291/37/3362, Gov. to Sec. St., 3 Jan. 1902.

82   TABA, SNA, 2/15/01, minutes by Wybergh and Lagden on the jacket of the file, 1 Oct., 7 Oct. 1901.

83   Ibid., 2/46/01, Memo. for H.E. on Indian Question by Comm. Native Affairs, 2 Jan. 1902. And see memo. by Super. Indian Imms. in same file. He was given verbal instructions by the Commissioner to deal with despatch no.223, 16 Mar. 1901, from the C.O. The memo. for Milner was a reply to the despatch.

84   Ibid., Lt.G. 97/97/4, Memo. by Comm. of Native Affairs and Asiatics on Indian Question, 18 Mar. 1902.

85   Ibid., minute no. CM46/02, by Comm. of Mines, 21 Mar. 1902.

86   See Marks and Trapido, op. cit., pp.55, 72, for the 'increasingly pervasive ideology of social imperialism' whose assumptions fed these views.

87   TABA, SNA, 10/54/02, memo. by Comm. of Mines, Feb. 1902.

88   Memos. by R Solomon, W E Duncan, quoted in Pillay, op. cit., pp.93-4.

89   In September 1902, on the advice of the Colonial Office, Asian affairs were handed over to a separate department which functioned as a sub-department of the Colonial Sectretary's Office. CO 291/56/13483, Report by Transvaal Assist. Col. Sec., c.Feb. 1902.

90   TABA, Lt.G. 97/97/4, minute by SNA (some time after 3 Apr. 1902); ibid., SNA 10/1255/02, Clerk to Exec. Co. to SNA, encl. memo. by Milner, 24 Mar. 1902.

91   Milner's alternative formed point three of the resolution.

92   TABA, Gov. 579/P.S.261, Gov. to Sec. St., tele., 26 Mar. 1902. And see Marks and Trapido, op.cit., pp.69-71 for the rural reconstruction programme which dictated clause 5 of the Resolution.

93   See, for example, Lambert's awareness that while Milner was driven by the pressure of local opinion, the CO was equally subject to pressure in parliament and from the government of India. 24 Apr. 1902, minute on CO 291/35/13080, Gov. to Sec. St., tele, 3 Apr. 1902.

94   Ibid., minute by Just. 30 Apr. 1902.

95   TABA, Gov. 579/P.S.261, Sec. St. to Gov., tele., 6 Aug. 1902.

96   Ibid., Sec. St. to Gov., tele., 27 Apr. 1903.

97   Ibid., Gov. to Sec. St., tele., 20 Jun. 1902.

98   A year later Milner was still demanding a clear statement of policy from the CO. TABA, Lt.G. 95/97/2/1, Gov. to Sec. St., 1 Feb. 1904.

99   Transvaal Govt. Notice 356 of 1903.

100   TABA, Gov. 577/P.S.250, Gov. to Sec. St., tele., 12 May 1903.

101   Ibid., Gov. 577/P.S.250, Sec. St. to Gov., 4 Jan. 1904. The government of India also demanded that 'respectable' Indians — meaning all traders and shopkeepers — be exempt from all restrictions on the use of footpaths and public conveyances, the curfew and pass law.

102   CO 291/67/6147, Gov. to Sec. St., 1 Feb. 1904.

103   TABA, Gov. 577/P.S.250, Gov. to Sec. St., tele., 20 Jan. 1904.

104   Ibid., Lt.G. 95/97/2/1, Gov. to Sec. St., tele., 15 Apr. 1904. For hostile legislative council, see ibid., Gov. to Sec. St., 1 Feb. 1904. For hostile white public see ibid., Smuts Collection, Private Papers, no.89, draft protest against introduction of Asiatic labour signed by De La Rey, Smuts, Botha and others, 10 Feb. 1904. And see similar protests by chambers of commerce in ibid., Lt.G. 95/97/2/1, Col. Sec. to Lt. Gov. 1 Mar. 1904 and ibid., Gov. to Sec. St., 8 Feb. 1904.

105   TABA, Lt.G. 95/97/2, Gov. to Sec. St., 18 Apr. 1904 and encl. Lt. Gov. to Gov. 13 Apr. 1904.

106   CO 291/70/21419, Gov. to Sec. St., 16 June 1904.

107   Ibid., 16319, minute by Lambert, 16 May 1904.

108   Ibid., minute by Sec. St., 26 May 1907.

109   Ibid., 66/45154, Bhownaggree to Sec. St., 21 Dec. 1903, minute by Lambert, 28 Dec. 1903.

110   Ibid., 70/17255, Gov. to Sec. St., tele., 14 May 1904.

111   TABA, Lt.G. 95/97/2, Sec. St., to Gov., 20 Jul. 1904.

112   Ibid., Gov. to Lt. Gov., 21 Jan. 1904.

113   CO 291/72/28902, Gov. to Sec. St., tele., 16 Aug. 1904. The commission was expected to prove that the consequences of the Lyttelton policy would be the virtual elimination of white retail trade.

114   Ibid., see, for example, minute by Lambert, 17 Aug. 1904.

115   Ibid., 70/27534, Gov. to Sec. St., tele., 5 Aug. 1904. This telegram contained proposals which closely resembled the resolution passed by the Transvaal legislative council some ten days later on 16 August. Graham, pointing out in a minute on 8 August 1904 that he had the longest South African experience of anyone in the office, advised that the Indian question 'is the very last question on which H.M.G. should have a difference with [Milner] if it can possibly be avoided. We have the whole of South Africa against us. Briton, Boer and Foreigner'.

116   Ibid., 16319, minute by Just, 18 May 1904, before the C.O. had even tried to impose the Lyttelton policy on the Transvaal.

117   Ibid., 27534, minutes on Gov. to Sec. St., tele., 5 Aug. 1904.

118   Ibid., 72/30986, Sec. St. to Gov., tele., 12 Sept. 1904.

119   Ibid., 99/20630, Gov. to Sec. St., 21 May 1906.

120   Ibid., 84/26270, minute by Graham, 13 Mar. 1905, on Gov. to Sec. St., 25 July 1905.

121   See, for example, minute by Just, 25 May 1906, on CO 291/99/181128, Gov. to Sec. St., 21 May 1906: 'It is due to the I.O. and to the attitude taken up in answer to questions in Parliament (viz. that H.M.G. do what they can to safeguard the position of the Indian) that the policy of leaving the matter over should be deliberately adopted as the safest and best in the circumstances'. Graham agreed with him in a minute dated 26 May 1906.

122   Ibid., 20630, Gov. to Sec. St., 21 May 1906.

123   *Johannesburg Star* (weekly ed.), 2 Dec. 1905.

124   C W, v, pp.312-3, 'Indian Permits', 12 May 1906, ibid., pp.323-4, 'Johannesburg Letter', after 18 May 1906.

125   TABA, Lt.G. 97/97/3, confidential report on the 'Position of Asiatics in the Transvaal' by Curtis, Assist. Col. Sec., 1 May 1906.

126   Ibid., Gov. to Attorney Gen., 12 May 1906.

127   Ibid., confidential report on the 'Position of Asiatics in the Transvaal' by M Chamney, Protector and Registrar of Asiatics, 17 Apr. 1906.

128   CO 291/99/18128, minute by Just, 25 May 1906 on Gov. to Sec. St., tele., 21 May 1906.

129   Ibid., 20630, minutes by Lambert, 15 Jun. 1906, Graham, 21 Jun. 1906, and Ommaney 21 Jun. 1906 on Gov. to Sec. St. 21 May

1906.

130   CO 291/103/39670, minute by Churchill, 4 Nov. 1906, on petition from Chinese Assoc. and others.

131   Ibid., 105/41130, minute by Ommaney, 10 Nov. 1906, on Gov. to Sec. St., 7 Nov. 1906.

132   *C W*, iii, p.281, 'The Indian Question', 23 Feb. 1903.

133   Ibid., p.273, 'Address to Chamberlain', 7 Jan. 1903.

134   See fn. 89 above.

135   Although BIA was much later said to have been established by Gandhi in 1902 (TABA, B S, Correspondence File no.A40, BIA to Acting Sec. of Interior, 20 Jan. 1916) this is highly unlikely since he did not return to the Transvaal until early 1903. BIA first appears in the records in March 1903. (*C W,*, iii, p.284, 'Indian Position in New Colonies', 16 Mar. 1903). It seems to have nothing in common with the British Indian Association listed under fn.10 above, except name.

136   *C W*, iv, p.250, 'Memorial to Colonial Secretary', prior to 3 Sept. 1904.

137   Ibid., iii, pp.389-90, 'Hajee Habib', 1 Aug. 1903.

138   In November 1906, at the request of NIC, Gandhi represented the party during his visit to London where he informed the Secretary of State for the Colonies that he had continued to be their adviser after he moved to the Transvaal. CO 179/239/40587, Gandhi to Sec. St., 2 Nov. 1906.

139   In 1916, Ahmed Cachalia, one of the early members of BIA and chairman of the party at the time, claimed that Gandhi had been 'the constitution' of the party. TABA, CIA, IV/1/M39/24/G20/5, Imm. Officer, Transvaal, to Sec. for Interior, 13 Jan. 1916.

140   Ibid., B S Correspondence File no. A450, notes on deputation of Indians who met the Min. of the Interior on 28 Jan. 1916. (Ahmed Cachalia's description of the working and organisation of BIA since its inception is contained in these notes.)

141   See below, p.108-109.

142   *Indian Opinion*, 24 May 1904.

143   *C W*, iii, p.86, Gandhi to British Agent, 21 Jul. 1899.

144   Ibid., pp.179-80, 'Telegram Regarding Permits', 25 Mar. 1901.

145   For deputations, see *C W*, iii, pp.280-2, 'The Indian Question', 23 Feb. 1903; ibid., pp.301-8, 'The British Indian Association and Lord Milner', 11 Jun. 1903; ibid., iv, p.33, 'Notes', 9 Nov. 1903; *Johannesburg Star* (weekly ed.) 2 Dec. 1905; *C W*, v, pp.236-8, 'Disabilities of Transvaal Indians', 17 Mar. 1906; ibid., pp.409-10, 'Johannesburg Letter', 3 Sept. 1906. For petitions see *C W*, iii, pp.322-31, 'Petition to Transvaal Governor', 8 Jun. 1903; ibid.,

pp.331-2, 'Petition to [Transvaal legislative council]', 10 June 1903; ibid., iv, pp.73-5, 'Petition to the Transvaal Council', 8 Dec. 1903; ibid., pp.243-52, 'Memorial to Colonial Secretary', before 3 Sept. 1904. For mass meetings see *C W*, iii, p.297, 'Cable to *India*', 9 May 1903; ibid., iv, p.79, 'Cable to British Committee', 12 Dec. 1903; ibid., pp.298-9, 'Cable to Dadabhai Naoroji', 18 Nov. 1904.

146   *C W*, iv, p.83, 'British Indians in the Transvaal', 17 Dec. 1903.

147   TABA, Gov. 173/671, Gov. to Sec. St., 7 Aug. 1905, encl. Schedule of Asiatic Bazaars in the Transvaal.

148   *C W*, iii, pp.380-82, 'Notes', 25 Jul. 1903; ibid., pp.386-7, 'On Trial', 30 Jul. 1903; ibid., iv, p.97, 'Last Year's Stock-Taking', 7 Jan. 1904; ibid., pp.145-7, 'The Asiatic Bazaar Johannesburg', 17 Mar. 1904; ibid., pp.165-6, 'Letter to the *Rand Daily Mail*', 14 Apr. 1904; ibid., 'Camp Life', 23 Mar. 1904; ibid., vi,pp.370-71, 'The Malay Location', 23 Mar. 1907.

149   Ibid., v, pp.236-8, 'Disabilities of Transvaal Indians', 17 Mar. 1906.

150   Ibid., iii, pp.386-7, 'On Trial', 30 Jul. 1903; ibid., iv, pp.5-6, 'Johannesburg Indian Location', 8 Oct. 1903; ibid., pp.44-6, 'Notes', 16 Nov. 1903.

151   CO 291/37/3362, Gov. to Sec. St., 3 Jan. 1902; *C W*, iv, pp.288-90, Gandhi to High Commissioner's Sec., 31 Oct. 1904.

152   *C W*, vi, pp.370-71, 'The Malay Location', 23 Mar. 1907.

153   Ibid., iv, p.13, 'Johannesburg Location', 15 Oct. 1903; 'If the Indians residing in the Location were all of them workmen pure and simple, there might be something to be said in favour [of moving the Location]'.

154   Ibid., pp.170-71, 'Camp Life', 23 Mar. 1904.

155   Ibid., pp.242-3, 'Mr Lyttelton's Despatch', 27 Aug. 1904.

156   *C W*, iv, pp.152-3, 'Plague in Johannesburg', 24 Mar. 1904; ibid., pp.155-7, 'The Plague', 2 Apr. 1904.

157   TABA, Gov. 579/P.S.261, petition by BIA, addressed to the Gov. of the Transvaal, 8 Jun. 1903.

158   Ibid.

159   See, for example, *Johannesburg Star* (weekly ed.) 2 Dec. 1905; *C W*, xi, pp.86-7, 'Statement of the British Indian Deputation to General Smuts', after 20 May 1911.

160   *C W*, iv, pp.466-7, 'Japan and Russia', 10 June 1905; ibid., pp.475-7, 'Corruption during War Time', 24 Jun. 1905; ibid., v, pp.82-3, 'The Chinese and the Americans', 30 Sept. 1905; ibid., pp.131-2, 'Russia and India', 11 Nov. 1905; ibid., pp.413-4, 'Russia and India', 8 Sept. 1906; ibid., 'Brave Bengal', 28 Oct. 1905. And see also, ibid., iv, pp.112-13, 'Self-Sacrifice', 21 Jan. 1904; ibid., pp.115-7, 'Sacrifice — 1', 21 Jan. 1904; ibid., pp.121-2, 'Sacrifice

— 2', 28 Jan. 1904.

161 Selby Msimang, one of the founder members of the ANC, believes that the leadership level of the African political community would, in any case, have found Indian politics too radical to countenance an alliance. Interview, Pietermaritzburg, Sept. 1976. But see *C W*, v, pp.241-3, 'The Coloured People's Petition', 24 Mar. 1906, and ibid., pp.243-4, for Gandhi's explanation of why, despite a certain identity of interests, Coloureds and Indians should not ally. This suggests that the possibility of an alliance may have been raised either by some Coloureds or some Indians.

162 See, for example, *C W*, iv, pp.292-3, 'Coloured Passengers on the Transvaal Railways', 5 Nov. 1904 or ibid., p.362, 'The Plague', 25 Feb. 1905.

163 As Gandhi phrased it in 1903, 'We believe also that the white race in South Africa should be the predominating race'. Ibid., iii, p.453, 'The Labour Question in the Transvaal', 24 Sept. 1903.

164 He did this in the case of the Transvaal railways in Dec. 1903 to 'avoid friction'. Ibid., iv, p.94, 'Coloured Railway Travellers in the Transvaal', 31 Dec. 1903.

165 See fn. 161 above.

166 *C W*, iii, p.453, 'The Labour Question in the Transvaal', 24 Sept. 1903.

167 Ibid., iv, p.89, 'The Transvaal Chambers and British Indians', 24 Dec. 1903.

168 Ibid.

169 Ibid., p.303, 'A Plague Spot', 26 Nov. 1904.

170 Ibid., pp.130-31, Gandhi to Medical Officer of Health, Johannesburg, 15 Feb. 1904. Gandhi seems not to have objected, though, to the fact that 'the Kaffir races . . . [were] largely employed by . . . [the Transvaal Indian merchants] as their servants'. Ibid., vii, pp.260-62, BIA to J A Neser, M L A, 28 Sept. 1907.

171 Ibid., v, p.238, 'Disabilities of Transvaal Indians', 17 Mar. 1906.

172 Ibid., iii, p.367, 'The Labour Importation Association', 16 Jul. 1903.

173 Ibid., p.377, 'East Rand Vigilants', 23 Jul. 1903.

174 Ibid., p.360, 'The Labour Question in the Transvaal', 9 Jul. 1903.

175 Ibid., iii, p.377, 'East Rand Vigilants', 23 Jul. 1903.

176 CO 179/239/44678, SABIC to Sec. St., 4 Dec. 1906, encl. Statement Regarding British Indian Position in Natal, signed by Gandhi, 1 Dec. 1906.

177 *C W*, iv, p.315, 'Indentured Labour on the Coal Mines', 17 Dec. 1904.

178 *Indian Opinion*, 18 Nov. 1905.

179   *Indian Opinion* reports on indentured labourers were generally reprints from the *Natal Witness*.

180   *Indian Opinion*, 25 Nov. 1905.

181   C W, iv, 'Letter to the Rand Daily Mail', 23 Apr. 1904.

182   See, for example, ibid., vi, pp.45-6, 'Elizabeth Fry', 19 Aug. 1905; ibid., pp.111-12, 'The Nelson Centenary: A Lesson', 28 Oct. 1905; ibid., pp.116-18, 'How England Won', 28 Oct. 1905; ibid., pp.119-20, 'Sir Thomas Munro', 28 Oct. 1905; ibid., pp.137-9, 'Mountstuart Elphinstone', 18 Nov. 1905.

183   Ibid., p.45, 'Elizabeth Fry', 19 Aug. 1905.

184   Raghavan Iyer, *The Moral and Political Thought of Mahatma Gandhi* (OUP, 1973), pp. 133-4.

185   Ibid., pp.150-76. And see also, C W, viii, pp.60-62, 'Triumph of Truth', 8 Feb. 1908, for Gandhi's conviction that 'Truth is God, or God is nothing but Truth . . . . It is a divine law that he who serves that Truth — that God — will never suffer defeat'.

186   Iyer, op. cit., pp.133-4.

187   See, for example, C W, iv, pp.121-2, 'Sacrifice — 2', 28 Jan. 1904 or ibid., v, 'Russia and India', pp.413-4, 8 Sept. 1906.

188   Ibid., v, p.366, 'Should Indians Volunteer or Not', 30 Jun. 1906.

189   Gandhi, *Autobiography*, op. cit., pp.172-3.

190   C W, iv, pp.104-5, 'A New Year's Gift', 14 Jan. 1904.

191   TABA, Lt.G. 92/97/1/2, Gandhi to Gov. 16 Jan. 1904.

192   C W, iv, pp.112-3, 'Self-Sacrifice', 21 Jan. 1904; ibid., pp.115-7, 'Sacrifice — 1', 21 Jan. 1904; ibid., 'Sacrifice — 2', 28 Jan. 1904.

193   TABA, CS (conf.), 1083/032/04, Asst. Col. Sec. to Sec. to Law Dept., 29 Apr. 1904.

194   *Indian Opinion*, 1 Sept. 1906.

195   C W, vi, pp.4-6, 'Letter to *The Times*', 22 Oct. 1906.

196   Ibid., v, pp.313-4, 'Russia and India', 8 Sept. 1906.

197   C W, vi, p.383, 'Transvaal Asiatic Ordinance', 30 Mar. 1907; and see Chapter 4.

198   I am grateful to James Hunt for raising this interesting possibility.

199   *Indian Opinion*, 22 Sept. 1906.

200   C W, v, p.460, 'Haji Ojeer Ally', 6 Oct. 1906.

201   *Indian Opinion*, 28 Jul. 1906; TABA, B S Correspondence File No. A450[A] Hon. Joint Secs. British Indian League to Min. Interior, 22. Apr. 1917, encl. minute (unsigned), 23 May 1916.

202   *Indian Opinion*, 31 Aug. 1907.

203   C W, v, p.460, 'Haji Ojeer Ally', 6 Oct. 1906.

204   Ibid.

205   Ibid., p.446, 'Johannesburg Letter', 6 Oct. 1906.

206   Ibid., vi, p.216, 'Gandhi to H O Ally, 26 Oct. 1906.

207   *Indian Opinion*, 31 Aug. 1907.

208   See for example, *C W*, v, p.404-5, 'Abominable', 1 Sept. 1906; ibid., pp.411-12, 'Criminal', 8 Sept. 1906; ibid., p.417, 'Speech on the Black Act', 9 Sept. 1906; ibid., 418, 'Speech at Hamidiya Islamic Society', 22 Sept. 1906.

209   Modliar had been chairman of the Tamil British Indian Association in 1902. He resurfaces in the records as chairman of a reception committee for a visiting Hindu dignitary in mid-1905 at which time Gandhi seems to have first made contact with him. Naidoo, a political unknown in September 1906, went on to become the highly popular president of the Tamil Benefit Society, and one of Gandhi's most devoted followers. *Indian Opinion*, 4 Nov. 1905; and see below, particularly Chapter 4.

210   *C W*, v, p.413, 'Russia and India', 8 Sept. 1906.

9 *Braamfontein 'Coolie Location' during the plague*, 1904 (HWPC, *from* The Star, *weekly edition, 26 March 1904*)

10 *Burning of the Braamfontein Location*, 1904 (HWPC, *from* Graphic, *4 June 1904*)

11 *Disinfection measures in the Braamfontein Location, 1904 (HWPC, from* The Star, *weekly edition, 26 March 1904)*

12 *Street scene, Johannesburg, early 1890s (HWPC, from* Graphic, *17 March 1906)*

CHAPTER FOUR

Passive Resistance, 1907 — 1909

The passive resistance pledge of September 1906 was put to the test early in 1907 when the new administration in the Transvaal reintroduced Selborne's registration ordinance with only minor modifications. The form which passive resistance took was deliberate disobedience of the law in order to court jail sentences. The political goal of the movement was repeal, or revision, of certain pieces of legislation — first the Registration Act, later others. For Gandhi himself there was another more important aim which, in fact, determined his political goals. That was to follow his conscience and, moreover, teach others to follow theirs.

There were four major phases in this lengthy campaign which lasted until April 1914. For the moment we are concerned only with the first two. The opening phase lasted from April 1907 until January 1908, spanning the months between the official notification that the Transvaal Indians would go to jail rather than register under the terms of the ordinance, and a truce with the government. This truce — an attempted settlement — followed close on the first waves of arrests and was largely a response to the weaknesses in the movement which became apparent as soon as commitment to jail-going was put to the test.

The movement resumed in May 1908 when the settlement broke down. The government had given Gandhi the opportunity to introduce a new demand and also to broaden the territorial base of the movement. By seeking to replace the Natal-type educational test in the Immigration Restriction Act with a clause which excluded all future Indian immigrants *ipso facto*, the government permitted Gandhi to include as one of the goals of passive resistance theoretical equality in immigration, and also to recruit educated resisters from Natal for the movement in the Transvaal. During the last months of 1908 the renewed campaign reached a peak of intensity which was not matched at any time during the next five years. By early 1909 active support for the movement was all but lost. The inadequacy of its major goals either as an elite strategy, or as a vehicle of mass mobilization, had become fully apparent. Nor were Gandhi's repeated calls for the opening of a second front in Natal successful: directed at the merchants, they suffered from the same weakness as the goals of the Transvaal movement. A second deputation to London later in the year, on the eve of the union of the South African colonies, received far less official attention than the 1906 deputation had done. This added a note of finality to the end of the second phase of the campaign.

Certain aspects of the campaign require separate mention at this point. One of these was the decision to forge an alliance with the Chinese,[1] the only instance during his two decades in South Africa in which Gandhi's political horizons encompassed constituents outside the Indian community. The alliance, struck during the 1906 deputation to London when Gandhi helped draft the Transvaal Chinese Association's[2] petition of protest against Selborne's registration ordinance,[3] was reaffirmed in Johannesburg on 13 April 1907 during a meeting between Gandhi and the Chinese leaders.[4]

Hitherto the strategy of the Indian merchants — and, indeed, petty traders — in the Transvaal had demanded that a careful distinction be made between themselves and other Asians. In the past their claims on the government had been based in part on the rights which they believed should accrue to them as British subjects.[5] But obviously alliance with the Chinese made good strategic sense. The laws which the Indians resisted were framed for the Transvaal Asians as a whole. At the ideological level the alliance was made possible by the shift in Gandhi's thinking which has already been discussed: the move away from claiming rights in terms of specific attributes and towards the belief that human dignity demands the preservation of certain rights which are fundamental to man *qua* man.

The alliance did not entail either integration of the Chinese and Indian political communities, or subordination of the Chinese to Indian leadership. The Chinese maintained and worked within the framework of their own political organization and leadership. Occasionally Indian leaders spoke at Chinese meetings, and vice versa. Joint decisions were made by Indian and Chinese leaders on some matters which were fundamental to the course of the movement; funding remained separate. The Chinese part in the struggle mirrored the course of the Indian campaign in that an apparent widespread commitment to the movement in 1907 soon dissipated once jail sentences were handed down. The Chinese resisters suffered an additional source of weakness when their party split late in 1908 over the question of continuing support for passive resistance. The opponents of resistance retained control of the party organization and funds.[6] Nevertheless a handful of Chinese continued to support passive resistance as firmly as Gandhi's most devoted followers. At no time, however, did the success of the movement, as conceived by Gandhi, rest on the Chinese alliance. The Chinese role in the struggle can, in fact, be viewed as a parallel movement. As such it need play no major part in a discussion of Indian passive resistance in the Transvaal.

Passive resistance was at all times accompanied by the more usual methods of attempting to bring pressure to bear on the Transvaal government. As in the past, the foci of such conventional protests were the imperial, Indian, and Transvaal governments. At first these protests were intended to serve as auxiliaries to passive resistance. Further development of Gandhi's moral and political thought elevated passive resistance above conventional modes of protest which he then viewed as ancillary tactics. Although these additional means of protest were seldom critical to the development of the movement, it is as well to outline them briefly here since they cannot be ignored altogether in the detailed history of the campaign which follows.

The South African British Indian Committee (SABIC) was established in London during the 1906 deputation's visit. The moving spirit behind the creation of this committee of notables, which included numbers of distinguished former Anglo-Indians, was Sir Mancherjee Bhownaggree.[7] SABIC bore a strong resemblance to the British Committee of the INC in composition, goals and tactics. Its secretary and most active member between 1906 and 1911 was Louis Walter Ritch. Jewish by birth and a theosophist by conviction, Ritch was one of Gandhi's closest political lieutenants after 1903 and one of his most devoted followers. He gave up a business in the Transvaal to become an articled clerk in Gandhi's Johannesburg law office only months after they met in 1903.[8] In 1905 he and his wife left for London where he began full-time legal studies. He was paid little as SABIC's secretary.[9] Despite this, and his wife's prolonged and serious illness[10], he remained committed to the South African Indian cause.

SABIC inundated the Colonial Office with memoranda and petitions on the course of the movement.[11] They were also responsible for keeping the question before the British parliament and in the press. Once the Transvaal had become self-governing, however, Colonial Office responsibility was significantly reduced. They were able, as they had anticipated earlier, to cite 'the general will of the Colony clearly expressed by its first elected representatives'[12] in assenting to the new registration ordinance and, indeed, in response to most criticism of Transvaal government policy.[13] With the Colonial Office a relatively minor party to negotiations, SABIC was thus of limited use.

As early as 1906 Gandhi suggested the establishment of an Indian equivalent of SABIC. But, again, his way seems to have been blocked by Pherozeshah Mehta.[14] In any event, the beginning of passive resistance in the Transvaal coincided with the confrontation of the 'extremists' and 'moderates' in the INC which rocked the Indian political elite and resulted in a split in the party at Surat in December 1907. Large-scale Indian support for the movement in the Transvaal came only after 1909 when Henry Solomon Leon Polak, Gandhi's closest political lieutenant, had undertaken a lengthy propaganda and fund-raising campaign in India.[15]

Like Ritch, Polak was a theosophist born of a Jewish family in England. Educated in Britain and Switzerland, he too 'left what might be termed a lucrative appointment [in the Transvaal], with promise of further pecuniary advancement' in order to work with Gandhi.[16] He spent two years living and working on the commune at Phoenix. In 1906 he also took articles with Gandhi, becoming at the same time assistant honorary secretary of BIA. In 1908 he was admitted as an attorney of the Supreme Court of the Transvaal. His law practice consisted almost entirely of defending passive resisters in court, free of charge. His expenses were covered by the party.[17] His visit to India in 1909 was the beginning of half a decade of travel on behalf of the South African Indians; and, again like Ritch, this commitment cost him dearly. His wife and two small children did not always accompany him on his travels. Moreover, his wife was reluctant to accept the stringent living conditions which were becoming increasingly the lot of a devoted Gandhi-ite.[18]

The success of Polak's first mission to India in 1909-10 was important for Gandhi's political future in two ways. The Transvaal movement received a large infusion of funds from India without which it is doubtful that it could have continued, even in the abbreviated form which it had assumed by 1910. Also, with an Indian investment in the movement Gandhi's name became increasnigly a household word among the Indian political elite — in 1911 he was 'seriously discussed' for the role of president of the INC.[19] Indian interest in the movement therefore helped it continue and, as it continued, Gandhi (and with him, passive resistance) became a far greater object of interest to the Indian political elite than he had been as a visiting South African barrister in the mid-1890s and again at the turn of the century. By the time he returned to India in 1914 he had thus acquired both the expertise and the stature lacking when he first attempted to penetrate nationalist politics in 1902.

Leaving aside the financial question, however, Indian support was unimportant in terms of immediate influence on the course of the movement. There was only one real lever which the Indian political elite could use to put pressure on the Transvaal. That was to demand that the government of India cite the mistreatment of South African Indians as a case for ending indentured immigration to Natal, where plantation owners in particular still relied heavily on a cheap Indian labour force. But as early as January 1908 Jan Smuts, in his capacity as Transvaal Colonial Secretary, had made it clear that the white Transvalers themselves wanted an end to the indentured immigration which brought most of the Asians to South Africa.[20] There was thus only one occasion on which the labour stoppage question could have discomfited the Transvaal. That was during the negotiations for the unification of the South African colonies in mid-1909 when the Natal government feared that the question could prejudice acceptance of their referendum on the draft Act of Union.[21] But the Colonial Office declared the limit on the government of India's power over the labour flow at this point. The Secretary of State prohibited the Indian government from interfering at least until the far more important question of South African union had been settled.[22] Indeed, when the government of India finally did give notice in April 1911 that indentured immigration to Natal would be prohibited as of 1 July, the timing and wording of their notification was carefully worked out to give the appearance that it was they and not Smuts (by then Minister of the Interior of the Union of South Africa) who was depriving the Natal planters of their major source of cheap labour.[23] Far from being used to put pressure on the Transvaal, the indentured labour question was thus finally settled to suit their needs.

In terms of immediate influence on the movement, the passive resisters' most important auxiliary activity was negotiation with the Transvaal government. Both Gandhi and Smuts, who were the principal negotiators for each side, were masters in the art of ambiguity. The practice of this art was assisted by the fact that most of their negotiations were carried on through intermediaries — a committee of Transvaal whites sympathetic to both parties and bent on achieving conciliation between the two.[24] Much of what was proposed by Gandhi and Smuts consisted of no more than subtly worded attempts to undermine the other's position, a device which seldom worked but which allowed each to play for time when he needed to. The bulk of their negotiations can therefore be dealt with briefly. They were, however, sometimes critical to the development of the movement, and they will be considered a little more fully as these occasions arise.

Finally, the Transvaal government's policy should be mentioned here. Smuts clearly wished to break the movement with the minimum possible concessions on his side. The actions of his government will therefore also be considered only where they are critical to understanding the course of the movement.

April 1907 - January 1908

On 21 March 1907 the first Transvaal parliament under responsible government was formally opened. By 23 March a new registration bill (Act 2 of 1907) had passed the third reading in the Transvaal legislative assembly.[25] Leaders of the British Indian Association and the Hamidia Islamic Society met on 24 and 25 March to discuss the bill. A mass meeting was called for 29 March.[26]

During the brief time span between the introduction of the bill on 23 March and its implementation on 1 July 1907, the full range of auxiliary tactics was exhausted by the movement in an attempt to prevent it passing into law. Resolutions condemning the bill were submitted to the Colonial Office by the British Indian Association, the Natal Congress and SABIC. A deputation waited on Smuts and an unsuccessful attempt was made to see Louis Botha, Prime Minister of the Transvaal. Interviews with Gandhi appeared in the Transvaal press. *Indian Opinion* carried numerous editorials explaining Indian objections to the bill.[27]

The major thrust of this activity was to gain acceptance for an Indian proposal that voluntary registration should be offered by the community. This compromise was intended to comply with the letter of the proposed law while destroying its spirit by eliminating the principle of legislation which discriminated against Indians *eo nomine*.[28] At the same time, it was made clear to the government that implementation of the law would be met with passive resistance.[29] The compromise was rejected by the Transvaal government; royal assent for the bill was received on 11 May,[30] and a Permit Office was opened in Pretoria on 1 July to process applications for registration certificates.[31]

The 'Permit Office' toured the colony between 1 July and 31 October. Initially a set period was fixed for receiving applications in each of the centres visited by the office — a full month in major urban centres such as Pretoria, a few days, or a week, in smaller rural centres. As the final date for registration passed in each centre with few or no applicants, the government extended its initial deadlines and allowed anyone from any centre to register before 31 October. On 4 October the government issued a notice in the Gazette stating that failure to comply with the law would be a punishable offence as of 1 December and that trading licences for the forthcoming year would not be issued to anyone who failed to produce a registration certificate.[32] This information was issued to prominent figures in every Indian community, reminding them that the final date by which application for registration certificates had to be made was 31 October.[33] Towards the end of the month, the deadline was extended to 30 November.[34]

Despite the government's compromises on deadlines, only 545 applications out of a possible 7 000 or so had been received by the end of November.[35] Nevertheless rumours of imminent capitulation swept the community as the date for testing the resolve of the jail-going pledge approached.[36] The first wave of arrests took place on 28 December 1907. The visible leadership level of the movement — some two dozen men, mostly pickets — was rounded up, along with a handful of Indians who had taken no active part in the campaign.[37] The arrests synchronized with royal assent to the Immigration Registration Bill which had been introduced in late June.[38] Under the terms of this Act, non-registered Indians were prohibited immigrants, subject to deportation. The first batch of resisters was therefore convicted under the Immigration Act rather than Act 2. They were given 48 hours to leave the colony, retried between 10 and 14 January for failure to leave, and sentenced to two months' imprisonment.[39]

By the end of January some 2 000 Asians — mostly Indian — had been jailed under the terms of Act 2, the Immigration Restriction Act or the licensing laws.[40] Amid widespread rumours that opposition to the Act was about to collapse, Gandhi, Thambi Naidoo (who was already becoming known as one of the strongest supporters of the movement), and Leung Quinn, chairman of the Chinese Association, concluded a compromise with Smuts.

The essence of the compromise was a plan for voluntary registration, contained in a document drafted by Smuts, amended by Gandhi, and signed by Gandhi, Naidoo and Leung Quinn. The document pointed out that since the official deadline for registration under Act 2 had passed, registering now would put an entirely different construction on the meaning of the Act and, indeed, would make it redundant. Gandhi later claimed that although the document did not guarantee repeal of the Act, Smuts had delivered a verbal promise that it would be repealed if voluntary registration took place successfully.[41] On this basis Gandhi considered the January 1907 compromise an honourable conclusion to the passive resistance campaign.

As soon as the necessity to redeem the 1906 resistance pledge had been put to the test, the weaknesses in the fledgling movement began to show. The success of the campaign was predicated on the assumption that not one single Indian would take out a registration certificate under Act 2.[42] The decision to defy the Act was conveyed to the government in mid-April. The Permit Office opened on 1 July. In two and a half months, some 7 000 Indians had to be mobilized for political action. BIA had made prior political contact — and fleetingly at that — with less than half of this number. There was insufficient organization, insufficient funds, and insufficient committment to goals both at the leadership level and among the rank and file to begin any mass movement in the Transvaal, let alone one as ambitious as this. Furthermore, Gandhi, whose vision the movement was meant to fulfill, by no means enjoyed an unchallenged position of leadership among the elite. Before analyzing the first phase of the campaign whose events have just been outlined, it is thus necessary to dissociate oneself finally from the idea prevalent in the literature that the success of Gandhian passive resistance in South Africa was guaranteed from the moment of its inception simply by virtue of Gandhi's involvement in it. It was not. The value of this perspective, from the point of view of Gandhian scholarship, is that it is only in the learning process involved in overcoming the weaknesses in the movement — many of which he created himself — that one can find the dynamics which changed Gandhi from a hired representative to a 'leader' responsive to the needs of his constituents, and which simultaneously fed the clarification of his moral doctrine. In the subsequent analyses of the various stages of the campaign it will become clear that the political and, indeed, the moral responses which were necessary in order to ensure its success were formulated only after Gandhi's attempts to impose his idiosyncratic ethical preoccupations on the movement had driven it close to the brink of total failure.

The ideological underpinnings of the passive resistance movement during its first stage were much less coherent than the pure doctrine of *satyagraha* which later emerged. In part, this reflects a certain ambiguity in Gandhi's own ideas. His moral teachings, as expressed in *Indian Opinion* and his letters to family and friends, had not yet achieved the clarity and purposefulness that is familiar from his later years as a nationalist leader in India. This ambiguity has already been discussed. In addition, ideological inconsistency seems to have derived simply from Gandhi's inexperience. In 1907 he was faced for the first time with the task of formulating a message capable of successfully communicating a call to action to a wide and varied audience. They were drawn from levels of society previously untouched, or little touched, by the politics of the elite on whom Gandhi depended to form the vanguard of the passive resistance movement. More importantly, the very idea of a mass movement was new and unpremeditated. In February 1908, Gandhi claimed that the movement had been started by the merchants, for the merchants.[43] An *Indian Opinion* editorial of January 1910 leaves no doubt that mass support for the movement came unexpectedly.[44] It is not clear, however, whether it was the successful mass meeting held in September 1906, or the interest shown by the popular classes in early 1907, which resulted in the decision to broaden the social base of the movement. In any event, in mid-1907 Gandhi was a politician of the elite, groping inexpertly for the means to become the leader of a mass movement.

The major theme in the merchants' own ideology, which had been used to mobilize them for the September 1906 mass meeting at which the passive resistance pledge was taken, continued to play a dominant role in the ideology of the movement during the first stage. On numerous occasions resistance to the Registration Act was directly linked to the protection of merchant interests. The rationale behind this continued to be the belief that if the principle of discriminatory legislation were once admitted, this would ultimately be used to attack vested commercial interests.[45]

The importance accorded to these interests in the ideology of the movement reflected Gandhi's desire to mobilize the elite. The clearest statement that he himself no longer subscribed to the same set of beliefs as the merchants came in a letter written to his elder brother Lakshmidas Gandhi in April 1907. 'You seek peace and happiness through money', he wrote, 'I don't depend on money for my peace; and for the moment at any rate my mind is quite calm and able to withstand any amount of suffering'. Gandhi reminded his brother that he had given all of the money which he had saved in Natal to his family members in India, and informed him that any savings which he had accumulated since then had been spent on public work. 'The change in my ideas', he wrote, 'is due to my pursuit of truth'.[46]

It is worth noting, however, that in this period of transition and clarification, Gandhi's indictment of the pursuit of material success had not yet transcended the case of the particular to become the general critique of western civilization that it was later. His own lifestyle had been considerably simplified.[47] He maintained his interest in Phoenix, writing frequent letters of advice to residents on how to achieve greater self-sufficiency.[48] The Transvaal merchants with whom he came in daily contact, and whose devotion to profit-making he knew only too well, were the major counterpoint to his new ideas.[49] In May 1907, however, far from condemning western competitiveness and materialistic notions of progress, he still thought that India needed the British. He believed that India needed further exposure to western education and further contact with the west in order to encourage the growth of 'public spirit',[50] all of which is a curious, roundabout, but definite early statement of Gandhi's dual notion of *swaraj*; India needed the British in order to become a nation; in the process of becoming a nation, Indians would learn to become spiritually free.[51]

A second and equally dominant theme in the ideology of the movement was the concept of honour, the belief that resistance to the Registration Act was necessary to uphold not only individual honour but also the honour of India. This was articulated in a number of ways, sometimes through specific references to honour, often in the claim that Act 2 was an insult to manhood, or in the simple but emotive assertions that the eyes of India were on the Transvaal Indians, to submit would be an act of cowardice, the man with a registration certificate would be a slave, a beast, a Judas.[52]

The notion of honour, inseparable from the commitment to moral autonomy, had already found a central place in Gandhi's philosophy as we have seen.[53] It is therefore natural to find it being put to political use in the ideology of the movement. Here it played the potentially important role, not unusual in social movements like this, of allowing the merchants to join the movement with the intention of protecting their own interests, while enjoying the social prestige of appearing to be committed for a higher purpose. Also, the notion of honour with its universal applicability lacked the in-built limitations of the economic aspects of the ideology.

Gandhi had great difficulty in fitting this concept to the needs of the movement however. He could not produce a convincing explanation why submission to the Registration Act should be considered dishonourable. That depended on a convincing explanation of why a man should follow his conscience, a decision which Gandhi had made for himself, but whose dynamics he was still unable to articulate.[54] Editorials in both the Gujerati and English sections of *Indian Opinion* on 3 November 1907 entitled, respectively, 'Why Do We Oppose Law?'[55] and 'Why We Oppose', listed the by then familiar assertions that submission would reduce men to slaves and beasts, but admitted that 'If we were asked to point out in which section of the law all this occurs, it would be difficult to reply'.

Inability to convey his own rebellious conviction that honour demanded resistance to the Act led Gandhi onto the limited ground of claiming that the dishonour of submission would lie in breaking the pledge taken at the September 1906 mass meeting.[56] The pledge had been taken by some 3 000 people, and he was now trying to mobilize some 7 000. The pledge served another purpose, however, as an element in the third and final dominant theme of the ideology: religion.

The religious aspects of Gandhi's own philosophy need no emphasis. Religion existed as an element in the ideology of the movement from its inception. It became predominant around August 1907. Merchant support was already in question by then,[57] and the movement had lost H O Ally, organizer of the September 1906 mass meeting. Ally was elderly and in poor health. Among the first to realize that he could not, or would not, redeem his passive resistance pledge, he left the colony on 24 August 1907 rather than take out a registration certificate.[58]

Ally's departure coincided with the emergence of several religious figures as key supporters of the movement. He was replaced as chairman of the Hamidia Islamic Society by Imam Abdul Kadir Bawazeer,[59] a Konkani who had been in the Transvaal for over a decade and who was a fairly substantial businessman like his fellow officers in the Society.[60] The Imam was supported by Moulvi Syed Ahmed Mukhtiar, a newcomer to the colony who was attached to both the Society and the Surti Mosque in Johannesburg.[61] Their Hindu counterpart was Ramsunder Pundit, also a newcomer to the colony, who quickly rose to prominence in the Johannesburg Hindu community as the moving force behind the erection of a temple and the creation of the *Sanatan Veda Dharma Sabha*.[62] By September prayers for the movement were being offered in the Transvaal mosques; and the Moulvi — who taught at the newly formed Hamidia Madressa, preached at the Surti Mosque and to congregations of the Hamidia Society,[63] as well as being a regular speaker at the society's weekly meetings — was presenting his followers with a choice of 'the law or the faith'.[64] Ramsunder Pundit was doing much the same for the Johannesburg Hindus.[65] Thus Gandhi had not only the sacred pledge to fall back on, but also the fiery speeches of scripture-quoting[66] religious functionaries. Increasingly after September 1907, Gandhi invoked the name Khuda-Ishvar on behalf of the movement.

Ideological expositions were usually simplistic, even pedagogic in manner, often listing in point form the disadvantages which would accrue to Indians who submitted to the Registration Act. An editorial in the Gujerati section of *Indian Opinion* entitled 'Point of Honour' illustrates this well:

Let us for the moment consider what will be gained by the Indian who submits to Law. Firstly, he will have forsaken his God. Secondly, his honour will have been lost. Thirdly, he will have incurred the curse of all India. Fourthly, there will come a time when he will have to go to a location and at last live a dog's life in the Transvaal. Is there an Indian who will gain such 'benefits' by submitting to the law? Now let us take the case of the Indian who does not submit. This Indian will have lived in fear of God and kept his covenant with Him. He will be rewarded as a hero and acclaimed by all India. The gaol he enters will be considered a palace. The utmost that he will suffer is that he may lose all his possessions and may have ultimately to leave the Transvaal. If he has to leave the Transvaal, and go elsewhere, is not God there also? The Lord who has given us teeth is ever present to give us something to chew. He needs no flattery. He whispers constantly into our ears, 'Trust in Me alone'. If

we do not listen to his sweet words, having ears we are deaf. If we do
not see Him sitting by our side, having eyes we are blind.[68]

This editorial is particularly revealing of the inability of the movement's ideology to resolve the contradictions in the strategy of
resistance for the merchants and the petty traders. On one hand
Gandhi urged resistance in order to avoid segregation in locations —
the economic rationale which had been the driving force behind all
previous merchant and petty trader political activity. On the other
hand, he admitted the very real possibility of total economic loss as a
result of the campaign to prevent limited economic loss. This was a
calculation which the commercial classes had already made for
themselves and which many of them were beginning to find unsatisfactory.[69] What the ideology offered them in exchange for commercial
ruin was a confused conception of honour, and the notion of avoiding
the wrath of God; the same rallying cry which Gandhi had used
unsuccessfully between March 1904 and September 1906. For the
mass of the people, the equation was the same: certain hardship and
financial loss as a result of jail-going, in order to avoid spiritual loss.
Again, this was a calculation which proved unsatisfactory to the
majority.

What the movement lacked in terms of an effective ideology was by
no means compensated for by efficient organization. Gandhi chose to
continue working within the already existing structures of merchant
politics. This assured him of access to the most wealthy and influential
members of the community on whom he counted to carry the
campaign. No attempt appears to have been made to build on the
success of the September 1906 mass meeting. Recruitment for the
movement therefore started from scratch in mid-1907, within the
framework of the loosely structured British Indian Association and
Hamidia Islamic Society. Although one or two references to local
committee meetings in the smaller urban centres appear in the
records,[70] the major vehicles of organization remained the central
meetings of BIA and the Hamidia Society, and *Indian Opinion*
editorials.

The Hamidia Society, under whose auspices the successful
September mass meeting had been organized, continued to be the most
effective institution for mobilizing the merchants. Its weekly Sunday
meetings were attended by the leadership level of BIA (many of whom
were officials in the Society as well), Tamil leaders, *Sanatan Veda
Dharma Sabha* leaders and occasionally Chinese leaders. The

meetings were thrown open to the public and usually attracted an audience of several hundreds. These gatherings served as the main distribution point for personal communications from the leadership. Here, the movement's ideology was expounded, tactics were reviewed and the commitment to resistance was constantly reaffirmed.[71] Although the meetings reached a limited audience, it was the audience which Gandhi intended to be the vanguard of the movement.

Gandhi identified the Hamidia Society as the backbone of resistance during its early stage,[72] but BIA remained the parent organization. As a secular institution, it played a role which the Hamidia Islamic Society could not, offering official leadership positions to non-Muslims. Gandhi himself had no official standing in the Society, nor had Tamil leaders such as A A Pillay, Thambi Naidoo, Ramsunder Pundit and Peter Moonlight Modliar who were, however, members of the executive committee of BIA in 1907.[73] In addition, BIA controlled the funds of the movement through its offshoot, the Anti-Asiatic Law Fund Committee, which had been established in September 1906. Little information is available on this committee which was disbanded by resolution of the executive committee of BIA in October 1907, when sole control over the movement's funds was simultaneously vested in Gandhi.[74] This, and the fact that funds were raised specifically for the movement rather than as subscriptions to the political and other associations, gave Gandhi what on the surface appears to be a considerable degree of power and independence. However, that power was circumscribed by the problems experienced in fund-raising, as well as by the methods employed, which will be discussed shortly.

BIA continued to operate on the same principles as it had since its inception — no formal branches were established, no permanent body of members created, no regular meetings held. The party continued to wait on events, responding to the significant junctures created by government policy with 'mass' meetings.[75] In 1907, these meetings, held in Johannesburg and Pretoria, were attended by between one and three thousand Indians and Chinese. The meetings were fed by the Hamidia Society, the Tamil Benefit Society, the *Sanatan Veda Dharma Sabha*, as well as BIA itself and, to a lesser extent, the Chinese Political Association. The success of the meetings therefore depended on the commitment of the leaders of these organization to passive resistance. After H O Ally had been replaced at the head of the Hamidia Society by Imam Abdul Kadir, that commitment was assured, at least for a time.

The mechanisms of recruitment for the meetings and, indeed, for recruiting and maintaining support for the resistance effort in general, do not seem to have differed from those of the September mass meeting. There is further evidence in 1907 of vertical links with the community being used as mediums of mobilization: creditors commanding the actions of debtors,[76] employers those of employees,[77] and big merchants those of petty traders.[78]

In addition, *Indian Opinion* consistently addressed appeals for support, and condemnation for lack of support, to specific sub-groups within the community. 'Heroes' and 'blacklegs' were listed not only by name, but also by religious, caste, or regional affiliation — a Memon hero or blackleg for instance; or a Kanmia, a Konkani, a Parsi, a Pathan, a Tamil.[79] These specific appeals served to make the movement more personal to individual members of a community which was far from being cohesive, and which was new to participatory politics. The extent to which horizontal linkages may also have served as mechanisms of recruitment by means of intra-group pressure is unclear, though. One knows, for example, that Alibhai Akuji, a prominent Kanmia, was credited with bringing the Kanmias into the movement,[80] and that Konkani support followed a special meeting of 200 Konkanis after the news had broken that some members of that sub-group had taken out registration certificates.[81] There is no information available on what — if anything — it meant to be identified as a member of such a sub-group, what social or economic advantages might have accrued, and thus what type of peer group pressure might have been brought to bear. There is abundant evidence, however, that social and even economic boycott was practised against 'blacklegs' in 1907,[82] and that resistance therefore made good sense (so much so that some former blacklegs publicly recanted),[83] no matter what the basis of one's social allegiances.

The timing and location of the mass meetings reflected a defensive strategy, a response to government pressure rather than an attempt to seize the political initiative. The meetings served to boost morale at moments when government policy was likely to weigh most heavily.

In Pretoria, where support for passive resistance was thought to be weak and where, in fact, most of the registrations did take place, meetings were held on 30 June and 31 July, the first and last days of the period originally allotted for receiving applications. These meetings reflect many of the deficiencies of the fledgling movement. The first, although written up in the Gujerati columns of *Indian Opinion* under the headline 'Huge Mass Meeting'[84] enjoyed a meagre turnout of around 500, of an Indian population of 1 500.[85] A tremendous organizational effort was therefore made to ensure the success of the second meeting. It was announced by the distribution of notices and in *Indian Opinion*.[86] As in September 1906 a work stoppage was decreed for the self-employed — traders, hawkers and news vendors.[87] Recent meetings of the Durban and Cape Town elites resulted in dozens of telegrams of support from Natal and the Cape Colony.[88] These were read out at the meeting. Some 600 supporters were brought in from Johannesburg, most of them on a train chartered by BIA. Their arrival, hours before the meeting was due to start, was marked by a formal procession from the station to the meeting ground, banner-bearers in front and a bicycle escort alongside.[89] The turnout at the meeting was estimated at 2 000 — virtually complete support from Pretoria. The local press noted the festive air of the proceedings and an apparently firm commitment to resistance.[90] The enthusiasm of the September 1906 mass meeting had thus been recaptured. But the effort which made this possible had resulted from the creation of an ad hoc committee under Haji Habib's direction only days before the meeting.[91] It is typical of one of the movement's most serious problems that no attempt was made to crystallize the enthusiasm generated at the meeting using the ad hoc committee as the basis for a permanent organizational infra-structure in Pretoria. It is not surprising that one-third of the city's Indian population took out registration certificates.[92]

In Johannesburg the work of rousing and maintaining support during the registration period in October was left mainly to the Hamidia Society where Imam Abdul Kadir and Moulvi Syed Mukhtiar continued to preside over weekly meetings which were described as packed by high-spirited audiences.[93] On 8 November Ramsunder Pundit was arrested for being in the colony without a residence permit. The Asiatic Department had refused to renew the temporary permit which he held as a religious functionary on the grounds that his political activity rendered him undesirable.[94] Both as a priest and as a well-known leader Ramsunder was perfectly suited to become the movement's first martyr. His arrest provided an opportunity to prevent a lull in the movement's momentum during November, which had been left free to allow the administration to process applications for registration. Gandhi responded by making Ramsunder's arrest, trial and sentencing the subject of numerous special meetings, petitions and work stoppages.[95]

On 1 December, the day on which prosecutions under the terms of Act 2 were expected to begin, a well organized mass meeting was held in Johannesburg. Over 60 delegates from other centres attended, and the crowd was estimated at 3 000 — the largest since the September 1906 meeting. The platform speakers suggest that the Hamidia Society was again the driving force behind this achievement.[96] Throughout December, as tension mounted and no further arrests were made, the Society continued to hold crowded weekly meetings. On 1 January, the day on which refusal of trading licences to non-registered Indians was expected to begin, another mass meeting was held in Johannesburg. The turnout was around 2 500 and there were a number of delegates from other centres.[97] On 27 December Gandhi had been informed by the Acting Commissioner of Police that orders had been given to arrest him and some two dozen others, most of whom had taken a prominent part in the movement.[98] Between then and mid-January, when they were sentenced to two months imprisonment, their arrests were made the subject of numbers of special meetings in both Pretoria and Johannesburg.[99]

Indian Opinion, like the Hamidia Society's meetings and the BIA mass meetings, was consciously[100] used by Gandhi to disseminate information about the movement, its ideology, goals and tactics, and to boost morale in moments of potential crisis. Tactics were usually reviewed in the paper in the form of answers to questions which had been raised by the public: what should people do when the Permit Office opened; who might be arrested, where and when; what should one do in case of arrest; what would happen to wives and children; how could a business continue to run if all employees were jailed; what if every adult Indian were jailed simultaneously; what if Gandhi were jailed first; where would the movement find the money to support dependants of jail-goers; how were people to put up with losses incurred in the struggle?[101] Gandhi provided answers for all these queries. But it is the questions themselves which are important. Published in the Gujerati columns of the paper, they illustrate the other major weaknesses of the movement. The questions came from the merchants whom Gandhi expected to be the vanguard of the struggle. They reveal insufficient or inadequate communication between the leaders and the rank and file; a gap, which was to become critical, between the merchants' conception of the movement's goals and Gandhi's conception; ignorance of tactics; lack of commitment to the movement's ideology; and, most of all, as Gandhi himself pointed out, they reveal fear — fear of going to jail, fear of pecuniary loss.

The paper's function as a morale booster was taken seriously. Imaginative, emotive epithets were applied to the opposition. The Permit Office became the Plague Office,[102] the permit officer a tout.[103] The Registration Act was likened to the 'god of destruction [who] goes on devouring new victims. The monster is fond of Indian blood'.[104] Supporters of the movement were invited to send their names to the paper which published them at regular intervals.[105] When a handful of Pretoria merchants approached the government with their own compromise solution for registration in July 1907, the Hamidia Society[106] countered by circulating a petition of protest against Act 2. The results of this campaign — 4 522 signatures were collected — were published in full in *Indian Opinion* early in November.[107] Outside support for the movement, such as meetings of sympathy held in Durban or Cape Town, or the work of SABIC, was reported regularly in the paper.

The paper also served as a diary of the course of the movement. Mass meetings were given extensive coverage under eye-catching headlines. The passage of the Permit Office through the colony was carefully charted, and supportive editorials were addressed to whichever centre was currently being visited.[108] Praise was lavished on centres which passed through the registration period without any applications being submitted. 'Blacklegs' were shrilly condemned, held up for scorn and listed by name or, more importantly, by sub-group affiliation.[109] 'Heroes' who refused to register in the face of unusual pressure such as being dismissed by a white employer, which happened to not a few resisters, were also listed by sub-group affiliation or name.[110]

To a certain extent, then, the paper, like the periodic mass meetings, also served to offset the lack of a solid organizational base. In terms of disseminating information it represented a possible substitute for a network of local committees in constant contact with the centre. Gandhi attached a great deal of importance to the paper's role. He claimed later that from 1907 onwards it existed solely to serve the movement.[111] In August 1907, readers were instructed to go through each issue carefully, to act on what they read, to make their copies available to others who did not (but should) buy it themselves, and to throw nothing away.[112]

Except as a valuable source of information about the movement, the role of the paper must not be overestimated however. Whatever Gandhi's intentions, the fact remains that *Indian Opinion* reached a very limited audience in the Transvaal. In 1907, only 100 copies were regularly sent to Johannesburg.[113] By that date the paper had already ceased to publish Tamil or Hindi editions. Some politically active Tamils such as Thambi Naidoo and David Ernest were bilingual.[114] Even so, and even allowing for widespread sharing of copies, it is clear that the paper did not regularly reach all supporters of the movement, far less the whole community. The best indication of this is the 'questions about the movement' which were periodically addressed in the Gujerati columns. The same, or similar, questions were raised time and time again.

One other important organizational technique requires mention. Gandhi attributed the success of virtually preventing registration in 1907 to pickets.[115] This should be qualified by adding that the initial publicity given to the movement through mass meetings and *Indian Opinion* helped spread political awareness, and that numbers of volunteers for active political work then emerged. These were the pickets.

Volunteers for picket duty were asked to come forward at mass meetings.[116] These pickets were important men in the Transvaal Indian community in 1907. They wore badges of identification, held special meetings, and received frequent mention in *Indian Opinion* and at Hamidia Society or BIA mass meetings.[117] An analysis of the names of the Pretoria and Johannesburg pickets reveal that many of them were political unknowns, a few of whom went on to become committed resisters.[118] The picket 'brigades' therefore performed a dual function. Besides acting as a deterrent to registration they served also to provide a definite role within the loose structure of Indian politics for numbers of new people, thus enlarging the active political community. Some pickets inevitably were attracted to the role rather than the movement it was meant to serve however. A few of them actually took out registration certificates themselves.[119]

Pickets were instructed to patrol the vicinity of the Permit Office and politely dissuade would-be applicants from registering.[120] In some small communities a continuous 'meeting' under the auspices of the most prominent trader took the place of picketing during the brief rural registration periods.[121] In Germiston, there was a spontaneous work stoppage, and for two days the entire community picketed. The prestigious role of the picket is reflected in the fact that the work stoppage ended only when the officially designated pickets persuaded others to return to work.[122] It is difficult to establish how closely the pickets followed their instructions to rely on reason and courtesy. There were one or two instances of violence,[123] and others in which people applied for registration in secret, at the same time signing affidavits which asserted that intimidation by pickets had prevented them from applying earlier.[124] Gandhi responded to criticisms in the white press and a 'sporting challenge' from a police officer by withdrawing the pickets from the immediate vicinity of the Johannesburg office for 24 hours. One registration took place during that period.[125] He then went so far as to have some would-be applicants escorted to the Johannesburg office by pickets. Nevertheless, the pickets, or 'watchmen' as they were sometimes called,[126] supported by the threat of social and economic sanctions, do seem to have played the critical role suggested by Gandhi. Most of the 500 or so registrations which occurred took place in secret.

The loosely structured nature of the movement, the reliance on BIA mass meetings and *Indian Opinion* editorials as major vehicles of organization, exacerbated one final weakness which further undercut an already weak structure — problems in funding. BIA had no standing fund. The costs of the 1906 deputation to London had been met by a special collection.[127] The question of further funding was discussed at length within a week of the Registration Bill's passage through the Transvaal Assembly in late march 1907.[128] Yet collecting for the movement did not recommence until two months later when Act 2 had actually been gazetted and the necessity for funds became indisputable.[129] Even then, fund-raising techniques — which will be discussed shortly — were haphazard, a natural corollary of the lack of structure in the movement itself. Despite this, by mid-1907, the movement had already committed itself to a path involving heavy expenditure

BIA's normal operating costs were low enough. The party had no hall of its own,[130] but most of its meeting were held in the Hamidia hall in Johannesburg or in mosque grounds in Johannesburg or Pretoria.[131] There was therefore little rent to pay, and Gandhi listed the party's 'recurring expenditure' at under £10 in 1907.[132] Presumably this covered postage and stationery and perhaps also the cost of advertising mass meetings. It could not have covered much else. For the rest, however, there is some confusion in the information which is available for expenditures between 1906 and 1907. In September 1907 Gandhi informed the Natal Congress that BIA had already spent around £1 500 'in this struggle'.[133] It is difficult to estimate how long a time period this covered (whether from the creation of BIA in 1903, or from the passive resistance pledge in September 1906), and which expenditures the figure covered. The problem is complicated by the summary of accounts which appeared in *Indian Opinion* in October and November 1907, reproduced on the following pages.

Apart from the gap of some £600 between the figure which Gandhi gave the Congress, and the total expenditures listed, the summaries present several problems in themselves. It is difficult to understand the use of the term 'balance' which appears in both debit and credit columns. More importantly, the first summary is by no means a complete list of expenditures from March 1906 to August 1907. Only one item is included for the September 1906 deputation: a return of £167.9.6d to BIA some time before August 1907. The costs of the deputation must therefore be added to the published figures in order to arrive at total expenditures for the movement up to late 1907. Again, conflicting information makes it difficult even to approximate costs, but BIA's share of the deputation's expenses was probably around £600.[134] The addition of this sum closes the gap between the published figures, and the figure which Gandhi gave the Natal Congress, putting the total expenditure up to late 1907 at around £1 500.

Leaving aside the cost of the deputation, all items listed in the published summaries are ordinary expenses inherent in the way the movement was conducted — telegrams and cables, transportation of leaders from one centre to another, typing, printing petitions, the regular receipt of important newspapers, occasional reliance on outside legal advice.[135] By far the largest single ordinary expense was the upkeep of SABIC (referred to as the London Committee in the first summary). BIA and the Natal Congress initially pledged £150 each to support SABIC during its first year.[136] Over 90 per cent of that was spent on Ritch's honorarium, the salary of the Committee's other employee, and office space in London, leaving a little over £20 for SABIC's activities. In March 1907, BIA therefore pledged a further £100 to the Committee of which the Congress was again expected to pay half.[137] By October, a total of £500 had been sent to London. Gandhi lobbied for continued support of SABIC, and late in 1907

British Indian Association, Johannesburg. Summary of Account of Receipts and Expenditure, March 1906 to August 1907[138]

To Cash	£	s	d
London Committee	280	6	6
Telegrams	27	10	11
Cables	192	1	9
Lichtenstein & Blake	88	16	0
Tram case etc.			
Stationary			
Papers, including daily Cape *Gazette* and supply of 30 copies of *Indian Opinion* weekly to London Committee	1	3	6
Typist	16	14	11
Printing petitions etc.	47	10	0
Hire of halls for meetings	47	11	4
Stamps	26	16	6
Fares (Railway for several deputations)	4	7	4
Press telegrams	29	2	2
Alexander	2	2	3
Sundries, including advertisements, etc	24	8	3
	2	10	6
	£781	**2**	**9**

By Cash	£	s	d
From Naidoo	18	10	0
The Tamil Community	20	0	0
The Hindu Society	25	0	0
Rander Committee	20	0	0
Hamidia Islamic Society	14	0	0
Refund by C S A R	1	8	2
Refund by Reuter	1	2	6
Refund re West End Hall	1	10	0
From the Gujerat Hindu Society	224	10	9
Collection by Alibhai Akoojee	17	0	0
Collection from Naidoo & Co	1	4	0
From M E Gatu	8	0	0
Balance from deputation a/c	167	9	6
From C M Valab	39	10	0
Collected at meeting	30	10	0
From A A Pillay	1	0	0
From I V Thomas		10	0
From Suliman I Mia & Co	1	10	0
From Nanji Ghela	7	0	0
Collection at Spelonken	1	0	0
From Vyas	10	2	4
Amount previously acknowledged	108	10	7
Balance available	94	17	5
	£781	**2**	**9**

Summary of Receipts and Expenditure from 1st September to 23rd November 1907[139]

To Cash

	£	s	d
Advertising re: Deputation and Association's a/c	4	15	0
Cables, Immigration Bill, Dadabhai's birthday, Professor Gokhale, S Banerjea, King's birthday	15	17	6
Fares to Germiston and Pretoria	3	7	8
Advocate Gregorowski for opinion re: Sinha Vassa Rangasamy	2	2	0
Papers — Cape Government Gazette, Leader, Mail, supply of 30 copies of Indian Opinion weekly to London Committee	10	1	0
Printing: K Dickionson & Co., printing and binding petition	14	1	6
Stamps	3	4	8
Telgrams re: Pundit's trial, etc.	8	12	4
Typist: September and November	10	0	0
Balance	140	18	1
	£213	5	2

By Cash

	£	s	d
Balance from last account	94	17	5
Cash collection by Kunbies per Dulab Bhaga	11	0	0
Cheque not cashed by conductor		10	0
Cash from Chinde Indians	33	15	9
From Allbret & Co (donation)	25	0	0
From G P Vyas re: Pretoria fare	1	0	0
Withdrawn from Association Account	18	15	0
By sale of chairs to Hindu Society	13	5	9
United Assembly Rustenburg	15	1	3
	£213	5	2

£1 000 was pledged for a second year. Natal was again requested to help meet the costs.[140]

Despite the difficulty of synthesizing the varied information which is available for BIA's expenditures, it is clear that by the end of 1907 the movement was operating on a scale which demanded around £1 200 a year, a figure which does not take into account the possibility of supporting the dependants of jail-goers.

The published lists of receipts illuminate the movement's fund raising, which, after the disbandment of the Anti-Asiatic Law Fund Committee, was done on an ad hoc basis. Influential individuals such as Thambi Naidoo or Alibhai Akuji[141] attempted to raise monies in their respective sub-groups: in Naidoo's case the Johannesburg Tamils, in Akuji's, the Kanmias. Remittances from non-political associations whose leaders supported the movement constituted another source of revenue. The published receipts reveal that for the most part these remittances, like those from the informal social sub-groups, were too low to be a real source of comfort, far less strength. The remittance of £224.10.9d. from the 'Gujerat Hindu Society', which dwarfed all others, is somewhat of a mystery. The society cannot be traced in the records. It seems likely, however, that this money was donated by the 'Gujerati Hindus' who had a hall in Vrededorp[142] and who were already indebted to the movement for successfully protecting the 60 or 70 merchants in the township from an attempt to evict them in 1906.[143]

In mid-1907 an attempt was made to raise money throughout the Transvaal by way of local collections. Evidence of some of these appears in the published receipts — collection at Spelonken (£10); United Assembly, Rustenburg (£15.1.3d). Gandhi had planned to have the movement's leaders tour the colony to spearhead the fund-raising drive[144] — much the same had been done by the Natal Congress leaders, and with some success, in the mid-1890s. The plan did not materialize, however, and the central leadership, in the absence of any suitable mechanism, whether general to the movement or specific to funding, failed to generate in the hinterland the necessary urgency. By November, 'there [had] been some collections in most places, but these [had] not been remitted to the Association'.[145] At that time, the movement's bank balance stood at just under £141 and BIA had already committed itself to send a further £500 to London.

From the first, Gandhi had attempted to broaden the movement's financial base. The published receipt of £33.15.9d from the 'Chinde

Indians' is evidence of his partial success; but Cape Colony Indians failed to respond. Natal was naturally a major target. The social links between the Natal and Transvaal merchants were so strong and their economic interests so closely intertwined that the colony represented a logical external base of support for the movement. But fund-raising there was not easy. *Indian Opinion* carried frequent calls for funds addressed specifically to Natal, and Gandhi made three trips to Durban in the latter half of 1907.[146] The Congress did pledge itself to help support SABIC but that was apparently done with reluctance (its share of the costs was slow to come), and no other monies were forthcoming from the colony in 1907.

By the end of 1907, then, the movement's financial foundations, like other aspect of its organizational infrastructure, were shaky. Gandhi controlled finances — the only aspect of the movement which he did control completely. His reliance on ad hoc collecting, money raised specifically for the movement rather than any of the established societies, gave him a great deal of apparent independence, but there were enormous constraints. External assistance was limited and difficult to come by. In the Transvaal, the community was so small, and the money generated by any one group so inadequate to the movement's needs, that Gandhi was, in fact, heavily dependent on every influential Indian in the colony.

At the end of 1907 refusal to register was virtually universal.[147] This magnificent success had been achieved primarily as a result of co-operation from Gandhi's chosen vanguard — the merchants, working through BIA, the Hamidia Society, and informal social networks. Additional important co-operation had come from the *Sanatan Dharma Sabha* and the Tamil Benefit Society. The leaders of these groups had given both material and moral support. They were responsible for raising most of the funds for the movement's heavy expenses, and they had recruited their associates, followers, or clients. Support had been maintained by the threat of social and economic boycott and by appeals to sub-group pride. The continuation of the movement, as it was then conceived and structured, thus depended on the continued cooperation of at least the merchants, if not also the petty traders. Throughout 1907 they had been called on to sacrifice time and money for the movement in limited, controllable quantities, and in the hope of a major return: securing their vested commercial interests. In January 1908 they simultaneously faced jail sentences and ineligibility to renew trading licences.[148] This double threat negated what was for many of them the very *raison d'etre* for supporting the movement. And for those who had refused to register through fear of boycott by the community, for the hundreds of hawkers whose livelihood depended on a trade licence, for the government employees and others who had already lost, or who feared for their jobs, whatever motivated their support, whatever they hoped to gain by resistance in the short or long run — unless moral victory, and moral victory alone — the losses which they faced in January 1908 were greater than the gains to be had from continued support of the movement. Some stood to be stripped of their wealth, and some to lose even the means of subsistence. All of this was avoidable by accepting the government's final offer, the possibility of late registration provided that it were done *en masse*.[149]

Gandhi, himself undergoing the first of many jail sentences, was 'kept posted . . . of the real difficulties of the people and the state of their mind'.[150] The movement had already received a severe blow when Ramsunder Pundit left the colony after his two-week sentence rather than be re-arrested.[151] On 4 January Gandhi tried to offset the demoralizing effect of one of the movement's most fiery leaders fleeing after his first taste of jail by declaring that 'as far as the community is concerned, Ramsunder is dead as from today . . . we should think of Ramsunder as a demon, and guard ourselves against being possessed by it'.[152] But there were few people left to exorcise demons. H O Ally had quit the colony in August 1907, Haji Habib in December.[153] Abdul Gani had stepped down from his long-time leadership position late in the year.[154] By the end of January 1908, Gandhi, Thambi Naidoo, Leung Quinn (Chairman of the Chinese Association), Essop Ismail Mia (Gani's successor as chairman of BIA), A F C Beg and M Patel (Habib's successors in Pretoria), M P Fancy (Secretary of the Hamidia Society), Imam Abdul Kadir Bawazeer, and all the identifiable Johannesburg and Pretoria pickets were either in jail or had just been sentenced.[155] And although in December Smuts had decided on a policy of 'not striking at the tail but at the head of the movement',[156] dozens of hawkers had also been sentenced to prison for hawking without a licence.[157]

The reports which Gandhi received from those who followed him to jail were 'discouraging':

They told me that people were losing courage. The hawkers, they told me, had stopped going their rounds for fear of prosecution for hawking without a licence. They wanted me to bring about a compromise as early as possible. Those who went to gaol lost their nerve in a few days and some of them hinted that they would not go to gaol again. General Smuts told me much the same thing when I met him: that I did not have the slightest idea of the number of people who had wanted to submit to the law. A few people had already sent applications to him in secret. I even know the names of some of them. All these things could not just be ignored by a person who had been deeply involved in the struggle for 16 months.[158]

On 28 January, with the movement collapsing around him, Gandhi signed a compromise with Smuts. Leung Quinn and Thambi Naidoo were co-signatories.[159]

The compromise consisted of voluntary registration of the Asian community — voluntary in that the official application period had passed — under regulations 'as near as possible' to those of Act 2. The registration certificates were to be validated by special legislation.[160] The compromise gained notoriety as the subject of a chapter in Gandhi's autobiography entitled 'Breach of Faith?'. The evidence for and against this tentative charge against Smuts has been considered many times. Briefly, Gandhi claimed that although the written compromise took note of the fact that 'it is not possible during the Parliamentary recess to repeal the Act, and we have noted your repeated public declarations that there is no likelihood of the Act being repealed', Smuts verbally promised him repeal provided that voluntary registration were completed successfully. Smuts denied making this promise;[161] and, indeed, if previous offers of voluntary registration had always demanded repeal of the Act, such demands had been consistently rejected by Smuts. Thus both Gandhi's and Smuts's interpretations of the compromise assumed virtual abandonment by the other of the principle which had led to confrontation. One can add nothing new to the many analyses of these negotiations except to point out that both Gandhi and Smuts manoeuvred well in muddy waters, and that the compromise bought time for each.[162]

The compromise exposed the widespread gap between Gandhi's understanding of the goal of the movement, and popular understanding. This gap must be attributed as much to the loosely based organization of the movement, the inadequate lines of communication between leadership and the rank and file, and the variety of dominant themes in the ideology, as to the politically unsophisticated nature of most of the Transvaal Indians. In the weeks following the compromise Gandhi was called on to explain his actions at meetings in the

Transvaal and Natal.[163] Repeated editorials in *Indian Opinion* offered
further explanations. The major source of misunderstanding was the
fine line which Gandhi drew between Act 2 and voluntary registration
in terms of the regulations of the Act. As far as Gandhi was concerned,
honour, conscience, human dignity — even the oath before God —
demanded only that compulsion be resisted. But this was one of the
most poorly articulated elements in the movement's ideology and it
now transpired that many Indians, struggling unsuccessfully with
Gandhi's concept of honour, had taken hold of the idea that it was
contained in resisting the regulations in Act 2 which called for a full set
of fingerprints from applicants for registration certificates. The
misunderstanding widened when it became known that Gandhi had
accepted Smuts's offer that the fingerprint requirement be waived in
the case of the wealthy or well-known Indians.[164] The Pathan
community[165] was particularly hostile to the idea of giving prints, and
Gandhi, having publicly declared his own intention to comply with
the regulations of the Act, was brutally assaulted by a Pathan on his
way to the registration office on 10 February.[166] Although Gandhi
publicly forgave his assailant, privately he tried to prevent the possible
radicalization of the movement. On 21 May, after Thambi Naidoo
and Essop Mia, the new chairman of BIA, had also been assaulted,[167]
he wrote to Smuts:

> Many more may be assaulted in the near future . . . . The most
> violent member of the Pathan community, who has remained behind the
> scenes but who has been an active agent in having the assaults commit-
> ted, has been arrested today on a charge of inspiring to do harm. If it is
> at all possible, I certainly think that this man should be deported. In my
> opinion he is more or less a maniac and many dissatisfied Indians simply
> hang around him . . . you will add to the peace of mind of well-
> behaved Indians . . . by dealing with the fanatic I have mentioned
> either by way of deportation or by treating him as a prohibited
> immigrant under the Immigrants' Restriction Act. I believe he possesses
> no documents.[168]

The man was not deported,[169] but the anticipated radicalization did
not take place. Early in March, however, Gandhi narrowly escaped a
second assault when he tried to explain the compromise to a NIC
meeting in Durban. He was mobbed by angry Indians and a revolver
shot was fired. A police escort drove him to safety 'amid much hissing
and booing'.[170]

The compromise also brought Gandhi face to face with another of the limitations inherent in the structure and nature of the movement. That was the consultative manner of 'decision making' in which decisions previously made by the leadership were discussed and ratified by resolution of the general assembly at mass meetings before being implemented. Although the general principle of voluntary registration had been agreed to in this manner, months earlier, the details had not, and Gandhi was exposed to criticism for having signed the compromise without consulting the community. His final defence against the criticism was the novel claim that 'those who are accepted as leaders must have a certain freedom [of action] in crises'.[171]

Despite confusion and criticisms, the apparent end to the struggle was welcomed by the Transvaal Asians. Voluntary registration, complete with fingerprinting in most cases, was successfully carried out between 10 February and 9 May 1908.[172]

May 1908 — December 1909

The cracks in the compromise began to emerge as early as 30 January when the Registrar of Asiatics implied in a conversation with Gandhi that Act 2 would not be repealed, but rather used to validate voluntary registration.[173] By mid-May when the Registrar had asserted, and Smuts confirmed, that anyone outside the colony during the voluntary registration period must register under the Act on his return, Gandhi had begun to speak of the need to resume passive resistance.[174] This was the beginning of three months' work aimed at saving the compromise. Repeated warnings to the government in the form of personal communications, announcements at meetings, and in *Indian Opinion*, that the campaign might be resumed and its demands increased,[175] resulted in a renewal of negotiations between Smuts and Gandhi. The course of the first new round of negotiations was determined by Smuts's belief that Gandhi lacked effective support.[176] Smuts's final offer was the repeal of Act 2 on condition that appropriate amendments be made to the Immigration Act. Since the Immigration Act treated non-registered Indians as prohibited immigrants, validation of voluntary registration under the Act was feasible enough. However, Smuts proposed additional amendments to confine the extension of permanent residence rights to those who had been issued permits under the terms of the Peace Preservation

Ordinance, as well as to eliminate the theoretical possibility of Indians qualifying for immigration under the Act's education qualification.

On 22 June Gandhi refused Smuts's offer, broke off the talks, declared the settlement breached, and revealed the substance of the negotiations in a letter to the press.[177] The following day, some of the leaders of the movement filed affidavits requesting the return of their applications for registration certificates on the grounds that the compromise had been breached.[178] The day after, a lone passive resister from Natal was brought in to test Smuts's defence of one of his proposed amendments: the assertion that the Immigration Act, as it then stood, could be used to prohibit the entry of even educated Indians.[179]

Gandhi declared the campaign reopened. The movement's goals were enlarged to include protection of the residence rights of all former *bona fide* residents, as well as the theoretical right to immigrate of educated Indians.[180] But the efforts to save the compromise by negotiation had not been abandoned. On 6 July, after the Supreme Court's refusal to return registration documents to those who had submitted affidavits, some 800 Indians resolved to burn their registration certificates the following week unless the government conceded their demands.[181] This 'ultimatum', as *Indian Opinion* called it, was conveyed to the government, and both sides accepted the offer of white sympathizers to mediate in a new round of negotiations. On 9 July the question of resuming full-scale passive resistance by burning certificates was suspended pending the outcome of the mediation.[182] On 18 July, amid rumours that Smuts was drafting a bill which would be acceptable to the Indian community, the burning was further postponed until the introduction of the new bill.[183]

The unacceptable offer which had ended the first round of negotiations grew out of Smuts's conviction that Gandhi lacked support for his demands. The resumed negotiations were therefore accompanied by limited passive resistance, which Gandhi hoped would pressure the government into submission.[184] The Supreme Court sidestepped the issue which Gandhi had hoped to clarify with the educated resister from Natal. Sorabji Shapurji Adajania was tried, convicted and sentenced to one month's imprisonment for being in the Transvaal without a registration certificate, and therefore in violation of Act 2.[185] The question of the legality of Smuts's interpretation of the Immigration Restriction Act was thus avoided. In the middle of Sorabji's trial when it had already become clear that he was not going to constitute a new source of embarrassment for the government, some of the movement's leaders began to court jail sentences. With the question of destroying registration certificates in suspension, they took to hawking, for which they were not licensed, in order to invite arrest and prosecution.[186]

The 'hawkers' served a second, and far more important purpose. The movement was in disarray, despite Gandhi's confident assertions that flexing its muscles would exert the necessary pressure on the government. The 'hawkers' were therefore seen as a means to regenerate momentum in the movement.[187]

The movement had recently lost two more leaders. Alibhai Akuji, the most influential of the Kanmia community, and Moosa Salooji Coovadia, BIA's treasurer, returned to India in April 1908.[188] At the mass meeting on 24 June which declared the reopening of the campaign, there were only 700-800 in attendance. Gandhi was exposed to renewed criticism for his handling of the compromise. The Pretoria delegate refused to support the resolutions condemning the government and calling for a resumption of resistance to Act 2 on the grounds that Gandhi had misled the movement over the compromise and he was still its adviser.[189] On 7 July the Registrar of Asiatics had sent a circular letter to Town Clerks informing them that Act 2 would remain on the statute books and that applicants for trading licences must therefore tender a registration certificate and a right-hand thumb print for examination in the registrar's office.[190] Many licence renewals — particularly hawkers — came due on 30 June and, despite pickets, hundreds of Indians had 'swarmed . . . like locusts' to comply with the terms of the circular, thus validating Act 2.[191]

In the meantime, few constructive changes had taken place in the movement. What momentum it had attained had been permitted to lapse after the compromise in much the same way that the enthusiasm of September 1906 had been allowed to dissipate. BIA began to hold regular mass meetings again in late June, but they were poorly attended.[192] Although Imam Abdul Kadir remained committed to resistance, there is nothing to indicate that the Hamidia Society as a whole continued to function as a driving force. And with the loss of Ramsunder Pundit, the *Sanatan Dharma Sabha* faded from the political scene as swiftly as it had entered it. Fund raising was confined to generalized appeals at mass meetings, and the movement's treasury was very low.[193]

Some important changes had occurred, however. A conscious effort was made to strengthen some of the weak spots which had become manifest at the time of the compromise, and to build on unexpected strengths. The movement's ideology was simplified, a determined effort made to clarify the new as well as the old goals, less importance attached to the role of the merchants and petty traders, and correspondingly more to the hawkers. These changes served less to redirect the movement than to confirm the shape which it had assumed by early 1908.

The economic imperative was dropped from the ideology.[194] This helped simplify the task of finding a place in the movement's philosophy for the new goals. More importantly, it reflected the liberating effect of loss of merchant and petty trader support. Most of those who continued to support passive resistance in mid-1908 were drawn either to the moral content of the ideology, or to Gandhi himself — it is not possible to separate the man from his ideas in this respect. Thus although Gandhi still hoped for backing from the commercial classes the movement was no longer posited on their support.

The other changes which took place in the ideology reflected the crystallization of the moral precepts which Gandhi had been trying to follow, and to convey to others in the political arena, at least since 1904. The cumulative experiences of stage one of the campaign, Gandhi's first jail sentence (particularly the readings which he did in jail — Tolstoy, the *Gita*, Ruskin, the *Koran*, Plato's *Dialogues*, the Bible, Bacon's essays on civil and moral counsel), and the compromise, all seem to have assisted the clarification of his ideas. By 1908 he was able, finally, to articulate the moral stance with which he sought to inform both his political and personal conduct. He did this by deifying 'Truth'. 'Truth is God, or God is nothing but Truth . . . it is a divine law that he who serves that Truth — that God — will never suffer defeat', he wrote in 1908.[195] The concept of 'Truth' dominated Gandhi's writings during this period. The compromise. while it stood, was a victory not for the Indians, but for Truth.[196] A series on Socrates, the perfect passive resister, was published in *Indian Opinion* between April and May 1908 under the title 'Story of a Soldier of Truth'.[197] A similar series, based on Ruskin's *Unto This Last*, translated Ruskin's 'Roots of Honour' as 'Roots of Truth' in Gujerati.[198] Implicit in Gandhi's translations of and commentaries on Ruskin is a definition of what he perceived to be the meaning of Truth, and of the central place which it held in the philosophy by which he tried to live. Truth, the universal god, when elevated to become the means and end of all endeavour, is nothing else than right action by a fearless man of conscience.

It was during this period too that Gandhi found the word to convey what passive resistance meant to him: *satyagraha*.[199] Its English equivalent, 'truth force', means little without a prior understanding of what Truth meant to Gandhi. As Rughavan Iyer describes it, 'The doctrine of *satyagraha* was meant to show how the man of conscience could engage in heroic action in the vindication of truth and freedom against all tyranny, in his appeal to justice against every social abuse and sectional interest'.[200] All this was already apparent in Gandhi's thinking early in 1908. It is set out most clearly in an *Indian Opinion* editorial entitled 'Secret of Satyagraha':

> A satyagrahi enjoys a degree of freedom not possible for others, for he becomes a truly fearless person. Once his mind is rid of fear, he will never agree to be another's slave. Having achieved this state of mind, he will never submit to any arbitrary action. Such satyagraha can be, ought to be, practised not only against a Government but against society as well [if need be].
>
> Such a wonderful remedy is this satyagraha . . . our satyagraha prompts us to become free and feel independent.
>
> Satyagraha is really an attitude of mind. He who has attained to the satyagrahic state of mind will remain ever victorious, at all times and places and under all conditions irrespective of whether it is a government or a people that he opposes, whether they be strangers, friends or relatives.[201]

From here Gandhi's thoughts ranged far beyond the South African Indians into the dual notion of 'self-rule' (*swaraj*) that was to characterize his later politics as a nationalist leader in India, and the concept of 'non-violent socialism' (*sarvodaya*) that was the nearest thing he ever had to an economic programme for India. He adopted and added to Ruskin's critique of industrial society, calling for 'social affection' as the motive force behind the creation of a socialistic economic order meant to advance the welfare of all.[202] But he saw the possibility of that economic order only within the framework of the '*satyagrahic* state of mind', and this he called *swaraj*, the rule of conscience. At the same time he said that political freedom, national *swaraj*, 'would be no better than hell' unless it were based on that other *swaraj*, the rule of conscience.[203]

By early 1908, then, in the wake of his first involvement in mass politics and his first experience as a political prisoner, Gandhi had thought out and articulated virtually every one of the major elements which matured into the body of moral and political thought collectively known as the Gandhian doctrine. To anyone familiar with that doctrine, there is a startling omission in the concepts which have been discussed above: non-violence (*ahimsa*). From the start, Gandhi had declared the passive resistance movement non-violent.[204] Indeed, *sarvodaya* assumes non-violence. What is missing is only the elaboration of *ahimsa* as an integral part of Gandhi's moral and political philosophy. It is as if he took non-violence so much for granted in the first decade of the century that there was little need for elaboration. This was appropriate enough to the kind of constituency which Gandhi had in the Transvaal, even after the social base of the movement had been widened to embrace petty traders, hawkers and small numbers of Indian labourers. The Transvaal Indian community was oppressed — politically, socially, and (some of them) economically. Of that there can be no doubt. But the oppression in this period was nowhere so severe for most of them as to breed the kind of rage and frustration that so often erupts in violence when the truly oppressed are drawn into, or force their way into, a social or political movement. If, for instance, there was anything in the Transvaal to compare with the widespread destitution among the ex-indentured labourers in Natal during this period, or the conditions of indentured labourers, it does not emerge in press reports or official documents. It is probably also significant that police action against the *satyagrahis*, which rarely even approached violence,[205] spared them, by and large, one of the severest tests of a non-violent resister. Thus although Gandhi declared from time to time that one of the properties of the Transvaal movement must be non-violence, he had not yet elevated *ahimsa* to the level that *sat* (Truth) enjoyed in his philosophy.

The clarification of Gandhi's own moral doctrine, and the virtual loss of support from the commercial classes, were the starting points for the simplification of the movement's ideology. The discussions of the properties of *satyagraha* combined with other entries in *Indian Opinion* and speeches at meetings to put the ideology on a purely moral footing. An editorial entitled 'Self-Sacrifice' stressed the fact that the self-interest which had characterized the first stage of the campaign was to be replaced with self-sacrifice. This sacrifice was meant to liberate the Transvaal Indians from a condition of moral slavery, in that liberation consisted simply of rebelling against that condition — it consisted of actively and fearlessly pursuing Truth. Religion continued to play an important role; but now, through the equation of Truth with God, it blended more easily into the ethical content of the ideology: to worship Truth and God was one and the same thing. The only discordant note in an otherwise humanistic message was the nationalism which continued to flavour the ideology.[206]

The movement's political goals — repeal of Act 2, preservation of the theoretical right of educated Indians to immigrate, and protection of the residence rights of all bona fide former residents — were communicated often and clearly at meetings and through *Indian Opinion*. Further attempts at clarification were made by also stressing what the campaign was *not* about; it was not to prevent the giving of fingerprints, nor to secure the immigration rights of clerks, an old merchant demand, and one which many people now thought the question of educated Indians was about.[207] Over all, though, and permeating the reconstructed ideology, was the moral goal which Gandhi had set for himself as early as 1904: to follow one's conscience. This was implicit in each of the movement's political goals in the second stage of the campaign. Thus in mid-1908, for the first time, the movement's goals flowed readily from its ideology. The price of these changes in the movement had already been paid: the virtual loss of merchant and petty trader support. Although Gandhi still hoped for their backing, it was to the Johannesburg hawkers in particular that he turned for *satyagrahis* at the beginning of the second stage of the campaign. Even apart from the loss of most of the merchants and petty traders, he had little choice but to appeal to the hawkers. The wage workers were in a very vulnerable position — there were numerous instances of Indian workers being fired for political activity in the first stage of the campaign.[208] Most importantly, perhaps, the hawkers' licences came due on 30 June. Hundreds of them had already 'accepted' Act 2 by giving thumb prints for their licences.

The limited *satyagraha* which accompanied the Smuts-Gandhi negotiations in the latter half of July and early August 1908 was thus meant to perform a dual function. On one hand Gandhi intended it to put pressure on the government. On the other hand, it served to pull the movement out of the deepening crisis whose beginning had been marked by the compromise in January. The handful of merchants and petty traders who remained committed to the movement and to Gandhi deliberately courted jail by hawking in July and August in an attempt to strengthen the resolve of the 400 or so hawkers who had refused to take out licences by giving thumb prints.[209] The resumption of jail-going provided the rationale for the resumption of 'mass' meetings during a period when the old style BIA meeting (and no attempt had been made to change that style) would otherwise have been inappropriate. The mass meetings, in turn, provided a forum for communicating the reconstructed ideology and the new goals. The jail sentences for hawking without a licence were brief (4 to 14 days), and the second stage of the campaign gained widening publicity through meetings and receptions to mark the sentencing and release of 'hawkers'.[210] This was the first time that Gandhi had attempted to seize the political initiative from the government.

On 11 August the second round of the Smuts-Gandhi negotiations was concluded with a 'Bill to validate the voluntary registration of certain Asiatics who failed to comply with the Asiatic Law Amendment Act, 1907'.[211] The Bill posited the repeal of Act 2, but made no concession on the immigration question. By this time, the movement had regained sufficient momentum to make widespread passive resistance feasible.[212] Gandhi broke off the negotiations for a second time and set 16 August as the date for a mass meeting at which registration certificates would be burned.[213]

The 16 August mass meeting was a repetition of the emotion-charged September 1906 rally and the July 1907 mass meeting in Pretoria. Repeated calls for registration certificates had been followed up by a house to house collecting tour by the leaders.[214] In all, some 1 300 certificates and 500 trade licences had been offered up by 16 August, and 3 000 Indians and Chinese turned out to witness the burning in the grounds of the Fordsburg mosque. *Indian Opinion* described the scene thus: 'the air vibrated with expectancy, and a tense feeling seemed to hold everyone in check — until the supreme moment came'.[215] The drama was heightened when a former blackleg appeared on the platform to recant and personally consign his certificate to the flames. Two hundred more certificates were surrendered once the burning got under way.

The chairman declared the meeting 'one of the most unique in Indian annals in South Africa' by virtue of the presence of a handful of prominent members of NIC, personal friends of Gandhi's who had weathered the storm of criticism over the compromise.[216] Each, as Gandhi said, represented a 'different faith or clan of India'.[217] They had been brought in as a final attempt to save the compromise after the unacceptable validating bill had been gazetted. Smuts was informed on 14 August that they were about to cross the border and challenge the law, a reflection of 'strong [gen]uine and invincible opposition to the Asiatic Act'.[218] Although their entry was ignored by the government, as platform speakers on 16 August they served as morale boosters and desirable role models. 'It speaks volumes for the courage of Mr Dawad Mohamed and his companions', *Indian Opinion* reported, 'that they should, for the sake of their countrymen in the Transvaal, forsake their avocations, suffer pecuniary loss, and invite trouble on themselves by entering the Transvaal'.[219] The *Rand Daily Mail*'s report of the meeting noted that Gandhi 'appeared to be suffering from mental stress'.[220] This, and the content of Gandhi's lengthy and unusually impassioned speech, reflected the importance of the meeting for the continuation of the movement, as well as the vulnerabilty of Gandi's own political position following the failure of the compromise. He took what was for him the unusual course of mounting a personal attack on the Registrar of Asiatics. He also found it necessary to defend himself against charges that widespread resistance would cause widespread hardship and to point out that the dimensions of the struggle and the method of resistance were the product of joint decisions on the part of the movement's leaders.[221]

The August mass meeting and the careful build-up which preceded it successfully launched the resumption of resistance. The Congress notables toured the rural areas bringing in more certificates and collecting money for the movement in much the same way that successful fund raising had been carried out in Natal in the mid-1890s.[222] Over 2 300 registration certificates had been destroyed by the end of the month. By now, though, Gandhi had learned to separate the easy promise given in the heat of the moment from a genuine abiding commitment to resistance. He estimated that many of those who had burned their certificates immediately applied for duplicates.[223]

For the next six months, still working with a loose organizational structure and communications network, Gandhi turned from one group to another in an effort to keep the movement going. If he followed a preconceived plan, it is not apparent from the course that the movement took. Changes in tactics or in the focal point of recruitment efforts appear as responses to the pressures of government policy and the weight of the movement as it collapsed for the second time.

Government policy in the latter part of 1908 cut at the movement's already weak roots outside Johannesburg. In Vereeniging,

Heidelberg, Pietersburg and Pretoria, those traders who continued to support *satyagraha* were denied the possibility of becoming jail-going 'heroes'. The courts adopted the 'annoying practice' of simply fining *satyagrahis* rather than offering them the alternative of a jail sentence. When they refused to pay the fine, their goods were auctioned to cover the cost.[224] This was a severe blow for a provincial petty trader. Gandhi tried to bypass government policy and at the same time rally up-country support by advising storekeepers to sell their shops nominally to sympathetic whites and then go out hawking to court arrest. If they were not prepared to do that, he advised them to 'prepare a servant or relative to go to gaol' and offer personal support to the movement in the form of contributions.[225]

By the end of September, the petty traders were suffering another financial assault. A letter, published in *Indian Opinion* and said to express 'the views of a number of Indians', complained that small storekeepers were being denied their customary source of credit by white wholesale merchants. Gandhi could offer little more in reply than the assertion that 'the leaders have ensured that the community carries only those burdens which it can bear. In view of this, not a single Indian should lose heart'. In the same issue of *Indian Opinion*, however, he turned back to the hawkers, claiming that 'this is really a movement on behalf of the traders — especially the hawkers'.[226]

At the end of September, Gandhi's search for *satyagrahis* took him to Durban again. The Natal notables who had entered the Transvaal in mid-August were now in jail and Gandhi used their example as the rallying call for more volunteers.[227] But he had already virtually exhausted his small stock of active supporters in Natal. In any event M C Camroodeen appears to have blocked the way to further support. Camroodeen was opposed to resistance,[228] and his managing partners in Durban and Johannesburg — Abdul Kadir and Abdul Gani — who had dominated Indian politics in Natal and the Transvaal for years, had resigned their positions as chairmen of the Congress and BIA since the movement started. But, with a personal credit network encompassing hundreds of Natal merchants and petty traders, Camroodeen's firm had no need of formal political positions in order to keep the Natal elite out of passive resistance. Gandhi returned to the Transvaal with only thirteen new *satyagrahis*, none of them merchants.[229]

In the Transvaal, the movement was kept going by the same mechanisms which had been used to rally support in late 1907 —

arrests, convictions and releases were attended by a constant round of meetings, *hartals*, parties and receptions, and given wide publicity in *Indian Opinion*.[230] Pickets operated in an attempt to prevent registration certificates being taken out under the terms of the new Act (Act 36 of 1908) which demanded re-registration by 30 November.[231]

This frenzy of activity swept hundreds of Indians into jail in the latter part of 1908. Some 1 500 sentences had been handed down by the end of the year, most of them to hawkers.[232] The petty traders had taken Gandhi's advice to secure their businesses by making them over to sympathetic whites or to their wives, but few of them had followed this up by courting arrest.[233] In January 1909 accusations began to flow that the 'Transvaal shopkeepers [had] betrayed the hawkers and ruined them'.[234] In a letter to *Indian Opinion*, Gandhi commented that 'many [Indians] have given up the fight. Others, it appears, are about to do so'.[235] Gandhi responded to the imminent collapse of the movement by turning back to the merchants again. An open letter to the press, written on 20 January 1909 by A M Cachalia, Mia's successor as chairman of BIA, called on all the Transvaal merchants to surrender their goods to creditors and dissolve their businesses.[236] Gandhi's declaration that 'the campaign has now reached a stage where everything depends on the businessmen',[237] highlights the poverty of the movement's human resources by early 1909. Not surprisingly, Cachalia and one other[238] were the only merchants willing to take the radical step of liquidating their businesses in order to free themselves for resistance.

By February 1909, 97 per cent of the Transvaal Asians had taken out registration certificates under Act 36 of 1908.[239] The movement was bereft of leadership. The primary leaders were an easy target, and Haji Habib, who had returned to the Transvaal, supplied the Registrar of Asiatics with lists of secondary leaders.[240] By March, every influential person who continued to support passive resistance was undergoing a three or six-month jail sentence with hard labour.[241] The report of the Superintendent of Asiatic Affairs on a mass meeting held in Johannesburg on 11 April estimated the crowd at less than 400, 'a very large number' of whom were in possession of registration certificates. The Superintendent claimed that 'many of them treated the whole affair as a joke. Several of them said to me, "why don't you arrest . . . [the platform speakers] and we shall have some peace" '.[242] Gandhi himself underwent a second and then a third term of imprisonment between October and December 1908, and February and May 1909. During his third sentence he learned that BIA was bankrupt and 'the people have been financially ruined'.[243] He broke down in front of a crowd which gathered to greet him in Johannesburg on his release from jail on 24 May.[244]

Objectively viewed, the movement appeared to be finished. The first jailings in January 1908 had broken the back of merchant and petty trader support, and confirmed the inadequacy of the goals and tactics of the movement as a vehicle for mobilizing the elite. Caught up by the holiday atmosphere of the mass meetings, hundreds of Indians — mostly hawkers — had been willing to try jail in late 1908, but they capitulated after a single sentence.[245] By May 1909, the vast majority of Transvaal Asians had emphatically repudiated the path of resistance. But Gandhi refused either to accept defeat, or to modify goals and tactics. 'God is with those who follow the right', he told the Johannesburg crowd on 24 May, and 'since we follow the right, victory is bound to be ours'. He accepted only that the struggle would be prolonged because 'a task that needs a thousand men cannot be accomplished by ten, as it were'.[246]

Gandhi's refusal to concede the end of the struggle led to a direct challenge to his leadership. On 6 June H O Ally and Haji Habib, both of whom had returned to the colony, set up a 'conciliation committee' to try to negotiate a final settlement with the government.[247] The questions which the committee addressed were not only how to bring about an end to passive resistance, but also who should comprise a deputation to England to add an Indian voice to the discussions on the union of the South African colonies which were scheduled to begin shortly in London. A special committee which was appointed to decide the personnel of the deputation reflected the brief flowering of a new political configuration in the Transvaal. On one side were six members of the conciliation committee, on the other five committed passive resisters.[248] There is no information available on the process which produced the deputation committee.[249] However, if the weakness of this challenge to Gandhi's leadership can be inferred from the high proportion of passive resisters on the committee, so too can the vulnerability of Gandhi's own position. Gandhi neither wanted, nor approved of, another deputation to England. He had reached a point where he believed — or professed to believe — that passive resistance was the *only* effective means of protest, while the conciliation committee already held the possibility of undercutting his role as leader by directly negotiating with the Transvaal government. Not surprisingly, Gandhi was also opposed to these activities.[250] Under the circumstances, a deputation of non-resisters, meeting Colonial Office officials and members of the Transvaal cabinet, in London, clearly threatened Gandhi's leadership position. He did not want another deputation to London, but he evidently did not want to be bypassed if there were one.

The summary of the deliberations of the deputation committee,[251] which is the only available documentation on this challenge to Gandhi's leadership, suggests that he won by default. Inexplicably, one of the representatives of the conciliation committee voted against a proposal that the deputation should consist solely of those who were not passive resisters. When Gandhi's proposal — that the delegates should be resisters — was put to the vote, two more members of the conciliation committee abstained, and the passive resisters won an easy six-three victory. The routing of the conciliation committee, both here, and in their unsuccessful attempt to negotiate with Smuts, secured Gandhi's position as the unchallenged leader of the Transvaal Indian community. But, though he had no political opponents, nor did he have many followers. Indian political activity in the Transvaal had virtually ceased to exist by early 1909, and the Natal Congress sent its own deputation to London where it was 'specially commission[ed] to wait on [Justice Ameer Ali] and seek [his] advice and be guided by it'[252] in presenting the standard grievances of the Natal elite.

Two of the proposed members of the Transvaal deputation — V A Chettiar, the chairman of the Tamil Benefit Society, and A M Cachalia, the chairman of BIA — were rearrested shortly before they were due to leave for England.[253] In the end, then, the deputation consisted of Gandhi and Haji Habib, whose lightning switch from conciliator to resister[254] had secured him a nomination as a delegate. Gandhi and Habib spent some four months in England during which nothing was accomplished. The Colonial Office held talks with Smuts on the possibility of conceding the Indian demands. The stumbling block remained the immigration question. Gandhi had long since declared that a formal ban on all but six educated immigrants a year would eliminate his objections to Smuts's determination to exclude Indians on principle. Smuts left London without conceding this demand.[255] In the meantime, Gandhi had followed the Colonial Office's advice not to publicize the Transvaal Indian case for fear of prejudicing the negotiations with Smuts. The deputation was thus effectively muzzled, and a statement of their case was sent to the press only on 5 November 1909, less than a week before their return when it had become obvious that they were to leave London empty-handed.[256]

The movement in the Transvaal was in a state of collapse, the deputation to London a failure. But still Gandhi's message was the message of the rebel. 'If we do not recognize the principles of the man [who may attempt to enslave us] and refuse to carry out his orders, we cease to be slaves', he told the press.[257] And still he was determined to spread the spirit of rebellion, to share the insight which sustained him, and which he wanted to sustain others. On the voyage back to South Africa he wrote *Hind Swaraj*,[258] a searing condemnation of western civilization which enlarged on the political and economic thought whose framework he had worked out early in 1908.[259] The title of the pamphlet — *Indian Home Rule* — reflects both the breadth and content of Gandhi's political vision since he had begun the resistance movement. Still mired in the politics of the Transvaal Indians — that community whom Naoroji in London had dismissed in a single sentence, whom Mehta in India would not adopt as a cause[260] — weighed down by the inadequacies of the first passive resistance movement, Gandhi wrote a pamphlet describing how and why Indian independence must be achieved through the practice of *satyagraha*. By late 1909, his long term political priorities were clear. He wanted a successful end to *satyagraha* in the Transvaal not only for its own sake, but also as the necessary prerequisite for returning to India, taking *satyagraha* with him, making it the basis of Indian nationalist politics.[261]

Any attempt to explain why the movement failed to retain support once passive resistance reached the logical conclusion of jail-going must be in part speculative. The structural weaknesses in the movement have already been pointed out. It seems reasonable to suggest, however, that these weaknesses could have been transcended had commitment to the movement's ideology and goals been strong enough. It is thus tempting to complete the explanation by concluding that the Transvaal Indians were not concerned with questions of honour or personal dignity — or, at least, that they valued their material possessions more than their spiritual well-being. Indeed, for many this was probably true, but there is too much evidence to the contrary to dismiss the collapse of the movement in 1909 in these terms. Hundreds of Indians (and Chinese) did go to jail. Hundreds, and sometimes thousands, continued to attend rallies or receptions for returning jailbirds, and even to pledge support to passive resistance, long after they had ceased activily to support it. Immanuel Wallerstein's comment on one of the distinguishing features of an effective social movement is not out of place here:

> It often can induce others within its social milieu to share its rhetoric, pay lip service to its ideals, and even applaud its victories. The ideas incarnate too many hopes and aspirations, assuage too many frustrations for them to be scorned publicly.[262]

Gandhi was ignored by many, but he was seldom scorned.

One cannot look, either, to the rigours of jail-going in the Transvaal for an explanation of the early collapse of the movement. There can be few, besides men like Gandhi, who actually enjoy a jail sentence.[263] But the complaints which the *satyagrahis* submitted to the Director of Prisons, and others — lack of Indian foodstuffs; being housed with, or near, blacks; the indignity of having to carry slop-buckets[264] suggest lack of understanding between two different cultures, rather than deliberate ill-treatment. The actions of the Transvaal police and prison warders seldom even approached violence. Similarly, the passive resisters seldom encountered violence from other prisoners.

One is entitled to assume, then, that by mid-1909 the movement's crippling weakness was lack of success. For Gandhi himself, 'success' lay in the mere fact of opposition; for the majority of his followers, this was evidently not enough. Rughaven Iyer, quoting Gandhi, claims that *satyagraha* in its pure form was practised only in South Africa.[265] Even the second stage of the campaign, when ideology and goals were strictly ethical with no reference to material reward, belies this. For Gandhi *satyagraha* was a moral doctrine. The collapse of the movement in 1909 suggests that for the majority of his constituents it was a political technique whose efficacy was to be measured by its ability to produce concrete results.

The major results of the passive resistance movement between 1906 and 1909 lay in Gandhi's maturation as a moral philosopher, and as a moral and political leader. By 1909 he had ceased to be simply the chief representative of the Transvaal merchants. The challenge posed by the conciliation committee reflected Gandhi's assumption of the role of leader in Transvaal Indian politics as well as his injection into those politics of a new element — conscience. *Hind Swaraj* reflected the depth and breadth of this new leader's ambition in what was for him the single field of morals and politics.

Notes

1   The Chinese community consisted of 981 Southern Chinese settlers
     in 1904, 952 of whom were resident in Johannesburg. They had
     migrated to South Africa during the last thirty years of the nineteenth
     century. P Richardson, 'Coolies. Peasants and Proletarians: The
     Origins of Chinese Indentured Labour in South Africa, 1904-1907',
     Collected Papers of the Centre for South African Studies (University
     of York), No.3 (1978), pp.73-4.
2   The TCA was created around the same time as BIA in 1903. *Indian
     Opinion*, 13 Feb. 1909.
3   C W, vi, p.27, Gandhi to Yuk Lin Lew, 26 Oct. 1906.
4   Ibid., p.427, 'Johannesburg Letter' (hereafter referred to as 'J L')
     20 Apr. 1907.
5   This distinction even appeared in the Indian deputation's representa-
     tion to the Sec. St. for the Colonies in October 1906. C W, vi, p.54,
     31 Oct. 1906.
6   *Rand Daily Mail*, 22 Dec. 1908; *Indian Opinion*, 13 Feb. 1909. The
     split ran deep enough to produce a fight during which five persons
     were wounded by revolver fire. *Rand Daily Mail*, 19 Apr. 1909.
7   C W, vi, pp.149-50, Gandhi to Bhownaggree, 12 Nov. 1906.
8   Ibid., iv, p.370, fn.1.
9   Ritch initially received an honararium of £25 per quarter. Ibid., vi,
     pp.371-2, 'South African British Indian Committee', 23 Mar. 1907.
     This was increased to £15 per month in 1907. Ibid., 'J L', 9 Mar.
     1907.
10   Ibid., ix, p.286, Gandhi to Polak, 14 Jul. 1909.
11   These are filed in CO 291, CO 879/106, and CO 879/108. See, in
     particular, CO 291/122, passim; CO 879/108, no.970 passim.
12   See above, Chapter 3, pp.102-103.
13   See, for example, Cd.3887, no.56, C O to SABIC, 3 Jan. 1908.
14   C W, vi, p.255, Gandhi to Gokhale, 3 Dec. 1906.
15   This is discussed in Chapter 6.
16   *Indian Opinion*, 3 Jul. 1909. Polak was a journalist.
17   Ibid.
18   See her own brief account of life at Phoenix; M G Polak, 'In the
     South African Days', *Incidents of Gandhiji's Life* (Bombay, 1949),
     pp.247-51.
19   C W, xi, p.177, Gandhi to Gokhale, 30 Oct. 1911.
20   Ibid., viii, p.54 'Interview to the Press', 8 Feb. 1908.

21   CO 879/106/934, no.101, Gov. to Sec. St., 19 May 1909.

22   CO 179/255/18498, I O to C O, 2 Jun. 1909. encl. I O to Viceroy, 28 May 1909.

23   TABA, Gov. Gen. 707/15/91, minute by Priv. Sec. to Gov. Gen., Secret, 12 Jan. 1911, encl. minute by P M., no.902A, 20 Dec. 1910 and ibid., 15/89 P M to Priv. Sec., to Gov. Gen., 5 Jan. 1911.

24   The Committee was established in 1908 at the start of the second stage of the campaign. Albert Cartwright, former editor of *Transvaal Leader*, was instrumental in its formation. For a summary of the committee's activities to mid-1911, see *Indian Opinion*, 17 Jun. 1911.

25   *Johannesburg Star*, (weekly ed.), 23 Mar. 1907.

26   *C W*, vi, p.389, 'J L', 30 Mar. 1907.

27   See, for example, *C W*, vi, p.389, BIA to Sec. St. for Colonies, 30 Mar. 1907; ibid., p.390, BIA to SABIC, 30 Mar. 1907; ibid., p.393, 'Transvaal Mass Meeting', 6 Apr. 1907; ibid., pp.408-9, BIA to Sec. St. for Colonies. 6 Apr. 1907; ibid., pp.409-10, 'Meeting of Natal Indian Congress', 13 Apr. 1907; ibid., pp.416-7, 'J L', 13 Apr. 1907. See also, *Indian Opinion*, 11 May 1907; and CO 879/106/874, no. 240, Gov. Natal to Sec. St. 15 Apr. 1907 and encl.; ibid., no.242, Gov. Cape to Sec. St., 17 Apr. 1907 and encl.

28   *C W*, vi, pp.407-8, 'Mass Meeting of Transvaal Indians', 6 Apr. 1907.

29   Ibid., pp.426-7, 'J L', 20 Apr. 1907.

30   Cd.3887, no.10, Sec. St. to Gov. 9 May 1907.

31   *C W*, vii, p.80, 'Mass Meeting at Pretoria', 6 Jul. 1907.

32   *Rand Daily Mail*, 5 Oct. 1907.

33   *C W*, vii, p.312, 'J L', 26 Oct. 1907.

34   Ibid., p.336, 'Letter to the Press', 9 Nov. 1907.

35   CO 291/127/28881, Gov. to Sec. St. 20 Jul. 1908. (It is difficult to assess the size of the adult Indian population during this period. Using 1904 census data and a rough estimate of the large number of Asians who left the colony during the last few months of 1907, the *Rand Daily Mail*, 3 Dec. 1907, put the figure at around 7 000, the great majority of whom must have been Indian.)

36   See, for example, *C W*, vii, p.232, 'J L', 14 Sept. 1907.

37   Ibid., p.449, fn.1; ibid., p.473, 'J L', 4 Jan. 1908.

38   CO 879/106/874, no.359, Gov. to Sec. St. 11 Jul. 1907.

39   *Rand Daily Mail*, 11 and 15 Jan. 1908.

40   *Transvaal Leader*, 31 Jan. 1908.

41   CO 291/132/32986, SABIC to C O, 9 Sept. 1908, encl. Petition by BIA addressed to Transvaal Leg. Assembly, 13 Aug. 1908.

42   See, for example, *C W*, vi, p.442, 'J L', 27 Apr. 1907, or ibid., vii,

p.57, 'J L', 26 Jun. 1907.

43   Ibid., viii, p.100, 'A Brief Explanation', 22 Feb. 1908.

44   Ibid., x, p.123, 'Duty of Hawkers', 8 Jan. 1910.

45   See, for example, ibid., vi, p.383, 'Transvaal Asiatic Ordinance', 30 Mar. 1907; ibid., p.399, 'Mass Meeting of Transvaal Indians', 6 Apr. 1907, and especially, ibid., p.481, 'The Transvaal Struggle', 18 May 1907.

46   Ibid., pp.430-5, about 20 Apr. 1907.

47   Ibid.

48   Ibid., v, pp.195-7, Gandhi to C Gandhi, 18 Feb.1906; or ibid., pp.307-8, Gandhi to C Gandhi, 5 May 1906.

49   Ibid., v, pp.413-14, 'Russia and India', 8 Sept..1906, or ibid., pp.366-7, 'Should Indians Volunteer or Not?' 30 June 1906.

50   Ibid., vii, pp.6-7, 'Unrest in India', 1 Jun. 1907.

51   This interpretation may seem to read too much into Gandhi's words, and, indeed, it is made possible only by hindsight.

52   *C W*, vii, pp.399-401, 'Why Do We Oppose Law?', 30 Nov. 1907; ibid., vi, pp.456-8, 'Will Indians be Slaves?', 11 May 1907; *Indian Opinion*, 3 Aug. 1907 (particularly speeches by Gandhi and Gani at Pretoria mass meeting).

53   Cf. Iyer, op.cit., pp.134, 147 and particularly 277.

54   See above, Chapter 3, p.115.

55   The English translation of 'Why Do We Oppose Law?' is printed in *C W*, vii, pp.399-401.

56   Ibid., vi, p.385, 'Transvaal Asiatic Ordinance', 30 Mar. 1907; or ibid., p.457, 'Will Indians be Slaves?', 11 May 1907; ibid., vii, p.59, 'J L', 29 Jun. 1907.

57   Ibid., vii, p.192, 'J L', 24 Aug. 1907. (A group of 'leading' merchants from Pretoria, Standerton, Pietersburg and Middelburg hired legal counsel to petition the government for minor modifications of the Act, such as exemption from finger-printing for educated Indians and exemption from the ban on immigration for merchants' clerks. CO 291/120/41955, Gov. to Sec. St., 11 Nov. 1907, encl. memo. by Smuts, 11 Nov. 1907.)

58   Ally returned to the Cape with his family, *C W*, vii, p.206, 'J L', 31 Aug. 1907.

59   The Imam began chairing meetings in July, ibid., p.137, 'J L', 29 Jul. 1907.

60   *Indian Opinion*, 1 Aug. 1908.

61   Ibid., 18, 25 Jan. 1908. Mukhtiar had been in the colony for about 14 months. *Rand Daily Mail*, 15 Jan. 1908.

62   *C W*, vii, p.363, 'Life Sketch of Punditji', 16 Nov. 1907.

63   *Indian Opinion*, 25 Jan. 1908.

64   *C W*, vii, p.220, 'J L', 7 Sept. 1907.

65   Ibid., p.221.

66   Ibid., p.309, 'J L', 26 Oct. 1907; ibid., p.328, 'J L', 2 Nov. 1907, or *Indian Opinion*, 10 Aug. 1907.

67   See, for example, ibid., vii, p.339, 'A Word to the Wise', 9 Nov. 1907.

68   Ibid., vii, pp.72-3, 6 Jul. 1907.

69   See above, fn.58.

70   *C W*, vi, p.489, 'J L', 18 May 1907, or *Indian Opinion*, 17 Aug., 28 Sept. 1907.

71   *C W*, vii, p.159, 'Speech at Hamidia Islamic Society', 11 Aug. 1907; ibid., pp.295-6, 329, *Indian Opinion*, 17 Aug. 1907.

72   *C W*, vii, pp.267-8, 'J L', 5 Oct. 1907.

73   Ibid., vi. p.491, 'Meeting of British Indian Association', 18 May 1907; ibid., p.416, 'J L', 13 Apr. 1907.

74   Ibid., vii, p.318, 'J L', 26 Oct. 1907.

75   But see below, p.165, for an instance in which Gandhi responded to a severe crisis in the movement by seizing the political initiative.

76   *C W*, vii, p.136, 'J L', 3 Aug. 1907. This case refers to Ali Khamisa, a prominent member of the Kanmia community.

77   Ibid., p.420, 'J L', 7 Dec. 1907. Although this case refers to an employer preventing his employees from joining the movement, it is clear that the process could have worked equally well in reverse.

78   See *Indian Opinion*, 21 Sept. 1907.

79   See, for example, *Indian Opinion*, 2 Nov. 1907, 4 Jan 1908, or *C W*, vii, p.97, 'Measure of Indian Strength', 13 July 1907; ibid., p.173, 'J L', 17 Aug. 1907; ibid., pp.143-4, 'J L', 10 Aug. 1907; ibid., pp.199-200, 'Need for Great Caution', 31 Aug. 1907; ibid., p.461, 'J L', 28 Dec. 1907. Gandhi also instructed Polak to use this tactic during his fund-raising trip to India in 1909. Polak was told to make separate appeals to Muslim Anjumans 'and lay stress upon the fact that Mahomedan interests are very much involved in South Africa', *C W*, ix, pp.412-5, Gandhi to Polak, 16 Sept. 1909.

80   Ibid., viii, p.194, 'J L', 18 Apr. 1908. The Kanmias were members of a Gujerati farmer caste from Broach district. And see also, *C W*, vii, p.309, 'J L', 26 Oct. 1907 for Akuji's offer to pull out the Kanmia employees of a certain 'blackleg'.

81   *Indian Opinion*, 30 Nov. 1907.

82   The most striking instance of boycotting a 'blackleg' was undoubtedly that of Ramsunder Pundit. See below, p.161. And see, *C W*, vii, pp.295-6, 'J L', 19 Oct. 1907; the Hamidia Society recommended that 'all contacts with . . . [the blackleg] should be cut off, his

employees should give notice and quit his service, and that other Indians should have no business dealings with him'. See also, *Indian Opinion*, 1 Feb. 1908.

83   *C W*, vii, p.347, 'J L', 9 Nov. 1907; ibid., p.393, 'J L', 30 Nov. 1907.

84   Ibid., p.80, fn.1.

85   *Indian Opinion*, 6 July 1907.

86   *C W*, vii, p.118, 'Struggle in Pretoria', 26 Jul. 1907.

87   *Indian Opinion*, 3 Aug. 1907.

88   Gandhi spoke at a meeting of NIC on 20 July. *C W*, vii, pp.113-15. A special meeting in support of passive resistance was held in Cape Town on the 19th. *Indian Opinion*, 27 July 1907. Telegrams from Natal and the Cape, printed in *Indian Opinion* on 10 and 17 Aug. 1907 reveal much duplication. There were some half-dozen from NIC alone, for instance.

89   *Indian Opinion*, 3 Aug. 1907.

90   *Pretoria News*, 1 Aug. 1907.

91   *Indian Opinion*, 10 Aug. 1907 and *C W*, vii, p.118, 'Struggle in Pretoria', 26 July 1907.

92   Gandhi claimed that most of the 'blacklegs' came from Pretoria. *C W*, vii, p.330, 'J L', 2 Nov. 1907.

93   Ibid., p.309, 'J L', 26 Oct. 1907.

94   *Rand Daily Mail*, 15 Nov. 1907.

95   Ibid., 15, 16 Nov. 1907. The work stoppage was called by means of telegrams from BIA to the rural centres. See also, *Indian Opinion*, 30 Nov. 1907, and *C W*, vii, p.389, 'J L', 30 Nov. 1907.

96   *Indian Opinion*, 7 Dec. 1907.

97   Ibid., 4 Jan. 1908.

98   *Rand Daily Mail*, 28 Dec. 1907.

99   *Indian Opinion*, 4, 11 and 18 Jan. 1908.

100   See below, p.153.

101   See, for example, *C W*, vi, pp.485-8, 'J L', 18 May 1907; ibid., vii, pp.172-3, 'J L', 17 Aug. 1907.

102   *C W*, vii, p.250, 'J L', 28 Sept. 1907.

103   Ibid., p.163, 'Implications of Indian Offer', 17 Aug. 1907.

104   Ibid., p.437, 'J L', 14 Dec. 1907.

105   May, June 1907, *Indian Opinion* (English eds.).

106   The suggestion was Gandhi's, but implementation had to be delayed due to initial opposition from M S Coovadia, Treasurer of BIA. *C W*, vii, p.222, 'J L', 7 Sept. 1907.

107   *Indian Opinion*, 2 Nov. 1907.

108   Ibid., 10, 17, 24 Aug. 1907.

109   There are countless examples of the use of this tactic. For instance,

the report under an *Indian Opinion* headline 'Blacklegs in November' read in part: 'Everyone felt sorry that Mr Khota's men had applied. The Surati community feels humiliated by the action of these men. The Gujerati Hindus are very much upset on account of Mr Ratilal's applications. It was observed that the Gujerati Hindus had so far remained clean'. *C W*, vii, p.420, 7 Dec. 1907.

110   *C W*, vii, p.169, 'J L', 17 Aug. 1907. The Pietersburg Indians had already been identified as Memons. Ibid., p.144, 'J L', 10 Aug. 1907. Also, ibid., p.300, 'J L', 19 Aug. 1907.

111   For example, ibid., x, pp.96-7, Gandhi to Gokhale, 6 Dec. 1909; ibid., p.189, 'Preface to *Indian Home Rule*', 20 Mar. 1910; ibid., pp.230-1, Gandhi to Gokhale, 25 Apr. 1910.

112   Ibid., vii, p.187, 'Suggestion to Readers', 24 Aug. 1907; ibid., vi, pp.392-3, 'Suggestion to our Transvaal Readers', 6 Apr. 1907.

113   Ibid., vi, pp.380-1, Gandhi to C Gandhi, 25 Mar. 1907.

114   *C W*, vii, pp.101-2, 'J L', 20 Jul. 1907.

115   *C W*, vii, p.255, 'Picket's Duty', 28 Sept. 1907.

116   *Indian Opinion*, 3 Aug. 1907.

117   *C W*, vii, p.288, 'J L', 12 Oct. 1907. See also a full page picture of the 'Indian Passive Resistance Volunteers in Pretoria', Supplement to *Indian Opinion*, 28 Sept. 1907.

118   P K Naidoo provides the most striking example. He was recruited at a meeting on 28 July 1907 (*Indian Opinion*, 3 Aug. 1907) and was still active during the 1913 strike.

119   *Rand Daily Mail*, 3 Dec. 1907; *C W*, vii, p.315, 'J L', 26 Oct. 1907.

120   *C W*, vii, p.258, 'Duty of Volunteers', 28 Sept. 1907.

121   *Indian Opinion*, 21 Sept. 1907 (Zeerust). But see *Transvaal Leader*, 2 Sept. 1907, *Rand Daily Mail*, 23 Sept., 27 Sept., 4 Oct. 1907, for formal picketing in respectively Heidelburg, Benoni and Zoutpansburg.

122   *C W*, vii, pp.262-3, 'Letter to *Rand Daily Mail*', 28 Sept. 1907.

123   *Rand Daily Mail*, 24 and 25 Oct. 1907.

124   *Johannesburg Star* (weekly ed.), 3 Aug. 1907; *C W*, vii, p.210, BIA to Col. Sec., 7 Sept. 1907 and ibid., p.246, 'J L', 21 Sept. 1907.

125   *Rand Daily Mail*, 29 Oct. 1907.

126   *C W*, vii, p.258, 'Duty of Volunteers', 28 Sept. 1907.

127   *C W*, v, p.378, 'J L', before 4 Aug. 1906.

128   Ibid., vi, p.389, 'J L', 30 Mar. 1907.

129   Ibid., vii, p.10, 'J L', 1 Jun. 1906.

130   Its postal address was Gandhi's Johannesburg law office.

131   But see also one of the items listed under the summary of accounts.

132   *C W*, vii, p.388, 'J L', 30 Nov. 1907.

133   Ibid., p.208, 'Speech at Congress Meeting', 7 Sept. 1907.

134   BIA voted £300 to H O Ally to cover domestic expenses, and an additional half share (with NIC) of the £600 which was estimated as the total cost of the deputation.

135   Lichtenstein and Blake's bill of £88.16.10d (see summary of accounts) was not strictly connected with the movement. However, outside legal advice was sought from time to time to confirm or clarify interpretations of legislative proposals which had a direct bearing on the movement.

136   *C W*, vi, p.363, 'J L', 9 Mar. 1907; ibid., pp.276-9, 'South African British Indian Committee', 12 Oct. 1907.

137   Ibid., p.371-2, 'South African British Indian Committee', 23 Mar. 1907.

138   *C W*, vii, appendix VII.

139   *C W*, vii, appendix VII.

140   Ibid., vii, pp.278-9, 'South African British Indian Committee', 12 Oct. 1907; ibid., p.318, 'J L', 26 Oct. 1907.

141   Gandhi identified Alibhai Akuji as an almost indispensable link between the movement and the Kanmias, *C W*, viii, p.194, 'J L', 18 Apr. 1908.

142   *Indian Opinion*, 1 Aug. 1908.

143   *C W*, vii, p.171, 17 Aug. 1907.

144   Ibid., p.10, 'J L', 1 Jun. 1907.

145   Ibid., p.375, 'Suggestion to Indians in Transvaal', 19 Nov. 1907.

146   Gandhi was in Durban on 20 July, 4 September and mid-November. On the first two occasions he made direct appeals to NIC for funds. On the third he spoke about the movement at a Diwali celebration where a small collection was made. *C W*, vii, pp.113-5, 207-10, 372.

147   545 applications for registration certificates had been received by 30 Nov. 1907 when the registration period expired. CO 291/127/28881, Gov. to Sec. St., 20 Jul. 1908.

148   Licences had to be renewed by the end of the month. On 3 and 6 January applicants in Pretoria and Johannesburg were refused renewal unless they could produce registration certificates. On 7 January BIA received a letter from the Receiver of Revenue confirming that anyone trading without a licence would be subject to prosecution under the Revenue Licence Ordinance. *Rand Daily Mail*, 4, 7 Jan. 1908.

149   Ibid., 7 Jan. 1908.

150   *C W*, viii, p.113, 'Further Considerations', 29 Feb. 1908.

151   *Rand Daily Mail*, 30 Dec. 1907.

152   *C W*, viii, p.314, 'Ram Sundar "Pundit"', 4 Jan. 1908.

153   *C W*, vii, pp.442-3, 'Hajee Habib', 21 Dec. 1907.

154   There is no information available to determine why Gani stepped down. But the gradual erosion of merchant support in both Natal and the Transvaal suggests that by withdrawing from formal politics, Gani and his partner might have hoped to stop the movement before it seriously threatened merchant interests, either by alienating the government, or by leading to the radicalization of Indian politics.

155   *Rand Daily Mail*, 11, 14, 15, 28 Jan. 1908. In addition, the Moulvi was notified on 17 January that his temporary residence permit would not be renewed and that unless he left the colony immediately he would be subject to arrest and imprisonment; ibid., 18 Jan. 1907.

156   TABA, Smuts Collection (Private), 187/S48, Gov. to Smuts, Conf. 9 Dec. 1907.

157   *Rand Daily Mail*, 14, 18, 21 Jan. 1908. The usual sentence was 14 days hard labour.

158   *C W*, viii, p.114, 'Further Considerations', 29 Feb. 1908.

159   Ibid., pp.40-2.

160   CO 291/127/28881, Gov. to Sec. St., 20 Jul. 1908.

161   The correspondence between Gandhi and Smuts is filed in CO 291/132/27629, SABIC to Sec. St., 29 Jul. 1908 and encls.

162   This observation is confirmed by C O minuting on 291/132/27629. See, in particular, minute by Lambert, 29 Jul. 1908.

163   *Rand Daily Mail*, 30 Jan., 7 Mar. 1908; *C W*, viii, pp.55-6, 'Speech at Meeting of British Indian Association', 8 Feb. 1908.

164   *Indian Opinion*, 8 Feb, 1908; *C W*, viii, pp.76-86, 'A Dialogue on the Compromise', 15 Feb. 1908; ibid., pp.99-101, 'A Brief Explanation', 22 Feb. 1908.

165   Gandhi estimated the size of this community at around 150.

166   *Indian Opinion*, 15 Feb. 1908.

167   *Rand Daily Mail*, 2 Feb. 1908.

168   *C W*, viii, pp.253-4, Gandhi to Smuts, 21 May 1908.

169   The government dealt with the matter by arresting two of the 'ringleaders'. CO 291/125/8354, Gov. to Sec. St. separate conf. 17 Feb. 1908.

170   *Rand Daily Mail*, 7 Mar. 1908.

171   *C W*, viii, p.85, 'A Dialogue on the Compromise', 15 Feb. 1908.

172   CO 291/127/28881, Gov. to Sec. St., 20 Jul. 1908, encl. minute no. 431, P M's Office, 11 Jul. 1908.

173   *C W*, viii, pp.49-51, Gandhi to Smuts, 1 Feb. 1908.

174   Ibid., pp.247-9, 'J L', 16 May 1908.

175   *C W*, viii, pp.260-1, BIA to Smuts, 30 May 1908; ibid., pp.261-2, Gandhi to Chamney, 26 May 1908; ibid., pp.266-9, 'J L' 30 May

1908.

176   Ibid., pp.290-92, Gandhi to Smuts, 13 June 1908. See also ibid., p.369, 'J L', 18 July 1908.

177   Ibid., pp.306-7.

178   Ibid., p.311.

179   Ibid., p.318, 'J L', 23 June 1908.

180   Ibid., pp.329-33, 'J L', before 2 July 1908.

181   Ibid., pp.342-5, BIA to Col. Sec., 6 July 1908.

182   Ibid., pp.352-3, Gandhi to Cartwright, 9 July 1908. See also ibid., pp.361-3, Gandhi to Cartwright, 14 July 1908.

183   Ibid., p.369, 'J L', 18 July 1908.

184   Ibid., p.370; ibid., p.378, 'Speech in Johannesburg', 20 July 1908.

185   *Rand Daily Mail*, 21 July 1908.

186   Ibid., 22 July 1908.

187   This was explicitly stated by Gandhi. *C W*, viii, p.370, 'J L', 18 July 1908.

188   Ibid., p.194, 'J L', 18 Apr. 1908.

189   *Rand Daily Mail*, 25 June 1908.

190   *C W*, viii, pp.353-4, 'Letter to the *Transvaal Leader*', 10 July 1908.

191   Ibid., p.367, 'J L', 18 July 1908.

192   *C W*, viii, pp.342-5, BIA to Col. Sec. 6 July 1908; ibid., p.370, 'J L', 18 July 1908; *Rand Daily Mail*, 25 June 1908.

193   Ibid.

194   *C W*, viii, p. 329, 'J L', before 2 July 1908; ibid., pp.335-6, 'Self-Sacrifice', 4 July 1908; ibid., pp.365-6, 'What Was, and Is, The Campaign About', 18 July 1908.

195   Ibid., p.61, 'Triumph of Truth', 8 Feb. 1908, and cf. Iyer, op. cit., p.155.

196   *C W*, viii, pp.58-9, 'Humility', 8 Feb. 1908.

197   Ibid., pp.172-4, 4 Apr. 1908; ibid., pp.185-7, 11 Apr. 1908; ibid., pp.196-9, 18 Apr. 1908; ibid., pp.212-14,. 25 Apr. 1908; ibid., pp.217-21, 2 May 1908; ibid., p227-9, 9 May 1908.

198   Ibid., p.241, 'Sarvodaya (I)', 16 May 1908.

199   The expression was coined after a competition sponsored by *Indian Opinion*, *C W*, viii, pp.131-2, 7 Mar. 1908.

200   Iyer, op. cit., p.252.

201   *C W*, viii, pp.91-2, 22 Feb. 1908 (from the Gujerati).

202   Ibid., p.289, 'Sarvodaya (V)', 13 June 1908.

203   Ibid., pp.370-5, 'Sarvodaya (IX)', 18 July 1908.

204   See, for example, *C W*, vii, p.331, 'J L', 2 Nov. 1907.

205   But see Cd. 5363, no.69, Dep. Gov. to Sec. St., 2 Oct. 1909, encl. Ministers to Dep. Gov. 20 Sept. 1909 (concerning Chella Nagapan who died six days after his release from prison. Nagapan's case was

unusual, but clearly some of the passive resisters were brutally treated in jail).

206   *C W*, viii, p.336, 'Self-Sacrifice', 4 July 1908; ibid., p.392, 'Speech at Mass Meeting', 23 July 1908.

207   *C W*, vii, pp.365-6, 'What Was, and Is, the Campaign About?', 18 July 1908.

208   The Johannesburg Town Council dismissed virtually all of its Indian employees, except those who worked for Parks and Estates and who could not readily be replaced by African workers. *Rand Daily Mail*, 25 Jan. 1908. See also, *Indian Opinion*, 5 Sept. 1908, 27 Mar. 1909, and *C W*, vii, p.319, Gandhi to Wedderburn, before 31 Oct. 1907.

209   *C W*, viii, p.391, 'J L', 21 July 1908.

210   Ibid., pp.407-10, 'J L', 1 Aug. 1908.

211   The Bill was gazetted on 11 Aug. 1908.

212   Attendance at mass meetings was back up to around 1 500 by early August. *Indian Opinion*, 1 Aug. 1908.

213   *C W*, viii, pp.451-2, Gandhi to Smuts, 14 Aug. 1908.

214   *Rand Daily Mail*, 8 Aug. 1908.

215   *Indian Opinion*, 22 Aug. 1908. See also, *Rand Daily Mail*, 17 Aug. 1908, *Transvaal Leader*, 17 Aug. 1908.

216   *Indian Opinion*, 22 Aug. 1908.

217   *C W*, vii, p.452, Gandhi to Smuts, 14 Aug. 1908.

218   Ibid. See also chairman's speech at 16 Aug. mass meeting. *Indian Opinion*, 22 Aug. 1908.

219   *Indian Opinion*, 22 Aug. 1908.

220   *Rand Daily Mail*, 17 Aug. 1908.

221   *Indian Opinion*, 22 Aug. 1908.

222   *C W*, ix, p.13, 'J L', 7 Sept. 1908.

223   Ibid., pp.1-2, 'J L', 31 Aug. 1908.

224   *Rand Daily Mail*, 15 Dec. 1908, 27 Jan. 1909.

225   *C W*, ix, p.2, 'J L', 31 Aug. 1908.

226   Ibid., pp.63, 65-6, 'J L', 26 Sept. 1908.

227   Ibid., pp.72-3, 'How Natal can Help', 26 Sept. 1908.

228   TABA, CIA II/7/M5/19/E/67/5, Burgess (Durban representative of Transvaal Col. Sec.'s office) to Dept. of Asiatic Affairs, 1 Oct. 1908. Burgess was reporting the substance of a conversation with Camroodeen.

229   *Indian Opinion*, 10 Oct. 1908.

230   Ibid., 12 Sept., 10 Oct., 21 Nov. 1908.

231   Ibid., 12 Sept., 10 Oct., 21 Nov. 1908.

232   *C W*, ix, p.63, 'J L', 26 Sept. 1908; ibid., p.109, 'Speech at Hamidia Islamic Society', 13 Dec. 1908; *Indian Opinion*, 10 Oct., 26 Dec. 1908.

233   *C W*, ix, pp.130-2, 'Shopkeepers versus Hawkers', 9 Jan. 1909. Of 111 resisters in jail in March 1909, only three had contravened the licensing laws. CO 291/137/7809, Gov. to Sec. St., 4 Mar. 1909.

234   *C W*, ix, pp.130-2, 'Shopkeepers versus Hawkers', 9 Jan. 1909. This was possibly only the tip of the iceberg. One of the hawkers claimed in a letter to *Indian Opinion* that fear of the merchants prevented hawkers from voicing 'their views freely at meetings'.

235   *C W*, ix, pp.151-3, 19 Jan. 1909.

236   *Rand Daily Mail*, 22 Jan. 1909.

237   *C W*, ix, p.184, 'The Transvaal Struggle', 6 Feb. 1909.

238   Ebrahim Aswat, secretary of BIA who became acting chairman of the party when Cachalia was jailed. *C W*, ix, p.166, 'Aswat to Creditors', 23 Jan. 1909.

239   CO 291/136/8942, Gov. to Sec. St., 22 Feb. 1909, encl. minute by Ministers no.82, 19 Feb. 1909.

240   TABA CIA II/9/M5/27/E67/7, Haji Habib to Registrar of Asiatics, 8 Feb. 1909; ibid., 31/E67/7, Haji Habib to Registrar, 13 Feb. 1909. And see also, Chinese informants, ibid., 60/E67/7, Ly Kai to Registrar 22 Mar. 1909; ibid., 52/E67/7, Ly Kai to Registrar 25 Mar. 1909; ibid., 39/E67/7, 'S R P' to Registrar, 24 Feb. 1909. This information was acted on: ibid., 27/E67/7, Registrar of Asiatics to Commissioner of Police, Pretoria, 10 Feb. 1909, and ibid., 49/E67/7, Registrar to District Commissioner of Police, 13 Mar. 1909.

241   *Indian Opinion*, 13 Mar. 1909. There were 11 men in jail at the time. CO 291/137/7809, Gov. to Sec. St., 4 Mar. 1909.

242   TABA, CIA II/9/M5/52/E67/7, Report by Supt., 11 Apr. 1909.

243   *C W*, ix, p.216, 'Speech at Pretoria Meeting', 24 May 1909.

244   Ibid., p.218, 'Speech at Johannesburg Meeting', 24 May 1909.

245   In July 1909, Gandhi claimed that there had been 'over 2 500 imprisonments' since the start of the movement. TABA, Gov. Gen. 716/15/669, A Statement of the Transvaal British Indian Case, July 1909. This seems to be an inflated figure. In October 1910, by which time jail-going had virtually ceased, the government put the total number of arrests for non-compliance with the registration laws, and trading and hawking without a licence at 2 124. Ibid., 706/15/57, minute from Ministers, no.570, 3 Oct. 1910, and encl. It is not possible to confirm either of these figures without access to police records for the period. These, I was informed by the chief archivist in the Pretoria Archives in September 1976, have been destroyed.

246   *C W*, ix, pp.218-9, 'Speech at Johannesburg Meeting', 24 May 1909.

247   Ibid., pp.249-50, 'J L', 12 June 1909. See also *Indian Opinion*,

5 June, 19 June, 26 June, 3 July 1909.

248   The members of the deputation committee were: H O Ally, Gandhi, Haji Habib, A M Cachalia, Thambi Naidoo, N A Cama, Shahboodeen. Omerjee Sale, Ali Kamissa, Dadabhai, G V Godfrey. *C W*, ix, Appendix XIII. Ally, Habib, Kamissa, Dadabhai and Godfrey were also members of the conciliation committee.

249   The deputation's statement for the Col. Sec. noted only that the delegates were nominated at a meeting of over 300 British Indians. TABA, Gov. Gen. 716/15/669.

250   *Indian Opinion*, 26 June, 3 July 1909, and *C W*, ix, pp.257-8, 'Deputation', 19 June 1909.

251   *C W*, ix, Appendix, XIII.

252   Ibid., pp.341-2, 'Letter to Ameer Ali', 7 Aug. 1909.

253   Ibid., pp.255-6, 'Letter to *The Star*', June 1909.

254   Ibid., Appendix, XIII.

255   Smuts was solidly backed by the C O in his handling of the movement. See, in particular, CO 291/141/27075, minute by Lambert, 19 Aug. 1909, on Ampthill to Sec. St., 11 Aug. 1909: 'The Indians are really the main obstacle to any settlement because they persist in asking what South Africans will not concede'.

256   *C W*, ix, pp.514-9, 'Letter to the Press'.

257   Ibid., p.522, 'Deputation's Last Letter', after 6 Nov. 1909. And cf. Albert Camus, *The Rebel* (New York, 1956), p.14: 'The very moment the slave refuses to obey the humiliating orders of his master, he simultaneously rejects the conditions of slavery'.

258   Erik Erikson's analysis of the document is extremely interesting; op. cit., pp.217-26. See also, *C W*, x, pp.203-7, Gandhi to M Gandhi, 2 Apr. 1910, for further explanation by Gandhi.

259   This is clear in any case. Also, in a letter to Polak dated 14 Oct. 1909, Gandhi wrote that the ideas in *Hind Swaraj* 'are not new but they have only now assumed such a concrete form and taken a violent possession of me', *C W*, ix, p.481.

260   *C W*, ix, p.395, fn.1.

261   This is implicit in *Hind Swaraj*, and see also fragments of a letter 'probably addressed to Maganlal Gandhi) 5 Feb. 1910, *C W*, xi, p.151.

262   I Wallerstein, *Africa, the Politics of Unity* (New York, 1967) p.221.

263   *C W*, ix, p.182, 'My Second Experience in Gaol (V)', 30 Jan. 1909.

264   For example, CO 291/142/27587, Gandhi to Sec. St., 16 Aug. 1909 and encl.

265   Iyer, op. cit., p.326.

13 and 14 *Indian and Chinese leaders during the passive resistance campaign,* January 1908. Gandhi *on far left,* Thambi Naidoo *fourth from left in top picture.* (HWPC, *from* Transvaal Leader, *weekly edition, 18 January 1908)*

15 *Crowd outside the police court while leaders were being sentenced,* January 1908 (HWPC, *from* Transvaal Weekly Illustrated, *18 January 1908)*

16 *Mass meeting, early 1908 (HWPC, from* Transvaal Leader, *weekly edition, 18 January 1908)*

17 *16 August 1908: burning the registration certificates (HWPC, from* Transvaal Weekly Illustrated, *22 August 1908)*

CHAPTER FIVE

Natal: The Politics of the New Elite, 1908 — 1912

The Natal Indian Patriotic Union, the new elite's first political organization, grew out of a slowly increasing dissatisfaction with the Congress at a time when the economic pressures of the post-war depression in Natal were beginning to lower the ceiling on upward mobility for Indian white collar workers. In late 1905 and early 1906 *Indian Opinion* published letters to the editor criticizing the narrowness of the party's social base and interests. The correspondents called for a broadening of its membership.[1] In January 1907, a handful of the emerging elite — most of them colonial-born white collar workers — convened a meeting in Durban to discuss the unrepresentative nature of the party. Two alternatives were proposed: asking the Congress to open up its membership to the young colonials by lowering the annual dues; or forming a separate organization if the Congress refused to co-operate. In an *Indian Opinion* editorial Gandhi attempted to dismiss this criticism of the party as a reflection of the discontent of men 'who feel aggrieved at not being able to figure prominently in the work of the Congress'. But the editorial also implied dissatisfaction with the extent to which the interests of the 'Tamils' (colonial-born white collar workers) were represented by the party.[2] Both suggestions, which were not unconnected, seem to have been valid.

These, and other rebukes,[3] were sufficient to delay the creation of a new party. It is not hard to find reasons for this delay. The emerging elite lacked political experience, funds, and legitimacy in the eyes of the colonial government. They had no desire to assume an independent political identity. As P S Aiyar and V Lawrence — two of their main spokesmen — pointed out: 'It would be the height of unwisdom and folly for a handful of young, inexperienced men to found a political institution without funds and without influence'. The 'Natal Congress . . . is recognized by the Imperial and Colonial governments as the representative institution of the Indian Community in Natal.'⁴ A second meeting was thus held in January 1907 where a decision was taken simply to approach the Congress with a request to lower its membership fee.⁵ Two months passed before the request was considered by the party on 8 April. Gandhi was in Durban at the time trying to rally support for passive resistance and he proposed that the question should be turned over to a special committee of the Congress. A group of party notables was duly elected.⁶ No further information on the request appears in the records.

More than a year later, some time around March 1908, NIPU was formed in Durban. Its first president was P S Aiyar, and its officers included several of the speakers at the 1907 meetings.⁷ Aiyar's newspaper, *African Chronicle*, which is the major source of information for the politics of the new elite, did not go into print until July 1908. *Indian Opinion* reports concentrated on voluntary registration in the Transvaal during March and April. There is therefore no direct evidence of the birth of NIPU. However, it seems to have followed closely on, and may have been connected with, the rowdy 6 March Congress meeting where Gandhi narrowly escaped a second assault while trying to explain his compromise with Smuts. One of the first recorded acts of NIPU was a letter of support for Gandhi and passive resistance.⁸ Indeed, despite Gandhi's failure to bestow approval on the politics of the new elite, a solid core remained committed to him throughout the next six years, wavering only once in their loyalty.

In April 1908 NIPU founded three more branches in rural centres close to Durban (Sea Cow Lake, Springfield, Isipingo).⁹ Other branches were opened in Pietermaritzburg in August, Tongaat (close to Durban) in September, and Newcastle in the northern coal district in January 1909.¹⁰ The work of opening up new branches was done by officials of the party's headquarters in Durban. Numbers of them were present at several of the inaugural meetings. Support for these meetings appears to have been mobilized by Hindu institutions or local petty traders, ¹¹ indicating that the urbanized new elite drew on whatever connections they had in the rural areas. Some idea of the appeal which was used to stir initial curiosity about the party is given by a report on the inaugural meeting in Isipingo which noted that word had been spread among the local Indian population that 'the proceedings would be conducted in . . . [Tamil] and that the promoters were local men, willing to gather information from them and impart to them that which was necessary for the betterment of their condition.'[12]

With the exception of the Pietermaritzburg branch, none of the up-country branches seems to have long outlived its inaugural meeting. Interest in the 'betterment of their condition' and in a Tamil language party was clearly high among colonial-born Indians, but NIPU had more ambition than experience, more enthusiasm than resources, and it proved difficult enough to keep the party going in Durban, let alone anywhere else.

Although the Durban branch of NIPU was still in existence late in 1910 the party functioned effectively only until around mid-1909, a little over a year. During that time NIPU organized some half-dozen 'mass' meetings in Durban and Pietermaritzburg attended by audiences of up to 500.[13] The overlap between officials of NIPU and the Hindu and Catholic Young Men's Association[14] suggests that the party drew on these organizations to mobilize support for the meetings. It is important to note, however, that NIPU's orientation was strictly secular. The party addressed itself to both the underclasses, to whom it looked for constituents,[15] as well as to the grievances of the new elite, its founders and leaders. A petition was presented to the Natal legislature by NIPU in 1908, and a second to the imperial government in mid-1909.

This bare recounting of the party's brief record does not look particularly impressive — the upcountry branches as quick to wither as they had been to blossom, the main branches themselves dead in less than a year and a half. But during that time NIPU successfully reintroduced the interests of white collar workers and of indentured and ex-indentured workers into Natal Indian politics, and in a more meaningful way than they had been represented by NIC in the 1890s.

On 3 August 1908, NIPU submitted a petition to the legislative assembly signed by 400 ex-indentured labourers claiming that they had failed to understand the implications of the £3 tax on ex-indentured workers when they signed their contracts. *African Chronicle*'s report on the petition illuminates both the depth of the problem faced by the tax payers and the fresh, aggressive approach which the new elite brought to bear on the question. The *Chronicle* described the effects of the tax law thus: 'the man with a wife and children, who does not enjoy robust health, and who has not a penny saved, to him the Act of 1895 stands like a monster of death'.[16]

This petition attracted the attention of Congress leaders. The mass meeting which was held on 5 September 1908 to discuss a second petition (to the throne) was attended by Congress members Abdullah Haji Adam and Dada Osman, as well as H S L Polak and Maganlal Gandhi.[17] The petition, which was nearly a year in preparation, called for the elimination of the major grievances of the Natal Indians: the system of importing workers under contract, the £3 annual tax on ex-indentured labourers, the Dealers' Licences' Act, and the barriers which prevented the western-educated from upward mobility in white collar occupations and locked them into an inferior social status.[18] The petition was endorsed by the Congress and its substance included in the statement of grievances which was presented to the Colonial Office by the Congress delegation during the final stage of the negotiations for the union of the South African colonies in London in August 1909.[19]

The Congress's lukewarm commitment to the priorities of its new political rival is evident, however, in the differential emphasis which was placed on particular grievances by the two parties. NIPU's petition reversed the old merchant order of priorities: it began with the indentured labourers, then moved on to the ex-indentured (noting in particular the widespread hardship which had pushed hundreds of Indians into disastrous work contracts on the Benguela railway), before touching on the merchants. The delegation's statement of grievances reverted to the merchants' traditional order of priorities, dealing first of all with the Dealers Licences' Act which was described as a 'matter of life and death to us'.[20] This was confirmed in a meeting between the delegates and the Under Secretary of State for the Colonies. When asked to state their most important grievance, the delegates replied unanimously that it was the licensing act;[21] and a minor modification of the act was in fact secured during the Union negotiations.[22]

Even in the earliest stages of their development as an independent political force the new elite thus made a potentially significant breakthrough. They reintroduced the grievances of the underclasses into Indian politics in a new and more effective way. The Congress responded to this first challenge to their claim to be the representatives of the entire Indian community by immediately enlarging their own platform. Later events suggest that they felt less threatened by the politicization of the new elite *per se*, than by the possibility — reflected in NIPU's priorities — that they might radicalize Indian politics by successfully drawing on the popular classes for support. But the Congress's submission to the London negotiations indicates that the merchants felt sufficiently secure in mid-1909 to avoid a significant commitment to the new political impulses which the Indian community was beginning to generate. This was no doubt partly due to the fact that NIPU was already disintegrating rapidly. However, the commentary of the governor of Natal on the delegates to London provides another important explanation for the Congress's confidence. By 1909 the party had achieved two of its basic aims: official recognition of both the superior status of the commercial elite, and the Congress's claim to be the legitimate voice of the Natal Indians. The governor described the party's delegates to London as 'reliable and respectable men . . . representatives of the Mussulman Indians from whom and from . . . [the Congress] the Hindus of the Colony, or at any rate a considerable section of them, have recently disassociated themselves'.[23] The delegates' submission was careful to confirm this impression of moderation[24] — a particularly revealing formulation given not only the emergence of a new political party in Natal, but also the fact that Gandhi was in London at the same time representing the Transvaal passive resisters.

Gandhi's reaction to the emergence of a new political party was ambivalent despite the support for passive resistance which NIPU had affirmed in April 1908 and continued to reaffirm in the following months. The party's earliest activities were reported in *Indian Opinion* but without editorial comment.[25] Later, the paper openly criticized NIPU, though less directly than it had the new elite's activity in January 1907.

It is difficult to assess why Gandhi was so unreceptive to the new party given the great gap which had opened up between his personal philosophy and that which informed merchant politics. Indeed, Gandhi shared at least one of the new elite's political priorities. He had been urging the Congress to make unconditional demands for the stoppage of indentured labour since late 1907.[26] In fact, by this time, opposition to the continuing flow of Indian labour was so widespread that it made good political sense for anybody to support the issue: the Transvaal government wanted to end the labour flow and the Natal legislature had gone so far as to introduce a bill to end indentured immigration in mid-1908.[27] It is not unlikely that Gandhi had already reached, or was at least working towards, the conclusion which he expressed later: 'It must be borne in mind that even if Indians were to give up the agitation for the prohibition of indentured labour, the Union Parliament will certainly prohibit it on its own. Indians would then look small and would lose the credit which they have a chance of earning today'.[28]

Gandhi's position on the hardships of the £3 tax payers was less clear-cut however, and it seems unlikely that at this time he had any real understanding of the problems faced by Indian workers during the post-war depression. In 1906 he had sympathized with a group of complainants in a rural centre close to Durban, but pointed out that it would be very difficult to do anthing now about the tax which had passed into law in 1895.[29] In 1908 when thousands of ex-indentured workers were being driven back under contract by the cumulative pressures of the depressed economy and the annual tax, *Indian Opinion* began to receive occasional letters of complaint about the hardships caused by the tax. The letters were published, but generally without editorial comment.[30] NIPU's petition to the legislative assembly in August, signed by 400 ex-indentured labourers, was treated with caution. *Indian Opinion* agreed that the weight of the tax on women and youths was so heavy that it was bound to reduce them to a condition of moral degredation. But the paper did not call for the repeal of the tax.[31]

When NIPU held its mass meeting in Durban on 5 September to discuss its proposed petition to the throne, H S L Polak and Maganlal Gandhi were in attendance. *Indian Opinion*'s English language report of the meeting was entitled 'The Old Prescription'. Gandhi criticized NIPU's tactics and claimed that if they really wanted to do something about the £3 tax the Natal Indians must assume the responsibility of 'initiating and carrying on a passive resistance campaign'. More importantly, Gandhi asserted the old claim that the Congress represented the entire Indian community, and denounced NIPU as the special representative of 'the interests of the colonial-born and bred section of the community'.[32]

Gandhi thus seems to have been far ahead of the Congress in identifying the direction which the politics of the new elite were to follow. Indeed, he may even have been ahead of the new elite themselves. NIPU claimed to represent the community as a whole, and the speeches and newspaper editorials of its president, P S Aiyar, did in fact cover the entire range of Indian grievances, from wage labourers' to white collar workers' to merchants'. But at the mass meeting two articulate young men, Lazarus Gabriel, the vice-president of the

Durban branch of the party, and R N Modaley, an official of both the Hindu Young Men's Association and the Pietermaritzburg branch of NIPU, spoke at length on the inherent rights and privileges of the colonial-born in a way which had never been done before by a Natal Indian. Although Modaley's speech was described by *African Chronicle* as 'forcible', the depth of emotion behind Gabriel's comes through more clearly in the newspaper report:

> I am proud to stand before this audience, and to own that I am a descendant of an immigrant Indian who shed his life blood for the welfare of this Colony — we have made this our home, and as Colonial Born Indians we have an inherent right to remain in this Colony and enjoy all the rights and privileges of a properly constituted British Colonist . . . . We know no other country than Natal, and this is our home. To many of us, India is only a geographical expression. [. . . in the] so called Higher Grade Indian School . . . when a boy attains the age of 16 years, no matter how great the boy's ambition for further knowledge, he is practically turned out of the school [. . . this] is like placing a loaf of bread in a glass case and showing it to a hungry man. By private study four Colonial Born Indians appeared [in] and passed the Civil Service Exam of this Colony. The government, determined to keep the Indian down, has now formulated some law by which they debar Indians from competing. Where is the British idea of justice and fair play? And where is the famous British constitution? . . . it is certainly not here in Natal.[33]

Gandhi's ambivalent reaction to the emergence of the new elite, which varied between non-commital and negative, thus appears to have stemmed from the fact that their driving force drew some of its strength from a consciousness that could not possibly be shared by much of the community, and least of all the Congress, to whom Gandhi still looked for supporters for the Transvaal movement. It is also possible that Gandhi's Indian nationalism served as an additional barrier to a sympathetic appraisal of the strong assimilative tendencies which were manifest in the emergence of the new elite.[34] However, before their politics had developed beyond the point where they could be ignored or dismissed, NIPU's leadership had split, and the party had ceased to be an effective institution.

The Market Boycott Movement

The central figure in the debate which split NIPU was a Hindu missionary, a former Arya Samajist who claimed that he had transcended formal religious distinctions.[35] Swami Shankeranand, a Punjabi *brahmin* turned *sunnyasin*, described by *Indian Opinion* as 'well-built and of commanding presence', arrived in the colony in 1908.[36] A successor to Swami Parmanand who had visited Natal for a time in 1905 and established the first branch of HYMA during his stay, Shankeranand was eagerly awaited by the Natal Hindus.[37] His arrival on 4 October was celebrated — like that of any other visiting Indian dignitary — by a reception held in the Congress Hall in Durban and attended by about 1 000 people.[38]

Despite the warm welcome which he received from the colony's Muslim merchants, the Swami began touring the Natal coastal districts within two months of his arrival to urge assemblies of Hindus to revive their neglected religious practices and to denounce the widespread Hindu participation in *Mohurrum*.[39] New Hindu societies sprang into existence in his wake. By early 1909, branches of what *African Chronicle* referred to as either the 'Hindu Society' or the '*Veda Dharma Sabha*'[40] existed in Pietermaritzburg, Durban, Avoca, Umgeni, Springfield, Prospect Hall and Sea Cow Lake.[41]

By April 1909, both the tension which was to split the new elite, and the commanding position which Shankeranand was beginning to assume among the coastal Hindus in general, and some of the new elite in particular, had become apparent — Shankeranand was called in to arbitrate a dispute between members of the Pietermaritzburg branch of HYMA.[42] Within a month of this initial dispute Shankeranand had destroyed the fragile unity of the new elite and split NIPU. In May the Pietermaritzburg branch of the party publicly announced the severance of its links with party headquarters in Durban.[43] *Indian Opinion* did not report this split, and *African Chronicle*'s reports are confused. It is clear, however, that the rhetoric of the dissidents was anti-Gandhi, anti-Muslim, and anti-Congress, and that NIPU was identified with this perceived network.[44] The dissidents, led apparently by Shankeranand, had met with the Congress leaders and informed them that the 'Natal Indian Congress and the Natal Indian Patriotic Union are not representative organs of the Indian people and that . . . an institution[45] recently established by [Shankeranand] both in [Pietermaritzburg] and in Durban, is the real representative organ of the people'.[46] It is not made clear whether they repeated the unsuccessful demand of January 1907 that the Congress open up its membership by lowering the annual dues. *African Chronicle* reported only that the Congress leaders agreed to consider the matter, and that the split in NIPU occured soon afterwards.[47]

Despite the dissidentss rhetoric, and the nature of the organization to which their allegiance was transferred (the *Veda Dharma Sabha*), the grievances which Shankeranand used to mobilize them were not religious, but economic. The confrontation with the Congress, the split in NIPU, and the establishment of the Pietermaritzburg and Durban branches of the *Sabha* were accompanied by rumours that 'about a million pounds is going to be brought from India and that the money will be utilized for the purpose of establishing co-operative stores, educational institutions, political bodies and what not, Heaven only knows it'.[48]

Shankeranand's own motivations must remain speculative. However the evidence suggests that he was simply a Hindu zealot pursuing religious reform which, particularly under the circumstances existing in Natal, favoured drawing a sharp, clear line between Hindus and Muslims. The diffuse economic and social grievances of the young colonial-born men, the Congress's failure to represent these grievances, the predominance of Muslims in the party, the links which NIPU retained with the party — all of these factors lent themselves to an attempt to channel discontent with the social and economic status quo into a Hindu revivalism which found its counterpoint in an anti-Islamic and therefore anti-Congress stance.

Shankeranand's real interests are much more apparent in the social movement which he set in motion in Durban. In Durban, the Swami completed the destruction of NIPU which was again identified with the Congress in what was primarily an anti-Muslim and therefore anti-Congress movement. An attempt to analyze the dimensions, far less the dynamics of this movement, suffers the same limitations as a discussion of the first stage of NIPU's disintegration. Since both Gandhi, and P S Aiyar in his capacity as president of NIPU, were among Shankeranand's antagonists, reports in *Indian Opinion* and *African Chronicle* — the only existing documentation on the move-ment — are fragmentary. This problem is mitigated in part by the fact that Aiyar was evidently ignorant of the movement's anti-NIPU orien-tation when it began and, indeed, had sufficient contacts among the new elite to gather information on the movement. Thus although the

Chronicle's later reports are polemical and lacking in data, its earliest reports on the movement are both sympathetic and informative.

On 20 May 1909 a fight broke out in the Durban Mosque Market between Hindus and several prominent Muslim members of the Congress.[49] The underlying hostility erupted over an apparently meaningless dispute about a religious picture and resurfaced some ten days later in a more articulate form. On 31 May a rowdy meeting dominated by members of the new elite — white collar workers and the more well-to-do vegetable hawkers[50] — was held at Cato Manor near Durban. The discussion at the meeting centred around 'the best method of boycotting the Indian [Mosque] Market, and carry[ing] on a religious crusade against the Mohammedans.'[51] A committee of eighteen held a second, closed meeting at Swami Shankeranand's house shortly afterwards, where it was resolved to apply to the Town Council for new market premises. Permission had already been obtained to establish a temporary market in Victoria Street. The boycott of the Mosque Market began on 1 June. It was virtually complete.

It is possible, as the *Chronicle* alleged, that Shankeranand's committed followers ensured the success of the boycott by intimidating the petty cultivators who normally sold their produce there. It does seem likely that Shankeranand had no real concern for the cultivators, and that he simply used them in an attempt to further the interests of his emerging constituency (congregation would perhaps be more appropriate) — Hindu white collar workers and the more well-to-do, higher caste hawkers and petty traders. The movement's goals were more directly related to the grievances of the new elite than anyone else. The primary demand was for a share of the market profits. Although this was allegedly to be used to help the 'poorer classes for education',[52] it is hard to see how this could have been a popular demand; or, indeed, how improved educational facilities could have benefited the poorer classes when, as *African Chronicle* was quick to point out, their daily lives centred around the struggle to avoid re-indenture for failure to pay the £3 annual tax on ex-indentured workers.[53] The other major complaint of the boycotters, that the 'Indian merchants do not employ colonial-born Indians as clerks in their offices'[54] seems even less likely to have been the focal point of a popular cause. However, Aiyar's first editorial on the issue had suggested that the 'reason why the present market movement has gained general sympathy is there is no doubt that the poor basket people [the lowest level of cultivators — petty market gardeners who were often elderly women] were not subjected to proper treatment at the hands of the old Indian market people'.[55] It thus seems likely that although intimidation may have played a part in mobilizing popular support for the movement, its success derived mainly from manipulating a fundamental grievance of the poorer cultivators. As *African Chronicle* worded it, the leaders had convinced the 'petty peasants, the majority of whom make no more than a hand to mouth existence, that they will lead them to a place which is no less than a paradise, and that they could make their fortune with as little trouble as possible and in fact . . . that the golden tree will be planted in their house doors, and gold will pour in without even exerting to go and pluck it'.[56]

Despite the close ideological links between the newly established *Veda Dharma Sabhas* and the boycott movement, the boycott was carried out under the auspices of the Indian Farmers' Association whose establishment had also been inspired by Shankeranand.[57] The IFA appears to have been organized specifically for this purpose; there is no mention of it in the press before this period. Any explanation for why Shankeranand chose to establish yet another new association must remain speculative; but it seems likely, given the neglected state of the Hindu religion in Natal, that the task of rapidly mobilizing the petty cultivators might have appeared easier to effect under the auspices of a 'farmers' association' than a 'Hindu society'.

Although the Mosque trustees agreed to discuss the question of feeding market profits back into the wider community, they refused to share control over the profits with the IFA, or anyone else, on the grounds that their religion forbade them 'to part with funds belonging to the Mosque'.[58] It is difficult to establish the extent to which this was the real reason for the trustees' obduracy. Obviously, control of the market was a significant index of power and prestige in the Indian community, and Shankeranand's mobilization of the cultivators was thus potentially a very threatening political development. In any event the trustees refused to concede Shankeranand's demand, and the IFA therefore continued to market Indian produce on the temporary site which the Town Council had allocated to them at the beginning of the boycott. In July, unable to agree on a suitable permanent site for the new market, the IFA accepted an invitation from the Town Council to arbitrate. The Council's decision to consult representatives of the Indian Christians and

Muslims, as well as the IFA, is a good indication of the religious rhetoric generated by the secular-sounding Farmers' Association. It also suggests that the Council shared the Indian merchants' desire to maintain the status quo in Indian politics.[59] In early August the committee which had been elected by the IFA to negotiate with the Town Council split after C R Naidoo, the secretary of the committee and a relative newcomer to Indian politics, had publicly declared that the Association was unfit to operate the Indian market.[60] Further criticisms were directed at the IFA by the Muslim and Christian representatives at the Town Council sessions. The Association, in its turn, criticized 'Arab merchants', Gandhi, and the Christian representative, V Lawrence, president of the Young Men's Catholic Society and also joint honorary secretary of the Durban branch of NIPU and a loyal supporter of Gandhi.[61]

On 31 August the Town Council took it on itself to choose a new site, erect premises, manage the market and add its profits to the Council's revenue.[62] Although this decision was accepted by the IFA at the time,[63] the association approached the Council early in December with a suggestion that the market should be controlled jointly by the two bodies. This suggestion was rejected.[64] When the new market was opened in August 1910, the IFA, still trying to gain the control over Indian marketing which they had let slip through their fingers a year earlier, attempted to organize another boycott. This was shortlived,[65] and the total receipts for the new market's first year of operation were £2 194.7.3d. By August 1912, the annual receipts had risen to £3 218.1.8d.[66]

The IFA disappears from the records after mid-1910, together with the more than £500 profits which P S Aiyar estimated they had collected from the temporary market.[67] Although Shankeranand remained in South Africa until May 1913,[68] his influence dwindled rapidly after the boycott of the Mosque Market. By the time he left, he had been publicly repudiated by numbers of Hindu bodies not only in Natal, but also in the Transvaal and the Cape.[69]

By introducing Hinduism into the politics of the new elite as a primary level of identification, Shankeranand retarded the process of unification whose beginning had been reflected in the creation of NIPU. The party itself was damaged beyond repair after the breakaway of the Pietermaritzburg branch and the inevitable erosion of the main Durban branch during the boycott movement. Shankeranand's tactics, however, served to reinforce the growing awareness of a far more relevant dichotomy in the daily lives of the Natal Indians — the patron-client nature of the relationship between the merchants and the rest of the community whose interests they purported to represent. Thus although Shankeranand's intrusion into new elite politics was in large part responsible for the early disintegration of NIPU and, indeed, helped keep their politics in disarray throughout much of 1909 and 1910, the effects of this intrusion were not wholly negative. The new elite emerged from the experience with a clearer perception of how they wished to identify themselves, and of what should be the nature of their relationship with the merchants, and the underclasses from whom they had risen.

Reintegration, 1909 — 1911

By mid-1909, the political activity of the new elite, though not dead, had become less confident, more diffuse. Associations which were not identified as political, but which functioned as proto-political bodies, re-emerged as the most effective media of elite self expression. HYMA, their earliest organization, now approaching its fourth anniversary, flourished in both Durban and Pietermaritzburg in late 1909 and early 1910. More importantly, the Durban Indian Society, a secular body, appears in the records for the first time in the latter part of 1909, while a branch was opened in Pietermaritzburg in April 1910. It was DIS, above all, which provided a forum for the regrouping of the shattered elite. HYMA, DIS, and individual political initiatives, kept elite political interest and activity alive between the collapse of NIPU and the establishment of its successor organizations in 1911.

During the period of uncertainty and searching after the collapse of NIPU, maximum interest and attention was focussed on the question of educational facilities, the lifeblood of the new elite. In part, this reflected colonial government policy. In October 1909, the upper age limit for Indian scholars in government schools had been reduced to fourteen.[71] It is also clear, however, that apart from being an urgent issue of the moment, education represented a 'neutral' question on which all parties could agree. Late in 1909 the Pietermaritzburg and Newcastle branches of HYMA opened private Indian high schools.[72] HYMA also attended, and contributed to, the annual prize-giving at the Wesleyan and Methodist School late in 1909.[73] Weekly discussions at the Association stressed the need for industrial training facilities for Indians, and the benefits of education for Indian women. The *Veda Dharma Sabha*, the Durban Indian Society, and, in particular, *African Chronicle*, contributed to the growing clamour for more, and better, facilities.[74] The Congress was criticized for lavishing money on 'pomp and show' while doing nothing about the need for improved educational opportunities. At the same time, DIS raised the familiar criticisms of the party: the unrepresentative nature of its politics, and the high annual dues.[75]

The elite also continued to make forays into the other problem areas which had been defined and reintroduced into the Indian political arena by NIPU. C R Naidoo, who had moved into the forefront of Indian public affairs during his brief stint as secretary of the IFA's market committee, turned back to his two earlier preoccupations, the £3 tax and the system of indentured labour.[76] On 7 and 15 November 1909, public meetings were convened at Tongaat to choose a delegate to the forthcoming INC session at Lahore. Naidoo was appointed the delegate, charged with publicizing the grievances of the Indian underclasses in Natal — the conditions of indentured labourers, the £3 tax, widespread unemployment — and with trying to obtain assistance in India to end the system of indentured labour.[77] This was the first time that a representative of the new elite had been sent abroad with a political mandate. Although this innovation forms a coherent part of the larger pattern of a gradually increasing effort to politicize the grievances of the Natal Indian underclasses, there is insufficient evidence available to determine exactly whose innovation it was. Only one of the five conveners of the meetings, whose names were listed in *African Chronicle*, has been traced in the records: Ramdutt Maharaj, a landowner in Tongaat who, as early as 1890, rented out small-holdings to Indians,[78] but whose name, like those of the other conveners, is otherwise absent from the leadership of the new elite. In fact, C R Naidoo was the only politically active person among those who were reported in the *Chronicle*. It thus seems probable that when he sailed for India on 22 November, funded by the participants at the Tongaat meetings, Naidoo was carrying out a task that he had set for himself.[79]

Naidoo was not the only colonial-born Indian to maintain an interest in the conditions of Indian labourers. On 15 January 1910, NIPU held a meeting in the new Indian market to discuss the hardships of the £3 taxpayers.[80] The meeting came only three weeks after NIPU's final successful mass rally, a gathering of over 1 000 to greet Gandhi on his return from England,[81] which seems to have breathed a final flicker of life into the moribund party. The renewed criticisms of the tax were not followed up by NIPU, but P S Aiyar's promise, in an editorial on 29 January 1910, to begin agitating for the repeal of the tax, bore fruit late in 1911. Aiyar's anti-tax campaign will be discussed later.

One other topic was pursued by the new elite in late 1909 and early 1910. The question of trading rights for colonial-born Indians was made the subject of a petition to the legislative assembly on 4 January 1910.[82] The petition is of interest for several reasons. Most notably, this is the first demand by the new elite that they, specifically, be given access to the commercial sector.[83] However, they explained their demand in terms of the limited employment opportunities for educated Indians, which is in keeping with their other concerns for the western educated. It is also significant that this was the elite's most determined formal (though not informal)[84] demand thus far for a higher ceiling on their mobility on the grounds that they were South African born. The petition thus reflects an important step in the formation of the new elite's ideology. They were South African first, and Indian second: India was a 'mere geographic expression' for them.[85] Finally, the nature of the demand reflects the growth in the gap between what the new elite perceived to be their interests, and the interests of the merchants.[86] Since the passage of the Dealers Licences' Act in 1898, colonial government policy had served to prevent Indian commercial expansion. Indian commercial opportunities were thus strictly limited. Indeed, the petition was a response to the announcement of the meagre concession which had resulted from the pre-Union negotiations in London some months earlier: the right of *established* merchants to appeal the refusal of a trade licence to the supreme court. If the colonial-born were to obtain access to the commercial sector, they could thus do so only by reducing the interests of established merchants.

The petition was signed by 300 colonial-born Indians and endorsed at a mass meeting held in Pietermaritzburg early in January.[87] Like the other political initiatives of the new elite during the same period, this one did not endure. P S Aiyar, according to the *Chronicle*'s report, was asked for advice on how to secure the demand for trading rights. Aiyar suggested a full-scale campaign directed by a central committee with a network of sub-committees throughout the colony 'in order to arouse public feeling'.[88] If an attempt was made to follow Aiyar's advice, it was not reported in the press.

Throughout 1910 *African Chronicle* criticized the inability to unite which it claimed vitiated Natal Indian politics. 'The educated Indians of Durban are fond of cheap notoriety', the *Chronicle* noted on 29 October, 'each one desires to be the leader in every public movement . . . through not having sufficient followers for all the leaders, the matter generally collapses'. When Lutchman Panday, who had also attended the Lahore Congress,[89] returned from India, he added his voice to the call for political unity, suggesting, as the *Chronicle* had often done, the creation of a new party representative of the entire Indian community and with branches throughout Natal.[90] By this time, the hostility which characterized the market boycott movement and the establishment of the *Veda Dharma Sabhas*, had, in fact, subsided sufficiently to permit a return to organized politics. But the new party, when it was formed, represented the colonial-born, rather than all Natal Indians as Aiyar and Panday had envisaged.

The Colonial Born Indian Association emerged as timidly as NIPU had done. On 16 August 1910 a deputation of western educated men who had been born in the colony approached NIC with yet another request that the party widen its social base by lowering the annual membership dues. The Congress leaders evaded a decision by refusing to reply until Gandhi had been consulted.[91] If consultations took place, they do not appear in the surviving records. At the end of September, however, Gandhi met with representatives of the western educated when he visited Durban to receive Polak who returned from his fund-raising tour of India on 28 September.[92] By this time, they were already discussing the formation of a separate party for the colonial-born.[93] Gandhi talked them out of it temporarily.[94] Thus the history of the birth of NIPU was repeated.

When the CBIA was finally formed on 13 March 1911 it represented a direct response to the Congress's failure to include the grievances of the new elite in the party's petition of protest against the 1911 Union Government immigration bill. The bill, which was the first of several attempts to replace the immigration laws of the four former colonies with a single new piece of legislation, violated numerous existing rights in its attempt to impose uniformity. For the

Congress, the most important violations were:

(a) Replacement of the existing education test which allowed intending immigrants to be tested in a European language known to them. The 1911 bill proposed to examine immigrants in a language chosen by the immigration officer, and the merchants objected, like those in the Transvaal earlier, to legislation which might interfere with their ability to continue to import confidential clerks and shop assistants.[95]

(b) Inadequate protection for the residence rights of legally domiciled Indian immigrants, their wives and minor children, especially if any of these persons were non-resident at the time, or should wish to leave Natal temporarily in the future. The biggest merchants, at least, made frequent trips outside Natal, often as far afield as India. The available information suggests that the overseas trips lasted for months, and sometimes more than a year. The possibility of losing domiciliary rights during a temporary absence was thus a real threat to the commercial elite. Their concern for the rights of wives and minors, by contrast, reflects the fact that many merchants had immigrated without their families.[96]

(c) The inability to have recourse to a court of law, in the case of a person declared a prohibited immigrant by an immigration officer. This was especially threatening since the bill held the possibility that even those who were legally domiciled could be declared prohibited immigrants in the case of a temporary absence.[97]

The Congress's objections to the immigration bill and its successor bills in 1912 and 1913 will be discussed again in the following chapter. In the present context, the Congress's position on the bill is significant for the problem which it omitted rather than for those which it addressed. The main concern of the new elite, and the immediate reason for the establishment of the CBIA on 13 March 1911, was the immigration bill's failure to provide freedom of movement within the Union for Indians — particularly those born in South Africa, and those who wished to move between Natal and the Cape province (whose existing immigration laws posited special rights for Indians born in South Africa). The question of inter-provincial migration was raised by P S Aiyar at a NIC meeting on 9 March where the discussion centred on the list of objections which appeared in the party's petition to the legislative assembly.[98] The best that Aiyar could achieve, despite what he described as 'vehement protest', was a qualified objection which noted that the restriction on inter-provincial migration was 'unfortunate', but that 'in view of the anti-Asiatic prejudice existing in many parts of the Union, those represented by your petitioners do not desire to raise, for the time being, any objection to the restriction'.[99] The Congress had claimed since its inception to represent all Natal Indians and it was accepted as their spokesman by the Natal and imperial governments. On 13 March, four days after the NIC meeting, before the petition had even been submitted, R N Moodley presided over a meeting of colonial-born Indians to form an association to protect their interests in general, and to protest in particular the encroachment on their rights made by the immigration bill.[100]

Two days later the Colonial Born Indian Association, as the new party was called, met to draw up a petition protesting the deficiencies in the bill.[101] However, H S L Polak who, after his return from India, had remained in Natal as editor of *Indian Opinion* and who continued to rank with W L Ritch as one of Gandhi's most trusted lieutenants, successfully steered the new party away from an effective statement of protest. Gandhi's major interest in the immigration bill, which over-rode all other considerations for him, was to mould it into a form which would remove the outstanding grievances of the Transvaal *satyagrahis* and produce a successful conclusion to the passive resistance campaign. Polak had been in touch with him by cable as early as 7 March about the 'right [of] Natal born Indians going to Cape'.[102] He also kept Gandhi informed about the new elite's view of the immigration bill as reflected in editorials in *African Chronicle*.[103] On 13 March therefore, Gandhi, deep in negotiations with Smuts, and juggling objections to the bill from NIC, the Cape British Indian Union, and now the Natal elite as well, advised Polak that the colonial-born should be promised only that 'immediately the matter is settled and the Bill is on the Statute Book we will have to present our Bill of Rights throughout the Union, and work away for it, leaving me out of account'.[104] Polak's mediation[105] was successful, at least for a time. The petition of protest which the CBIA submitted to the legislative assembly on 15 March, while reserving the right to make further representations at a later date, simply repeated NIC's assertion (drafted by Gandhi)[106] that no formal objections would be raised at the moment 'in view of the anti-Asiatic prejudice existing in many parts of the Union'.[107]

Though the CBIA reflected the full flowering of a self-conscious political identity for the new elite, the old problems of timidity and indecisiveness, born of vulnerability and lack of experience in the political arena, had not been solved. The officers of the party — several of whom were members of Congress as well — were drawn from the group which had dominated the public life of the colonial-born Indians since the establishment of the first branch of HYMA in 1905. However, neither P S Aiyar nor C R Naidoo (who, alone among the leadership level of the new elite, demonstrated a capacity for independent action) appears to have been a member, far less an officer, of the CBIA. Naidoo moved to Dundee in the northern coal district at some time between his return from India in mid-1910 and his re-emergence in public life as the representative of the Dundee 'Madrasis' in November 1912.[108] Aiyar ceased to hold political office after he resigned as president of NIPU when the party was breaking up in November 1909.[109] But he continued to maintain an active interest in the new elite's politics, offering advice, encouragement and often severe criticism, through the columns of *African Chronicle*. In an editorial on 25 March, he railed against the CBIA's swift surrender to the Congress's policy line. 'If they also repeat like parrots what the Congress is doing', he wrote, 'then, we say deliberately, there is no need for a superfluous body and in name [the] Colonial Association'.

Aiyar's criticisms were followed by a radical reassessment of the Gandhi-Polak advice. On 8 April the CBIA called a mass meeting of colonial-born Indians in Durban, successfully mobilizing support from many coastal and up-country communities.[110] The chairman's opening speech noted that 'on further consideration . . . the provincial restriction contained in the [immigration] Bill was an unjust and unfair one to impose upon those born in South Africa who . . . had a birthright'; and 'they regretted' that Gandhi had not seen fit to include their grievances in his negotiations on the bill.[111] The first resolution passed by the meeting called on the government to remove or amend the provincial restriction in the immigration bill so 'as to exclude Indians born within the Union from the operation thereof'.[112]

The immigration bill was withdrawn on 25 April by the government, which had its own problems trying to gain acceptance of the bill by the Orange Free State which refused to compromise its existing discriminatory legislation. *African Chronicle* claimed that only the withdrawal of the bill prevented an open breach between the CBIA and the Congress.[113] It is still hard to believe, though, that the bold resolution of 8 April would have come to much under any circumstances. The CBIA spun like a weather-vane amid gusts of criticism, and *Indian Opinion* was unequivocally critical of the party following the 8 April meeting:

> Apart from this self stultification, which might be excused, by reason of the political inexperience of those responsible for the meeting, the resolution is bad in principle, inasmuch as it seeks for privileges specially for Colonial-born Indians that other domiciled or lawfully resident Indians may not have.[114]

What Gandhi did not know, and evidently had not bothered to explore, was the fact that the Colonial-born did not seek a *new* privilege, but simply the protection of their existing right, as South African-born Indians, to migrate to the Cape. Nevertheless, it seems highly unlikely that only the withdrawal of the immigration bill prevented a confrontation between the Natal elites. The resolution on the bill was not the only business discussed by the CBIA on 8 April. The third resolution called for a five-member deputation to approach the provincial government 'with a view to urge them to afford better facilities in respect of the issue of trading licences to colonial-born Indians and generally to do such other things as . . . seem meet in the premises aforesaid'. In addition, the chairman's speech raised the old grievance of the £3 tax, taking note of the fact that their future constituency would increasingly include numbers of Natal-born Indians who were subject to the tax.[115] However, the discussions at this meeting represented the peak of the CBIA's assertiveness. It did nothing about the £3 tax, and the proposed deputation to the government does not appear to have materialized. In August 1911 there was talk of passive resistance after the refusal of a trader's licence to a colonial-born man.[116] But it remained talk, despite the fact that in May a limited liability trading company whose founder was a vice-president of the CBIA,[117] and most of whose board of directors were Natal-born,[118] had been refused permission to assume the licence of an existing Indian business.[119] In March 1912 the CBIA finally submitted a petition to the government requesting special preference in traders' licences for the colonial-born.[120] The Association was goaded into this by a series of rejected applications to trade; in particular, a case in which established merchants objected to the application of a member of the CBIA which was ultimately rejected by the licensing officer.[121] If the party had any objections to the second immigration bill, which was under discussion between January and June 1912 and whose terms were at least as discriminatory as those in the first bill, these objections were not strenuous enough to merit attention in the press.

The CBIA at least served to keep the question of the £3 tax in the Indian political arena. On 15 May 1911 in a petition to the Colonial Secretary which dealt primarily with the immigration bill, the Congress called for the abolition of the tax which they referred to as 'a cruel and tyrannical imposition'.[122] In June H S L Polak, visiting England en route to India, was requested by the Colonial Secretary to produce a written statement of South African Indian grievances. Armed with the Congress's petition, Polak included the £3 tax in a statement issued over the name of the London-based South African British Indian Committee. But the tax still took a subordinate place to the vulnerability of vested commercial interests.[123]

The new elite's next political organization was more active, if not immediately more effective, than the CBIA. At some time between the 7 and 14 October 1911 the South African Indian Committee was formed. P S Aiyar was the driving force behind the Committee, whose sole purpose was to secure the repeal of the £3 tax.

Aiyar's interest in the tax was an old one, dating at least from the formation of NIPU in April 1908. Under Aiyar's leadership the party had collected signatures of £3 tax payers for a petition to the Natal legislature. The hardships generated by the tax had also featured prominently in the joint NIPU-NIC petition to the throne in July 1909, and the question was aired regularly in *African Chronicle*. In January 1910, the Natal legislature reviewed the workings of the tax act in the light of the Indian complaints and the needs of the Natal planters. They rejected a proposal to exempt women from the annual payment.[124] Aiyar responded by advocating, for the first time, systematic agitation for the repeal of the tax law.[125] But this was the period of maximum disjunction in the new elite's politics. Aiyar's only significant activity during the remainder of 1910 appears to have been to recommend at a public meeting in Charlestown that the law's capacity to imprison tax defaulters should be challenged in the courts.[126] In February 1911 he sought the opinion of W P Schreiner, the liberal Cape Senator, on the legality of the Tax Act. Although Schreiner agreed that the law was harsh, he pointed out that 'having been permitted to pass and having been promulgated it is legally unassailable'. His advice was that 'your objective should be to persuade the Union Parliament and Government of the injustice of the law, with a view to its repeal or amendment. To spend money on litigation in the matter will be simply to waste it'.[127] In late August Aiyar reported in his column 'Talk of the Town' in *African Chronicle* that an anti-tax movement was about to begin.[128] On 16 September the first official meeting was held.[129] Some three weeks later the central committee of the South African Indian Committee was constituted.

The Committee was unique in Natal Indian politics in many respects. Before it had even been formed, Aiyar made it clear that he had no wish to control the organization himself. His intention was simply to provide a 'common platform for sympathizers of whichever shade to come together and take up the £3 cause'.[130] The 64-man central committee was composed of 'representatives of all societies'. It included the leadership level of the Congress, but was overwhelmingly dominated by the new elite who comprised 55 of the 64 members.[131] Although the names of several are familiar from their other organizations, many of them are new. This reflects another striking feature of the Committee — the heavy representation of communities outside the traditional centres of Indian politics, Durban and Pietermaritzburg. At least one-third of the central committee, and possibly many more, were up-country representatives.[132]

Aiyar's goal was to bring massive popular pressure to bear on the government in order to force the repeal of the tax.[133] The strategy and tactics which he outlined for the Committee were thus also unique in Natal Indian political history. He planned a province-wide series of meetings to 'deepen into activity the interest of the people', particularly in 'country districts wherein reside the bulk of those who must pay the tax'.[134] *African Chronicle* served as a major medium of communication for the Committee. But, faced with a high rate of illiteracy in the labouring population, and a constituency virtually untouched by institutional politics, Aiyar also called on 'Preachers, Missionaries, Schoolmasters, Storekeepers, Sirdars and educated Indians generally' to take the campaign to the people.[135] Through the *Chronicle*, he invited requests to address meetings and form local sub-committees, 'essential to the success of the scheme', which were to have complete autonomy in enrolling members and collecting subscriptions.[136] Aiyar's tactics also included the press and pamphlet campaigns which had characterized the earliest stages of the Congress's politics. The

Committee's first activity, before its officers had even been chosen, was a deputation to the *Natal Mercury*.[137] By February 1912, copies of a pamphlet entitled, *The £3 Tax: An Appeal to the Empire* had been sent to leading South African newspapers, and MPs in South Africa, Britain and India.[138]

The campaign enjoyed some initial success, and then slowly dissolved into nothing, like the new elite's other political initiatives. Between late October and early December 1911, the Committee organized and addressed about a dozen workers' meetings. Participation at the meetings was mobilized in a variety of ways. A particularly successful rally at the huge Natal Government Railways Barracks in Durban resulted from a particularly appropriate choice of locale. Another Durban meeting was advertised by handbills. A branch of HYMA served as the focal point for a meeting in Sydenham. Handbills were distributed in one rural centre after the first meeting scheduled there was cancelled due to lack of participation; a local petty trader's store served as the meeting point in another rural centre.[139]

It cannot have been very difficult to attract audiences once the word had been spread that a committee of influential Durban Indians intended to do something about the £3 tax. The workers had a great deal to gain, and nothing to lose, by attending the meetings. As Aiyar noted in *African Chronicle*, the Committee seemed to have 'all the elements of success'.[140] Indeed, even during its brief active stage in late 1911, the powerful potential of an anti-tax campaign became apparent. In late November Aiyar received a letter from a *sirdar* at Burnside Colliery informing him that a mass meeting of Indian labourers on the mine had voted unanimously to support the Committee's actions.[141] The Burnside workers were far better organized, and more highly politicized than most Indian labourers; some eight months earlier they had staged a highly successful mass walkout from the colliery on behalf of a fellow worker.[142] However, the difference between the Burnside workers and a significant number of other Indian workers was one of degree, not of kind. There is information to make it abundantly clear that some degree of worker organization and cohesiveness existed in several other mines, among the railway workers, and, to a lesser extent, on the plantations. It thus seems reasonable to assert that Aiyar's hopes for widespread mobilization of the free labouring population would have been fulfilled, and with little assistance from the centre, if the Committee had remained active for a longer time.

One of the Committee's major weaknesses was lack of support from the merchants who represented the main source of funding for any significant political undertaking in Natal. Shortly after the beginning of the campaign *African Chronicle* ran a number of articles explaining that the merchants would lose a great deal of their business if, as seemed likely, the £3 tax forced large numbers of workers to leave the country. The paper noted that Natal whites would no longer tolerate the merchant presence in the absence of the labourers.[143] Nevertheless, the campaign funds remained low. Collections were made at meetings, but these were naturally small: 17s.9d. was subscribed at one Durban meeting, and £3.0.11d at another.[144] By the end of January, the *Chronicle* was issuing weekly appeals for subscriptions to the Committee's funds, but the active stage of the campaign had already ceased.

The Committee's strategy must also be questioned. The campaign did not last long enough to make clear what action Aiyar intended the workers to take once they had been mobilized. It seems highly unlikely, however, that he planned anything other than conventional constitutional protest. Two prominent members of the CBIA — J Royeppen and V Lawrence — who had spent time in the Transvaal as *satyagrahis*[145] unsuccessfully urged the use of passive resistance at the first formal meeting of the Committee. *African Chronicle* wrote a front page report on the meeting describing the would-be passive resisters as a 'few recalcitrants who are vainly trying to wreck the scheme'.[146] Lawrence and Royeppen found no support from others either. Abdullah Haji Adam, who chaired the meeting, dissolved it prematurely after Lawrence made an unsuccessful bid for the secretaryship of the Committee 'amid an uproar'.[147]

The use of strike action by the workers was never considered, despite the fact that Aiyar's writing on worker conditions was uncompromisingly critical. In April 1912 he wrote a highly favourable article on the Industrial Workers of the World, ending with the assertion that, 'the time is not far distant when the evils of capitalism as we know it will be done away with, and a more rational, and in every sense a sounder system of the employment of capital will be substituted'.[148] However, despite this flowing rhetoric, Aiyar did not articulate any strategy for transforming capitalist relations, or even question the floundering committee's tactics. His philosophy remains elusive. It seems certain that he was genuinely concerned with ameliorating the lot of Indian workers. But it is highly doubtful that he wished to provoke any disturbance, far less radical alteration, of the social order.

Besides a shortage of funds and a strategy which at best would have taken a great deal of time to become effective, the Committee evidently suffered from lack of leadership. The CBIA, well represented on the Committee, had little to offer in this respect. Aiyar himself had made it clear at the beginning of the campaign that he did not intend to direct it; and indeed, it is doubtful that he could have. A close reading of the *African Chronicle* editorials between 1908 and 1914 leaves the distinct impression that Aiyar was a talker rather than a doer. His calls to action were frequent, his schemes grand, he was a ready critic of other people's activity, but his own active involvement at the leadership level of Indian politics was quite limited. The Congress's activities both before and after the campaign suggest that it was interested in the £3 tax only insofar as it might be used by the new elite to mobilize the Indian workforce for political action, thus possibly radicalizing Indian politics and endangering the fragile but workable relationship which had developed between the merchants and the Natal government. The Congress notables who were officers of the Committee were influential and experienced enough to have taken charge of the campaign: their network of influence extended throughout Natal and they alone had access to large scale funding. The brief life span of the campaign thus permits the assumption that the Congress leadership made no attempt to achieve its success.

In terms of direct results Aiyar's anti-tax campaign was a complete failure. Indirectly it was of great significance for Natal's ex-indentured workers, representing a major possibility that the new elite could, and might, mobilize the workers for political action. The Congress, as noted, did nothing to assist that mobilization. But both the Congress and Gandhi responded to the campaign by swiftly elevating the abolition of the £3 tax to the top of their lists of grievances. The CBIA's reminder that its constituency would increasingly include £3 tax-payers had already been reflected in the Congress's and Polak's submissions to the Colonial Secretary in May and June 1911. At that point the tax was low on the list of South African Indian grievances. By the time Polak left London in October, shortly after the start of Aiyar's campaign, he ranked the tax with the Transvaal question as the most pressing of the South African Indians' problems.[149] This could only have been done on Gandhi's orders, and is in marked contrast to the instructions given to Polak on his trip to India in 1909 when he was simply told to do whatever he 'consider[ed] to be necessary on the Natal question'.[150] The Congress confirmed the new importance of the tax as a political issue in late 1911. Shortly after Polak's arrival in India in mid-November he received a cable from the party instructing him to 'lay great stress' on the abolition of the tax.[151] On 18 November the party addressed a petition to the Minister of Justice stating its intention to agitate for the repeal of the tax.[152] *Indian Opinion*, which offered little coverage of the Aiyar campaign, called on the Congress to work for the repeal of the tax 'at any cost'.[153] In a number of articles betwen November 1911 and February 1912, the paper highlighted SABIC and NIC correspondence on the tax under eye-catching headlines such as 'The £3 Tax: The Congress Follows the Matter Up.'[154]

The flurry of activity provoked by Aiyar's campaign died with the campaign. But in Britain, South Africa and India, the £3 tax had been brought to the forefront of South African Indian grievances. In late 1912 when Gokhale accepted Gandhi's longstanding invitation to visit South Africa on a fact-finding mission, the tax was on his agenda. Gokhale's belief that the Union ministers had promised the repeal of the tax, and their denial that they had done so, offered Gandhi a second 'breach of faith' which became the means to turn *satyagraha* into the truly mass movement that he had unsuccessfully sought for seven years. The final stage of the passive resistance campaign, the 1913 Natal Indian strike which will be discussed in the next chapter, secured both an end to the seven year old campaign, and the abolition of the tax.

The new elite's political record between 1908 and 1912 leaves unanswered certain questions which are difficult to approach in the absence of writings by the elite about themselves. It is by no means clear how profound was the commitment to the underclasses which is apparent even in their earliest political activity, and which intensified gradually, culminating in Aiyar's anti-tax campaign. That some of them increasingly sought to include at least the upper levels of the popular classes in their perception of themselves as 'South Africans' — with all that that connoted — is evident. Still, the question of motivation remains elusive.[155] It is difficult to judge with accuracy whether the failure to develop the mass-based politics on whose brink the elite hovered for five years derived from lack of real commitment to popular interests, or from the other problems which plagued the politics of the new elite. The failure to pursue effectively even their own interests suggests that the problem was broader than lack of commitment. Throughout the period under review the new elite was unable to produce anyone capable of independent political leadership. The weekly English editions of *African Chronicle* reveal a community with a lively existence of its own and an intricate network of social and political organizations appropriate to the needs of a group which was rapidly assimilating to a set of circumstances far removed from those into which their parents had been born. But the *Chronicle* also reveals the vulnerability and insecurity of the group as they sought to establish a political identity separate from the Congress in an increasingly threatening environment. Perhaps one of the best commentaries on the extent to which this may have been at the root of the new elite's failure to fulfill the promise of their politics — whether in respect to the underclasses or themselves — is the group's extraordinary loyalty to Gandhi, the only Indian in South Africa who demonstrated leadership ability and a real sense of direction in the political arena. However, the elite's limitations, their failures, do not alter the fact that they successfully politicized the question of the £3 tax — the final burden which broke thousands of ex-indentured labourers and drove them back into servitude during the first decade of the century. Within four years of their emergence as a separate political unit the new Natal elite thus achieved more for the underclasses than the merchants had achieved in over 20 years of political activity.

Notes

1   *Indian Opinion*, 28 Oct. 1905, 17 Mar. 1906.
2   C W, vi, p.291. 'Will there Be Dissension Among Indians?', *Indian Opinion*, 26 Jan. 1907.
3   Ibid.
4   *Indian Opinion*, 26 Jan. 1907.
5   Ibid.
6   C W, vi, p.410, 'Meeting of Natal Indian Congress', 8 Apr. 1907.
7   A D Pillay and V Lawrence became joint hon. secs. of the party. CO 179/253/27317, Gov. to Sec. St. 22 July 1909, encl. petition by NIPU and NIC, 10 July 1909.

8   *Indian Opinion*, 4 Apr. 1908.

9   Ibid., 11, 25 Apr. 1908.

10   *African Chronicle*, 22 Aug., 26 Sept. 1908, 6 Feb. 1909.

11   Ibid., and *Indian Opinion*, 11, 25 Apr. 1908.

12   *Indian Opinion*, 25 Apr. 1908.

13   For example, ibid., 12 Sept. 1908, and *African Chronicle*, 22 Aug. 1908, 25 Dec. 1909.

14   CO 179/253/27317, Gov. to Sec. St., 22 July 1909, encl. petition by NIPU and NIC, 10 July 1909. See also *Indian Opinion*, 4 May 1907, for other officials of HYMA.

15   *Indian Opinion*, 25 Apr. 1908.

16   *African Chronicle*, 1 Aug. 1908.

17   Ibid., 12 Sept. 1908.

18   CO 179/253/27317, Gov. to Sec. St., 22 July 1909, encl. petition by NIPU and NIC, 10 July 1909.

19   Ibid., 255/2936, Statement made on behalf of Natal delegates by M C Anglia, 12 Aug. 1909.

20   Ibid.

21   Ibid., Nicholson to Hirtzel, 31 Aug. 1909.

22   The Natal government agreed to pass a bill permitting an appeal to the supreme court in the case of a licence being withdrawn, in exchange for the government of India's agreement not to put into effect their enabling bill to prohibit further indentured emigration to Natal before the union of the South African colonies. CO 179/254/34757, Sec. St. India to Viceroy, tele., 22 Oct. 1909. See also CO 879/106/934, no.101, Gov. Natal to Sec. St., 19 May 1909; ibid., no.118, Sec. St. to Gov. Natal 2 June 1909; ibid., no.184, Sec. St. to Officer Admin. Natal Gov. 1 Oct. 1909; ibid., no.195, Gov. Natal to Sec. St., 21 Oct. 1909; ibid., no.201, Under Sec. St. Col. to Gov. Natal, 28 Oct. 1909; ibid., no.203, Gov. Natal to Under Sec. St. Col., 5 Nov. 1909; ibid., no.222, Gov. Natal to Sec. St., 25 Nov. 1909.

23   CO 179/253/26400, Gov. to Sec. St. 15 July 1909.

24   'It is not our profession to agitate, as we are born traders, and what we only ask for is justice, which if denied now, it will be difficult for us what to say to the people', CO 179/255/29361, Statement by M C Anglia, 12 Aug. 1909.

25   For example, 4, 11, 25 Apr. 1908.

26   *Indian Opinion*, 23 Nov. 1907, 29 Feb. 1908, 12 Dec. 1908. By early 1910 Gandhi's original views on the conditions of indentured labourers had changed radically: he referred to them as existing in a condition of slavery (*C W*, x, p.179, 'Indentured Indians', 2 Mar. 1910). It is hard to know exactly when Gandhi reached this point of

view. Less than a year earlier, Polak, his closest confidant, testified in writing before the Natal Educ. Comm. that 'on the large estates, the covenanted employees are as a rule well looked after, the employers . . . making the conditions of service as tolerable as possible' (*Indian Opinion*, 3 Apr. 1909).

27   The Natal planters, farmers and mine owners still relied heavily on a cheap Indian labour force and the bill was withdrawn before the end of the session.

28   *C W*, x, p.201, 'Duty of Natal Indian Congress', 2 Apr. 1910.

29   Ibid., vi, p.261, 'Reply to Welcome Address at Verulam', 29 Dec. 1906.

30   For example, *Indian Opinion*, 18 July, 1 Aug., 8 Aug. 1908.

31   Ibid., 29 Aug. 1908.

32   Ibid., 12 Sept. 1908. See also CO 291/141/10348, SABIC to C O, 23 Mar. 1909, informing the C O that 'the Natal Indian Congress virtually represents the whole of the Natal Indian population'. Much later, in India, Gandhi consistently made the same claims for the INC.

3   *African Chronicle*, 12 Sept. 1908.

34   *Hind Swaraj* came approximately a year after this, preceded by contentions such as 'it was in South Africa that the Indian nation was being formed', *C W*, ix, p.452, 'London', after 1 Oct. 1909. Also, in 1912, praising the introduction of vernacular education in government-aided Indian schools, Gandhi commented that 'as much as we admire the bright intelligence of our Colonial-born young men, we feel that there is something missing, and that is a knowledge of real Indian thought, history and literature', ibid., xi, p.353, 'Education in Vernaculars', 7 Dec. 1912.

35   *Indian Opinion*, 10 Oct.1908. But see also *African Chronicle*, 19, 26 Nov. 1910, describing Shankeranand's followers as Arya Samajists.

36   *Indian Opinion*, 10 Oct. 1908.

37   Ibid., 21 Mar. 1908. His travelling expenses were financed by public subscriptions, ibid., 20 June 1908.

38   Ibid., 17 Oct. 1908.

39   See, for example, *African Chronicle*, 9 Jan. 1909.

40   It is possible, though it seems illogical, that Shankeranand established, or inspired the establishment of, parallel organizations. It seems more reasonable to assume that 'Hindu Society' was a loose English translation of *Veda Dharma Sabha*.

41   *African Chronicle*, 9 Jan. 1909, 9 Apr. 1910. By mid-1910 there were also branches of the *Sabha* in Ladysmith, New Guelderland and Clare. TABA, Gov. Gen., 706/15/62, teles. to Gov. Gen. from secs. of branches, Nov. 1910.

42   *Indian Opinion*, 3 Apr. 1909.

43   *African Chronicle*, 22 May 1909. Charlie Nulliah, chairman of the Pietermaritzburg branch of the party, became a close follower of Shankeranand. See TABA, Gov. Gen. 706/15/62, Handbill by secs. of Durban and Pietermaritzburg *Veda Dharma Sabhas*, 15 Oct. 1910.

44   *African Chronicle*, 22 May, 5 June 1909.

45   This clearly refers to the *Veda Dharma Sabha*. The Pietermaritzburg branch was established in Apr. 1909. *African Chronicle*, 23 Apr. 1910.

46   *African Chronicle*, 5 June 1909.

47   Ibid.

48   Ibid.

49   Ibid., 14 Aug. 1909.

50   P S Aiyar's elliptical prose is not always easy to follow. *African Chronicle* reports of 12 June, 3 July, and 9 July 1909 must be read in conjunction with the report of the 31 May meeting in order to recognize that by 'Banian Hindoos' he meant 'passenger' hawkers of some substance, and that 'Hindoostanee gentries' refers to white collar workers.

51   *African Chronicle*, 5 June 1909.

52   Ibid., 26 June 1909.

53   Ibid., 3 July 1909.

54   *African Chronicle*, 26 June 1909.

55   Ibid., 5 June 1909.

56   Ibid., 12 June 1909.

57   Ibid., 4 Sept. 1909.

58   Ibid., 26 June 1909.

59   In this respect, the presiding magistrate's comments on the fracas which preceded the boycott are of interest. He could not understand how 'respectable', well-known merchants came to be in court, and concluded that they had been 'framed'. *African Chronicle*, 14 Aug. 1909.

60   Ibid., 7 Aug. 1909. See also ibid., 21 Aug., 13 Nov. 1909.

61   Ibid., 4 Sept. 1909. Lawrence signed the 10 July 1909 petition to the throne as president of the YMCS.

62   Ibid.

63   It was accepted by everyone except the Muslim representative who pressed for the continuation of the Mosque Market. Ibid., 11 Sept. 1909.

64   Ibid,, 4 Dec. 1909.

65   The IFA had lost the support of the hawkers. *African Chronicle*, 6 Aug. 1910. In any case the Town Council procured an interdict

constraining Indians to use the new market. Ibid., 1 Oct. 1910. Shankeranand wrote to the Gov. Gen. requesting (unsuccessfully) his intervention. Gov. Gen., 706/15/35, ibid., 15/38. Shankeranand to Gov. Gen., 20, 28 July 1910, 9 Aug. 1910.

66 *African Chronicle*, 17 Aug. 1912.

67 Ibid., 2 July 1910.

68 He returned to India on 21 May 1913, reportedly because of the illness of 'a brother disciple'. *African Chronicle*, 31 May 1913.

69 Ibid., 26 Nov. 1910, 15, 22 June, 6 July 1912; TABA, Gov. Gen. 707/15/76 Hon. Sec. *Sanathan Dharam Maha Mandal* to Gov. Gen., 21 Nov. 1910; ibid., 15/78, Hon. Sec. *Sanathan Dharam Sabha* of Hillary's to Gov. Gen., 24 Nov. 1910.

70 On 18 Dec. 1909, *African Chronicle* commented on the vitality of HYMA's weekly meetings. Its membership probably at least equalled the 112 reported in the paper on 22 Oct. 1910, when it appears to have been less active.

71 Although the government defended the age reduction as a necessary result of the cut in the Indian education vote, C O minuting interprets both measures as part of a policy to restrict Indians to a primary education. It was noted that Indian education received £3 225 of a total education vote of £111 548. CO 179/252/4357, minuting on Gov. to Sec. St., 13 Jan. 1909. The age restriction was withdrawn in 1910. Ibid., 256/9755, Gov. to Sec. St., 8 Mar. 1910.

72 *Indian Opinion*, 31 July 1909; *African Chronicle*, 13 Nov., 11 Dec. 1909, 1 Jan. 1910.

73 *African Chronicle*, 1 Jan. 1910.

74 For example, *African Chronicle*, 4 Dec. 1909, 15, 21, 29 Jan. 1909, 19 Feb. 1909.

75 Speeches at the weekly meetings of DIS, ibid., 26 Sept., 2 Oct. 1909.

76 For Naidoo's earlier activities see ibid., 22 Aug. 1908, 9 Jan. 1909.

77 Ibid., 20 Nov., 4 Dec. 1909.

78 NA, II, 1/58/972/1890, statement by Maharaj before Verulam magistrate, 1 Sept. 1890.

79 *African Chronicle*, 4 Dec. 1909.

80 *Indian Opinion*, 22 Jan. 1910.

81 Ibid., 25 Dec. 1909.

82 The petition is printed in *Indian Opinion*, 8 Jan. 1910.

83 In mid-1908, NIPU, like NIC, had condemned a proposed bill to discontinue the issue of trade licences to Indians. The rights of the colonial-born were noted almost in passing. During a lengthy speech at a NIPU meeting, Aiyar observed that 'without discrimination as to the status and education of people licences are refused even in the case of colonial born Indians'. *African Chronicle*, 1 Aug., 12 Sept. 1908.

84   See, for example, speeches at the NIPU mass meeting of 5 Sept. 1908, ibid., 12 Sept. 1908.

85   Clause 9 of the petition, *Indian Opinion*, 8 Jan. 1910.

86   This is corroborated by an *Indian Opinion* report on 21 May 1910, (*C W*, x, p.256) which stated that a few 'Hindus and colonial born Indians' had successfully obtained trade licences by asserting that they should not have to buy from established (Muslim) merchants since 'Hindus and Muslims were not united'.

87   *African Chronicle*, 15 Jan. 1910.

88   Ibid.

89   Ibid., 30 Apr. 1910. Panday was chairman of the Shri Vishnu Temple, Umgeni, and a prominent member of HYMA, NIPU and DIS. But the press reports on his trip to India do not discuss who, if anyone, he represented at Lahore, nor even whether he visited India specifically to attend the INC session.

90   *African Chronicle*, 4 June 1910.

91   Ibid., 8 Oct. 1910.

92   *C W*, x, p.326, fn.1.

93   The matter had been under discussion at least since mid-September. *African Chronicle*, 17 Sept. 1910.

94   Ibid., 1 Oct. 1910.

95   This is spelled out in *C W*, x, p.455, Gandhi to Natesan, Gokhale and SABIC, 11 Mar. 1911. See also ibid., xi, pp.70-74, NIC memorial to Sec. St. Colonies, 15 May 1911.

96   *C W*, x, p.455, Gandhi to Natesan, Gokhale and SABIC, 11 Mar. 1911.

97   This list is taken from *C W*, x, pp.441-3, NIC petition to Leg. Assembly of the Union of South Africa, 9 Mar. 1911.

98   *African Chronicle*, 18 Mar. 1911.

99   *C W*, x, pp.441-3, NIC petition to Leg. Assembly of the Union of South Africa, 9 Mar. 1911. The petition was drafted by Gandhi, ibid., p.435, Gandhi to Polak, 7 Mar. 1911.

100   *African Chronicle*, 25 Mar. 1911.

101   *Indian Opinion*, 15 Apr. 1911.

102   *C W*, x, p.439, fn.1.

103   Ibid., p.459, Gandhi to Polak, 13 Mar. 1911.

104   Ibid.

105   Polak made a lengthy speech at the inaugural meeting of the CBIA, *Indian Opinion*, 18 Mar. 1911. He was less successful in trying to persuade P S Aiyar of the 'efficacy of . . . [Gandhi's] hair-splitting logic'. By the time the second bill was introduced, Aiyar was criticizing not only the bill, but the Gandhi-Polak approach to it. *African Chronicle*, 17 Feb. 1912.

106   C W, x, p.435, Gandhi to Polak, 7 Mar. 1911.

107   *Indian Opinion*, 15 Apr. 1911.

108   Ibid., 30 Nov. 1912.

109   *African Chronicle*, 27 Nov. 1911.

110   There were representatives, or messages of support, from Charlestown, Ladysmith, Dundee, Buffalo's Drift, Pietermaritzburg, Stanger, Greytown, Cato Manor, Overport and South Coast Junction, *Indian Opinion*, 15 Apr. 1911.

111   Gandhi's interest in freedom of movement within the Union extended only to the handful of educated Indians whom he wished to be allowed to immigrate, as by right, each year.

112   *Indian Opinion*, 15 Apr. 1911.

113   29 Apr. 1911.

114   *Indian Opinion*, 15 Apr. 1911.

115   Ibid.

116   *African Chronicle*, 26 Aug. 1911.

117   Ibid., 15 Apr. 1911. This refers to R N Modaley, who was elected VP on 21 Mar. 1911. Ibid., 25 Mar. 1911.

118   Ibid., 17 Sept. 1910.

119   *Indian Opinion*, 20 May 1911.

120   *African Chronicle*, 6 Apr. 1912.

121   Ibid., 2, 9 Mar. 1911, 2 Mar. 1912. This was by no means an unusual procedure. In 1913 the Licensing Officer for Durban claimed that 'of the people who opposed licences to Indians, at least 50% were Indians'. He also noted that there was strenuous opposition from both whites and Indians to the heavy trade in household articles which was carried on by unlicensed Indians. *Natal Mercury*, 7 Feb. 1913.

122   C W, xi, pp.70-74.

123   TABA, Gov. Gen. 708/15/152, Sec. St. to Gov. Gen., 1 July 1911, encl. Polak to Under Sec. St. for Colonies, 17 June 1911.

124   Act 19 of 1910 gave magistrates the discretionary power to waive the tax on women in cases of severe hardship. The Act also made provision for suspending (but not nullifying) tax arrears in the case of reindenture.

125   *African Chronicle*, 29 Jan. 1910.

126   Ibid.

127   Ibid., 2 Sept. 1911, Schreiner to Aiyar, 6 Mar. 1911.

128   Ibid., 26 Aug. 1911.

129   Ibid., 30 Sept. 1911.

130   Ibid., 9 Sept. 1911.

131   Ibid., 14 Oct. 1911. In the case of unfamiliar names, it has been assumed that South Indians were not members of NIC.

132   It is difficult to follow the system of categorization which Aiyar used to list members. Unless the name of a town appears immediately after a member's name, it has been taken that the member represented Durban since several without regional identification are known to have lived in Durban.

133   *African Chronicle*, 4 Nov. 1911.

134   Ibid., 7 Oct. 1911.

135   Ibid., 2 Sept. 1911. And see also, 7 Oct., 4 Nov. 1911.

136   Ibid.

137   Ibid., 30 Sept. 1911.

138   Ibid., 3 Feb. 1912,

139   Ibid., 11, 18, 25 Nov. 1911.

140   Ibid., 4 Nov. 1911.

141   Ibid., 2 Dec. 1911.

142   Ibid., 29 Apr. 1911.

143   *African Chronicle*, 14 Oct. 1911.

144   Ibid., 25 Nov., 16 Dec. 1911.

145   C W, x, p.103, 'Speech at Durban Meeting', 20 Dec. 1909; ibid., pp.103-4, Gandhi to Polak, 22 Dec. 1909.

146   *African Chronicle*, 30 Sept. 1911.

147   Ibid.

148   Ibid., 13 Apr. 1912.

149   *Indian Opinion*, 28 Oct. 1911.

150   C W, ix, pp.268-9, Gandhi to Polak, 26 Aug. 1909. It is also noteworthy that Gandhi ignored the £3 tax question in the Natal delegation's submission to the Sec. State for the Colonies in 1909. He decribed NIPU's petition as raising 'an issue which is a very old one'. Ibid., p.339, 'London', 6 Aug. 1909. See also, ibid., x, p.164, an *Indian Opinion* report (Gujerati ed.) on a series of Congress resolutions passed in Feb. 1910. The £3 tax is ignored here, but resolutions on the stoppage of indenture, and the Transvaal movement, are described as 'of the highest imperial importance'.

151   Ibid., xi, p.317, fn.1.

152   Ibid., p.235, fn.3.

153   Ibid., p.188, 25 Nov. 1911.

154   *Indian Opinion*, 24 Feb. 1912. See also, ibid., 18 Nov., 2, 9, 16, Dec. 1911.

155   For a fascinating parallel see P L Bonner, 'The Transvaal Native Congress 1917-1920: The Radicalization of the Black Petty Bourgeoisie on the Rand', unpub. paper, Univ. of London, Centre of International and Area Studies, Conference, January 1980.

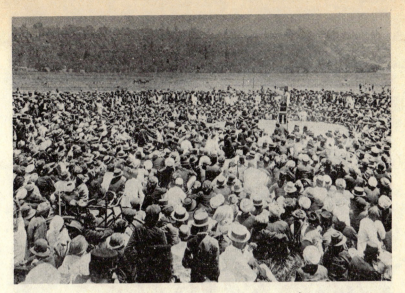

18 *Thambi Naidoo addressing a mass meeting at the Durban Indian football ground during the strike, 1913 (HWPC, from 'Golden Number' of* Indian Opinion, *1914)*

19 *The strikers march through Volksrust (HWPC, from 'Golden Number' of* Indian Opinion, *1914)*

20 *Widow and orphan of Pachiappan, an Indian striker on the Coast, shot dead during the strike. Photo by B Gabriel. (The original caption of this photograph as it appeared in the 'Golden Number' of* Indian Opinion, *1914. HWPC. 'B Gabriel' is almost certainly Brian Gabriel — see page 12.)*

CHAPTER SIX

Passive Resistance, 1910 — 1914

The third stage of Gandhian passive resistance in South Africa began with Gandhi's return from London in December 1909. The campaign continued to be characterized by the purely ethical ideology which Gandhi had formulated for the movement in 1908. The twin goals remained the repeal of Act 36 of 1908, and an amendment of the Transvaal's immigration legislation to eliminate discrimination against Indians in principle. At the beginning of this third stage the movement's active supporters had declined to about a hundred.

In April 1911, the Union government failed in its first attempt to pass an immigration bill which would replace the immigration laws of the four former colonies, and meet the demands of the passive resistance movement in the Transvaal. By written agreement with Smuts, who continued to be the main adversary of the movement in his capacity as Union Minister of the Interior, Gandhi suspended *satyagraha* pending the reintroduction of the immigration bill. Smuts chose to treat Gandhi as the principal Indian spokesman on immigration, thus formally extending his influence to a national level. The 'provisional settlement' of April 1911 was extended in July 1912 following the government's second failure to pass new immigration legislation. During this period Gandhi's minimal involvement in public affairs increased only when Gopal Krishna Gokhale accepted Gandhi's long-standing invitation to visit South Africa.

By April 1913, when the third immigration bill was introduced, Gandhi's active supporters had dwindled to a handful, and the Natal elites had begun to articulate the opposition to Gandhian strategy which culminated in a formal leadership challenge and a split in the Natal Congress six months later. The weakness of the movement, and the emergence of opposition, caused Gandhi to widen the scope of the movement's objectives to permit an indirect appeal to the specific interests of the elites, and a direct appeal to the underclasses.

By September, negotiations with the government had failed to produce results. The negotiations were abruptly broken off, and the fourth and final stage of the campaign launched. The repeal of the £3 tax on ex-indentured labourers — an issue which had been co-opted first by NIC, then Gandhi, in response to the growing political potential of the new elite — was now added to the movement's goals. This allowed Gandhi to call a workers' strike in Natal which provided the movement with the committed army of supporters that Gandhi had unsuccessfully sought for years.

The First Immigration Bill

The success of H S L Polak's fund-raising tour of India, which had begun when Gandhi and Haji Habib left for London in June 1909, confirmed Gandhi's victory in the May 1909 Transvaal Indian leadership struggle. In November Ratan Tata, a wealthy Bombay industrialist, made the first of several large donations to the movement. A few other wealthy Indians followed suit, and over £8 000 was received from India during the course of the next two years.[1] Gandhi refused to be accountable to anyone in South Africa for the disbursement of these funds.[2] The money was used, in part, to keep *Indian Opinion* and the communal settlement at Phoenix running, paying off the heavy debts incurred since Gandhi had given up his private law practice which had helped finance both the paper and the settlement.[3] Throughout 1910, one hundred or so passive resisters continued to court arrest. Most of them were members of the Tamil Benefit Society, the only Transvaal Indian organization which remained actively committed to *satyagraha*. A handful of the original leaders of the movement also remained loyal. Jail sentences for multiple offenders, as most of these were, ran to three or six months with hard labour.[4] In addition, the government tried hard to crush the remnants of the movement by treating *satyagrahis* as prohibited immigrants, deporting them to Natal, Mozambique, and even India, under the terms of the Transvaal Immigration Act.[5] The expense of supporting resisters and their dependants therefore rose steadily. By late 1910 the costs were over £300 per month, even though Gandhi refused to support the many who chose not to live on a second communal settlement, Tolstoy Farm, which he had established outside Johannesburg in mid-1910.[6]

Gandhi's political goals, both short and long term, demanded a satisfactory conclusion to passive resistance in the Transvaal. But by early 1911, the 'movement' existed in name only. The government had stopped making arrests pending the inroduction of new immigration legislation. Funds were again low: the merchants in Natal and the Transvaal had long since withdrawn their financial support from the movement; there was no way of knowing yet whether adequate further funding would be received from India. When the immigration bill was introduced in March, Gandhi's political future therefore hinged on the clauses which dealt with the objectives of the movement. His initial response to the bill, whose terms he found far from clear, was to advise the Cape and Natal elites to petition the government on clauses which seemed to erode existing rights in those provinces,[7] but to limit his own negotiations with Smuts to an unambiguous settlement for the Transvaal passive resisters.[8]

Smuts's concerns were wider. His major problem was to gain acceptance of the bill by dissenting factions in the Union parliament.[9] But the Indian question, though secondary, was by no means irrelevant. As early as August 1909 Smuts had told the Secretary of State for the Colonies that he expected the first Union government to deal with the passive resisters' grievances.[10] In November 1910, in exchange for a promise from the Colonial Office that the exportation of Indian labourers to Natal would cease in mid-1911, the Union government confirmed Smuts's earlier statement to the Colonial Secretary.[11] Thus for Smuts, like Gandhi, the major significance of the immigration bill, insofar as it affected Indians, was to enable a final settlement with the passive resisters.[12] Smuts was prepared to negotiate that settlement with Gandhi, within the wider framework of gaining parliamentary acceptance for the immigration bill.

The Smuts-Gandhi negotiations were complicated by both parties. On 4 March 1911, after receiving legal counsel on the implications of the bill, Gandhi extended the demands of the movement to include theoretical right of entry for Indians into the Orange Free State.[13] The logic of this new demand, in terms of the passive resistance movement's goals, is straightforward. Without the repeal of existing discriminatory O F S legislation, or the insertion of a special provision in the immigration bill, the 'colour bar' as Gandhi now called it, would continue to operate in that province of the Union. As such, the colour bar could be said to be contained within the immigration bill itself. The old demands of the movement, for both the repeal of the

Transvaal registration law and the theoretical right of Indians to immigrate into the Transvaal, represented a fight against a colour bar. The immigration bill, by virtue of its Union-wide application, therefore necessitated a Union-wide extension of those demands.[14]

Analyzing the new demand in terms of conventional political logic presents certain difficulties however. The demand virtually eliminated the possibility of achieving a final settlement by means of the immigration bill. The OFS had the most restrictive anti-Asian legislation in South Africa. All but a handful of Indians had been expelled from there twenty years earlier, and the possibility of inducing the province to accept even the theoretical right of Indians to immigrate was remote indeed. There is no means to understand the adoption of this politically unsound demand in terms of conventional political bargaining. On 4 March 1911, Gandhi seems to have ceased, for the moment, to be a politician, and become a *satyagrahi* pure and simple.

The O F S refused to compromise on the Asian question.[15] Gandhi responded with a blend of politicking and moral hair-splitting. He tried to save the possibility of a settlement by asking Smuts to withdraw the immigration bill and remove the old passive resistance grievances by an amendment of the existing Transvaal immigration legislation.[16] Gandhi saw in this a solution to a number of his moral and political problems. The bill eroded the existing rights of the Natal and Cape Indians. They could not be prevented from raising objections; and, indeed, Gandhi's first public statement on the bill had advised the Cape and Natal elites to submit petitions of protest. But additional demands threatened to undermine the already delicate Smuts-Gandhi negotiations. Gandhi successfully steered the Congress away from pressing the most contentious issue, the question of Asian interprovincial migration which could not be raised without confronting the resolute refusal of every other province in the union to open its doors to the Natal Indians.[17] However, the Congress's failure to include interprovincial migration in its list of demands led directly to the emergence of the CBIA, and yet another dissenting Indian voice raised against the immigration bill. Through Polak's mediation Gandhi was able temporarily to dissuade the new party from pressing the interprovincial question.

By mid-March however, it was clear that negotiating with Smuts within the framework of the Union immigration bill created a network of problems on both sides. The Orange Free State refused to accept what Smuts was willing to give Gandhi, and less than which Gandhi would not take. The Cape and, particularly, Natal Indian elites demanded even more. 'Personally', Gandhi wrote to Louis Ritch on 17 March, 'I would like an indefinite postponement of the Bill and the desired alteration to the Transvaal Immigration Law. Then we need raise no question as to the Free State, there would arise no question as to the Cape and Natal, and the whole thing would be quite satis-factory'.[18] By the time he made this statement Gandhi had evidently recovered some of his political acumen. It is almost superfluous to comment that tortuous rationalization is necessary in order to follow the moral logic of this argument. But, though Gandhi had ceased to be a *satyagrahi* pure and simple, he had not by any means made a full commitment to political expediency. It was a waste of time to ask Smuts for new provincial immigration legislation when he had pledged himself to replace the old laws of the colonies with a Union-wide bill.[19]

Much of the Smuts-Gandhi negotiations were conducted by letter and cable: Smuts was in Cape Town, the seat of the Union parlia-ment, and Gandhi in Johannesburg. Louis Ritch, who had returned to Cape Town at the end of 1910 after four years as secretary of SABIC, was authorized by the British Indian Association to represent them personally in the negotiations.[20] Smuts however declined to deal with anyone other than Gandhi.[21] On 25 March, after a 'temporizing and threatening' letter from Smuts on the O F S question, Gandhi therefore left for Cape Town to negotiate in person and canvass the support of sympathetic MPs.[22] Ritch took Gandhi's place in Johannesburg,[23] Polak remained active in Durban. Between the three, a united South African Indian response to the immigration bill was co-ordinated.[24] Gandhi used the same mixture of diplomacy and threat that had characterized the negotiations with Smuts in 1907 and 1908; but the proportions of the ingredients had been changed. Of necessity, diplomacy played a far more prominent role than threat in early 1911.[25]

It seems clear that by mid-April both Smuts and Gandhi had accepted the need for a truce and for leaving the Transvaal question over until the next parliamentary session.[26] Smuts's major concern — which had not been stated explicitly to Gandhi — was to avoid making a formal bargain which would enhance Gandhi's prestige and allow him to think that he could dictate terms.[27] By contrast, Gandhi needed a public and well defined agreement for more than one reason. For him, the main obstacle to a truce seems to have been the fear of a second unsuccessful agreement like the 1908 compromise which had had serious political repercussions for him. He continued to mistrust Smuts;[28] and the Natal Congress, whose approval was necessary for a settlement which derived from the Immigration Bill,[29] continued to doubt his ability to deal with Smuts. In a clear allusion to the 1908 compromise, a hostile cable from NIC at the beginning of the 1911 negotiations had warned Gandhi against another 'blunder'.[30] Thus on 19 and 20 April, when it had become clear that the Immigration Bill could not be passed that session, Gandhi began pressuring Smuts to conclude an acceptable formal truce. The need for a temporary suspension of passive resistance had already been broached by Smuts[31] when Gandhi wrote to him on 19 April, 'I do not know how I could promise inactivity on the part of the passive resisters'.[32] The following day Smuts was presented with cables from BIA and NIC, and written support on behalf of the Cape British Indian Union, threatening the continuation of passive resistance if the demands of the movement remained unfulfilled at the end of the session.[33]

Gandhi's tactic brought the necessary pressure to bear. Smuts responded by reaffirming that it would be impossible 'for the Government to proceed with immigration legislation in any form this session'. But, at the same time, he noted that the question would continue to receive government attention during the parliamentary recess with a view to reaching a satisfactory solution, and he called for an interim truce.[34] Within half an hour of receiving Smuts's proposal, Gandhi had arrived at his private secretary's office to begin the work of hammering out a watertight agreement.[35]

The 1911 'provisional settlement', as it came to be known, unequivocally stated Smuts's intentions to fulfil all the passive resisters' demands (including 'legal equality for all immigrants') during the next session of parliament.[36] Smuts also pledged himself to seek the early release of imprisoned resisters if Gandhi kept his part of the bargain and brought passive resistance to a halt. The terms of the agreement were made public by Gandhi in *Indian Opinion* and in a press interview in Johannesburg where he stressed that all possible precautions had been taken 'to avoid misunderstanding or ambiguity'.[37] Despite these precautions, the agreement was ratified at an 'overflow meeting' in the Hamidia Hall in Johannesburg on 27 April only after a four-hour discussion which 'was at times heated, if not actually stormy'.[38] The meeting demanded, and was accorded, an additional promise by Smuts that besides fulfilling the terms of the provisional settlement, new immigration legislation would not erode existing rights. It is noteworthy that most of the hundreds of Indians who attended the meeting were not, or had long since ceased to be, passive resisters themselves. Although the burden of achieving a settlement was carried by the *satyagrahis*, the Transvaal and Natal merchants had since early 1908 consistently opposed any action that could be construed as a surrender by the movement.

The Second Immigration Bill

During the negotiations on the immigration bill Gandhi had been confronted by government attempts to define the movement's goals as the sum total of South African Indian grievances.[39] This reflected Smuts's desire to deny Gandhi the possibility of reopening the passive resistance campaign with a widened set of objectives: Smuts mistrusted Gandhi as much as Gandhi mistrusted him.[40] Following the provisional settlement Gandhi took immediate steps to ensure that the broader Indian question remained open. This was necessary if for no other reason than that the price of cooperation by the CBIA during the negotiations had been a promise by Gandhi that a national 'bill of rights' would be drawn up as soon as the passive resistance question was settled. The 'bill of rights' was contained in petitions to the imperial government by NIC, BIA and the Cape British Indian Union in May 1911, and in Polak's written submission to the Colonial Secretary in June. These four documents, covering the long standing grievances of the merchants as well as several new ones, focussed most directly on the vulnerability of vested commercial interests under the terms of the Natal and Cape Dealers' Licences Acts, Transvaal Law 3 of 1885 and the Transvaal Gold Law and Townships Amendment Acts (1908).[41] At a more general level, Polak also cited widespread indirect attempts to defeat the provisions of the South African Act which were meant to protect the rights of the black population. He noted that a given piece of legislation might appear acceptable but that 'regulations framed thereunder, which very seldom come before parliament for sanction, often contain provisions of a highly objectionable racial character'.[42] In addition to the familiar merchants' grievances, the emergence of the CBIA in Natal dictated the inclusion of the £3 tax on ex-indentured labourers. However, this remained a minor consideration in the 'bill of rights' until P S Aiyar began his anti-tax campaign in September 1911. By the end of the year, the abolition of the tax had been elevated to the top of the commercial elite's list of political priorities.

In the months following the 1911 provisional settlement, Gandhi's supreme political objective remained the confirmation of that settlement. He intended, as he had since at least 1909, to return to India as soon as the passive resistance campaign was successfully concluded. The 'bill of rights' may have reflected the beginning of an awareness by Gandhi that a final settlement could ultimately demand widening the movement's scope to include other long-standing grievances; but it did not reflect a reassessment of his personal objectives. Throughout the remainder of 1911, *Indian Opinion* carried the familiar articles and editorials on Indian grievances. At the end of the year during Aiyar's anti-tax campaign, coverage of the £3 tax question intensified notably. However, Gandhi was less active, politically, than he had been for years. He lived almost in retreat on Tolstoy Farm marking time until the immigration bill was re-introduced.

When the second immigration bill was introduced in January 1912, Gandhi resumed negotiations with Smuts in an attempt to clarify the ambiguity which still surrounded clauses concerning the goals of the movement. However, his strategy had altered since 1911. The intensity which had characterized the earlier negotiations was missing. Paradoxically, Gandhi had also shifted ground, blurring the edges of the requirements for a final settlement.

In a commentary on the bill which was published in *Indian Opinion*, Gandhi urged the Cape British Indian Union and the Natal Congress to object to what amounted to a virtual ban on inter-provincial migration, and asserted that 'even the *satyagrahis* cannot remain silent [on this point]'.[43] He also objected to the government's attempt to meet one of the complaints submitted by the Cape and Natal elites in 1911: the possibility of the loss of domicile rights in the case of a temporary absence from the Union. The new bill provided for (but did not make mandatory) the issue of a permit which would entitle the holder to leave the country and freely re-enter the province in which he was domiciled within a three-year time limit. Gandhi hypothesized that 'the poor' would leave without permits and be subjected to harassment and imprisonment when they attempted to return. He urged the Natal Congress to 'vehemently oppose' this clause, and warned that 'the *satyagrahis* may [oppose it] too; but it cannot be asserted just yet that they should fight'. Although Gandhi approved the clause which provided in theory for new immigrants to enter and reside in any province of the Union, including the O F S, his commentary on the clause raised the decades-old inability of Indians to own land in the Transvaal or the O F S and to farm or trade in the latter. He made it clear that these disabilities would not be challenged during the current passive resistance campaign, but asserted that 'another campaign, and that on a big scale, should, however, be launched to secure the rights to own land etc.'[44]

There is no information available on the decision-making process behind the new strategy. But its implications make it hard to avoid the inference that by early 1912 Gandhi was beginning to admit the possibility that *satyagraha*, as it had been conceived and practised since early 1908, would not work. The strategic modifications of early 1912 opened up the possibility of elevating the campaign from a regional to a national basis by broadening the movement's goals. The ban on interprovincial migration had been the new Natal elite's major objection to the 1911 bill: Gandhi's refusal to press the question then had led to the emergence of the CBIA. Athough the party was inactive during early 1912, there is nothing to suggest that their views on interprovincial migration had changed. The question of permits to ensure domiciliary rights presented the only possibility of drawing the Natal Indian underclasses into a fight against the immigration bill. The issue was more than academic: thousands of ex-indentured labourers had temporarily left the province to work in Angola in 1909. The immigration bill offered no specific grounds on which to mobilize the merchants for passive resistance, but the call for a future campaign on behalf of their grievances in the Transvaal and OFS did.

The contents of the 1912 bill, and the low intensity of the 1912 negotiations, support the contention that Gandhi was beginning to doubt the power of the Transvaal *satyagraha* movement. A final settlement for the passive resisters hung on the immigration bill. But it differed little from its predecessor whose passage through the legislature had been impossible. Intense negotiations with Smuts were obviously a waste of time. Gandhi's commentary on the bill reflects a reversal of the proportions of threat and diplomacy which had characterized the 1911 negotiations. And the commentary cannot be construed as an empty threat. It was not relayed to Smuts in private, but printed in *Indian Opinion* for all to see. It seems clear that the second immigration bill provoked Gandhi into a fundamental reassessment of the movement's potential. By early 1912 he was prepared to adopt new goals in an attempt to put the campaign on a nation-wide footing.

A striking feature of the new strategy is that although it created the possibility of a nation-wide campaign, its inherent limitations suggest that it was designed primarily to achieve Gandhi's personal political objective, a final settlement for the Transvaal passive resisters. The strategy provided a basis for appealing to the merchants, the new Natal elite, and the underclasses, but it did not address the most pressing grievances of *any* of these groups. The major threat to the merchants in the Transvaal continued to be the possibility of compulsory segregation in designated Locations, the more so since the Transvaal administration had resumed the surveying of bazaar sites in 1911. For the Natal merchants, the main problem remained the workings of the Dealers' Licences Act. Although an attempt to prevent interprovincial migration had sparked the emergence of the CBIA, this grievance was more symbolic than real: few colonial-born Indians had attempted to migrate out of Natal in the past. The more pressing problems of the new elite were limited job opportunities for the western educated, the Dealers' Licences Act, and inadequate educational facilities. And, for the mass of the Indian people resident in Natal, the £3 tax was a particularly serious grievance.

Thus the new strategy, although providing the potential to adopt a wider set of goals, avoided the long-standing grievances which seemed most likely to mobilize widespread opposition to the government. The compensation for this limitation was that the issues which past governments had adamantly refused to rectify were also avoided, thus eliminating the possibility of submerging a final settlement for the Transvaal *satyagrahis* in conditions for a wider settlement even less likely of achievement.

The Third Immigration Bill

The question of adopting new goals was postponed on 24 June 1912 when the Union parliament was prorogued with the second reading of the immigration bill left unfinished.[45] On 19 July, after prompting from Gandhi and the Governor General,[46] Smuts had extended the terms of the provisional settlement pending the passage of suitable legislation. In October, Gokhale's long awaited tour of South Africa began, and Gandhi re-emerged at the forefront of Indian public life after more than a year, as the *Transvaal Leader* described it, of 'comparative retirement'.[47]

Throughout his tour, Gokhale, accompanied by Gandhi, was received and lavishly feted by crowds of Indians in dozens of centres in Natal, the Transvaal and the Cape.[48] One of Gokhale's stated intentions was to gain first-hand experience of Indian conditions in South Africa.[49] But he rarely moved beyond the elites. Indeed, the tour was subjected to criticism from the elites more than once on the grounds that those in disagreement with Gandhian policy were also denied access to Gokhale.[50] However, several mass rallies to greet Gokhale were organized by the merchants in and around Durban: 10 000 petty cultivators and agricultural labourers were assembled at Isipingo, another 10 000 (mostly indentured workers) on the Mount Edgecombe sugar estate at the invitation of its owner, Marshall Campbell, and 5 000 in Durban.[51] Gokhale's message to the underclasses was far from radical. He promised to urge the government to repeal the £3 tax, but avoided confronting the issue of indentured labourers' conditions, and did not call for mass political mobilization. The closest that Gokhale came to mixing with the people was at the Durban rally where he personally heard the complaints of selected £3 tax payers in a *durbar*-like setting.[52]

Although Gokhale's visit was unofficial, he was cordially received by all levels of the South African administration.[53] On 14 November he discussed Indian grievances with Botha, Smuts and Fischer, a Free State minister who shortly afterwards succeeded Smuts as Minister of the Interior. The next day he met the Governor General. Besides the provisional settlement, the issues on which Gokhale concentrated were those covered in the 1911 'bill of rights': the vulnerability of vested commercial interests, and the £3 tax. Gokhale's views on merchant grievances were no more radical than his approach to the problems of the people. He accepted the Union ministers' contention that no improvement could be expected in trade licensing or in immigration. The talks held the promise of some success, however. Gokhale was left with the impression that the provincial settlement would become final before the end of the year, and the conviction that the government would 'do their best to remove the [£3 tax] as early as possible.'[54]

The major consequence of Gokhale's tour was that it served, inadvertently, as a significant step towards mass Indian mobilization. A year later Gandhi viewed the government's failure to repeal the £3 tax as the 'breach of faith'[55] which allowed him to include the abolition of the tax in the goals of the movement and call a miners' strike in northern Natal. The success of the strike is largely attributable to its rapid spread in the coastal sugar districts where Gandhi's name had been linked to the £3 tax question during Gokhale's tour, and where first Aiyar, then Gokhale flanked by Gandhi, had promised to work for the repeal of the tax.

When Gandhi saw Gokhale off at Dar-es-Salaam on 1 December 1912, he wore Indian dress for the first time in his adult life.[56] He expected to conclude a final settlement for the passive resisters and return to India within six months. Some time in January 1913 he therefore closed the settlement at Tolstoy farm and took its handful of settlers south to Phoenix where most of his family lived and where he hoped to sit out the rest of his time in South Africa.[57] But although the assurances given to Gokhale by the Union ministers allowed Gandhi to hope that the third immigration bill would give effect to the 1911 interim agreement with Smuts, Gandhi had clearly refined his modified 1912 strategy still further to meet the possibility of renewed threats to the agreement. From March onwards, when new barriers in the way of a settlement began to appear, Gandhi's negotiations with the government were accompanied by unequivocal statements that passive resistance would be resumed unless the terms of the 1911 settlement were given legal effect.

On 14 March 1913, a judgement given in the Cape division of the Supreme Court by Justice Malcolm Searle found that the wife of a marriage celebrated according to rites which recognized polygamy did not have the right to emigrate to South Africa even though she was the only wife of that marriage.[58] Gandhi, extrapolating from the Searle judgement, concluded that all 'Hindu or Muslim wives living in South Africa lose their right to live there . . . [and] it is quite on the cards that the government will not permit any more wives to come in.'[59] Within days of the publication of this article in *Indian Opinion*, Gandhi had mobilized the committed core of the *satyagraha* movement. On 30 March at a BIA 'mass' meeting held in Johannesburg, the party resolved to adopt passive resistance unless the government introduced 'remedial legislation recognizing the validity of [non-Christian] marriages throughout the Union'.[60] On 1 April Gandhi linked the Searle judgement directly to a final settlement for the movement, informing Fischer, the Minister of the Interior, that in order to give effect to the terms of the 1911 interim agreement it would be necessary 'to so frame the Immigration Bill as to restore the position as to wives as it availed before Justice Searle's decision'.[61]

On 9 April the third immigration bill was published. Although it fulfilled the original demands of the movement, it violated the provisional settlement in many other respects. Gandhi telegrammed Fischer at once, outlining the revisions which were necessary to avoid 'the revival of passive resistance and all consequent sufferings'.[62] A copy of the telegram was sent to Smuts's private secretary asking for Smuts's support and repeating the assertion that 'if the objections are not met a revival of the awful struggle is a certainty'.[63]

On 12 April *Indian Opinion* carried several articles on the bill. Detailed criticisms appeared under the heading 'Its Effects'. Gandhi stated that existing rights were eroded by the following provisions:

(a) the Supreme Court's jurisdiction over immigration appeals was replaced by the authority of the immigration boards;[64]

(b) the Minister of the Interior was empowered to declare persons or classes of persons prohibited immigrants to the Union or a province, other than the province of domicile, 'on economic grounds or on account of standards or habits of life considered to be unsuited to the requirements of the Union or any particular province thereof'. In the event that such persons were permitted to immigrate, the Minister was also entitled to delimit their possible port of entry;[65]

(c) the definition of 'those who shall not be prohibited immigrants' excluded the £3 taxpayers in Natal who, though they may have been resident in the province for over a decade, did not have the usual domiciliary rights which entitled them to be classified as 'non-prohibited';[66]

(d) domiciliary rights were to be forfeited in the case of absence from the province of domicile for three years or more;[67]

(e) the existing theoretical right of educated and/or South African-born Indians to migrate from other provinces into the Cape or Natal was limited by the sweeping powers granted to the Minister of the Interior.[68]

The last of these objections to the bill, which became part of an ultimatum to the government in September 1913, is ironic in view of the fact that Gandhi's ignorance of, and refusal to support, colonial-born rights in 1911 had led to the emergence of the CBIA and to the only instance — apart from Shankeranand's and Aiyar's criticisms —

of new elite opposition to Gandhi. The inclusion of this grievance in the list of objections was probably in part responsible for the revival of the new elite's support for Gandhi which was evident by mid- 1913.

Indian Opinion also criticized the 1913 bill 'from the passive resistance standpoint only' in that:

(1) Sub-clause (a) sub-section I of Section 4 seems to contemplate the prohibition of the entry into the Free State of new immigrants who may pass the education test.

(2) Even if it does not prohibit such entry, the bill seems to require a declaration from an educated immigrant which would not be required from any other immigrant as an immigrant.

(3) Sub-clause (g) of Section 5 does not recognize the right of the wives and minor children of new immigrants to enter the Union with their husbands.

(4) And the bill does not correct the defect, discovered by the Searle judgement, in the existing South African laws as to Indian marriages and minor children born of such marriages.[69]

Fischer replied to Gandhi's list of objections with a lengthy telegram, dated 15 April, which reflected the government's determination to push through the third immigration bill and also Colonial Office and India Office acceptance of the draft bill.[70] In marked contrast to the conciliatory tone of the 1911 and 1912 Smuts-Gandhi negotiations, Fischer refused to consider any of Gandhi's demands. He ended with the words:

> Minister strongly deprecates references in your telegram and other communications to passive resistance. The threats therein contained might very possibly, in view of feeling throughout the Union on matter under consideration, lead to results far different from those anticipated by the representatives of the Indian community when making them.[71]

Gandhi found Fischer's reply 'unsatisfactory' and immediately responded with a restatement of his demands.[72] By the end of April he had heard nothing further from Fischer.

Confronted by this show of strength, Gandhi's most immediate problem was to demonstrate the intention to defy the government which had been explicitly stated in his correspondence with Fischer and Smuts. Through *Indian Opinion*, he called for opposition throughout the country to Searle's judgement and the immigration bill.[73] BIA had already pledged itself to *satyagraha* in consequence of the Searle judgement. There is nothing to indicate that Gandhi openly called for passive resistance resolutions from the Cape and Natal elites before the end of April, but his *Indian Opinion* editorials were shot through with the old rallying cries: the assertion that the government was encircling the Indian community with damaging legislation which could ultimately 'compass our ruin', and the reminder that others — even women — had gone to jail for their beliefs.[74]

Although *Indian Opinion* had not openly advocated widening the passive resistance front, Gandhi's repeated editorials, whose effect seems to have been heightened by his brooding presence at Phoenix,[75] provoked a decision on the question by the Natal elites. On 26 April the joint secretaries of NIC convened a meeting to tender their resignations 'owing to differences of opinion between themselves and our leaders in South Africa'.[76] The meeting was extraordinary in that it was thrown open to the public and everyone present was invited to participate in the discussion and to vote for new officers. However, the Congress's sudden lurch towards democracy was limited by the fact that no attempt had been made to inform workers about the meeting.[77] Nevertheless, the crowd of 500 was unusual in that it included the *new* as well as the old elite — a revolutionary enough turn of events given NIC's adamant refusal to widen its membership in the past, and a strong indication that the party sought the security of a unitary Natal approach to the passive resistance question.

There could have been little doubt about the outcome of the meeting. The Congress had sent a telegram of protest against the immigration bill to the Minister of the Interior five days earlier. Although it ended with the assertion that the party would 'oppose bill with all resources in its power', there was no mention of passive resistance, nor even of the peculiarly Gandhian objection to the Free State issue.[78] On 26 April, despite some dissent from the new elite, led by a former *satyagrahi*, the public meeting voted overwhelmingly to reject the resignations tendered by the secretaries,[79] thus formally repudiating the Gandhian strategy with which the secretaries were in disagreement.[80]

Within 24 hours of the NIC meeting, Gandhi was back in the Transvaal speaking at a BIA rally on the immigration bill. The rally, which was attended by numbers of provincial representatives,[81] must have been planned some time in advance. It seems highly likely, however, that Gandhi's presence there was a response to his repudiation by the Natal elites — an effort to keep alive the possibility of further passive resistance.[82] The shape of the renewed campaign, which was outlined in speeches by Gandhi and A M Cachalia, the president of BIA, and in an *Indian Opinion* editorial on 3 May,[83] reflected the movement's past failures and present problems as much as its new needs. Gandhi wanted national demonstrations of support for passive resistance in order to bring pressure to bear on the government.[84] In an effort to achieve that support he made it clear from the outset that few instead of many would be expected to go to jail, that there would be no attempt to round up reluctant participants, nor to define support for the movement only in terms of jail-going, nor to discredit those who — for whatever reason — rejected jail-going. Gandhi called simply for widespread visible demonstrations of support for the move- ment — formal resolutions endorsing *satyagraha*, financial assistance for the dependants of jail-goers, the donation of time and labour to the movement.

The BIA mass meeting forwarded a resolution to the government which embodied the new spirit of the campaign. Instead of pledging themselves to jail-going, the participants resolved only that unless the objections against the immigration bill were met 'passive resistance, which has remained under suspense since 1911, be revived and con- tinued'.[85] This carefully limited commitment to passive resistance,[86] which replaced the tentative widening of goals that Gandhi had toyed with in 1912, received relatively widespread support. Despite the fact that the remodelled campaign remained capable only of achieving Gandhi's personal political objective, numbers of elite organizations in Natal (though not the Congress *per se*) sent endorsements of the BIA resolution to the Minister of the Interior within a week.[87] The most striking endorsement, however, came from the Transvaal Indian Women's Association, which went beyond the stock messages of sup- port relayed by other organizations. The members of IWA — a small group established early in 1909,[88] and consisting almost exclusively of the wives of committed *satyagrahis*[89] — resolved to seek arrest unless the Searle judgement was overturned.[90]

Gandhi's objections to the bill and the Searle judgement were raised by sympathetic opposition MPs while the bill was passing through the House of Assembly. It is difficult to assess the extent to which the passive resistance resolutions, and subsequent telegrams of protest,[91] helped Gandhi's case in the House. The Governor-General claimed that the 'truculent and minatory attitude of the Indian community generally and of Mr Gandhi in particular', *impeded* the government from meeting Gandhi's demands.[92] In any event, in order to secure the passage of the bill, Fischer had to steer a narrow course between members who criticized the proposed legislation for its restrictiveness, and those who thought the bill was too easy on the Asians.[93] Thus by the time the bill had passed both Houses and received the Governor-General's assent on 14 June 1913, some minor amendments had been made,[94] but a number of Gandhi's demands remained unfulfilled: confirmation of the permanent residence rights (that is, domicile rights) of £3 taxpayers and their descendants; restoration of the right of all colonial-born Indians to migrate from Natal to the Cape province;[95] restoration of the legal status of wives married in accordance with non-Christian rites; theoretical equality in respect to Indians immigrating or migrating to the Free State.[96]

Gandhi refused to accept the passage of the immigration bill as the final breach of the provisional settlement that it so clearly was. During the last week of June[97] he went back to Johannesburg to begin another, abortive, round of negotiations with Smuts and Fischer who were in Pretoria. The most interesting aspect of the negotiations is the extraordinary length to which Gandhi was prepared to go in order to avoid a resumption of passive resistance. He seriously suggested yet another extension of the provisional settlement if the government undertook yet again to pass the necessary legislation in the course of the year.[98]

There is no information available to determine conclusively why Gandhi made this proposal,[99] and it is difficult to assess what he hoped to achieve by it. The movement was weak — Gandhi expected no more than about 100 people to answer a call for passive resistance.[100] But, given the failure of the 1908 Smuts-Gandhi agreement, the breach of the provisional settlement made explicit in the passage of the immigration bill, and the already widespread belief that *satyagraha* was ineffective, it is hard to believe that Gandhi hoped to increase the support from his old constituents in Natal and the Transvaal by concluding another truce. It is equally difficult to accept that Gandhi still believed 100 *satyagrahis* — whether endorsed by the elites or not — could achieve the final settlement that he had unsuccessfully sought for six years. The widening of goals that Gandhi had toyed with in 1912, the restructuring of the campaign strategy in 1913, confirm the contention that though Gandhi continued to believe in the power of passive resistance, he had ceased to believe in the power of a small number of resisters to move the government. A letter which Gandhi wrote on 23 or 24 June 1913 to Herman Kallenbach, the owner of Tolstoy farm, offers the only coherent explanation for the proposal to extend the provisional settlement. In a scrawled postscript to the letter Gandhi wrote: 'I am resolving in my own mind the idea of doing something for the indentured men.'[101] Never before had Gandhi addressed himself to the Natal underclasses. It is reasonable to assume therefore that this was the germ of the idea which produced the Natal Indian strike, and that the proposed extension of the settlement was an attempt to buy time to make firm contact with the mass of the people before trying to draw them into the movement.

The Minister of the Interior did not accept Gandhi's proposal to extend the provisional settlement. Negotiations did however continue. They were resumed on 28 June but suspended shortly afterwards while the government concentrated on breaking a widespread strike of white mineworkers in the Transvaal.[102] After prompting from Gandhi the negotiations again resumed on 19 August.[103] On 3 September Gandhi informed the Minister of the Interior that if the negotiations proved abortive, 'the struggle [would] be revived on a wider issue'.[104] By 10 September, although the Minister had moved close to meeting Gandhi's demands, he refused to negotiate further on the questions of South African-born Indian migration from Natal to the Cape, or on non-Christian marriages.[105] Gandhi replied immediately with a telegram which asserted that the government's position made the 'revival [of the] struggle imperative.'[106] Two days later, on 12 September 1913, passive resistance was formally resumed as long as:

1. A racial bar disfigures the Immigration Act;
2. the rights existing prior to the passing of the Act are not restored and maintained;
3. the £3 tax upon ex-indentured men, women and children is not removed;
4. the status of women married in South Africa is not secured;
5. generally so long as a spirit of generosity and justice does not pervade the adminstration of the [Immigration Act, Cape and Natal Licensing Acts, and the Gold and Township Acts of the Transvaal].[107]

The new phase of the campaign combined the strategy modifications which Gandhi had formulated in 1912 and 1913. The movement's goals opened up the real possibility of widespread passive resistance involving

Indians throughout South Africa and from all levels of the social and economic hierarchy. Like the widened set of objectives which Gandhi had considered in 1912, the new goals set for the campaign offered something for everyone, with the crucial difference that they now addressed fundamental grievances. It is important to note, however, that the movement still stopped short of making demands which past governments had long since refused to concede, thus continuing to avoid linking the original goals of the movement to others even less likely of attainment. This is particularly clear in the different forms of the demands which were made on behalf of the underclasses and of the elites.

The repeal of the £3 tax, which Gandhi had avoided in May 1912, but demanded in September 1913, gave the movement the potential to recruit thousands of indentured and ex-indentured workers and, indeed, numbers of the new Natal elite. The continuing opposition of the Natal legislature to the repeal of the tax had been demonstrated as recently as June 1913 when Natal Act 17 (1895) was amended, but to allow only for the remission of the tax on women. However the assurance given to Gokhale by Botha, Smuts and Fischer that the tax would be repealed made it clear that this demand was no longer impossible to achieve. By contrast, the most deep-seated grievance of the merchants, and the only issue which had proved capable of mobilizing them in the past, remained out of reach: Gokhale had been assured that there could be *no* radical change in the laws affecting Indian commerce. The formula which Gandhi devised to appeal to the merchants was thus a half measure. He demanded only that a more liberal spirit be brought to bear in administering the existing laws. In mid-October when the merchants had failed to respond to the call for passive resistance, the formula was modified slightly to demand a *declaration* from the government that existing laws would 'be administered in a liberal spirit, and with due regard to vested rights'.[108]

The initial campaign tactics differed little from the proposals which Gandhi had outlined in April. The strident condemnation of non-participants which had characterized the earlier stages of the campaign between 1907 and 1909 was replaced with a low-key call for a few volunteers in every town of 'those who feel inclined to take an active part in the campaign'.[109] Far from calling on merchants to sacrifice their businesses and undergo prolonged suffering in jail, Gandhi made it clear that if *satyagrahis* courted arrest by hawking without a licence, their businesses would remain safe and the jail sentences would be brief.[110] Despite the inclusion of the £3 tax question, the tactics outlined in *Indian Opinion* and in speeches at mass meetings[111] made no provision to take the campaign to the people. Indeed, Gandhi had not formulated a 'programme or plan of action for the campaign'.[112] However, the course of events between mid-September and mid-October suggests that Gandhi hoped to avoid an attempt to mobilize the underclasses, with whom he had no direct contact, and that he relied on an elite campaign, supported by the threat of mass mobilization which was implicit in the inclusion of the £3 tax question, to put pressure on the government.

The campaign started with a handful of *satyagrahis* — including women for the first time — seeking arrest by illegally crossing the Natal-Transvaal or Natal-Free State border.[113] By early October, after Gandhi, Polak, Ritch and other committed Gandhi-ites had addressed elite rallies in Johannesburg, Cape Town and Durban,[114] a number of organizations in the three provinces had passed resolutions supporting the principle of passive resistance.[115] But few of their members were willing to court arrest. The total number of *satyagrahis* remained around three dozen,[116] too few to put pressure on the government. On 28 September Gandhi informed the Minister of the Interior — but did not make it public — that the next step of the campaign would consist of a strike of indentured labourers.[117] On 15 October when the government had failed to respond positively either to the limited passive resistance which was all that Gandhi could muster, or to the threat of a strike, Gandhi issued an official press statement which noted inter alia that strike action by indentured labourers would form part of the campaign.[118] On 16 October the strike began in the coal district of northern Natal.

There is very little direct information concerning the decision to call a strike. It is clear however that it was begun with minimal preparation beforehand,[119] and with less than full support from the elites. Gandhi started the strike at a moment when his leadership was again being formally challenged.

At a special meeting of the Natal Congress on 6 October a decision had been taken to organize an all-South African Indian conference to present the grievances of the elites to the government. This decision was endorsed by several prominent members of the new elite. A circular was addressed to major Indian associations inviting their participation. Minor associations were invited through the press to contact the Congress's secretaries directly.[120] On 12 October Gandhi answered questions and criticisms of his policy at a public meeting in Durban, convened by the Anjuman Islam because Gandhi refused to attend a Congress meeting as long as the secretaries who had rejected his policy in April remained officers of the party.[121] The severest critics at the meeting blamed Gandhian policy for the steady deterioration of merchant rights over the past twenty years. At a more reasonable level, the discussion focussed on Gandhi's increasing assumption of the leadership mantle, and his unwillingness to adopt alternative policies. Gandhi was questioned about the possibility of an all-South African Indian conference, and the reason why he had failed to support Aiyar's anti-tax campaign. His replies to both questions were evasive. His failure to use Indians at the leadership level of the passive resistance movement was also criticized. One of NIC's secretaries asked why Gandhi chose white lieutenants over educated Natal-born Indians like K R Nayanah, S R Pather, a barrister, or 'Gabriel' — presumably Bernard Gabriel who was also a barrister. Gandhi's reply, that Pather, Nayanah and Gabriel could not be compared with Polak, his principle lieutenant, in terms of 'ability, talent, purity and ideals' provoked a prolonged attack on Gandhi's own abilities.

The 12 October meeting ended with an undertaking by Gandhi to seek consensus at a second meeting a week later, provided the proceedings were more orderly than they had been that day, when police intervention was required to prevent fist fights breaking out. In return, the crowd promised to support Gandhi provided that he proved willing to 'abide by the decision and wishes of the people'. Two days later, committed *satyagrahis* began trying to bring out Indian workers in northern Natal. The strike which followed thus has the appearance of a last ditch stand by Gandhi in South Africa: a tactic which he was so ill-prepared to use that he was uncertain of how successful it would be,[122] but whose use was demanded by the alienation of a powerful group of his original constituents, and by the consistent failure of the movement even after it had been shifted as far back from an ethical to a material plane as Gandhi could go without endangering his original goals.

The Strike

Before discussing this lengthy and widespread strike it should be pointed out that since the initial call to action was issued by Gandhi, the strike has conventionally been viewed simply as 'a new phase'[123] in his long-running passive resistance campaign. The dominant themes of the literature, which portray Gandhi as the prime mover in early South African Indian history, and as the 'champion of indentured labourers'[124] from the mid '90s onwards, have allowed historians to bypass key questions such as, how and why did the strike occur; why *then*; why was it so widespread; how and why was it able to last so long; why was it suppressed with such brutality? In the simplistic Gandhi-centric framework which most historians have used, the strike ceases to have any intrinsic interest. The striking workers are dismissed as 'volunteers for *satyagraha*',[125] and the strike as an almost reflex response to the Gandhian imperative.

Not the least extraordinary gap in this historiography is the fact that the form of the workers' action — a prolonged and widespread work stoppage — is taken for granted. Yet these workers were at most only a few years removed from the pre-industrial Indian countryside. George Rudé's detailed study of eighteenth and nineteenth-century Britain has shown how, in that context, it could take five decades or more for workers to adapt the nature and style of their protest to suit the exactions of advanced industrial society. He notes the 'tendency for protest at this stage to be spontaneous, unstructured, and to possess a minimum of organization.'[126] Indeed, these are among the key characteristics of indentured workers' protests which were noted in Chapter 1. To this one might add the use of what Rudé calls a 'traditional' or 'inherent' ideology[127] — that is, an ideology unsuited, by its very nature, to organizing and structuring protest appropriate to advanced industrial society. Thus part of the fascination of the close examination of the strike which follows is that it places passive resistance in perspective and, in so doing, reveals the uneasy and incomplete transition from what Rudé terms 'pre-industrial' to 'industrial' workers' protest. In short, the strike emerges as not only the finale of Gandhian passive resistance, but also a crucial moment in the making of the modern South African Indian working class.

The strike was preceded on 13 October 1913 by a public meeting held in Newcastle, one of the major urban centres in the Natal coal mining district. Gandhi's principal representative at the meeting was Thambi Naidoo, the veteran *satyagrahi* and popular president of the Johannesburg Tamil Benefit Society. Naidoo was accompanied by the wives or female relatives of several other well known *satyagrahis* who were also Tamils, like the majority of the workers.[128] Naidoo successfully mobilized the Newcastle elites for what was described in *Indian Opinion* as 'an extraordinarily enthusiastic meeting.' Notable participants included several men who had been officers of the local branch of NIPU, or regional representatives of Aiyar's anti-tax Committee. If strike action was discussed, it was not reported in the press, but the meeting resolved to 'abide by the [*satyagraha*] movement till redress is obtained.'[129] A 'passive resistance committee' was formed and four men including a *sirdar* from a Natal Government Railway work gang volunteered to seek arrest as soon as possible.[130] The following day, Naidoo and a party of committed *satyagrahis*, which included eleven women and six infants, unsuccessfully attempted to bring out the workers at the N G R barracks in Newcastle. Naidoo and two other men were arrested for trespassing on railway property, but released on the morning of the 15th. That afternoon, the passive resistance party addressed the 78 Indian workers at the Farleigh Colliery, who struck the next morning. They were taken to court and advised by the resident magistrate that they would be prosecuted unless they resumed work by the 17th. On the 17th, however, 'the movement spread beyond expectations' and within a week 2 000 Indians had struck work in northern Natal.[131]

At the most fundamental level, the swift success of the strike call, which was supported by between 4 000 and 5 000 Indian workers in northern Natal within two weeks,[132] derived from the fact that Gandhi had expressed a deeply-felt economic grievance by demanding the repeal of the tax. The records also show that some of the workers (perhaps many: the records are incomplete) struck work with the intention of articulating other grievances besides the one which Gandhi chose to represent.[133] Above all, though, it was the tax which paved the way for this unprecedented upsurge of mass resistance. Previously workers had suffered the extreme privations of contract work with the sure knowledge that in five years they would be able to return to India; or, as so many of them chose to do, pursue one of the variety of opportunities for a modestly successful living in Natal. The tax, in conjunction with the depressed economy, fundamentally altered the terms of this exchange by removing the time limit from indentured labour. Workers forced back under contract by tax debts and unemployment (and, indeed, those who had yet to complete their first period of indenture) faced, for all they knew, a lifetime on the plantations or the mines. At this point it is worth recalling that in 1913 over 65 per cent of the entire indentured workforce was undergoing second or subsequent terms of indenture. In this context even the familiar grievances of contract work must have assumed much greater significance.

But none of this addresses the question why the workers who, in the main, lacked even rudimentary labour organization, or a worker ideology, responded to a strike call issued by Gandhi. Again Rudé's work on the first generation of the British proletariat is suggestive. He has found that the leaders of 'pre-industrial' popular protest came from without, as often as within, the 'protesters' own ranks', and that in the former case 'it was usual to find the "crowd" responding to the direction, or believed direction, of a leader from a higher social group.'[134] Gandhi himself provided this sort of legitimacy. Moreover his call to action had been preceded by some two years of groundwork by *other* representatives of higher social groups. Aiyar's shortlived South African Indian Committee had begun the process by demanding the repeal of the tax in late 1911; Gokhale had carried it on in 1912. Fragments of this information had filtered down into the indentured workforce, inevitably undergoing distortion en route. Indeed, as we shall see, these fragments were crucial legitimating factors for the workers in southern Natal, who wove together complex patterns of fact and fiction to describe the external leaders under whose orders they believed they were protesting.

Under these conditions, starting a strike for the repeal of the £3 tax was not difficult. Maintaining solidarity and organizing the striking workers was, however, less simple. As soon as the strike began to spread Gandhi rushed in numbers of veteran passive resisters, as well as making use of those who now volunteered to join the movement, notably Tamil-speaking Natal-born Indians.[135] These organizers, who included Gandhi himself at times, travelled around the mining district helping to bring out labourers and discouraging others who showed signs of returning to work. Mass meetings attended by as many as 3 000 workers were addressed by Gandhi, Thambi Naidoo, and C R Naidoo, one of the earliest representatives of workers' grievances in Natal, who had been living in the north of the province since at least 1912.[136]

Neither the government nor the mine owners eased the task of keeping the striking workers out. The government adopted a policy of limited intervention. In his capacity as Minister of Defence, Smuts ordered armed police protection for every colliery in the strike area. Special constables were enrolled from the white colliery staff, and reinforcements for the local detachments of the South African Mounted

Rifles were drafted in from outstations. The SAMR were ordered to prevent violence, protect mine property and afford 'every protection [to Indian mine labourers] if they wish to work.'[137] But few arrests were made.[138] Government policy remained essentially defensive and no real attempt was made to break the strike.

Most collieries continued to provide striking workers with their daily food ration.[139] In addition, within days of the beginning of the strike the Natal Coal Owners's Association publicly dissociated themselves from a government statement that the 'majority of Natal employers are averse to the repeal of the [£3] tax'.[140] The statement, issued during the preceding parliamentary session, had been quoted by Gandhi in a telegram sent to the Prime Minister from the strike area some time around 23 October.[141]

Gandhi responded to the policy of non-intervention by trying to force a confrontation. On 23 October he issued a public statement announcing his intention to lead the striking workers out of the mine compounds in an attempt to seek arrest, which would culminate in an illegal border crossing into the Transvaal if necessary. This decision was explained, in a characteristic Gandhian blend of political expediency and moral integrity, as a function of the fact that Gandhi considered it 'improper that the men should live on mine rations when they do not work'.[142] The government did not respond to this announcement; but the Coal Owners' Association called for a meeting with Gandhi in Durban. On 24 October, the removal of the workers from the mine compounds was deferred, pending the outcome of this meeting.[143]

On 25 October Gandhi met with the Coal Owners and other major employers of Indian labour at the Durban Chamber of Commerce. He explained the strike as resulting from the government's failure to redeem its promise to Gokhale to repeal the £3 tax, and stated that the strikers would be 'immediately advised to resume work, regardless of any other grievances, as soon as the Government give assurance that they will carry out their promise'.[144] The Coal Owners' Association therefore telegrammed the government for a commentary on the alleged promise to Gokhale. When the government denied promising the repeal of the tax, the Association treated the strike as a misunderstanding which they were willing to forgive provided that there was immediate acceptance of the official version of Gokhale's discussion with the Union ministers. Bypassing Gandhi, the coal owners instructed colliery managers to inform their Indian workers that rations would be withheld if they continued to strike, but that if they resumed work within 24 hours, the 'time they had lost would be treated as a holiday, and no steps would be taken against them for breach of contract'.[145]

The mine managers had difficulty assembling the workers, let alone issuing the owners' statement. However, the fairly cohesive wall of defiance which the workers were able to present as long as rations were actually being issued, and very little done to attempt to break the strike, could not be expected to long outlive the introduction of punitive measures: the leaders of the movement were well aware of this.[146] The coal owners' ultimatum therefore provided a new imperative both to remove the strikers from the mine compounds, and to attempt to get them into jail, passing the responsibility for their upkeep to the government. On 29 October, the day that the coal owners attempted to issue their ultimatum, Gandhi led 200 strikers and their dependants out of Newcastle towards the Transvaal border.[147] Within 24 hours he was followed by a second party of 300, led by Thambi Naidoo. A day later Albert Christopher, the secretary of the CBIA, left Newcastle at the head of a column of 250.[148] Within days, 4 000 strikers and their dependants were on the move towards the Transvaal, organized and assisted by other colonial-born Indians and veterans of the earlier stages of the campaign.[149]

Gandhi appealed to the Transvaal government to arrest the column of strikers before they actually entered the Transvaal.[150] But Smuts played a waiting game, confident that the strike would collapse of its own accord in due course, as the movement in the Transvaal had done between 1910 and 1911. He observed that 'Mr Gandhi appeared to be in a position of much difficulty. Like Frankenstein he found his monster an uncomfortable creation and he would be glad to be relieved of further responsibility for its support'.[151] It was an accurate assessment of the situation. Smuts's continued refusal to order the wholesale arrest of the strikers, even as they crossed illegally into the Transvaal,[152] placed an enormous economic burden on the movement.

Rallying the support of the merchants, whose contribution to feeding the striking workers was essential, was made difficult by the formal split in the Natal Congress which had taken place on 19 October when an unsuccessful attempt was made to pass a no-confidence vote against Gandhi. The no-confidence motion was a logical progression from the heavy criticism which Gandhi had been subjected to a week earlier, before he unilaterally started the strike. However, according to *African Chronicle*[153] — the only existing documentation on the 19 October meeting — the motion alarmed even many of Gandhi's opponents. Thus Gandhi survived his confrontation with the Congress by default, in much the same way that he had survived the 1909 leadership challenge in the Transvaal, and the brief mutiny of the new Natal elite in 1911: even when they no longer supported Gandhi, the elites in Natal and the Transvaal could not replace him. However, although the majority of the Congress were unwilling to condemn Gandhi outright, they would not support him either. On 19 October, therefore, Gandhi split the party, pulling out most of the new elite and his supporters from among the traders — some fifty men in all — to form a new party.[154] The hastily-created Natal Indian Association started a strike fund soon afterwards.[155] In one of the Natal elites' most successful organizational efforts, food for the striking workers was distributed along the line of march from the coal district to the Transvaal border.[156] By the end of the first week of November, though, it was clear that the government's policy of non-intervention seriously threatened the success of the strike. The cost of maintaining the striking workers on a minimal ration of bread and sugar[157] was averaging around £250 per day.[158] £1 000 had been cabled from India,[159] the strike committee was gathering funds and provisions, but Gandhi estimated that the shortfall in funds would be in excess of £6 000 per month.[160]

While Gandhi and an exhausted leadership[161] struggled to maintain the solidarity of the strikers under increasingly unfavourable circumstances in northern Natal, the success of the strike was ensured when it spread to the coastal sugar districts. Although Gandhi had announced as early as 23 October that he would attempt to bring out the southern workers if necessary,[162] neither he nor anyone else from the leadership level of the movement was responsible for the spread of the strike to southern Natal:[163] it began spontaneously and slowly in the first days of November; by around the 7th it had begun in earnest.[164]

The course of the strike in the south, where no leadership was imposed from outside, was very different from what it had been in the north. Although leaders emerged among the workers,[165] and many workers knew they were part of a movement for the repeal of the £3 tax,[166] the strike in southern Natal was also marked by disunity and by apparent uncertainty of purpose. This must be attributed mainly to the lack of leadership which transcended barracks or plantation boundaries, as well as to the much higher number of workers involved in the south (over 15 000 concentrated in groups as large as 2 000).[167]

In this swirling mass of confusion the workers explained their actions in a variety of ways, all of which posited the existence of a significant outsider as leader. They drew on both their incomplete knowledge of elite politics, and popular forms of Indian culture, to portray this mythical leader in a fashion that, reminiscent of upsurges in pre-industrial protest in Europe, was often millenarian. Workers on one big plantation were alleged to have struck because they believed a powerful rajah was going to pay them £3 not to work; on another they struck for fear that a rajah was coming to decapitate non-participants.[168] Yet another came out for some reason (it is not clear what) connected with the alleged visit of a rajah to a neighbouring plantation.[169] The Protector, some of the plantation managers, and some of the strikers themselves, claimed that many people struck because they learned that their neighbours had done so.[170] One worker claimed that a Tamil language handbill was circulated which announced that Gokhale was coming from India to abolish the tax at once.[171] Although there is no evidence to corroborate the existence of such a handbill, it is clear that word somehow spread that Gokhale was en route to assist the workers. It was even rumoured that he was bringing troops — as much as a regiment — with him.[172] And finally, some of the workers who knew of Gandhi, and his connection with the strike in the north, believed that they were acting on his orders.[173]

In the absence of leadership, an appropriate ideology, or even a precise set of demands, some of the coastal workers left the plantations and congregated in nearby townships,[174] and others made their way to Gandhi's communal settlement at Phoenix,[175] but most simply remained in their barracks, refusing to work.[176] This apparent uncertainty of purpose helped generate numerous reports in the white press, and statements by plantation managers and owners, or the Protector, which dismissed the strike in the south as the product of agitation,[177] implicitly denying that it might have been an attempt to articulate deep-seated grievances. It was only an occasional more sympathetic observer such as the superintendent of Indian mission schools, the Reverend A A Bailie, who noted that thousands had struck work without being able to express a coherent reason for their actions, not because they had *no* grievances, but because they had so many.[178]

The reaction of employers and officials to the striking workers in the south also differed greatly from that in the north. From the beginning the coastal strike was characterized by tension which was absent in the north: 'cane fires and rioting' were anticipated long before any violence occurred;[179] arrests of suspected ringleaders began at once.[180] This tension was the product of several inter-related factors. The sheer number of workers who were or who might become involved, posed a potential law and order problem far greater than any that could occur among the relatively small number of Indians in the north. In addition, the sugar industry was totally dependent on their labour, and the year's crop was still being cut and crushed when the strike began. General H T Lukin, Inspector General of the Permanent Force of South African Mounted Rifles, who was responsible for maintaining control in Natal, was as concerned about the 'disastrous effect on the sugar industry if the movement spreads'[181] as he was about a breakdown of law and order. In fact, much of the crop had already been cut and milled when the strike began, but a call for harsh measures against the strikers came from men like W A Campbell, managing director of the vast Mount Edgecombe estate, whose mill closed down on 14 November with some three weeks of harvesting left unfinished.[182] A final cause of tension in southern Natal, which is difficult to assess, was the widespread rumour that the Indians were calling on the Africans for support, or that they would come out in support of the Indians in any case.[183] It was even reported that some Africans were only waiting for the Indians to give the word for a general uprising against the whites.[184] These rumours were submitted to Pretoria, but it is hard to know how much credence was given to them by either the government or the white population at large. Indians and Africans had not cooperated politically before, but, with the Zulu rebellion only seven years in the past,[185] it is reasonable to suppose that there was some apprehension about the possibility of Africans being drawn into another — possibly violent — resistance movement.

The state of tension among the employers and officials which accompanied and, indeed, preceded the strike in southern Natal[186] was soon translated into police brutality. In the most serious confrontations between police and strikers, a number of workers were shot dead and others gravely injured. Naturally the police claimed that they had acted in self-defence, but although official reports indicate that the police were faced with sticks, stones and even cane knives in some instances, it is also clear that they generally overreacted.[187] The most senseless act of brutality, however, was carried out by a planter named Armstrong, who 'grievously assaulted' two innocent, unarmed Indians on the flimsiest of suspicions.[188]

By the end of November the strike had, at one time or another during the preceding weeks, paralysed the Durban and Pietermaritzburg produce markets, closed down some of the sugar mills, and stripped many coastal hotels, restaurants and private residences of their domestics (although these were reluctant to come out), resulted in some 150 acres of cane being illegally burned, and had inconvenienced the coal industry, the N G R, and other, smaller industries in coastal Natal.[189] Smuts had been forced to modify his policy of non-intervention and order the mass arrests which rendered the campaign a success for Gandhi. Gandhi himself was arrested on 9 November, Polak and Kallenbach on the 10th,[190] and other leaders and rank and file gradually during the next two weeks. In order to accommodate the hundreds of mine workers who were charged with illegal entry into the Transvaal, and at the same time get the men back on the job, numbers of the mine shafts were converted into temporary prisons, and miners sentenced to mine labour.[191] Most of the miners, who were transported out of the Transvaal by train, returned to work quietly. However, at Ladysmith there was a riot which was quelled by mounted police charges and baton-wielding constables.[192] It is difficult to know who provoked whom in this instance, but at Ballengeich colliery defenceless workers were driven into the mine shaft by *sjambok*.[193] The use of mine compounds as prisons, and the police and employer actions during November, received thorough press coverage. Cabled Reuter reports carried the news to India and Britain where press, parliamentary and public criticism grew as the violence in Natal escalated.[194] In India, the Viceroy, Lord Hardinge, was requested by the non-official members of his Council to call an emergency session to discuss the South African situation.[195] Numbers of mass meetings were held to protest the recent events and demand action by the government of India.[196] On 27 November, Hardinge, pressured on all sides, publicly criticized the government of South Africa himself, and called for a commission of enquiry on which Indian interests would be represented.[197] In early December, when most Indians had already returned to work,[198] Smuts announced the appointment of a commission to enquire into the cause of the strike.

Gandhi, Polak and Kallenbach were released from jail within days of the announcement of the forthcoming commission, in order that they could testify before it.[199] As the final round of negotiations approached, Smuts and Gandhi were more evenly matched in terms of bargaining power than they had been in the past. The scale of the strike, and the violence which it produced, had subjected the Union government to far heavier criticism in Britain, India and, indeed, the Union,[200] than any of the earlier stages of the campaign. But the government were by no means the losers in the final stage. Smuts's policy of non-intervention did not fail completely. The government was forced to make several thousand arrests, but, as Smuts had predicted, the workers' slender resources had been consumed,[201] and the strike collapsed of its own accord in many areas. In addition, the Natal Indian Association, which had attempted to assume responsibility for the strike in the south, had panicked when it spread and violence began to erupt. On 18 November a mass meeting convened by NIA had demanded imperial government intervention in view of the 'increasing difficulty of feeding the strikers and keeping order.'[202] Two members of NIA, with official permission, had even toured the southern strike area urging workers to remain on their plantations, not to resist the police, and not to commit any illegal acts.[203]

Smuts and Gandhi each used their respective strengths, and the other's weaknesses, in an attempt to concede the minimum possible during the final round of negotiations. Gandhi objected to the composition of the three-man commission on the specific ground that two of the commissioners had known anti-Indian biases, and the more general ground that the commission, appointed without consultation with the leadership of the community, reflected the very indifference to Indian opinion which lay at the root of South African Indian grievances. Gandhi demanded an additional commissioner approved by the Indian community; and he refused to testify before the commission as it was originally constituted.[204] The Natal Indian Association, which by December comprised the majority of the Natal elites, supported Gandhi's rejection of the commission.[205] Gandhi further strengthened his demand by informing the government that passive resistance would be resumed unless his objections were met.[206] But Smuts refused: in a pointed reminder of the Indian community's major weaknesses, and the government's strength, Smuts noted the 'gratuitous infliction of grave sufferings on the innocent', which would be entailed by a renewal of passive resistance.[207] In addition, Smuts now enjoyed the added strength of support from the Viceroy and Gokhale, who pressed Gandhi to cooperate with the commission.[208]

Each having stated his irreducible minimum, and demonstrated his strength, Smuts and Gandhi then began the slow process of finding a formula which would break the deadlock without giving the appearance of concession on either side. The formula proved to be a NIA boycott of the commission, in exchange for private consultations between Gandhi, Smuts, Sir Benjamin Robertson, and the Rev. C F Andrews, the latter two sent from India for the occasion.[209] The bargain was sealed in an exchange of letters between Gandhi and Smuts on 21 January 1914, in which Gandhi promised to suspend passive resistance pending the outcome of the commission and the introduction of legislation which would fulfil the goals of the movement.[210]

The commission's recommendations, issued in April 1914, passed into law as Act 22 of 1914 — the 'Indian Relief Bill', as it came to be known. The £3 tax on ex-indentured workers was abolished. One wife, and the minor children, of an Indian marriage — even if it were polygamous — were given the right to join husbands resident in South Africa. Plural wives, living or who had lived in South Africa, were guaranteed the continued right to do so, provided that the husband remained resident.[211] No provision was made either to guarantee the right of South African-born Indians to migrate from one province to another, or to provide for a more just administration of the laws affecting Indian commerce. Gandhi had clearly included these in the list of objectives of the final stage of the campaign simply in order to mobilize support; and he had already conceded them in the exchange of letters with Smuts on 21 January.

Gandhi left South Africa on 18 July 1914, some three weeks after the Relief Bill was read for the third time. During his final weeks in South Africa, he was subject to virulent criticism by the segments of the Natal and Transvaal elites who had broken with him in late 1913, and who pointed to the gap between the objectives of the campaign and the Bill.[212] But elsewhere in South Africa, and in India and Britain, the Relief Bill was celebrated as a magnificent achievement. When Gandhi returned to India in January 1915, he was already being hailed as a *mahatma*.[213]

Notes

1   £8 509.13.0d. had been received by Apr. 1912. *Indian Opinion*, 6 Apr. 1912. Tata pledged a third donation of 25 000 rupees in July, ibid., 10 Aug. 1912.

2 *C W*, x, p.230, Gandhi to Gokhale, 25 Apr. 1910.

3 By Jan. 1905, Gandhi had already placed £3 500 at the disposal of the paper, ibid., iv, p.332, Gandhi to Gokhale, 13 Jan. 1905. See also, *Indian Opinion*, 6 Apr. 1912.

4 Sorabji Shapurji Adajania (the first of the Natal *satyagrahis*), and the son of V A Chettiar, president of the Tamil Benefit Society, were both undergoing their seventh sentence by mid-1910. *C W*, x, p.220, 'Tamil Sacrifice', 16 Apr. 1910; *Indian Opinion*, 4 June 1910.

5 The policy of deportation began at the end of stage two of the campaign. 198 resisters had been deported by June 1909. CO 291/138/21201, Gov. to Sec. St., 7 June 1909, encl. minute by Ministers, no.281, 5 June 1909.

6 Gandhi moved to Tolstoy on 4 June 1910, *C W*, x, pp.272-3, 'Johannesburg', 13 June 1910.

7 *C W*, x, pp.410-11, 'Johannesburg', 1 Mar. 1911.

8 Ibid., pp.412-3, Gandhi to Lane (Smuts's private sec.), 2 Mar. 1911.

9 The main reason for the failure of the bill was strenuous objections by some British and Jewish members to an education test which could equally well be used to prevent augmentation of their numbers by further immigration. TABA, Gov. Gen. 708/15/122d, Gov.Gen. to Sec. St. conf., 26 Apr. 1911, encl. Smuts to Gov.Gen., 22 Apr. 1911.

10 Cd.5363, no.42, Smuts to Sec. St., 26 Aug. 1909.

11 CO 879/106/952, no.92, Gov. Gen. to Sec. St. 4 Nov. 1910.

12 In his notes of a conversation with Smuts on 27 Mar. 1911, Gandhi recorded Smuts as saying, 'I hope you will keep the Cape and Natal Indians silent', *C W*, xi, p.496. And see also, CO 879/108/970, no.63, CO to IO, 2 Mar. 1911.

13 *C W*, xi, pp.424-5, Gandhi to Priv. Sec. to Min. of Interior, 4 Mar. 1911.

14 The logic of the new demand was articulated by Gandhi on a number of occasions. See for example, ibid., x, pp.464-5, Gandhi to Ritch, 16 Mar. 1911; ibid., pp.469-70, Gandhi to Ritch, 17 Mar. 1911.

15 *Rand Daily Mail*, 14 Mar. 1911; SABA Gov. Gen. 708/15/1229ᵃ, Gov. Gen. to Sec. St., urgent, private and personal.

16 *C W*, x, pp.467-8, Gandhi to Lane, 17 Mar. 1911; ibid., pp.482-3, Gandhi to Lane, 22 Mar. 1911. See also, ibid., pp.469-70, Gandhi to Ritch, 17 Mar. 1911. At Smuts's request these proposals were submitted in writing on 7 Apr. 1911, ibid., xi, pp.10-11, Gandhi to Lane.

17 The Union govt. had made it clear from the outset that it was 'not possible to ignore Provincial boundaries in the administration of the Asiatic or Immigration Acts'. SABA, Gov. Gen. 707/15/91, minute by PM no.902A, 20 Dec. 1910. See also, CO 879/106/952, no.92,

Gov. Gen. to Sec. St., 4 Nov. 1910.

18   *C W*, x, p.469. See also, ibid., xi, pp.16-17, Gandhi to Ritch, 8 Apr. 1911.

19   During an interview on 27 Mar., Smuts reminded Gandhi that he was 'bound to the Imperial Government to pass this Bill'. *C W*, x, pp.494-6. The impossibility of producing a separate bill for the Transvaal was spelled out in SABA, Gov. Gen. 708/15/122a, Gov. Gen. to Sec. St., urgent, private and personal, 12 Apr. 1911.

20   *C W*, x, p.437, BIA to Ritch, 7 Mar. 1911.

21   Ibid., p.443, Gandhi to Ritch, 9 Mar. 1911.

22   Ibid., p.489, Gandhi to Ritch, 24 Mar. 1911. Gandhi was introduced to sympathetic MPs by Morris Alexander, a Jewish MP from Cape Town. See, for example, ibid., xi, p.5, Gandhi to Ritch, 5 Apr. 1911; ibid., p.9, Gandhi to Ritch, 6 Apr. 1911. Dr Abdurahman, president of the APO introduced him to two others. Ibid., pp.12-13, Gandhi to Ritch, 7 Apr. 1911.

23   *Rand Daily Mail*, 4 Apr. 1911.

24   The extensive correspondence between Gandhi and Ritch and Gandhi and Polak in Mar. and Apr. 1911 is printed in *C W*, x and xi. See, in particular, Petitions to the Leg. Assembly by NIC and the Cape British Indian Union, dated Mar. 1911. Ibid., x, pp.411-3 and Appendix IX.

25   Gandhi made certain that Smuts was kept informed of his private meetings with opposition MPs in Cape Town. *C W*, xi, pp.17-18, Gandhi to Ritch, 9 Apr. 1911.

26   SABA, Gov. Gen. 708/15/122a, Gov. Gen. to Sec. St., urgent, private and personal, 12 Apr. 1911.

27   Ibid., 15/122b, Gov. Gen. to Sec. St., secret, 14 Apr. 1911.

28   See, for example, *C W*, xi, pp.17,19,21-2,29, Gandhi to Ritch, 9, 10, 12, 18 Apr. 1911. See also, ibid., pp.31-4, 'Abstract of Interview with General Smuts', 19 Apr. 1911.

29   Smuts had made this clear to Gandhi in a conversation at the end of March. Ibid., x, pp.494-6, 'Letter to Sonja Schlesin', 27 Mar. 1911. Gandhi had accepted the necessity of a joint settlement by early April. Ibid., xi, pp.12-13, Gandhi to Ritch, 7 Apr. 1911; ibid., 15, Gandhi to Lane, 8 Apr. 1911.

30   Ibid., x, p.433, fn.6, Acting Pres. NIC to Gandhi, 7 Mar. 1911.

31   Ibid., xi, pp.31-4, 'Abstract of Interview with General Smuts', 19 Apr. 1911.

32   Ibid.,pp.30-31, Gandhi to Smuts, 19 Apr. 1911.

33   Ibid., p.36, Gandhi to Lane, 20 Apr. 1911.

34   Ibid., Appendix II, Lane to Gandhi, 21 Apr. 1911.

35   Ibid., p.37, Gandhi to Ritch, 21 Apr. 1911, 5.45pm.

36   Ibid., pp.38-40, Gandhi to Lane, 22 Apr. 1911; SABA, Gov. Gen.
      708/15/122d, Gov. Gen. to Sec. St., conf. 2 Apr. 1911, encl. Lane
      to Gandhi, 22 Apr. 1911.
37   *C W*, xi, pp.44-6. See also, *Indian Opinion*, 27 May 1911.
38   *Indian Opinion*, 6 May 1911. The Chinese passive resisters voted in
      acceptance of the settlement at a similar meeting where the factions
      into which their party had split in 1908 were reunited. Ibid.
39   See, for example, *C W*, x, Appendix XI, Lane to Gandhi, 24 Mar.
      1911; ibid., xi, pp.17-18, Gandhi to Ritch, 9 Apr. 1911. And see in
      particular, ibid., pp.12-13, Gandhi to Ritch, 7 Apr. 1911.
40   In particular Smuts viewed the inclusion of the O F S question as a
      new demand, ibid., x, Appendix XI, Lane to Gandhi, 24 Mar. 1911.
41   *C W*, xi, pp.50-56, BIA Petition to Sec. St., 1 May 1911; ibid.,
      pp.70-4, NIC memorial to Sec. St., 15 May 1911, SABA, Gov. Gen.
      708/15/146, Gov. Gen. to Sec. St., 9 June 1911, encl. Cape British
      Indian Union petition to Sec. St., 3 May 1911; ibid., 708/15/152,
      Sec. St. to Gov. Gen., 1 July 1911, encl. Polak (on behalf of SABIC)
      to Under Sec. St. for Colonies, 17 June 1911.
42   Ibid.
43   *C W*, xi, p.222, 3 Feb. 1912.
44   Ibid., p.223.
45   The second bill failed to pass for the same reason as the first: the
      parliament's hostility to legislative proposals which could be used to
      exclude selected groups of white immigrants. CO 879/111/994,
      no.108, Gov. Gen. to Sec. St., 25 June 1912.
46   Fn.45 above, and *C W*, xi, pp.271, 275, 280, Gandhi to Lane, 25
      June, 6, 17 July, 1912.
47   23 Aug. 1912.
48   The details of the tour appear in a special ed. of *Indian Opinion*,
      entitled *Honourable Mr G K Gokhale's Visit to South Africa, 1912.*
49   See for example, *C W*, xi, Appendix XXIII, 'Gokhale's Speech at
      Bombay', 14 Dec. 1912.
50   *Honourable Mr G K Gokhale's Visit to South Africa, 1912*, p.24;
      African Chronicle, 9, 16 Nov. 1912, 14 Dec. 1912.
51   *Indian Opinion*, 23 Nov. 1912.
52   Ibid. At Isipingo Gokhale paid a tribute to the European planters
      who formed part of his reception committee, 'and thanked them for
      the treatment of their servants which he was satisfied was humane
      and tolerant'. At Mt. Edgecombe, after dining with Campbell, he
      spent a few minutes with the labourers, promising 'to do all that he
      could to make their condition happy and comfortable'.
53   See, for example, *Indian Opinion*, 16, 23 Nov. 1912.
54   CO 879/112/1002, no.13, Sec. St. to Gov. Gen., 18 Jan. 1913,

encl. extract *Times of India* (Mail ed.), 21 Dec. 1912.

55   Since this is another of the very contentious issues in Gandhi's career
        in South Africa, and since it offers a significant commentary on his
        political style, it is important to note that the Governor-General
        informed the CO two days after Gokhale's meeting with the Union
        ministers that, 'as regards the £3 tax, the PM told me that he thought
        it would be possible to meet Mr Gokhale's views, though there might
        be strong opposition in Natal. From what Gokhale said, I gathered
        that the PM had given him satisfactory assurance'. CO
        879/111/994, no.151, Gov. Gen. to Sec. St., 16 Nov. 1912. Cf
        W K Hancock, *Smuts*, I (Cambridge University Press, 1962),
        pp.341-3, and R Huttenback, *Gandhi in South Africa* (Cornell
        University Press, 1971), pp.301-3, who, using government
        statement issued months after the event, contend that, 'it is . . . clear
        that [the Union ministers] stopped short of giving a binding pledge to
        repeal the £3 tax'.

56   *C W*, xi, p.415, 'Diary 1912'.

57   Ibid., pp.449-50, Gandhi to H Gandhi, 26 Jan. 1913.

58   Ibid., xii, Appendix I.

59   Ibid., xi, pp.497-8, 'Attack on Indian Religions', 22 Mar. 1913.

60   *Indian Opinion*, 5, 12 Apr. 1913. The resolution was strongly
        supported by veterans of the earlier stages of the campaign, such as
        Thambi Naidoo, P K Naidoo, and A M Cachalia. The fact that the
        meeting was preceded by one of the Tamil Benefit Society suggests
        that Gandhi continued to rely heavily on the TBS, as he had done
        since 1908.

61   *C W*, xii, pp.1-2.

62   Ibid., pp.7-8, Gandhi to Min. Interior, 9 Apr. 1913.

63   Ibid., pp.9-10, Gandhi to Lane, 9 Apr. 1913. See also *Cape Times*,
        11 Apr. 1913 (interview with Polak).

64   *C W*, xii, Appendix VI, Sec.3, draft immigration bill.

65   Ibid., sec. 4(1)(a), 4(3).

66   Ibid., sec. 5.

67   Ibid., sec. 5(g).

68   Ibid., sec. 5(g) in conjunction with sec. 4(1)(a).

69   12 Apr. 1913.

70   CO 879/112/1002, no.81, Gov. Gen. to Sec. St., 2 Apr. 1913;
        ibid., no.89, Sec. St. to Gov. Gen., 26 Apr. 1913.

71   *C W*, xii, Appendix III, Min. of Interior to Gandhi, 15 Apr. 1913.

72   Ibid., pp.27-9, Gandhi to Min. of Interior, 15 Apr. 1913.

73   Ibid., pp.20-1, 'Reply to the Association', 12 Apr. 1913; ibid.,
        pp.34-5, 'Snare', 19 Apr. 1913; ibid., p.36, 'New Bill', 19 Apr. 1913.

74   Ibid., p.14, 'The New Bill', 12 Apr. 1913; ibid., p.32, 'The

Immigration Bill', 19 Apr. 1913; ibid., p.36, 'New Bill', 19 Apr. 1913; ibid., p.37, 'Mrs Pankhurst's Sacrifice', 19 Apr. 1913.

75   In a lengthy article in the 19 April ed. of *African Chronicle* entitled 'Why Mr Gandhi is a Failure', P S Aiyar criticized Gandhian strategy in general, and the failure of the provisional settlement in particular. Commenting that 'there is no use sulking in the tent at Phoenix and say[ing] that "people won't join me"', Aiyar called (unsuccessfully) for Gandhi to come into Durban and engage in a 'free and frank exchange of ideas with the people'.

76   Ibid., 3 May 1913.

77   Ibid. See Francis Joseph's protest which 'fell flat of course, causing spasmodic laughter'.

78   Ibid., 3 May 1913. See also SABA, Gov. Gen. 712/15/387, NIC to Gov. Gen. 22 Apr. 1913.

79   *African Chronicle*, 3 May 1913.

80   In fact, NIC had virtually ceased to support passive resistance in 1909. *African Chronicle* claimed on 19 July 1913 that they rejected the strategy because it had proved a failure.

81   *Indian Opinion*, 3 May 1913.

82   Ibid. This was the first time that Gandhi had left Phoenix since his arrival there in January. He was described as having come 'specially from Phoenix' for the meeting. Pessimistic editorials in *Indian Opinion* on 12 and 19 Apr. 1913 (*C W*, xii, pp.20,36), and a letter to Gokhale dated 14 Apr. 1913 (ibid.,p.41) strongly suggest that Gandhi anticipated NIC's decision on passive resistance.

83   *Indian Opinion*, 3 May 1913.

84   *C W*, xii, pp.58-62, 'The Campaign', 3 May 1913.

85   *Indian Opinion*, 3 May 1913. See also SABA, Gov. Gen. 713/15/397, Cachalia to Gov. Gen. 30 Apr. 1913. Cf. the passive resistance resolution at the BIA mass meeting against the Searle judgement on 30 Mar. 1913: 'Unless the relief requested is granted, it will become the *bounden duty of the community* . . . to adopt passive resistance' (emphasis added).

86   See Gandhi's detailed explanation of the limited meaning of the resolution in *Indian Opinion*, 3 May 1913.

87   Ibid., 10 May 1913. The organizations included the Anjuman Islam, Zoroastrian Anjuman, Mastic Society, Sydenham and Mayville Shri Hindi Jigyasa Sabhas and the Kathiawar Arya Mandal.

88   *Indian Opinion*, 3 Apr. 1909. Transvaal Indian women lagged behind Natal women in this respect. As early as October 1908 the Durban Indian Women's Association (consisting mainly of colonial-born women whose male relatives were politically active) was passing critical resolutions on government policy. *African Chronicle*,

24 Oct. 1908.

89   *C W*, xi, p.174, 'A Fruit of Passive Resistance', 28 Oct. 1911.

90   *Indian Opinion*, 10 May 1913.

91   See, for example, SABA, Gov. Gen. 713/15/412, Cape British Indian Union to Gov. Gen., 16 May 1913; CO 551/41/23023, Gov. Gen. to Sec. St., 18 June 1913, encl. BIA to Gov. Gen., 16 June 1913.

92   CO 551/41/23197, Gov. Gen. to Sec. St., conf., 16 June 1913.

93   Ibid., and CO 879/112/1002, no.98, Gov. Gen. to Sec. St. very conf., 5 May 1913.

94   A comparison of the clauses of the draft bill which affected Asians, and the Act as gazetted, is printed in *C W*, xii, Appendix VI.

95   The Act, as passed, restored the right of colonial-born Indians to migrate to the Cape provided that they were *not* born of parents indentured after Natal Act 17 of 1895 (that is, £3 taxpayers).

96   *C W*, xii, pp.120-21, Gandhi to Lane, 28 June 1913.

97   Gandhi was in Durban on 21 June, in Johannesburg by the 28th. Ibid., pp.117, 120.

98   Ibid., pp.120-22, Gandhi to Lane, 28 June 1913.

99   In a letter to Gokhale on 20 June 1913 (ibid., pp.112-15), Gandhi wrote that he intended 'to adopt all legitimate methods that prudence may dictate to avert the misery that must result from a renewal of the struggle'. But see below for reasons why an extension of the provisional settlement was unlikely, in itself, to avert passive resistance.

100   Ibid.

101   Sarvodaya Library, Phoenix, Natal, unnumbered document, Gandhi to Kallenbach. The letter, dated 'Tuesday', concerned the death of Gandhi's brother, Karsandas, the day before. Karsandas's date of death is given as Sunday, 22 June 1913 (*C W*, xii, p.649).

102   *C W*, xii, p.148, Gandhi to Bhavani Dayal, 23 July 1913. Gandhi returned to Phoenix when the negotiations were suspended.

103   Ibid., p.161, Gandhi to Min. Interior, 11 Aug. 1913; CO 551/44/39024, Gov. Gen. to Sec. St., secret, no.2, 22 Oct. 1913, encl. Min. Interior to Gandhi, 19 Aug. 1913.

104   CO 551/44/39024, Gov. Gen. to Sec. St., secret, no.2, 22 Oct. 1913, encl. Gandhi to Ass. Min. Interior, 3 Sept. 1913. Gandhi had returned to Johannesburg for the funeral service of his friend and supporter, Rev J J Doke on 24 Aug. *C W*, xii, pp.175-7, 'Speech at Memorial Service', 24 Aug. 1913.

105   *C W*, xii, p.175, fn.1, Ass. Min. Interior to Gandhi, 10 Sept. 1913.

106   CO 551/44/39024, Gov. Gen. to Sec. St., secret, no.2, 22 Oct. 1913, encl. Gandhi to Min. Interior, 10 Sept. 1913.

107   *Indian Opinion*, 20 Sept. 1913. 'The Indian Demands',

A M Cachalia to Min. of Interior, 20 Sept. 1913. The Minister of the Interior belived that Cachalia (president of BIA) had probably gone over Gandhi's head in issuing the ultimatum. The Gov. Gen. believed that the demand for the repeal of the £3 tax had been introduced by Cachalia. CO 551/43/35684, Gov. Gen. to Sec. St., secret, 25 Sept. 1913; ibid., 36464, secret, 2 Oct. 1913.

108   *C W*, xii, pp.239-41, 'An Official Statement', 15 Oct. 1913.

109   *Indian Opinion*, 20 Sept. 1913.

110   Ibid.

111   Ibid., and see also *C W*, xii, pp.187-8, 'No Settlement', 13 Sept. 1913; ibid., pp.204-6, 'The £3 Tax', 24 Sept. 1913 and *Rand Daily Mail*, 29 Sept. 1913.

112   *C W*, xii, pp.187-8, 'No Settlement', 13 Sept. 1913.

113   *Transvaal Leader*, 18 Sept. 1913; *Rand Daily Mail*, 18, 19 Sept. 1913. There were twelve men and four women in the original party.

114   SABA, Gov. Gen. 714/15/478, V R Vartak to Gov. Gen., Cape Town, 26 Sept. 1913; *Rand Daily Mail*, 28 Sept. 1913, 10 Oct. 1913. No 'public' meeting was held in Durban until 12 Oct. For the meetings at which passive resistance was discussed see refs. to K A Mandal and Anjuman Islam in the following fn.

115   SABA, Gov. Gen. 714/15/478, V R Vartak to Gov. Gen., 26 Sept. 1913; ibid., 15/481, Anjuman Islam, Durban, to Gov. Gen. 2 Oct. 1913; ibid., 15/483, R G Takamdas, Port Elizabeth to Gov. Gen. 2 Oct. 1913; ibid., 15/487, chair. mass meeting Kimberley Indians to Gov. Gen., 9 Oct. 1913; ibid., 15/488, chair. mass meeting Pietermaritzburg Indians to Gov. Gen. 5 Oct. 1913; *Indian Opinion*, 8 Oct. 1913 (report of meeting of Germiston British Indians on 5 Oct.); ibid., 22 Oct. 1913 (Kathiawar Arya Mandal to Min. Interior, nd.).

116   *C W*, xii, p.241, 'An Official Statement', 15 Oct. 1913.

117   The correspondence between Gandhi and the Min. Interior during Sept. is enclosed in CO 551/44/39024, Gov. Gen. to Sec. St., 22 Oct. 1913.

118   *C W*, xii, pp.239-41.

119   At a meeting in Johannesburg on 30 Nov. Ritch pointed out that 'the strike had been largely spontaneous, it had not been organized or engineered', *Transvaal Leader*, 1 Dec. 1913.

120   *African Chronicle*, 11 Oct. 1913. Those who endorsed the decision included Nayanah, president of the CBIA, and Panday and Gabriel, vice-presidents.

121   The following description of the proceedings of the meeting is taken from *African Chronicle*, 18 Oct. 1913. It is reasonable to assume that Aiyar's report of the meeting was not unbiased, but a synopsis of

a police report corroborates the contention that the majority of the merchants were opposed to Gandhi's policy, both on 12 Oct. and at a successor meeting on 19 Oct. after the strike had started: SABA, Jus. 180/4/572/13, Natal Attorney Gen. to Min. of Justice, 22 Oct. 1913.

122   *Rand Daily Mail*, 28 Oct. 1913.

123   For example, Huttenback, op. cit., p.316.

124   Fischer, op. cit., p.63.

125   Ibid., p.126.

126   Rudé, *Protest and Punishment*, p.53.

127   Rudé, *Protest and Punishment*, pp.52-54; Rudé, *Ideology and Popular Protest*, pp.30-33.

128   The list of female passive resisters appears in *Indian Opinion*, 25 Feb. 1914.

129   Ibid., 22 Oct. 1913.

130   Ibid., and *African Chronicle*, 25 Oct. 1913.

131   *Indian Opinion*, 22 Oct. 1913; SADF Archive, Sec. Def. 158/2/6388, Lukin to Under Sec. for Def., conf., 22 Oct. 1913; *Transvaal Leader*, 24 Oct., 1913; *Rand Daily Mail*, 24 Oct. 1913.

132   The number of Indian workers on the mines was 3 883. CO 551/56/12682, Gov. Gen. Sec. St., 21 Mar. 1914, encl. Report of Protector of Indian Imms. 1913, Section VI. The strikers included N G R workers and possibly some farm labourers, although newspaper reports are inconsistent on this point.

133   See, for example, *African Chronicle*, 25 Oct. 1913, report by Kallenbach after meeting with workers at the beginning of the strike: 'they wished to strike for many grievances apart from the £3 tax'.

134   Rudé, *Protest and Punishment*, p.53.

135   Kallenbach and Polak were sent to the strike area. Also, on 28 Oct., Albert Christopher (sec. of the CBIA), Ruben Joseph, S B Chetty, A D Pillay and C E Lalmohamed left Durban for the strike area. *African Chronicle*, 1 Nov. 1913. Organizers from the Transvaal, numbers of whom were veterans of the previous stages of the campaign included Bhawani Dayal, Gulabhdas, T C Naidoo, N K Pillay, P K Naidoo, L B Naik, Ramnaryan Singh, S B Medh, Pragji K Desai. *Indian Opinion*, 4, 11 Mar. 1914. See also, ibid., 25 Feb. 1914, for a more complete list of the men and women from the Transvaal who were involved in the strike. The names are overwhelmingly South Indian which, while appropriate to the demands of organizing South Indian labourers, also reflects the fact that the Johannesburg Tamil Benefit Society alone of the original supporters of the movement remained consistently loyal to Gandhi.

136   *Transvaal Leader*, 28 Oct. 1913, *African Chronicle*, 25 Oct., 1 Nov.

1913. See also SADF Archive, Sec. Def. 158/5/6388; ibid., 7/6388; ibid., 2/6388, telegrams from officers commanding detachments of the SAMR to H Q, 27 Oct. 1913, and Lukin to Under. Sec. Defence, 22 Oct. 1913.

137   Ibid., 1/6388, Under. Sec. Defence to Lukin, 22 Oct. 1913; ibid., 2/6388, Lukin to Under Sec. Defence, 22 Oct. 1913.

138   As late as 5 Nov. the Public Prosecutor in Dundee was advised that the 'Government has no desire that these men should be placed in gaol where they manifestly are trying to get to . . . if mine owners insist on prosecuting the wise course at present is to formally ask for remand from time to time until definite line of action decided upon and men released on their own recognizance', SABA, Jus. 177/4/572/13, Min. of Justice to Pub. Prosecutor, Dundee, conf. 5 Nov. 1913.

139   *Rand Daily Mail*, 24 Oct. 1911. The decision to withhold rations was taken a week later. SADF Archive, Sec. Def. 158/8/6388, Officer commanding SAMR Dundee to H Q, 31 Oct. 1913.

140   *African Chronicle*, 25 Oct. 1913.

141   C W, xii, pp.247-8, Gandhi to Botha, before 23 Oct. 1913.

142   *Rand Daily Mail*, 24 Oct. 1913.

143   The suspension was publicly announced by Polak, *Rand Daily Mail*, 24 Oct. 1913. On the reason for the suspension see C W, xii, pp.253-4, 'Interview to the *Natal Mercury*', 25 Oct. 1913.

144   Ibid., p.252, 'Statement at Chamber of Commerce', 25 Oct. 1913.

145   *African Chronicle*, 1 Nov. 1913.

146   Ibid.

147   *Rand Daily Mail*, 31 Oct. 1913.

148   Ibid., 1 Nov. 1913.

149   *Indian Opinion*, 4 Mar. 1914, lists numbers of the veteran passive resisters who assisted with the march to the Transvaal. A D Pillay, one of the earliest of the politically active Natal-born Indians, also led one of the parties. *African Chronicle*, 8 Nov. 1913.

150   *Tranvsaal Leader*, 4 Nov. 1913. See also, SADF Archive, Sec. Def. 158/9/6388, SAMR Dundee to HQ, 5 Nov. 1911.

151   CO 551/45/40709, Gov. Gen. to Sec. St., secret, 6 Nov. 1913.

152   SABA, Jus. 177/4/572/13, Min. Justice to Public Pros. Dundee, 5 Nov. 1913. Despite their ultimatum even the mineowners were far from unanimous on the question of prosecuting strikers, still 'hoping they . . . [would] return to work', SADF Archive, Sec. Def. 158/8/6388, SAMR Dundee, to HQ, 31 Oct. 1913.

153   *African Chronicle*, 26 Oct. 1913.

154   Ibid. Both the Natal elites were represented at the leadership level of the new party. Dawd Mahomed was elected president, Omar Johari

and Lazarus Gabriel the joint secretaries, and E M Paruk, the treasurer.

155   *Indian Opinion*, 22 Oct. 1913. The Officers of NIA were also officers of the fund-collecting committee.

156   *African Chronicle*, 8 Nov. 1913. See also SABA, Jus. 180/4/572/13, Assist. Mag. Volksrust to Sec. for Just., 7 Nov. 1913.

157   *C W*, xii, p.262, 'Letter to Indians', before 11 Nov. 1913 ('one and a half pounds of bread and a little sugar per day per adult').

158   *Transvaal Leader*, 8 Nov. 1913.

159   By 3 Nov. 1913, Gokhale had cabled £1 000 for the strike fund. Conversation between Gandhi and Res. Mag. Volksrust, reported in SABA Jus. 180/4/592/13, Res. Mag. to Sec. for Just., 3 Nov. 1913.

160   *C W*, xii, Gandhi to Gokhale, before 6 Nov. 1913.

161   Rhodes House, Oxford, MSS Brit. Emp.s. 327/2 Polak to Ampthill, 12 Nov. 1913.

162   *Transvaal Leader*, 24 Oct. 1913.

163   Rhodes Hse. Oxford, MSS Brit. Emp.s. 372/2 Polak to Ampthill, 12 Nov. 1913. Also SADF Archive, Sec. Def. 158/10/6388, Lukin to SAMR Pietermaritzburg, 8 Nov. 1913 and SABA, Jus. 180/4/593/13, Res. Mag. Volksrust to Sec. Just. 3 Nov. 1913 — conversation with Gandhi in which he claimed he had advised Indians on the Natal coast not to strike.

164   *Rand Daily Mail*, 10 Nov. 1913. See also CO 551/56/12682, Gov. Gen. to Sec. St., 21 Mar. 1914, encl. Report of the Protector of Indian Imms., 1913, Sec. VIII. The Protector claimed that by 5 Nov. some of the coastal workers had already anticipated a general strike.

165   See, for example, *Natal Mercury*, 24 Nov. 1913.

166   Ibid., 24 Nov. 1913 and CO 551/56/12682, Gov. Gen. to Sec. St., 21 Mar. 1914, encl. Report of Protector of Indian Imms., 1913, Sec. VIII.

167   SADF Archive, Sec. Def. 158/28a/6388, Lukin to Min. Defence, 14 Nov. 1913. There were 2 300 workers on the Mt Edgecombe plantation for instance.

168   *Report of the Indian Enquiry Commission*, 1914, UG 16, p.7.

169   *African Chronicle*, 15 Nov. 1913.

170   *Natal Mercury*, 3 Feb. 1914.

171   Ibid., 29 Jan. 1914.

172   SADF Archive, Sec. Def. 158/83/6388, Lukin to Min. of Defence, 27 Nov. 1913. See also, *African Chronicle*, 29 Nov. 1913.

173   See, for example, SADF Archive, Sec. Def. 158/35/6388, Lukin to Min. of Defence, 17 Nov. 1913, and SABA, Gov. Gen. 715/15/

564, Report on the Indian strike in the division of Durban by Chief Mag., Durban (nd), p.5.

174   SADF Archive, Sec. Def. 158/26/6388, Lukin to Min. of Defence, 12 Nov. 1913. Around 1 00 strikers made their way to Verulam. And see also, ibid., 35/6388 Lukin to Min. of Defence, 17 Nov. 1913, for striking plantation workers trying to enter Durban.

175   Ibid., 80/6388, Lukin to Min. of Defence, 26 Nov. 1913. Some 600 workers from Mt Edgecombe made their way to Phoenix.

176   *Rand Daily Mail*, 14 Nov. 1913.

177   See, for example, *Natal Mercury*, 24 Nov. 1913, 27, 29 Jan. 1914 and *Rand Daily Mail*, 14, 19 Nov. 1913.

178   *Natal Mercury*, 3 Feb. 1914.

179   SADF Archive, Sec. Def. 158/10/6388, Lukin to SAMR Pietermaritzburg, 8 Nov. 1913.

180   Ibid., 16/6388, SAMR Pietermaritzburg to HQ, 10 Nov. 1913.

181   Ibid., 10/6388, Lukin to SAMR Pietermaritzburg, 8 Nov. 1913.

182   *Rand Daily Mail*, 15 Nov. 1911. Campbell 'strongly advocate[d] the calling out of the Defence Force to show the Indians that the Government is determined to use force if necessary to put down the strike'. See also SADF Archive Sec. Def. 158/40/6388, Lukin to Min. of Defence, v. urg., 15 Nov. 1913. Lukin believed that the planters might object to strikers receiving food from external sources. But cf. ibid., 41/6388. Min. of Defence to Lukin, clear line, 16 Nov. 1913, warning that the government would not support refusal to allow the strikers external support.

183   See, for example, SABA, Jus. 180/4/592/13 Mag. Inanda Div. to Min. for Justice, 31 Oct. 1913; ibid., 184/4/751/13, copy, Rex versus Mzayana ka Hliyehla, 1 Dec. 1913, Greenwood Park Branch Court; ibid., copy, memo by Mag. Verulam, 5 Dec. 1913; ibid., Mag. Inanda Div. to Chief Native Comm. Natal, 20 Dec. 1913. But this was no new phenomenon in Natal. See also, 'Alleged Sedition by Indians. A Startling Story', *Natal Witness*, 18 Feb. 1893.

184   SABA, Jus. 180/4/592/13, copy. Extr. from minute by Chief Mag. Durban, 27 Nov. 1913.

185   On which see S Marks, *Reluctant Rebellion*, (Oxford University Press, 1970).

186   SABA, Jus. 180/4/592/13, Mag. Inanda Div. to Min. of Justice, 31 Oct. 1913.

187   See, for instance, SADF Archive Sec. Def. 158/42/6388, Lukin to Min. of Defence, 16 Nov. 1913, reporting incident at Mt Edgecombe where one white constable suffered several scalp wounds and a sprained ankle, while around 30 Indians were 'wounded by sticks, some seriously'; ibid., no.69/6388, Lukin to Min. of

Defence, 21 Nov. 1913 reporting several Indians injured at Avoca and no police casualties; ibid., no.79/6388, Lukin to Min. of Defence, 25 Nov. 1913, reporting one policeman stabbed in the thigh at Geneva, and two Indians shot dead and 'ten wounded, two dangerously'; ibid., 86/6388, Lukin to Min. of Defence, 27 Nov. 1913, reporting two policemen seriously injured, two others slightly injured, and four Indians shot dead and 24 wounded, some dangerously, at Mt Edgecombe.

188   SABA, Gov. Gen. 716/15/674, Report of Armstrong's trial, Durban and Coast Circuit Court, Local Div., 11 Mar. 1914. The assault was so brutal that the case gained particular notoriety. The minuting on this file notes that Armstrong should have been 'punished much more strenuously'. He was fined £25.

189   The strike spread to Durban on 17 Nov. Ibid., 15/564, report by Chief Mag. Durban. Pietermaritzburg was brought out by Thambi Naidoo just before he was arrested on 22 Nov. 1913. NA, Pietermaritzburg: Minutes of the Town Council, 1/1, report submitted at special meeting of TC on 15 Dec. 1913.

190   *Rand Daily Mail*, 10, 12 Nov. 1913.

191   This was done on the recommendation of the Res. Mag. Dundee. SABA, Gov. gen. 716/15/636, memo. nd, (early Jan. 1914?). And see also, *Rand Daily Mail*, 15 Nov. 1913.

192   SADF Archive Sec. Def. 158/58/6388, SAMR to Min. of Defence, 18 Nov. 1913.

193   *Rand Daily Mail*, 21 Nov. 1913.

194   See, for example, *Rand Daily Mail*, 19, 20, 22, 28 Nov. 1913. In particular, 'Imperial Government's Responsibilities', ibid., 20 Nov. 1913. See also ibid., 2 Dec. 1913.

195   Ibid., 21 Nov. 1913.

196   Ibid., and SABA, Gov. Gen., 714/15/515, Viceroy to Gov. Gen., 15 Nov. 1913, and ibid., 715/15/586, Sec. St. to PM 27 Nov. 1913.

197   SABA, Gov. Gen., 715/15/546, minute by PM, 27 Nov. 1913.

198   CO 551/46/2673, Gov. Gen. to Sec. St., 11 Dec. 1913, and encl. Smuts to Gov. Gen., 9 Dec. 1913.

199   *C W*, xii, pp.277-81, Gandhi to Min. Interior, 21 Dec. 1913.

200   CO 551/46/44988, Gov. Gen. to Sec. St., 11 Dec. 1913.

201   Ibid., 56/12682, encl. report of the Prot. of Indian Imms, 1913, sect. VIII. The Protector estimated the total loss of savings to be in excess of £30 000.

202   SABA, Gov. Gen. 714/15/514, encl. Gabriel to Gov. Gen. 21 Nov. 1913.

203   Ibid., Jus. 177/4/572/13, Lukin to Min. of Defence, 16 Nov.

1913. See also Gov. Gen., 716/15/674, 11 Mar. 1914 (managing director Mt Edgecombe testifying that Rustomjee and another Indian were called in to calm the strikers following a conflict with the police on 19 Nov. 1913).

204   *C W*, xii, p.283, Gandhi to Gokhale, 22 Dec. 1913; ibid., pp.277-81, Gandhi to Min. of Interior, 21 Dec. 1913.

205   Ibid., pp.276-7, 'Speech at Mass Meeting', 22 Dec. 1913.

206   Ibid.

207   Ibid., Appendix XV, Smuts to Gandhi, 24 Dec. 1913.

208   CO 551/53/4218, Gov. Gen. to Sec. St., 14 Jan. 1914, encl. Gov. Gen. to Smuts, private, 1 Jan. 1914.

209   On the role played by Andrews and Robertson in the negotiations, see for example, ibid., 53/4218, Gov. Gen. to Sec. St., 14 Jan. 1917; ibid., 53/2770, Gov. Gen. to Sec. St., 22 Jan. 1914, and minute by Sec. St., 23 Jan. 1914; ibid., 53/5101, Gov. Gen. to Sec. St. 22 Jan. 1914.

210   SABA, Gov. Gen. 716/15/642, Gandhi to Min. of Interior, 21 Jan. 1914 and Min. of Interior to Gandhi, 21 Jan. 1914.

211   *C W*, xii, Appendix XXV.

212   See, in particular, editorials in a new Anglo-Gujerati paper, *Indian Views*, started by M C Anglia in early 1914.

213   H Mukherjee, *Gandhiji: A Study* (Calcutta, 1958), p.15.

CHAPTER SEVEN

Conclusions

This book has sought to explore Indian political processes in Natal and the Transvaal between 1893 and 1914 and, by so doing, to test the consensus of the existing literature.

The book has argued that Indian politics in Natal and the Transvaal were crucially shaped by the social and economic stratification of the Indian population. Essentially, the Indian political community comprised only the highest strata of that population: merchants, petty traders and western educated white collar workers. The ideological basis of their politics was consistent with maintaining their relatively privileged position in the economic hierarchy. At no time did Indian politics seek a radical transformation of the social order.

Organized Indian political expression in Natal and the Transvaal did not 'owe its origins to M K Gandhi'[1]: it pre-dated his arrival in South Africa by several years. Gandhi was inducted into merchant politics as a hired representative at a time when there was an urgent need for a full-time organizer. His legal training, fluency in Gujerati and English, and ideological compatibility with the merchants (it is worth remembering that Gandhi himself had been socialized within the milieu of a Gujerati merchant caste), rendered him particularly suitable for the task.

The 'leadership' role in South African Indian politics which is generally attributed to Gandhi has been consistently over-rated. There is no evidence of 'leadership' before 1906. The new merchant political parties whose creation followed Gandhi's arrival — NIC and BIA — were the direct descendants of the pre-Gandhian Indian Committee in terms of leadership, ideology, goals, strategy and tactics: the parties sought to protect Indian commercial interests, by means of polite constitutional protest. The only discernible new element in Indian politics between 1893 and 1906 was evidence of more careful planning which derived from the use of a full-time organizer.

The development of the moral doctrine which came to inform Gandhi's politics can be dated — in writing, at least — from 1904 rather than the Zulu rebellion in 1906 as has been assumed in the past. By mid-1908 he had articulated all of the major elements of the body of moral and political thought which, collectively, has become known as the Gandhian doctrine. The stress on moral individuation, on the individual's duty to himself — and thus to all mankind — to follow his conscience, and (though with rather less emphasis during this period) the need for *ahimsa* in both public and private life, had all been thought out and articulated by 1908. Besides the intellectual traditions which so obviously informed Gandhi's philosophy (both Hindu and Judaeo-Christian), its development also emerges as a clear expression of Gandhi's perception of the crisis in Natal and Transvaal merchant politics between 1903 and 1906 — his belief that political apathy derived from moral degradation, and that a moral transformation was necessary in order to revitalize both the individual and the 'community' of which he was a part.

However, the increasingly universalist and humanistic tone of Gandhi's personal ideology should not be, as it is in the existing literature, conflated with the passive resistance movement which it produced. The movement was cautiously and selectively reformist in nature; Gandhi sought only to block erosion of the status quo for Indians in the Transvaal. It is noteworthy, however, that one of the most distinctive features of Gandhi's idiosyncratic political style was already apparent during this period — the self-defeating attempt to impose his personal ethical preoccupations on his constituents, as he did in the Transvaal between 1908 and 1913. During this period the elimination of the particular pieces of discriminatory legislation against which passive resistance was directed became, for Gandhi, a moral rather than a political challenge. Thus the lack of support from his notional constituents after his assumption of leadership in 1909 was met not with responsiveness to their needs and aspirations, but with assertions that Gandhi had chosen the right path, that God was with him, that the ultimate success of the movement was therefore assured. Moreover, by 1909 Gandhi had determined to use his new-found moral insights and political technique to reorganize not only Transvaal Indian politics, but also the Indian nationalist movement whose upper ranks he had tried, and failed, to penetrate in 1901. Nevertheless, Gandhi drove the Transvaal passive resistance movement virtually into the ground before he began to make the moral and political adjustments which were necessary in order to ensure its success.

The fact that in the past the nature and extent of these adjustments has not been appreciated, far less understood, is rooted in the main weaknesses of the existing literature: the failure to explore either the basis of division within the Indian communities, or exactly who was (and who was not) represented by the Indian political parties. The *a priori* assumption that *all* South African Indians were part of the political community permits, indeed demands, two further false assumptions: that Gandhi was the leader of *all* South African Indians, and that passive resistance was therefore a popular movement from its inception. This obscures the course of the passive resistance movement as a whole, and the events of 1913 in particular. However, the more careful examination of the dynamics of Indian politics which reveals that Gandhi was forced by the failure of his earlier strategy to make profound political adjustments to the movement in 1913, reveals also why they took the form they did. The nature of these adjustments was dictated by the emergence of new political parties in Natal as the upwardly mobile strata of the underclasses began to redefine their relationships with both the merchant class and the mass of the people. By 1912 it had become clear that they had the potential to mobilize the people (and there seemed to be a very real possibility that they might do so) thus possibly radicalizing Indian politics, and certainly further undermining Gandhi's already tenuous claim to be the sole representative of the South African Indians. It was this threat which resulted in the £3 tax — one of the most profound specific grievances of Natal Indian workers — being pushed to the top of the political priorities of both the Natal Congress and Gandhi. Thus in mid-1913 when the passive resistance movement had finally run aground after seven years, despite ethical compromises on Gandhi's part, and when he had been unequivocally repudiated by most of his former constituents, it was abolition of the £3 tax which he used in order to mobilize the committed army of supporters which he had unsuccessfully sought since 1906.

The 1913 Natal Indian strike, which resulted from including abolition of the tax in the passive resistance platform, was ensured of success only after its spontaneous spread to the coastal sugar plant-ations. The strike cannot therefore be dismissed, as it has been in the past, simply as a 'new phase'[2] in Gandhi's long-running passive resistance campaign. A more complex explanation must be sought for the scale and duration of the strike. I have argued that labour conditions on the plantations were among the worst for Indian workers in Natal. More importantly, the cumulative pressures of the £3 tax and a depressed economy had removed the time limit from indentured labour by driving thousands of ex-indentured workers back onto the plantations under second or subsequent contracts. These workers faced, for all they knew, a lifetime of extreme privation. It was this which brought them out in their thousands, without leadership, and often with no clear-cut idea of what the strike was about. Their seething frustration was reflected in outbreaks of violence and arson on the plantations during the course of the strike. The SAMR and the Natal Constabulary responded with increasing brutality. The escalating violence in Natal gained a barrage of international publicity for Gandhi and 'passive resistance'. This was the wave whose crest he rode into Indian nationalist politics.

For the South African Indians, the longer term results of the passive resistance movement were rather less dramatic. After Gandhi's departure the merchants' politics resumed the shape which he had helped entrench. Until the 1940s Indian politics continued to be dominated by the merchant class, and their political struggles remained what they had always been: an attempt to protect and expand their economic interests through the means of polite constitutional protest, seeking assistance from the governments of Great Britain and India.

The Natal white collar elite also repeated their own history with the creation of the Colonial Born and Settlers Indian Association in 1933, during a second period of perceived crisis when the merchants' politics again seemed to be inimical to their specific interests. Many of the CBSIA's officials had posed their first ephemeral challenge to trader politics as officials of the CBIA a quarter of a century earlier. Although this new organization again had the potential to incorporate the underclasses, it proved no more effective than its predecessor.

The brief inclusion of the underclasses in the passive resistance movement brought them an important if temporary victory. Abolition of the £3 tax — which had helped keep them in, or force them back into, contract wage work — allowed many of them to resist full proletarianization for a time. But new pressures replaced the old between the two world wars. Particularly during and after the Depression, the descendants of the indentured immigrant community were powerless to prevent their being pushed out of the countryside into urban wage labour. Conditions for these workers were often no better than those which had caused the groundswell of militancy which, in a unique combination of circumstances, helped produce the 1913 strike. Not until the 1940s, when a new generation of profoundly committed South African radicals — Indians and others — set in motion large scale labour organization underpinned by the ideology of class struggle, did this begin to change.[3]

Notes

1   B Pillay, op.cit., p.112.
2   For example, Huttenback, op.cit., p.316.
3   This is of course, a separate study, and one on which I am currently working. My first, tentative findings appear in M J Swan, 'Ideology in Organized Indian Politics 1890-1948', S Marks and S Trapido (eds) *South Africa in the Study of Class, Race and Nationalism* (forthcoming, Longmans).

Tables

Table 1 Return of Trading Licences Issued to Indians in Natal During the Years 1895 to 1908

	1895	1896	1897	1898	1899	1900	1901	1902	1903	1904	1905	1906	1907	1908	Remarks
Boroughs															
Pietermaritzburg City	-	-	-	-	-	-	-	-	-	-	109	105	93	82	Not possible to furnish returns prior to 1905
Durban	-	-	-	-	-	-	387	459	368	457	408	389	421	319	Ditto, prior 1901
Newcastle	-	-	-	8	8	-	13	27	23	23	21	16	16	14	No record 1900 and prior 1898
Ladysmith	23	24	23	22	22	25	27	25	26	35	29	31	26	26	
Dundee	-	-	-	18	16	12	13	28	21	18	16	15	16	15	Township Est. 1897
Townships															
Greytown	-	-	-	6	8	8	8	6	6	6	6	4	4	4	Township Est. 1897
Verulam	20	22	18	22	18	19	21	22	19	20	19	18	16	16	
Estcourt	-	-	-	-	-	-	-	-	-	-	5	18	13	9	Township Est. 1905
South Barrow	-	-	-	-	-	-	-	-	-	-	-	-	-	-	Nil
Charlestown	-	-	-	-	-	-	-	-	-	-	-	-	-	7	
Vryheid	-	-	-	-	-	-	-	-	-	-	1	-	-	-	Nil
Utrecht	-	-	-	-	-	-	-	-	-	-	-	-	-	-	

Table 1   277

Table 1 Continued

Magisterial Divisions	1895	1896	1897	1898	1899	1900	1901	1902	1903	1904	1905	1906	1907	1908	Remarks
Pietermaritzburg City	-	-	-	-	-	-	-	-	-	-	-	-	-	-	See City and Borough Pietermaritzburg
Umgeni	-	-	-	-	-	19	26	29	32	22	27	31	34	30	
Camperdown	-	-	-	-	-	-	-	-	-	19	13	12	13	10	
Lions River	10	13	13	12	15	21	23	20	19	20	22	20	20	17	
Richmond	10	12	15	14	12	13	13	16	18	16	15	14	15	14	
Ixopo	1	1	1	2	2	3	5	5	5	3	3	3	3	3	
Polela	4	1	4	4	4	3	5	5	3	3	4	5	5	5	
Underberg	-	-	-	-	-	-	-	-	-	-	-	-	-	-	Nil
Impendhle	1	3	6	5	4	3	2	2	2	2	4	4	5	5	
New Hanover	-	3	7	5	3	5	6	8	10	9	10	11	7	8	
Bergville	-	-	-	-	-	-	-	-	-	5	6	5	3	3	Records prior 1904 disappeared
Umvoti	13	9	15	12	44	9	12	13	14	15	11	9	9	9	
Estcourt	23	28	33	28	26	28	33	35	38	30	27	18	16	16	
Weenen	4	7	11	8	6	6	7	12	11	7	10	10	10	9	
Krantzkopf	-	1	3	4	2	2	4	3	3	3	3	3	3	3	
Klip River	-	-	-	-	-	-	-	-	-	22	24	19	4	4	Records prior 1904 disappeared
Newcastle	28	31	38	34	15	12	10	27	59	51	22	30	53	38	
Umsinga	-	-	-	-	-	10	11	-	8	11	16	4	11	7	Records other years destroyed by fire

Table 1 Continued

	1895	1896	1897	1898	1899	1900	1901	1902	1903	1904	1905	1906	1907	1908	Remarks
Dundee	57	74	77	44	38	11	15	29	33	27	27	33	34	31	
Durban	-	-	-	-	-	-	-	-	-	-	-	-	-	-	See borough of Durban
Umlazi	91	99	106	114	124	128	135	139	155	162	155	156	136	117	
Inanda	85	101	119	122	98	97	110	106	100	105	104	116	99	79	
Lower Tugela	-	-	-	-	-	-	-	-	-	104	113	88	94	77	Records prior 1904 disappeared
Indwedwe	-	-	-	-	-	-	-	-	-	-	-	-	-	-	Nil
Mapumulo	-	-	-	-	1	1	1	1	1	1	1	1	1	1	
Alexandra	18	25	25	24	25	27	26	26	23	19	26	24	24	19	
Alfred	4	8	7	8	7	7	7	8	8	7	7	7	7	7	
Lower Umzimkulu	1	2	2	2	3	3	3	3	4	4	4	3	3	3	
Utrecht	-	-	-	-	-	-	-	-	-	-	-	-	-	-	Nil
Vryheid	-	-	-	-	-	-	-	-	-	-	-	-	-	-	Nil
Paulpietersburg	-	-	-	-	-	-	-	-	-	1	1	2	2	-	
Bahanando	-	-	-	-	-	-	-	-	-	-	-	-	-	1	
Ngotshe	-	-	-	-	-	-	-	-	-	-	-	-	-	-	Nil
TOTALS:	393	464	523	520	461	472	923	1 056	1 009	1 225	1 269	1 226	1 216	1 008	11 765

Source: NA Gov. 1599/374/1908

Table 2   279

Table 2   *Statement of the Gross Turnover of Indian Trading Businesses in the Transvaal for the Year Ended 31 December 1904.*

District	No. of Licences	Amount of Turnover		
Krugersdorp	18	£29 934	11s	7d
Johannesburg	120	£279 194	-	-
Belfast	2	£2 030	16s	5d
Vereeniging	9	£6 429	19s	-
Volksrust	4	£1 040	01s	7d
Caroline	1	£953	15s	-
Lichtenburg	1	£3 988	10s	1d
Potchefstroom	56	£96 380	-	-
Germiston	5	£1 743	-	-
Boksburg	9	£5 487	-	-
Lydenburg	10	£3 249	17s	8d
Marico	14	£18 000	-	-
Heidelburg	20	£44 188	7s	6d
Swaziland	-	-	-	-
Klerksdorp	16	£24 823	18s	2d
Middelburg	9	£11 167	-	-
Pretoria	157	£352 709	-	-
Standerton	23	£42 622	-	-
Barberton	7	£8 531	8s	9d
Bethal	1	£447	16s	-
Ermelo	5	£5 877	-	-
Waterberg	6	£2 853	11s	5d
Rustenburg	7	£11 899	18s	1d
Wakkerstroom	-	-	-	-
Piet Retief	-	-	-	-
Kristiana	3	£1 200	1s	-
Pietersburg	78	£85 791	6s	4d
Wolmaranstad	-	-	-	-
TOTAL:	581	£1 040 542	18s	7d

Source: TABA, Gov. 823/P.S. 15/9

Table 3   Officials and Prominent Members of New Elite Organizations

Hindu Young Men's Assoc.	Natal Indian Patriotic Union	Durban Indian Society	£3 Tax Committee	Colonial Born Indian Assoc.
	Aiyar, P S		Aiyar, P S	
	Bayat, A		Bayat, A	
Bhugwatidin			Bhugwatidin	
		Christopher, A		Christopher, A
	Francis, J M	Francis, J M		
	Gabriel, L	Gabriel, L		Gabriel, L
				Gabriel, B
			Godfrey, J	
	Lawrence, V	Lawrence, V	Lawrence, V	Lawrence, V
	Lazarus, D		Lazarus, D	
	Maharaj, S	Maharaj, S		
Moodley, R N			Moodley, R N	Moodley, R N
Naicker, T M		Naicker, T M	Naicker, T M	
			Naidoo, M N	Naidoo, M N
Naidoo, R C	Naidoo, R C			
Naidoo, R M	Naidoo, R M			
Nayanah, K R				Nayanah, K R
Nulliah, C	Nilluah, C			
	Panday, G			Panday, G
	Panday, L		Panday, L	Panday, L
Pather, S R		Pather, S R		
Pather, V S C		Pather, V S C		
	Pillay, A	Pillay, A		Pillay, A
	Royeppen, J		Royeppen, J	Royeppen, J
Singh, G			Singh, G	

Source: *African Chronicle, Indian Opinion*, passim.

Table 4   281

Table 4   *Madras: Caste Breakdown of Random Sample of Migrant Labourers*

	M	F		M	F		M	F
Vannia	277	133	Paria	215	133	Malabar	71	29
Christian	60	27	Mala	56	35	Muslim	55	17
Vellala	52	12	Balija	43	21	Reddy	42	12
Kapu	38	22	Odda	34	31	Ajamudia	33	13
Edaya	30	8	Guntur	30	9	Madiga	30	21
Kamma	25	5	Gounden	18	5	Panchama	18	4
Golla	17	4	Kavaray	17	10	Padayachee	17	4
Chukla	15	7	Yadava	14	3	Chetty	13	4
Nair	13	4	Palla	13	6	Wodda	12	6
Dhobi	11	11	Kallah	10	2	Shauar	10	6
Washerman	10	3	Mudali	9	7	Telaga	9	3
Uppara	9	9	Velama	9	-	Koravan	8	3
Panisava	8	5	Shepherd	8	-	Thiyan	8	1
Ediga	7	1	Gavara	7	9	Naik	6	2
Gramany	5	2	Konar	5	2	Paligar	5	1
Palli	5	4	Parabannam	5	2	Sali	5	1
Vettakar	5	1	Weaver	5	3	Barber	4	3
Davanga	4	3	Hindu	4	1	Kurubaru	4	4
Muthrasi	4	7	Yanadi	4	2	Choyan	3	-
Dusari	3	-	Garia	3	-	Jogi	3	2
Kaikala	3	-	Kammavalu	3	-	Kandu	3	4
Komati	3	-	Labbai	3	3	Oilmonger	3	3
Sedagu	3	1	Ambalagaran	2	3	Besta	2	-
Blacksmith	2	2	Bulgigur	2	-	Chakali	2	2
Dudakula	2	-	Esuvan	2	-	Kapa	2	1
Kavandan	2	-	Kosava	2	-	Mophla	2	1
Mopila	2	3	Muthria	2	1	Nadar	2	-
Nagasali	2	-	Naidu	2	-	Pandaram	2	1
Pauisao	2	-	Pillay	2	-	Potter	2	1
Savapathy	2	-	Sudra	2	1	Udayar	2	2
Velli	2	5	Yelama	2	1	Boya	1	2
Cauady	1	-	Chamar	1	1	Chembadar	1	-
Cobbler	1	-	E. Indian	1	-	Erular	1	-
Fisherman	1	4	Goldsmith	1	-	Gollalu	1	1
Kambalathan	1	-	Kammavor	1	1	Kohatna	1	-
Madrasi	1	2	Maharati	1	-	Marava	1	3
Nambiar	1	-	Navilhan	1	-	Panikar	1	-
Raja	1	-	Rajput	1	-	Sakkili	1	-
Saleelu	1	2	Saliar	1	-	Sania	1	-
Satani	1	-	Sembada	1	-	Settigalu	1	2
Settigulu	1	-	Shorunker	1	-	Singanda	1	-
Solai	1	-	Subadavan	1	-	Surgunth	1	-
Thauda	1	-	Thottiah	1	1	Ulaja	1	-
Vadabaljie	1	-	Baljigur	-	1	Boi	-	1
Edachi	-	1	Endra	-	1	Kaliugulu	-	1
Kykala	-	1	Muppa	-	1	Pallakapu	-	1
Sathu	-	1	Woopera	-	3			

TOTAL MALES = 1 572   TOTAL FEMALES = 751

Source: Department of Indian Affairs, Durban, Ships' Logs, 1860-1910.

Table 5   Calcutta: Caste Breakdown of Random Sample of Migrant Labourers

Caste	M	F	Caste	M	F	Caste	M	F
Chamar	152	80	Ahir	93	46	Kori	80	33
Muslim	71	74	Kurmi	58	17	Thakur	47	13
Kahar	25	9	Chuttree	24	12	Pasi	21	6
Gareria	20	2	Dusadh	18	9	Rajput	18	8
Gowala	17	2	Jat	17	2	Kumhar	17	7
Brahmin	15	11	Gujar	14	2	Lodh	14	9
Lohar	14	6	Barhai	10	4	Bhooyear	10	2
Taili	10	6	Moosahyr	9	9	Dhoby	7	3
Kachi	7	2	Kewat	7	8	Murawo	7	1
Kunbi	6	2	Ateeth	5	2	Noonia	4	4
Arakh	4	-	Bania	4	1	Dhanook	4	1
Ghatwar	4	-	Gosain	4	3	Jaiswar	4	2
Kalwar	4	1	Khatik	4	1	Lonia	4	2
Maujhee	4	-	Nao	4	3	Bhoojwa	3	-
Gond	3	4	Kandu	3	2	Mali	3	1
Mallah	3	2	Murai	3	1	Rawt	3	2
Sonar	3	-	Bari	2	-	Beldar	2	2
Bhur	2	1	Dome	2		Kabari	2	1
Kaisth	2	-	Maina	2	-	Moochee	2	-
Tamoly	2	-	Tsoreea	2	-	Zamidar	2	1
Bagdee	1	1	Balur	1	-	Bansfore	1	-
Bhar	1	-	Bhoomiz	1	-	Bind	1	1
Dhurker	1	-	Gaddi	1	-	Gara	1	-
Gour	1	1	Gumtihar	1	-	Howaighur	1	1
Jaleea	1	-	Kisan	1	-	Konjra	1	-
Koulloye	1	-	Madrasi	1	-	Maratha	1	-
Mehter	1	1	Ooria	1	-	Panka	1	2
Shepherd	1	2	Tauti	1	1	(Illegible)	-	1
Aghrahari	-	1	Banmanus	-	1	Bawoory	-	1
Ghausse	-	3	Hazam	-	1	Julaha	-	3
Koibutti	-	1	Mala	-	1	Mehter	-	3
Moorawree	-	2	Pathan	-	3	Sheikh	-	1

TOTAL MALES = 929   TOTAL FEMALES = 455

Source: Department of Indian Affairs, Durban. Ships' Logs, 1860-1906.

Table 6   283

Table 6   *Madras: Districts of Origin of Random Sample of Migrant Labourers*

District	M	F	District	M	F	District	M	F	District	M	F
N Arcot	472	230	Chingleput	275	168	S Arcot	152	45	Vizagapatam	105	76
Godaveri	61	28	Malabar	51	13	Nellore	49	24	Salem	45	21
Chitor	43	9	Kistna	42	5	Tanjore	39	21	Kurnool	31	20
Coimbatore	29	9	Madura	24	12	Trichinopoloy	20	6	Cuddapah	18	8
Ganjam	17	5	Madras	15	22	Tinnivelly	10	3	Mysore	9	1
Cochin	8	1	Pondicherry	8	-	Bellary	7	9	Guntur	7	4
Travancore	7	1	Bangalore	6	1	Cuddalore	5	1	Hyderabad	3	2
Puducottah	3	1	Niligri	2	-	Anantpur	1	-	Bedar	1	-
Benares	1	1	Jubbulpore	1	1	Masulipatum	1	1	Nallakunda	1	-
Secunderabad	1	-	Sattara	1	-	Trivandaram	1	-	Warangal	-	2

TOTAL MALES = 1 572   TOTAL FEMALES = 751

Source: Department of Indian Affairs, Durban. Ships' logs, 1860-1910.

Table 7   Calcutta: Districts of Origin of Random Sample of Migrant
Labourers

District	M	F	District	M	F	District	M	F
Gonda	71	12	Basti	66	32	Sultanpur	47	15
Ghazipur	37	29	Rai Bareilly	35	11	Azamgarh	34	35
Fyzabad	33	22	Gya (Gaya)	33	15	Partabgarh	32	5
Patna	29	23	Allahabad	28	20	Gorakhpur	27	11
Lucknow	25	20	(Illegible)	21	7	Raipur	20	17
Moughyr	19	5	Shahabad	19	4	Barabanki	18	7
Bahraich	18	5	Jaunpore	18	19	Arrah	16	9
Benares	14	14	Cawnpore	14	4	Fatehpur	14	4
Jaipur	14	6	Hardoi	13	2	Unao	11	8
Mirzapore	9	7	Muzaffarpur	9	2	Alwar	7	3
Ballia	7	8	Bareilly	7	2	Chuprah	7	2
Hazaribagh	7	1	Saran	7	9	Aligarh	6	-
Dholepur State	6	1	Tirhut	6	1	Farrukhabad	5	6
Hamirpur	5	3	Nepal	5	2	Shahjahanpur	5	-
Agra	4	2	Bhaugulpore	4	-	Bharatpore	4	1
Etah	4	-	Etawah	4	2	ChotaNagpore	3	1
Gwalior	3	1	Meerut	3	-	Poreolia	3	10
Rewa	3	-	Agoodha	2	-	Ajmere	2	1
Bulandsahar	2	-	Banda	2	-	Bush (?)	2	-
Gurgaon	2	1	Hoshiapur	2	-	Lodhiana	2	-
Nawabgunj	2	1	Orai	2	-	Oudh	2	1
Pilibhit	2	1	Sitapore	2	2	Badaun	1	1
Bardwan	1	-	Bhopal	1	-	Bhumihar State	1	-
Bancoona	1	1	Bundelkhand	1	-	Batia	1	-
Çheetagunj	1	-	Delhi	1	-	Dulamow	1	-
Dinapore	1	-	Dattia	1	1	Girdaspur	1	-
Ganjam	1	-	Hoogly	1	-	Haripur	1	-
Hazaribagh	1	-	Indore	1	-	Jodhpur	1	1
Jhansi	1	2	Kheri	1	-	Kalpi	1	1
Kashnagarh	1	-	Karauli	1	-	Kusbah	1	-
Lahor	1	-	Madras	1	-	Mymunsing	1	1
Manipuri	1	2	Moradabad	1	-	Muksoodabad	1	-
Muthra	1	2	Muzaffernagar	1	-	Panipat	1	-
Poorneea	1	-	Patiala	1	-	Ranchee	1	-
Rohtak	1	-	Rampore	1	-	Sohunghardty	1	-
Sirauhi	1	-	Surat	1	1	Sowooth	1	-
Umbala	1	1	Cuttack	-	1	Durbhanga	-	1
Doomka	-	1	Deoghur	-	1	Jubbulpore	-	1
Midnapore	-	1	Samtar	-	1	Tikamgarh	-	2

TOTAL MALES = 929   TOTAL FEMALES = 455

Source: Department of Indian Affairs, Durban: Ships' Logs, 1860-1906.

Table 8   Madras: Age Distribution of Random Sample of Migrant Labourers.

	Missing	1-4	5-9	10-14	15-19	20-24	25-29	30-34	35-39	40-44	45-49	50-54	55-59	60-64	Total
Male:	48	99	80	25	176	463	366	205	93	10	4	1	1	1	1 572
Female:	27	115	75	12	93	206	151	41	24	4	2	–	–	1	751

Source: Department of Indian Affairs, Durban: Ships' Logs, 1860-1910.

Table 9   Calcutta: Age Distribution of Random Sample of Migrant Labourers.

	Missing	1-4	5-9	10-14	15-19	20-24	25-29	30-34	35-39	40-44	45-49	50-54	55-59	60-64	Total
Male:	30	41	28	9	113	383	232	69	19	4	1	–	–	–	929
Female:	14	36	34	12	51	177	100	28	2	1	–	–	–	–	455

Source: Department of Indian Affairs, Durban: Ships' Logs, 1860-1906.

Table 10   *Percentage of (Time-expired) Labourers who Re-indentured Between 1901 and 1913*

Year	Percentage of Re-indentures
1901	13,60
1902	19,65
1903	16,52
1904	8,64
1905	13,81
1906	47,16
1907	52,28
1908	53,93
1909	55,05
1910	70,53
1911	74,86
1912	95,29
1913	81,05*

*   The general Indian strike which began in October 1913 prevented re-indentures during the last quarter of the year. Using the figures for the first three quarters, the Protector estimated that the 1912 percentage would have been equalled had it not been for the strike.

Source: CO 551/56/12682, Gov. Gen. to Sec. St., 21 Mar. 1914, encl. Protector of Immigrants Report, 1913, part V.

Table 11   287

Table 11   Number of Male and Female Labourers under Second or
Subsequent Terms of Re-indenture in 1913

Terms of Re-indenture	Males	Females
2nd	1 287	540
3rd	389	145
4th	301	124
5th	93	27
6th	29	20

Source: CO 551/56/12682, Gov. Gen. to Sec. St., 21 Mar. 1914, encl.
Protector of Immigrants' Report 1913, part V.

Table 12   Biographical Outlines of Prominent Indians Mentioned in the Text

AMEER, ALI

Justice; President of All-India Muslim League, London; appointed Privy Councillor, 1909; Member of the South African British Indian Committee.

BHOWNAGGREE, MANCHERJEE

1851-1933; Barrister, settled in England; MP for Bethnal Green. London, 1895-1906.

GOKHALE, GOPAL KRISHNA

1866-1915; Member of Legislative Council of India, 1901-1915; President of the Indian National Congress, 1905.

MEHTA, PHEROZESHAH

1845-1915; Barrister of Bombay High Court; President of the Indian National Congress, 1890.

TILAK, BAL GANGADAHAR

1856-1920; Journalist and teacher in the Bombay Presidency; jailed for sedition between 1897-1898 and 1908-1914.

Bibliography

This bibliography has been divided into:

I UNPUBLISHED SOURCES

    A Official
       1 British
       2 Natal
       3 Transvaal
       4 Union of South Africa

    B Non-official
       1 Private Papers

II PUBLISHED SOURCES

    A Official Records
       1 British
       2 Natal
       3 Transvaal
       4 Union of South Africa

    B Other

    C Newspapers
       1 Natal
       2 Transvaal

III SELECT SECONDARY SOURCES

    A Books

    B Published Articles and Theses

    C Unpublished Theses and Papers

I. UNPUBLISHED SOURCES

A Official

1 Public Records Office (PRO)
     CO 179/182-256, Dispatches, Gov. Natal to Sec. St.,
     1892-1910.
     CO 182, Natal Government Gazette.
     CO 417/4-148, Africa, South, Dispatches and
     Correspondence, 1885-1893.
     CO 291/27-144, Transvaal Dispatches and
     Correspondence, Original, 1901-1910.
     CO 551/2-57, Union of South Africa, Correspondence,
     Original, 1910-1914.
     CO 879/106-112, Confidential Prints African (South).

2 Natal Archives, Pietermaritzburg (NA)
   (i) Government House Records
        GH 1589-1601, Indian Affairs, 1857-1910.
   (ii) Colonial Secretary's Office
        CS 2572-2602, Minute Papers, Confidential.
        CS 2854, Commission on the Treatment of Indians on
        Messrs. Reynolds Brothers, Esperanza, Alexandra.
        CS 2857, Mines Commission, Evidence and Papers, 1909.
   (iii) Protector of Indian Immigrants
         II 1/54-1/185, Indian Immigration Papers, 1890-1910.

3 Transvaal Archives (TABA)
   (i)   Transvaal Town Police
         TTP 17, 1908, Correspondence.
   (ii) Minister of Interior (Binnelandse Sake)
         BS Correspondence Files A450-A450ᴬ, 1916.
   (iii) Colonial Secretary's Office
         CS 63-682, Correspondence, 1902-1906.
   (iv) Military Governor, Pretoria
         MGP 79, 1901, Correspondence.
   (v)   Secretary for Native Affairs
         SNA 2-10, Correspondence, 1901-1902.
   (vi) Commissioner for Immigration and Asiatic Affairs
         CIA II-VII, Correspondence, 1903-1913.
   (vii) Lieutenant Governor

Lt. G. 95-97, Dispatches and Correspondence, 1903-1905.
(viii) Governor
G. 5-1056, Dispatches and Correspondence, 1901-1907.

4 Union Archives (SABA)
(i) Governor General
G.G. 706-709, Dispatches and Correspondence, 1910-1913
(ii) Secretary of Justice
J. 177-184, Correspondence, 1913.
(iii) South African Defence Archive (SADF)
Secretary for Defence Collection, Sec. Def. Box 158,
Correspondence, 1913.

B Non-Official

1 Private Papers
(i) Transvaal Archives, Smuts Collection: Public Papers (b),
CI-CXI, 1902-1914; Smuts Collection, Private Papers,
186-190, 1904-1914.
(ii) Sarvodaya Library, Phoenix, Natal, unnumbered letter,
M K Gandhi to H Kallenbach, 21 July 1913.
(iii) Killie Campbell Library, Durban, MS DAW 2.042, Dawes
Collection; MS CAM, 1.04, Campbell Collection.
(iv) India Office Library and Records, MSS Eur. B.272, 3
Letters from M K Gandhi to H S L Polak.
(v) Rhodes House Library, Oxford, MSS, Brit. Emp. S 372/2,
Miscellaneous Articles and Correspondence on the Indian
Question in South and East Africa, 1906-1944; MSS Afr.
r.125, Asiatic Passive Resistance in South Africa (typescript
by H S L Polak, 1908).

II. PUBLISHED SOURCES

A Official

1 British
(i) Parliamentary Papers
C4213, 1885. Further correspondence respecting the affairs
of the Transvaal and adjacent territories.
C5249-7, 1888. Natal: Report on the Blue Book for 1887.

C5588, 1888. Report by HM's Agent at Pretoria on the session of the Volksraad of the SAR in 1888.

C5620-18, 1889. Report on the Blue Book of Natal for 1888.

C5897-34, 1890. Report on the Blue Book of Natal for 1889.

C6487, 1890-1891. Correspondence relating to the proposal to establish Responsible Government in Natal.

C6857-61, 1892. Annual report on Natal for 1891-1892.

C7911, 1895. Papers relating to the grievances of HM's Indian subjects in the South African Republic.

C7946, 1896. Further Papers (in continuation of C7911).

Cd. 1683, 1903. Transvaal and ORC Correspondence re proposal for Indian Coolies on the Railways.

Cd. 1684, 1903. Transvaal, Correspondence re British Indians.

Cd. 2239, 1904. Transvaal, Correspondence re British Indians.

Cd. 2400, 1904. Despatch transmitting Letters Patent and Order in Council providing for constitutional changes in the Transvaal.

Cd. 2408, 1905. Memo on the state of the Southern African Protectorates.

Cd. 2479, 1905. Papers relating to constitutional changes in the Transvaal.

Cd. 2239, 1905. Correspondence relating to the position of British Indians in the Transvaal.

Cd. 2482, 1905. Further correspondence relating to labour in the Transvaal Mines.

Cd. 2563, 1905. Further correspondence relating to affairs in the Transvaal and ORC.

Cd. 2479, 1905. Papers relating to constitutional changes in the Transvaal.

Cd. 2786, 1906. Further correspondence relating to labour in the Transvaal mines.

Cd. 3308, 1907. Correspondence relating to legislation affecting Asiatics in the Transvaal.

Cd. 3887, 1908. Further Correspondence relating to legislation affecting Asiatics in the Transvaal.

Cd. 3892, 1908. Further Correspondence relating to

legislation affecting Asiatics in the Transvaal.
Cd. 4327, 1908. Further Correspondence relating to
legislation affecting Asiatics in the Transvaal.
Cd. 4584, 1909. Further Correspondence relating to
legislation affecting Asiatics in the Transvaal.
Cd. 5363, 1910. Further Correspondence relating to
legislation affecting Asiatics in the Transvaal.
Cd. 5192, 1910. Report of the Committee on emigration
from India to the Crown Colonies and Protectorates.

2 Natal
  (i) Departmental reports, 1890-1910.
 (ii) Emigrants' Information Handbooks, 1885-1905.
(iii) Report of the Coolie Commission, 1872.
(iv) Report of the Indian Immigrants' Commission, 1885-1887.
 (v) Report of the Indian Immigration Commission, 1909.
(vi) Census Report, 1891, 1904.

3 Transvaal
  (i) Census Report, 1904.

4 Union of South Africa
  (i) Census Report, 1911.

B *Other*

Collected Works of Mahatma Gandhi, I-XII, Government of India,
1958-1964.

C *Newspapers*

1 Natal
The Natal Witness
The Natal Mercury
The Natal Advertiser
The Times of Natal
Indian Opinion
African Chronicle
The Natalian
Indian Views
Colonial Indian News

2   Transvaal
   The Johannesburg Star (weekly edition)
   The Transvaal Leader
   The Rand Daily Mail
   The Zoutpansberg Review and Mining Journal

III. SELECT SECONDARY SOURCES

A   Books

Aiyar, P S, *Conflict of Races in South Africa* (Durban, nd).
— *The Indian Problem in South Africa* (Durban, 1925).
Andrews, C F, *Documents Relating to the Indian Question* (Cape Town, 1914).
— *Mahatma Gandhi's Ideas* (London, 1929).
— *The Asiatic Question* (Durban, nd).
Bondurant, J, *Conquest of Violence* (Princeton, 1958).
Brooks, E H and Webb, C, *A History of Natal* (Pietermaritzburg, 1956).
Bundy, C, *The Rise and Fall of the South African Peasantry* (London, 1979).
Burrows, H R, *Indian Life and Labour in Natal* (Johannesburg, 1943).
Calpin, G H C, *Indians in South Africa* (Pietermaritzburg,   1949).
Camus, A, *The Rebel* (New York, 1956).
Chattopadhyaya, H, *Indians In Africa. A Socio-Economic Study* (Calcutta, 1970).
Datta, D M, *The Philosophy of Mahatma Gandhi* (University of Wisconsin Press, 1953).
Davie, C J Ferguson, *The Early History of Indians in Natal* (Johannesburg, 1952).
Dhawan, G, *The Political Philosophy of Mahatma Gandhi* (Ahmedabad, 1951).
Diwakar, R R, *Satyagraha — Its Technique and Theory* (Bombay, 1946).
Doke, J J, *M K Gandhi: An Indian Patriot in South Africa* (Madras, 1909).
Eriksen, E, *Gandhi's Truth* (London, 1970).
Evans, H M S, *The Problem of Production in Natal* (Durban, 1905).

Eybers, W G, *Select Constitutional Documents Illustrating South African History 1795-1910* (London, 1918).

Feit, E, *African Opposition in South Africa* (Stanford, 1967).

Freeman, J R, *Gandhi in South Africa* (Madras, 1950).

Gandhi, M K, *Hind Swaraj* (reprint, Ahmedabad, 1938).

— *Satyagraha in South Africa* (Ahmedabad, 1928).

— *The Story of My Experiments with Truth* (2 vols., Ahmedabad, 1927-9).

— *Grievances of British Indians in South Africa* (Ahmedabad, 1896).

Gangulee, N, *Indians in the Empire Overseas, A Survey* (London, 1947).

Hancock, W K, *Smuts, I: The Sanguine Years, 1870-1919* (CUP, 1962).

Hattersley, A F, *The British Settlement in Natal* (CUP, 1950).

— *More Annals of Natal* (London, 1938).

— *Later Annals of Natal* (London, 1938).

Headlam, C (ed), *The Milner Papers* (London, 1931).

Hey, P D, *The Rise of the Natal Indian Elite* (Pietermaritzburg, 1961).

Hunt, J D, *Gandhi in London* (New Delhi, 1978).

Huttenback, R A, *Gandhi in South Africa* (Cornell UP, 1971).

— *Racism and Empire* (Cornell UP, 1976).

Hutton, J H, *Caste in India* (OUP, 1961).

Indian Institute of Advanced Study, *Gandhi, Theory and Practice* (Simla, 1969).

Iyer, R, *The Moral and Political Thought of Mahatma Gandhi* (OUP, 1973).

Joshi, P S, *The Tyranny of Colour, A Study of the Indian Problem in South Africa* (Durban, 1942).

— *The Struggle for Equality* (Bombay, 1951).

Konczacki, Z, *Public Finance and Economic Development of Natal 1893-1910* (Duke UP, 1967).

Kondapi, C, *Indians Overseas, 1838-1949* (New Delhi, 1960).

Kuper, H, *Indian People in Natal* (Natal UP, 1960).

Kuper, L, *Passive Resistance in South Africa* (London, 1956).

Le May, G H L, *British Supremacy in South Africa 1899-1907* (Oxford, 1965).

MacMillan, W M, *Bantu, Boer and Briton: The Making of the South African Native Problem* (Oxford, 1963).

— *Mahatma Gandhi, Essays Presented to Him on his 70th Birthday* (London, 1949).

Marks, S, *Reluctant Rebellion* (OUP, 1970).

Masani, R P, *Dadabhai Naoroji: The Grand Old Man of India* (London, 1939).

Meay, G, *Methodist Missions to the Indians of Natal* (Rondebosch, 1957).

Mehta, V, *Mahatma Gandhi and his Apostles* (Penguin, 1977).

Meer, F, *Portrait of Indian South Africans* (Durban, 1969).

Menon, K N, *Passive Resistance in South Africa* (New Delhi, 1952).

Menon, V L, *Ruskin and Gandhi* (Varanasi, 1965).

Misra, S C, *Muslim Communities in Gujerat* (London, 1964).

Mukherjee, H, *Gandhiji, A Study* (Calcutta, 1958).

Mukherjee, H and Mukherjee, U, *Bande Mataram and Indian Nationalism (1906-1908)* (Calcutta, 1957).

Mukherji, S B, *Indian Minority in South Africa* (New Delhi, 1959).

Nanda, B R, *Mahatma Gandhi* (London, 1958).

Narain, I, *Politics of Racialism* (Delhi, 1962).

Natal Agriculture (Durban, c 1885).

Neame, L E, *The Asiatic Danger in the Colonies* (London, 1907).

Nundy, E, *The Transvaal Asiatic Ordinance 1907: An Exposure* (Johannesburg, 1907).

Pachai, B, *Mahatma Gandhi in South Africa* (South African Institute of Race Relations, nd).

Palmer, M, *The History of Indians in Natal*, Natal Regional Survey, 10 (Cape Town, 1957).

— *Natal's Indian Problem* (Johannesburg, 1945).

Pillay, B, *British Indians in the Transvaal* (London, 1976).

Polak, H S L, Brailsford, H N, and Lord Pethick-Lawrence, *Mahatma Gandhi* (London, 1949).

Polak, H S L, *Indians of South Africa; Helots Within the Empire* (Madras, 1909).

— *Indians of South Africa, Part II* (Madras, 1909).

Polak, M G, *Mr Gandhi: The Man* (London, 1931).

Power, P F (ed), *The Meaning of Gandhi* (U P of Hawaii, 1971).

Prabhu, R K, and Rao, U R, *The Mind of Mahatma Gandhi* (Ahmedabad, 1967).

Pyarelal, *Mahatma Gandhi: The Early Phase* (Ahmedabad, 1965).

Radhakrishnan, S (ed), *Mahatma Gandhi: Essays and Reflections on His Life and Work* (London, 1939).

— *Mahatma Gandhi — 100 Years* (New Delhi, 1968).

Reflections on 'Hind Swaraj' by Western Thinkers (Bombay, 1948).

Rolland, R, *Mahatma Gandhi* (London, 1924).

Roux, E *Time Longer than Rope* (Madison, 1964).

South African Institute of Race Relations, *The Indian South African Papers Presented at a Conference Held Under the Auspices of the SAIRR, Natal Region* (Durban, 1967).

Sheean, V, *Lead, Kindly Light* (New York, 1949).

Shukla, C (ed), *Incidents of Gandhiji's Life* (Bombay, 1949).

— *Reminiscences of Gandhiji* (Bombay, 1951).

Simons, H J, and Simons, R E, *Class and Colour in South Africa, 1850-1950* (London, 1969).

Tendulkar, D G, *Mahatma: Life of Mohandas Karamchand Gandhi, I, 1869-1920* (Bombay, 1951).

Thurston, E, *Castes and Tribes of Southern India* (New Delhi, 1975).

Tinker, H, *A New System of Slavery* (OUP, 1974).

Tongaat Sugar Company, *Amanzunnyama* (nd).

Van Onselen, C, *Chibaro* (London, 1976).

Wallerstein, I, *Africa: The Politics of Unity* (New York, 1967).

Welsh, D, *The Roots of Segregation* (OUP, 1971).

B Published Articles and Theses

Bhana, S, 'M H Nazar, Gandhi and the *Indian Opinion*', *Historia*, 23, no.1, May 1978.

George, H, 'Gandhi, *Indian Opinion* and freedom', *Gandhi Marg. A Quarterly Journal of Indian Thought*, April 1958.

Huttenback, R A, 'Indians in South Africa 1860-1914; the British imperial philosophy on trial', *English Historical Review*, LXXXI, 1966.

— 'Gandhi in South Africa, the last phase', *Africa Quarterly*, VIII.

Marks, S, 'The ambiguities of dependence: John L Dube of Natal', *Journal of Southern African Studies*, I, no.2, April 1975.

Marks, S, and Trapido, S, 'Lord Milner and the South African state', *History Workshop*, 8, Autumn, 1979.

Mookerjee, S B, 'The Indian struggle in South Africa under Mahatma Gandhi: the birth of *satyagraha*, 1907-1910', *Calcutta Review*, 139, June 1956.

— 'The Indian struggle in South Africa under Mahatma Gandhi: the birth of *satyagraha*, II', *Calcutta Review*, 139, August 1956.

— The Indian problem in South Africa: Smuts-Gandhi agreement —

the Cape Town agreement (1914-1927)', *Calcutta Review*, 139, October 1956..

— 'The Indian problem in South Africa: Cape Town — success (1927-1946) II', *Calcutta Review*, January 1957.

Mullens, E T, 'The economic side of agriculture in Natal' *Natal Agricultural Journal and Mining Record*, X, part 7, 1907.

Narain, I, 'The Gandhi-Smuts agreement', *Agra University Journal of Research*, V, part 2, July 1957.

— 'Beginning of emigration to Natal', *India Quarterly*, XI, no.1.

Pachai, B, 'History of the *Indian Opinion*', *Archives Year Book of South African History*, 1961.

— 'South African Indians and citizenship: a historical survey, 1885-1934', *African Quarterly*, IV, (1964).

Pillay, P, 'Gandhi in South Africa; the origins of his philosophy of non-violent protest', *Dalhousie Review*, IL, 1969.

Richardson, P, 'Coolies, peasants and proletarians: the origins of Chinese indentured labour in South Africa, 1904-1907', *Collected Papers of the Centre for South African Studies* (University of York), no.5, 1978.

Songam, S D R, 'The Polaks and Gandhiji', *The Indian Review*, 63, May-June 1964.

Tayal, M J, 'Indian indentured labour in Natal, 1890-1911', *Indian Economic and Social History Review*, XIV, no.4, 1978.

Thompson, L M, 'Indian immigration into Natal 1860-1872', *Archives Year Book of South African History*, 1952.

Trapido, S, 'The origin and development of the African Political Organization', *Collected Seminar papers on the Societies of Southern Africa in the 19th and 20th Centuries*, I (London, 1970).

Van Onselen, C, 'The world the mineowners made: social themes in the economic transformation of the Witwatersrand, 1886-1914', *Review*, III, 2, Fall 1979.

— 'Randlords and rotgut, 1886-1903: an essay on the role of alcohol in the development of European imperialism and Southern African capitalism', *History Workshop*, 2, Autumn 1976.

C *Unpublished Theses and Papers*

Bonner, P, 'The Transvaal Native Congress, 1917-1920: the radicalisation of the black petty bourgeoisie on the Rand', University of London, Centre of International and Area Studies, conference,

January 1980.

Bradlow, E, 'Immigration into the Union, 1910-1948: policies and attitudes', PhD thesis, University of Cape Town, 1978.

Ginwala, F N, 'Class, consciousness and control: Indian South Africans 1860-1946', DPhil thesis, University of Oxford, 1975.

Vickers, S A C, 'Official attitude towards Indian emigration within the Commonwealth 1870-1947', PhD thesis, University of Delhi, 1976.

Virasai, B, 'The emergence and making of a mass movement leader: portrait of Mahatma Gandhi in South Africa', PhD thesis, University of California, Berkeley, 1968.

Index